Personal Aspects of the Roman Theatre

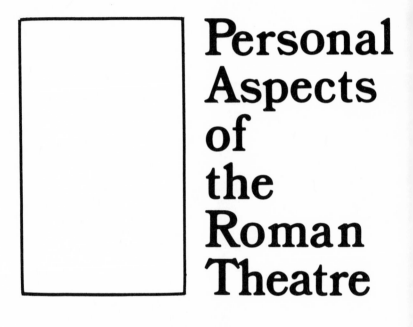

Personal Aspects of the Roman Theatre

BY

CHARLES GARTON

HAKKERT TORONTO 1972

Set in Aldine Roman
by A.M. Hakkert Ltd.

Printed in Canada

Standard Book Number
88866-518-0

Library of Congress Catalogue Card Number
72-78017

A.M. Hakkert Ltd.
554 Spadina Crescent
Toronto 179, Canada

Cover Design by R. Mitchell Design

Figure on Cover: masked actor playing procurer (*pronoboskos*, leno) wearing large
wreath (Webster, MNC2 MT10). Terracotta statuette from Myrina, second century B.C.
Reproduced by permission of the British Museum.

PATRI MATRISQVE MEMORIAE FILIVS

CONTENTS

LIST OF PLATES

Plate 1. Scene from Act 2 of Menander's *Phasma*, the original of Luscius Lanuvinus' play (see pp. 99 ff.). Mosaic at Mytilene, third century A.D. Reproduced, by permission, from S. Charitonidis, L. Kahil, R. Ginouvès, *Les Mosaïques de la Maison de Ménandre a Mytilène* (*Antike Kunst*, Beiheft 6 [1970]), pl. 8.2; pl. 24.2.

Plate 2. Papyrus fragments of Menander's *Phasma*, the original of Luscius Lanuvinus' play (see pp. 103 ff., 112 ff.). POxy XXXVIII 2825, early 1 cent. A.D. Reproduced by permission of the Egypt Exploration Society and the Editors of *The Oxyrhynchus Papyri*.

Plate 3 (a). Goat, showing *hirquina barba*, Plaut. *Pseud.* 966 (see pp. 186-187). Photo, author.

Plate 3 (b). Roman stilus from Lanuvium (see p. 47). Reproduced by permission of Leeds Museum.

Plate 4 (a). Medallion struck in 1805 in honour of William Betty, the young Roscius (see pp. 226-228). Reproduced by permission of the Victoria and Albert Museum, Enthoven Collection.

Plate 4 (b). Figures of Andronicus (?), Demosthenes, Roscius, and Cicero, on frontispiece of John Bulwer's *Chironomia*, 1644. Reproduced by permission of the British Museum Library.

(Plates follow page 338.)

ABBREVIATIONS

AC	*L'Antiquité Classique.* Louvain.
AClass	*Acta Classica. Proceedings of the Classical Association of South Africa.* Cape Town.
AJA	*American Journal of Archaeology.* Princeton.
AJPh	*American Journal of Philology.* Baltimore.
AK	*Antike Kunst.* Olten.
ASMG	*Atti e Memorie della Società Magna Grecia.* Rome.
BCH	*Bulletin de Correspondance Hellénique.* Paris.
Beare	W. Beare, *The Roman Stage*³ (London 1964).
BICS	*Bulletin of the Institute of Classical Studies of the University of London.*
Bieber *HGRT*²	Margarete Bieber, *The History of the Greek and Roman Theater*² (Princeton 1961).
Bonaria, "Dinastie"	M. Bonaria, "Dinastie di Pantomimi Latini," *Maia*, N.S. 11 (1959) 224-242.
Bonaria, *Fasti*	*Fasti Mimici et Pantomimici* in fasc. ii of the following work.
Bonaria, *MRF*	M. Bonaria, *Mimorum Romanorum Fragmenta* (Genoa 1956).
Bonaria, *RM*	M. Bonaria, *Romani Mimi* (Rome 1965) = *Poet. Lat. Rel. Aetas rei publ.* VI.2.
Broughton, *MRR*	T. R. Broughton, *Magistrates of the Roman Republic*, I (New York 1951), II (1952).
CIL	*Corpus Inscriptionum Latinarum.*
CPh	*Classical Philology.* Chicago.
CQ	*Classical Quarterly.* Oxford.

CR	*Classical Review*. Oxford.
CW	*Classical World*. Bethlehem, Pa.
Degrassi, ILLRP	Atilio Degrassi, *Inscriptiones Latinae Liberae Rei Publicae*, I² (Florence 1965), II (1963).
Del Corno	Dario Del Corno, *Menandro: Le Commedie*, I (Milan 1966).
Duckworth, NRC	George E. Duckworth, *The Nature of Roman Comedy* (Princeton 1952).
Edmonds	J. M. Edmonds, *The Fragments of Attic Comedy*, Vol. I (Leiden 1957), II (1959), III A (1961), III B (1961).
Fleisch-hauer	G. F. Fleischhauer, *Etrurien und Rom*, in H. Besseler and M. Schneider, *Musikgeschichte in Bildern*, Bd. 2, *Musik des Altertums*, Lieferung 5 (Leipzig 1964).
GRBS	*Greek, Roman and Byzantine Studies*. Durham, N. C.
Henry	G. K. G. Henry, "Roman Actors," *SPh* 16 (1919) 334-384.
HSPh	*Harvard Studies in Classical Philology*. Cambridge, Mass.
IG	*Inscriptiones Graecae*.
JDAI	*Jahrbuch des Deutschen Archäologischen Instituts*. Berlin.
JHS	*Journal of Hellenic Studies*. London.
Kern	O. Kern, *Die Inschriften von Magnesia am Maeander* (Berlin 1900).
Kock	Theodor Kock, *Comicorum Atticorum Fragmenta*, Vol. I (Leipzig 1880), II (1884), III (1888).
K-T I	A. Koerte, *Menandri quae supersunt*, I³, addenda adiecit A. Thierfelder (Leipzig 1957).
K-T II	A. Koerte, *Menandri quae supersunt*, II, addenda adiecit A. Thierfelder, ed. auct. (Leipzig 1959).
MAAR	*Memoirs of the American Academy in Rome*.
Migne, PL	*Patrologiae Cursus Completus* ... accurante J.-P. Migne, series latina (Paris 1837-).
MLN	*Modern Language Notes*. Baltimore.
NC	*Numismatic Chronicle*. London.
OCD	*Oxford Classical Dictionary* (Oxford, first ed. 1946, second ed. 1970).

O'Connor J. B. O'Connor, *Prosopographia Histrionum Grae-corum* = pp. 67-143 of his *Chapters in the History of Actors and Acting in Ancient Greece* (Chicago 1908).

PACA *Proceedings of the African Classical Association.* Salisbury, Rhodesia.

Parenti Iride Parenti "Per una nuova edizione della 'Prosopographia Histrionum Graecorum,'" *Dioniso* 35 (1961) 5-29.

Pickard-Cambridge, *Festivals*² A. W. Pickard-Cambridge, *The Dramatic Festivals of Athens,*² rev. by J. Gould and D. M. Lewis (Oxford 1968).

PMLA *Proceedings of the Modern Languages Association.* New York.

POxy *The Oxyrhynchus Papyri.* London.

RAL *Rendiconti delle Classe di Scienze morali, storiche e filologiche dell' Accademia dei Lincei.* Rome.

RCCM *Rivista di Cultura classica e medioevale.* Rome.

RE *Paulys Real-Encyclopädie der classischen Altertumswissenschaft.* Stuttgart.

RecPap *Recherches de Papyrologie.* Paris.

REG *Revue des Etudes Grecques.* Paris.

RFIC *Rivista di Filologia e di Istruzione Classica.* Turin.

RhM *Rheinisches Museum.* Frankfurt.

Ribbeck, CRF² O. Ribbeck, *Scaenicae Romanorum Poiesis Fragmenta*, II = *Comicorum Romanorum Fragmenta*, ed. 2 (Leipzig 1873, repr. Hildesheim 1962).

RSC *Rivista di Studi Classici.* Turin.

SEG *Supplementum Epigraphicum Graecum.* Leiden.

SHAW *Sitzungsberichte der Heidelberger Akademie der Wissenschaften*, Philos.-Hist. Klasse. Heidelberg.

Sifakis G. M. Sifakis, *Studies in the History of Hellenistic Drama* (London 1967).

SIFC *Studi Italiani di Filologia Classica.* Florence.

SPh *Studies in Philology.* Chapel Hill, N. C.

Spruit J. E. Spruit, *Die Juridische en Sociale positie van de Romeinse Acteurs* (Assen 1966).

Sydenham, CRR E. A. Sydenham, *The Coinage of the Roman Republic*, revised ed. (London 1952).

TAPhA	*Transactions and Proceedings of the American Philological Association.* Cleveland, Ohio.
Warmington, *ROL*	E. H. Warmington, *Remains of Old Latin* (Loeb Classical Library).
Webster, *GB*	T. B. L. Webster, *Griechische Bühnenaltertümer* (Göttingen 1963).
Webster, *HPA*	T. B. L. Webster, *Hellenistic Poetry and Art* (New York 1964).
Webster *MNC²*	T. B. L. Webster, *Monuments Illustrating New Comedy²* = *BICS* Supplement No. 24 (London 1969).
Webster, *SM²*	T. B. L. Webster, *Studies in Menander²* (Manchester 1960).
WS	*Wiener Studien.* Vienna.

PREFACE

The studies which compose this book are, with the exception of the introductory chapter, largely self-explanatory and may be read independently of each other. The appendices, though they are integral to the idea of the book, also form entities in themselves and are usable independently, with a certain amount of cross-reference.

The spelling of Greek names which do not have an established English form is always problematic, and in the present case has been more than usually so. The preferred practice of our times, with which I agree in the abstract, is to spell them in the Greek way. In many passages of this book, however, they are being cited from Roman authors, who naturally spell them in the Roman way; and even when not so cited they are for the most part intended to be looked at from the Roman point of view. Do we, then, write Dionysos or Dionysus? When we envisage Sulla's assault on Athens, is it to be the Ode(i)on or the Odeum which suffered such tragic damage? At all events I have felt justified in practice in using a large amount of Roman spelling, at cost of some slight inconsistencies which I hope will not exercise the reader unduly. Appendices 1 and 2 are a special case, requiring more objectivity. Here the spelling of Greek actors' names has generally been given in both forms, one or other taking precedence according to a rule set out in Appendix 1. In the Index, inevitably, a mixture of spellings will be found — just as happened in real life. As for the indexing of Roman names, they are generally placed under the *nomen*, but where a different usage is strongly established among

English speakers, as with the names Plautus and Cicero, I have
followed it. Borderline cases are cross-referenced.

Many portions of the book have at some stage of their
growth, been tried out as papers read to learned audiences
and/or articles published in journals. The third chapter first saw
light in the *American Journal of Philology* and the fifth in
Latomus. The sixth chapter began as a paper read to the Institute
of Classical Studies of London University and later published
in *Phoenix*, the seventh as an offering read to the Classical
Association of the Atlantic States, and the eighth as one read to
the Classical Association of England and Wales and published in
Classical Philology by the University of Chicago Press (all rights
reserved). The ninth was offered in response to an invitation from
the new journal *Mosaic* and appeared in its first volume. Of the
Appendices, the first incorporates the substance of an article in
Studies in Philology, and the second was submitted by invitation
in 1970 to *Aufstieg und Niedergang der römischen Welt* (Berlin, de
Gruyter) on the understanding that it was also to form part of the
present book. To all in those audiences who listened and criticized
I am grateful, and to all the journals mentioned I am indebted for
permission to reprint in revised form. The editors of *The
Oxyrhynchus Papyri* very kindly allowed me to see and use
portions of their Volume XXXVIII in advance of its date of
publication. And Janet Lembke's verse-translation of the epitaph
of Naevius is reprinted by permission of Mrs. Lembke and of
Arion.

My work was generously assisted in its earliest stages by a
grant from the Research Fund of the University of Newcastle
upon Tyne, and later by a grant-in-aid from the Research
Foundation of the State University of New York and a faculty
research grant from the State University of New York at Buffalo.

It remains to thank the many friends and correspondents who
have helped me. This I do. Among them my gratitude goes at its
liveliest to Professors T. B. L. Webster, Eric Turner, Ernst Badian,
and Geoffrey Arnott, who have all read over and discussed with
me portions of the book at various stages of its composition.
Obviously I alone am to blame for any mischievous consequences
of my own *incuria*, or of *authadia* maintained in their despite. The

typing of a snarled manuscript was handled with dauntless skill and patience by Mrs. Agnes Mitrision. My last thanks go to Professor Alan Samuel and the staff of Hakkert for seeing the book through the press.

State University of New York
Buffalo   C.G.

Personal Aspects of the Roman Theatre

1. PERSON, *PERSONA*, PERSONALITY

A sense of identity, a sense of the mystery and particularity of persons, when through its own operation it is deepened and overstrung by enjoyment of the characters portrayed in literature and drama by great writers, is one of the stabler comforts of our precarious existence. In the topography of the mind, such a sense occupies a place of some consideration. What we may call its next neighbour to northward is the feeling for language and style, and its next neighbour to westward the faculty of narrating, dramatizing, and acting; on the southward side it links hands with the open imagination, and when it faces east it looks upon the gardens of *Agapê*.

Thus defined and located, the sense of identity embraces fact and fiction, and present, past, and future. It is concerned with the living, but also with the dead of whom we have record, and with any record it can supply for the comfort of others hereafter. It is concerned with the work of authors who have, at the least, preserved personalia from oblivion; and with those who have given us lively images of real or fictive identities, including their own, in biography or autobiography, in sketch or essay, in novel, poem, or play. English literature contains a host of such writers, among them (after Shakespeare) Izaac Walton, James Boswell, and Charles Lamb. Among ancient authors Plato, Menander, and Plutarch stand out beyond the rest. The Romans, in objective record and portrayal, hardly reach the level of these, though Suetonius and in his own small way Hyginus deserve more honourable mention than historians and students of myth have, as a rule, been willing to make of them. In self-portrayal, on the other hand, Roman subjectivity has given us, in the writings of Cicero, the elegiac poets, and in a more reserved and diffracted way Virgil, works which can hold the candle to the brightest of Hellenic paragons. One purpose of this book is to further interest in identities both real and fictive by seeking to repair the Roman record at points where time has left it disengagingly ragged and torn. Even in the essays devoted to the technicalities of plot-reconstruction for lost plays, I hope that this aim will not be wholly forgotten.

The metaphor in the word "individual" has faded, but travellers find it vividly renewed when they meet the modern Greek word *atomon* in its sense of "person." A human *atomon* is literally indivisible, as of course the atoms of physics were formerly believed to be. He is the irreducible human unit, and also the only unit which a sense of identity can properly inhabit. And although persons do not resemble atoms in many respects — for example they are not interchangeable, as atoms often appear to be — there is at least one further important sense in which they are atomic, and this is that they very often depart leaving either no trace of themselves or a trace so infinitesimal that only an expert in such matters can pick it out. The sense of identity is awake to the slightest traces of individuals in past record. It sees them on gravestones — stones broken, whole, or even pressed into a second stint of duty, with the second name cut bolder and the first fading to evanescence. It pauses on attesting signatories, in some cases otherwise unknown, of charters, writs, warrants, wills, quitclaims, and like instruments. It tracks them with Münzerian fervour in genealogies and stemmata, even at points where the *atomon* is only inferable, and inferable only (let us say) as male or female. In this last case the student of identity, here acting as genealogist, may in the same way as the geneticist be in need of symbols, but whereas the geneticist sides with other scientists in his use of ♂ or ♀, the humanist dissents, he feels these to be inadequate as symbols of persons, and invents others.

By his sense of identity, and with the help of the neighbouring faculties in the mind, a man inveterately tries to put himself in the shoes of others and partly succeeds. This is different from having an interest in people. A man with the latter quality will often say such things as "I was curious to know what made him tick." One with a sense of identity would never say this because he is already partly inside the other person and knows that he does not tick. He is also partly inside the speaker of such words and knows that he is using a façon de parler. He knows, too, that in both there will be regions of no admittance. He finds that to be so much as aware of another − or, in writing, even to make him the subject of a sentence − is to be partly already within him. He differs from many other men in his way of looking at people. Whereas to a historian Luscii or Roscii "occur" in republican Praeneste, to him they lived or died there. And this "inlook" or empathy can apply by transference even to an animal, to a snake, or to anything sentient. Thus to begin a sentence "The snake lived . . . " immediately confronts him with the snake's own problems of existence and half personalizes it; and if he hears a prosing archaeologist explain that "the wineskins varied with the size of the animal concerned," the featureless last word, in this context, ignites like a firework.

Besides this, a sense of identity quickly recognizes its counterpart in others. Thus it knows, for example, when A, in narrative, is tacitly putting himself to some extent in the shoes of B, and it neither needs to have this fact laboriously spelled out nor accuses A of B's partialities. It is a sense in which historians are often weak − a weakness which is the defect of their virtues. Witness their unhappiness over Plutarch and general depreciation of Suetonius. The historical sense, which all writers on the past must try to use, seeks to explain men in terms of background and process: the sense of identity seeks, so far as may be, to be with them and in them, and if it succeeds, much of the scaffolding of explanation can then be dismantled.

There were not, so far as is known, any parent-teacher associations in Rome, but Juvenal includes it among the nuisances incident to the life of a schoolmaster that he is liable to be stopped on the street and asked such questions as

(1) who was Anchises' nurse,
(2) what were the name and country of Anchemolus' stepmother,

    (3) how many years Acestes lived, and
    (4) how many flagons of Sicilian wine Acestes gave to his
Phrygian visitors.[1]

Exegesis agrees univocally that "fascination with such *recherché* scraps of knowledge" existed and is "surprising," but that these particular questions are a parody of the usual type, since "the point of the conundrums seems to be that they have no answers."[2] That is to say, Juvenal represents them as asked merely for the sake of tweaking the schoolmaster's nose. It is forgotten by both Juvenal and his exegetes that there is at least one context in which such questions arise perfectly naturally; that this context is the study of identity (on which even the number of flagons could throw light); that, in the case of the *Aeneid*, the questions posed cannot be known to be unanswerable until they are asked; that if they were answerable they would contribute to the delineating intricacy of the poem's design; and that in the novel of the nineteenth century and after — in Balzac or Hardy or Conrad — the modern counterparts to such questions would indisputably be answered and for an indisputably artistic reason.

    The study of identity, with all that it means in knowledge of human nature, in the growth of sensibility, and in the fruition of literature, and near though it is, or should be, to the centre of humanistic learning, fits doubtfully into the pattern of subjects offered by our educational system. When pursued with reference to the ancient world it does not fall into any one of the recognized classical specializations. I know one or two scholars who are equally interested in Menander and Plutarch, but this is felt to require some apology — a person cannot have them both as his "real specialty" — and it would usually be thought anomalous to blend the two in a course offered to students. For similar reasons young prospective doctorandi with an interest in epitaphs as memorials of persons feel pressed to disguise it as an interest in the themes, or forms, of epitaphs, or some other dissertationable aspect of them. Amateurs of identity have their two main stakes in literature and history, but they repeatedly cross the borders — into philosophy and patristics, for obvious reasons; into linguistics and philology, especially for the origin of names and for verbal overtones and hidden nuances of meaning; into epigraphy and papyrology, the former mainly in pursuit of real persons and families, the latter also for the delicate reconstruction of lost works of the imagination; and into those reaches of archaeology, the unearthing, for example, of graves containing personal possessions or of mosaics showing scenes from life or the theatre, which carry us forward from the undifferentiated collective and begin to speak of a "he" or a "she."

The underlying concern of this book will be with the three aspects of identity in the world of the Roman theatre which form the title of this chapter. The essays, studies, and appendices to be found in the book will be exercises in the observation of these, partly as they appear to us now, and partly as they appeared in ancient times. The two viewpoints, ancient and modern, are often similar; sometimes they are in contrast, and sometimes their relationship is uncertain. With the exception of this introductory essay, the several parts of the book will be self-contained and self-explanatory, and may be read independently of each other. They will all rest, however, upon three assumptions. These are (1) that the three aspects of identity with which the book is concerned are, in the theatre world, closely interrelated, (2) that identity, embracing all these aspects, is a valid and important part of the theatrical experience as a whole, even though not perhaps at all levels a legitimate abstraction from it, and (3) that a sense of identity and a love of the theatre (even of a theatre now mediated mainly through literary texts and archaeology) go together and foster each other.

I am aware that to make these assumptions is seemingly to fly in the face of much critical theorizing of our day, tending as it does to lock the mind inside the dramatic illusion, to emphasize the centrality of praxis as taught by Aristotle, and to represent the tragic hero (an identity par excellence) as a modern concept wrongly foisted on to the ancient theatre.[3] The opposition is more seeming than real. In fact it will be found, in the discussion of Seneca, that I half concur, or more than half concur, with such criticism, because I believe it to be half or more than half correct. Praxis in the sense of doing and faring, in the sense that something is effected and someone affected, is central to ancient drama, or at least to tragedy (less central to Greek New Comedy and Roman comedy), but it is a mistake to think that this centrality renders identity in the widest sense — the self-consciousness of author, of actors, of the *dramatis personae*, and of the audience — trivial, irrelevant, or meaningless. After all, it is identity which effects and which is affected, witness the naming of the overwhelming majority of tragedies after *personae* without specification of the praxis or *pathos*. And the *prattontes*, as will be shown, are ultimately not just the dramatic characters but all involved, including the audience. The purpose of the present essay is to set forth the three aspects of identity mentioned above and to justify the assumptions made about it.

The three aspects, then, are person, *persona*, and personality. I intend each word in its ordinary acceptation. Each could be expressed by a variety of synonyms or periphrases, and sometimes will be as we go on. It is the concepts, not the terms, which matter.

To begin at the beginning, a *person* is an individual or self in real life. Persons are people. Within the context of this book they are anybody connected with the ancient theatre world *except* the personages enacted on stage or orchestra. They are authors, actors, judges, patrons, audience, and so on. Acquaintance with them, as will be shown, is part of the theatrical experience of identity. But as the names of the authors and of the most eminent among the spectators are already widely known, whilst the names of the rank and file of the audience we can never hope to know, our principal concern under this head will be with the actors. Awareness that such people exist, and that they do not exist merely for the purpose of effacing themselves is, among students of the classics, a mark of cultural health. The task of identifying Graeco-Roman actors, dating them, and listing them by period or place is ongoing, and perhaps, owing to the gradual accretion of new material, will never be complete. To identify an actor we must be able to fix him by name or name-substitute (some kind of identifying label) and at least one ancient testimonium. If at all possible we should also say when and where he performed, and if the available information about him has already been collected in some reference book (which of course need not be a book dealing solely with actors) we should indicate this fact.

There exist certain large general registers of more or less notable Greeks and Romans. Experience shows that these cannot be conveniently used as reference books on actors. There are four reasons for this. First, in some cases such books are expressly oriented in other directions, with the result that their coverage of actors may be very inadequate and desultory. Second, even if actors are included in large numbers, they are so scattered that finding them may be a lengthy business and one which precludes any conspectus. Third, even if a conspectus were extracted it would lack any kind of rational or appropriate subdivision by period or place. And fourth, such registers or prosopographies exclude persons who formerly had names but are now anonymous. Many individuals of the Graeco-Roman world are today known to us by something other than their name, and any conspectus of actors which omitted the anonymous would give a far from adequate picture of what is known. The last two of these reasons explain themselves: the first two can best be substantiated by instances. The *Prosopographia Imperii Romani*, in both its editions, and the *Prosopography of the Later Roman Empire*,[4] even if, and when, they are alphabetically complete, will always come most to life when dealing with persons of standing, persons who had some kind of career of office, that is, who played some part in civic or military administration, or who belonged to the families of men who did. In the nature of things the actors who satisfy this criterion are relatively few. As for the *Real-Encyclopädie*, though it had no reason to omit actors, it did in fact omit them with melancholy frequency until its tenth supplementary volume (1965). In that volume hundreds were suddenly included, the articles being written by Mario Bonaria, drawing for Rome and the empire upon his own earlier mimic and pantomimic fasti and for Greece upon the work of O'Connor and Parenti.[5] But the arrangement of this encyclopedia impairs its utility. Before you can be sure that a given actor is not listed you have to check for the name alphabetically in some six or more different places, and we are not promised any early improvement. In view of so tedious a rigmarole it is not surprising that scholars sometimes conclude prematurely that so-and-so is "Not in *RE*." I shall try to avoid such oversight, but it would be rash to hope for entire success.

There also exist certain registers especially devoted to actors, and these of course eliminate some of the inconveniences mentioned above. Chief among such registers is John B. O'Connor's *Prosopographia Histrionum Graecorum* (1908) and the supplement to it by Iride Parenti (1961).[6] The former of these contains 565 entries, and the supplement 120 more, but neither of them has much to say on actors who did not perform in regular comedy or tragedy. Moreover, the meaning to be attached to "Greek" becomes increasingly imprecise after the first century B.C., so much so that it virtually breaks down as a category. Of Roman actors — whatever meaning we are to attach to "Roman" — there is no good prosopography. Henry's work[7] is out of date, and Bonaria's fasti are of course not primarily prosopographic. There are some good lists in unpublished theses but they are hard to obtain.[8] Perhaps the greatest need has been for handlists of actors of (1) the Roman republic, (2) the Augustan age, and (3) the Graeco-Roman world in post-Augustan times. In the appendices to this book (which are integral parts of it), I shall try to supply the first two of these needs and so put the reader on the track of some of the centrally important persons of the ancient theatre.

A *persona* (Greek *prosopon*) is the dramatic counterpart of a person. He is, if we remember that the qualifying word may subtly but radically alter the meaning of the noun, an enacted person — in tragedy, comedy, satyr-play, mime, pantomime, or other kind of dramatic piece. He is often called a character, though this word has other uses. A *persona* belongs, properly speaking, to his play (*dramatis personae, dramatos prosopa*) or to the playwright. In another sense he might be said to belong to his actor, but a *persona* looked at from this point of view is more appropriately called a part or role.

In both ancient and modern criticism *personae* are sometimes consciously or unconsciously equated with (1) persons, (2) figures of mythology, (3) characters in non-dramatic literature, and (4) masks. Obviously they have much in common with all of these. They differ, however, from figures in myth, epic, or other forms of story in that their doing and faring is dramatized rather than narrated. Their differences from persons and their relation to masks are less easy to formulate. Like persons they always have a name or label and they seem to have identity, or at least a measure of it. A *persona* seems to live in the ambience of his play as we live in our proper world (he may of course be continued through a series of connected plays). *Personae* consequently are often taken to be individuals or selves on virtually the same footing as persons are, but the fact that they have their being in a medium other than real life should warn us to expect differences which are not to be glossed over. Some of these differences will be pointed out presently.

The relationship between *persona* and mask is partly an evolutionary one. The early history of the word *persona* is obscure, but from the beginning of theatrical record it is used practically as the equivalent of *prosopon*. The latter word, if we pretermit uses of it which do not concern us, passed by a metaphor from meaning "human face" to mean "mask." By the fading of the metaphor, "mask" became an accepted, proper, and permanent meaning of the word. At first no distinction was made between mask and *persona* in the modern sense, or role. But though the Greeks and Romans lacked a ready terminology to express the distinction, it is evident that, to them as to us, the two things came to be conceptually separable. Linguistically the process of metaphoric extension is repeated: *prosopon* and *persona*, from meaning "mask," came to be used figuratively for *persona* in the modern sense, and then this meaning became semi-proper, i.e. almost if not quite non-figurative. Mime, though we must allow it to contain characters or *personae*, did not use masks. In masked drama, the normal assumption was that the *persona* (in our sense) should suit the mask. This in itself betrays the conceptual distinction. Thus it was felt that a playwright or actor might well look at the mask while working out the *persona*, or that a complex *persona* might defy portrayal on a single mask. A scholiast on Euripides makes this very point, though his way of putting it is to say that Medea's weeping does not suit her *prosopon* (mask).[9] The number of masks used in the whole range of New Comedy seems to have been limited to forty-two,[10] but neither ancient writers nor the surviving parts of the plays give any impression that the possible *personae* or roles were considered to be limited to that number. If they had been, there would have been no point in ever giving different names to two or more *personae* who wore the same mask. There was indeed a good deal of re-using of names, but this element of conventionalizing seems entirely free from constraint and in any case comes nowhere near the severe ratio of 1 mask: 1 name. The general position, then, is that the spectator expects the *persona* to suit the mask (i.e. not contradict it), but to develop the implications of the mask freely, different developments being possible for different plays.

There is a simple-subtle Aesopic story[11] of a fox rummaging among an actor's properties, finding a horror-comic mask or headpiece, and admiring its appearance, but on closer inspection saying "What a pity there is no brain inside it." The story seems, though it is teasingly difficult to be sure one has got hold of the right end of the stick, to recognize the modern distinctions between actor, mask, and *persona*.

Personality is the total impression, qualitatively considered, made upon an ideal observer by a person. To be meticulous, it is not the impression itself but that which produces the impression; but since, to an ideal observer, any given quality, faculty, motive, choice, act, etc. produces an impression of that quality, faculty, motive, etc., we can perhaps afford to neglect the distinction. Personality is the qualitative aspect of a person's identity; it is the same as character when the latter word is used with reference to persons. There is a latent tendency in Aristotle to quantify character, through suggesting that it can be measured in terms of the moral value or the rectitude of our choices.[12] No one doubts that the moral worth of our choices is an important aspect of personality, many would say the most important, but the temptation to quantify personality in this way leads to an imbalance which, when we are considering the personalities of actors and other people connected with the theatre, becomes glaring. Fortunately the imbalance was redressed already in the fourth century B.C. by the *Characters* of Theophrastus, in which the qualitative foundations of personality are handsomely recognized, while purely *moral* qualities are, if anything, given somewhat less than their due.

The theatrical experience is a social experience. Within it, the theatrical experience of identity includes experience of personality, and it does so in more ways, the experience is keener and has more facets, than is generally detected. First, the theatre exposes us via the *persona* to the personality of the author and that of the actor. Second, if we encounter *personae* who are strongly and subtly delineated, a mutual heightening and intensification goes on between our awareness of these and our general awareness of personality. Third, constant exposure and encounter of this kind have historically tended to increase the colourfulness of theatrical personalities themselves, so that they become intrinsically more stimulating. And fourth, being such, they have historically drawn into their circle, and thus into ours, other persons with well-marked character and a strong sense of identity, whose presence then likewise becomes contributory to the theatrical experience. Such colourful or strong personalities may, by their impact, give a distinctive quality to the contemporary atmosphere and may even instill something into it which affects the future permanently. In eighteenth-century England one might instance David Garrick and Charles Churchill, both of whom will feature in the closing chapter of this book. Out of many personalities in the Roman theatre who similarly tinge our perceptions and sensibilities — they include the dramatic poets, Cicero, Augustus, and several later Roman emperors — I shall choose three for special attention: an author, a Roman dictator drawn into the circle, and an actor. The author is Luscius Lanuvinus, whose personality has permanently tinted our impression of the age of Terence and our reception of his plays. We shall consider both the background of Luscius and his dramaturgy in its own right. The dictator is Sulla, whose personality and interest in actors forms the crucial link between the dramatically and the monumentally most creative phases in Roman theatre history. The actor is Roscius, the impact of whose personality was so large as to achieve an enduring Nachleben, to furnish a pseudonym of honour for many of his greatest successors, and to inspire a long series of pieces of theatre criticism in the eighteenth and nineteenth centuries which, as we shall see, constitute "the Rosciad idea."

It was said above that the theatre exposes us via the *persona* to the personality of both author and actor. How this happens will become plain if we inquire further into the general nature of a *persona* and how he comes into existence. That is, we are now concerned with the total impression, qualitatively considered, made upon an observer by a *persona*: we are concerned with the "character" of a "character." The terminological quandary is so nice that instead of using an existing term for this entity, such as personality, character, or ethos, or coining a new one, I shall continue to speak simply of the *persona* and his general nature or qualities. Like a person, he is endowed with qualities, faculties, motives, reactions, etc., makes choices, performs acts, and may meet with good or evil fortune. And historically his image, like those of persons, has been compromised by the latent Aristotelian tendency to quantify. Indeed it has been a little more compromised, because Aristotle not only believes, as with the character of a person, that the best criterion for evaluating him is his pattern of choices — by implication moral choices — but further assumes as a starting-point that it is natural to rank *personae* on a moral scale as better or worse than, or on a plane with, ordinary men; and he recommends in the case of tragedy that they be better.[13] No one fails to see that tragedy, including what is left and what can be guessed at of Roman tragedy, contains heroes, saints, villains, fools, mediocrities, and (especially) unstable mixtures of these, and that the diverse moral factors in their make-up may be of critical moment; but if we do put them on any scale, it is surely one of bigness, depth, or intensity rather than moral worth. And, taking the first six ancient *personae* who come to mind — the Orestes and Electra of each of the three great Greek tragedians — who is there whose primary response to any of them significantly includes contentment with their moral superiority, or disappointment at their moral inferiority, to ordinary men? Next after pity and terror at what is tragic should come, not judgment, but the attempt at understanding. What Aristotle says about plausibility[14] is no doubt in implicit agreement with this, but his hints of moral quantification seem partly out of key.

One big difference between personality and the general nature of a *persona* is that a true summation of the former could not be made except by an ideal observer, whereas the latter only requires, and only can require, actual observers. The attributes of a *persona* differ from those of a person in that the sum of them is totally accessible. To put it another way, our acquaintance with a person is always less than complete, and there is practically no limit to the theoretically answerable questions we might ask about him. For example, if he is old, we might ask, how did he behave in his youth? The answer exists, at least potentially or in theory, and research may bring it to light. The question is valid. This principle does not apply to *personae*. If the play happens not to tell us how X behaved in his youth, we cannot find out. Our acquaintance with the *personae* consists of what the play discloses: this and the theoretically possible knowledge of them are coterminous. Questions asked about them are either answerable by reference to the play itself or are not answerable at all, even theoretically. They may come pretty close to being invalid questions.

A *persona*, in his totality, may best be explained as an analogue and a function. I have examined elsewhere, with reference to Greek tragedy,[15] and need here only briefly resume, the consequences of neglecting this fact and taking the *persona* as an individual or person in the full sense. What ensues when this mistake is made is a critical cycle such as occurred in classical scholarship in the first half of the twentieth century. The "individualizing" viewpoint orthodox in the times of Jebb and of the elder (Ulrich) Wilamowitz, father of Tycho, breaks down and precipitates the rest of the cycle. The viewpoint breaks down partly because it fails to recognize the invalidity of the kind of question mentioned above. Frustration at not finding the answer in the play leads to speculation and the subjective answering of what is objectively unanswerable. And besides this kind of incompleteness certain of the figures in the plays may seem dully repetitive of other figures, or too vaguely delineated; many more, including major ones, may show elements of the inconsistent or the irrational; and some may seem the mere embodiment of this or that impersonal idea. Having thus demolished the "individualizing" premise from which it began, criticism tries to solve the problem by analyzing the *persona* in a variety of other terms — as a type, as a vehicle of allegory, as a symbol or idea, and as a chameleon who changes colour with his context or background, in which case dramatic effect in successive scenes is bought at the cost of what, to our thinking, is psychological undovetailedness.

These categorizations, which played a role not only in the criticism of Greek tragedy but, as we shall see, in that of Seneca and also in Shakespearian and other modern criticism, do not go to the heart of the matter. The end of the critical cycle is the recognition that a *persona* is neither an individual or person in the full sense, nor is he fully accounted for by any of the other proposed categories. He is something *sui generis*. He is, as I have said, to be explained as an analogue and a function. He is an analogue in one sense and a function in three. Physically he as a rule (not always) looks like a person, a human being, and his general nature is sufficiently like that of a person for us to call it an analogue to personality. In this matter the dramatist is concerned to promote verisimilitude. The immediate enjoyability of most *personae* probably depends more on this than on any other single factor. But practical limits may be set to such "likeness to persons" by other concerns which engage the dramatist from time to time. He may wish to show Furies in converse with Athena, Prometheus in converse with Io, Hephaestus in converse with Might and Force, Apollo in converse with Death, Madness directly addressing the audience. If the list of *personae* can include such gods, abstractions, and beings midway between the two, and if these are as germane to the play as the ostensible human beings in it, and are "characterized" by the same means, then clearly we are dealing, not with personality itself, but with an analogue to it limited by some kind of functionality. That the *persona* is an analogue to a (single) personality, that he is, analogously to this, an aspect of identity, verging towards individuality and selfhood and having in consequence as much unity as his complex functionality will allow — is not likely to be denied nowadays. It is much less likely to be denied now than was the case earlier in the twentieth century, when the critical cycle was passing through the "chameleon" phase, in which it was strenuously denied that unity and likeness to selfhood were either among the necessary impressions received by the audience or among the conscious aims of the playwright.

In calling the *persona* a function we are drawing a term by strict metaphor from mathematics. A function, mathematically, is a variable quantity in relation to another, or others, in terms of which it may be expressed or on which its value depends.[16] If we were speaking of real life we might say, by strict metaphor, that our hereditary endowment is a function of the endowments of our ancestors, and this would be true in all regards, bating the case of the mutation of genes. Correspondingly, in the world of the theatre, a *persona* is a function in three separate senses. He is (1) in one sense a function of the action, (2) in another sense a function of the dramatist's personality, and (3) during any actual or remembered performance, in yet another sense a function of the personality of the actor. The second and third of these functionalities would, so far as I can see, be no bar to selfhood in the *persona*, but the first one is decisive against this. It is because the *persona* is, in his ultimate nature, a function of the action of the play that, while he may and does verge towards independent selfhood, he cannot fully attain it. As the making of a play goes on, action, character, and language become inter-constituted or consubstantial, but insofar as there is an order of priority the genesis of the action precedes the genesis of – and projects the main lines of – the characterization, the language coming third and being attuned to both.[17] This is as true of the Senecan Agamemnon and Oedipus as it had been of their Aeschylean and Sophoclean counterparts. It is as true of Seneca's Medea as it had been of the corresponding *persona* in Euripides. It is true of Othello and Iago. Ostensible self-justification or apologia, ostensible self-portrayal in such characters, is framed in the light of an action or praxis which is, relatively to them, a datum.

To Seneca we shall return at a later point in this book, but since the larger part of the book is concerned with comedy, it is appropriate to ask at this point how far the foregoing aetiology of characterization is valid for comedy, and especially New Comedy and Roman comedy. The answer is that it holds good, though less fully and less obviously. Superficially, the principle may seem not to apply: go beneath the surface and you find it there. Subject to one large qualification, the critical cycle described above with reference to tragedy operates for comedy also. That is to say, it becomes logical for critics who begin by postulating individuals to be driven by the exigencies of their own acumen through the recourses of type, symbol, chameleon, and so on, towards a sense of the characters as analogous to persons but arising in the first instance through functionality. That characters in comedy are analogous to, rather than authoritative instances of, personality, is intimated on a certain level by the give-away fact that once again we are from time to time confronted on the stage by deities, abstractions, or entities intermediate between the two. It suffices to mention Pan in the *Dyskolos*, Agnoia in the *Perikeiromene*, Tyche in the *Aspis*, Auxilium in the *Cistellaria*, Arcturus in the *Rudens*, and Luxuria and Inopia in the *Trinummus*. It is true, of course, that these are, more strictly than in tragedy, prologue figures cordoned off from converse with the other *personae*; but the very fact that they speak from the same stage, and that they rig this stage for the action and are, up to a point, prognostic of the course and outcome of that action, sufficiently recalls to us that this is not life but drama-land, and that both classes of *personae* are ultimately instruments of the mythos to be enacted. Aristotle might have said almost as truly of the comedians who were to come after him as he did of the tragedians he knew, that in characterizing they choose the ethos according to the action to be dramatized, *symparalambanousi ta êthê dia tas praxeis*.[18]

The one large qualification is that the *personae* of New Comedy and Roman comedy, much more than those of tragedy, cry out to be categorized as types or, more precisely, as variations on types. It is on types that the critical cycle described above, when dealing with comedy, lingers longest, and with good reason. Consider the recurrence of comic names and the tendency for the same name (e.g. Pamphila) to be attached to somewhat similar *personae* in different plays; consider further Julius Pollux' enumeration of the masks in this art-form as no more than forty-two, and compare this with the total number of roles, which must have run into thousands. It would be absurd to deny the aptitude of the type-category. It is perfectly reasonable to say that Ballio in the *Pseudolus* is a palmary instance of the procurer-type.

Beneath the surface, however, the types in this form of drama are nearly as much an outgrowth from function as are the characters in tragedy. There may be a difference here between

New Comedy and Old, and there fairly clearly is a difference between Roman comedy and atellan or mime. It would take us too far out of our way to discuss characterization in these other genres, but obviously the starting-point, in many cases at least, must have been "Take a funny/interesting given character — take an Alazon, a Maccus, a Bucco, a jealous husband — and see what we can make him do." Unless I am greatly mistaken, however, this was not the ultimate rationale of New Comedy and its Roman offspring. Their forty-two types surely began as functions in mythoi or praxeis and acquired their basic traits directly from that circumstance. It is the story that is elemental.

The course of true love never did run smooth.

To us so trite, to the audience of this art-form during its first two hundred years a proposition so rich, so fascinating, so infinite in capabilities. And so profound. For beneath all its disguises it was the story of the civilizing of sex, that is, the discovery of romance. Not the whole story in any one play, but one contingent aspect of it in the *Dyskolos*, another in the *Phasma*, another in the *Pseudolus*, and so on.

And it is the story that projects the characters — the love-smitten fecklessness of the *adulescens*, the mute, bridled reciprocity of his girl (*anti-phila*), the obstructive, worried, worldly, plan-match designs of his father the *senex*, the thick skin and double-dealing of the leno, the *alazoneia* or braggartry and the fool's paradise of the rival, the contriving slickness of the *servus callidus*, prying open the fence-work of society to get at its weak points, the professionalism of the cook at sacrifice or wedding-feast, and the varying qualities of all the other minor characters, each determined in the first instance according to his function. The poet may play ironically with the projected qualities, as Terence in the *Andria*, for example, befools the *calliditas* of the slave, but the ironic outcome does not essentially change the functional basis of the slave's role. The proof of this aetiology is very simple. A cook, a doctor, a leno, a flattering crony, cannot himself be seriously cast as a son, a father, a lover, or a rival. In life he could, as a *persona* he cannot. To make him such might make him more like a person, but it is ruled out because in the economy of the praxis it would make him dysfunctional.

Less directly, and we may say this of all kinds of drama, a *persona* is a function of his author's personality. This does not of course mean that the author presents an epitome of himself, least of all an epitome of his moral self, in each role he designs. It means that if X and Y each portray, let us say, a tyrant, the *modal* differences between the two portrayals correspond to something in the respective authors. It also means that the total number, range, and quality of an author's *personae* are a token of his identity. They might be regarded as arcs of a circle. The author is both the centre of the circle and the compasses which describe the arcs; and to a spectator, experience of a circle always includes some kind of consciousness of its centre. Hence, after a successful new play, the cry "Author, author!" From another point of view we might say that the author signs his *personae*, and this is what enables us to speak of them as Menandrean, Plautine, Machiavellian, Shakespearian, Goldonian, and so on. One of the most indisputable ways in which they reflect their author is in their simpleness or complexity. In the case of Shakespeare the aggregate of their complexities places his own identity, so to speak, beyond our measure. With a lesser author it is easier for us to link what he creates to what he is. This is what Arnold meant by "Others abide our question." Less directly again, a *persona* during performance or remembered performance is a function of the personality of the actor. The greater the actor the subtler and more latent may be his ties with the *persona*: the less accomplished he is, the more obvious they will be. For a great role, a great actor is needed: for lesser roles, the art of casting is largely the art of minimizing the necessity to act. These facts come home when actors take a bow, or address the audience outside their roles, or are interviewed after a play on television. Casting in antiquity, because of the smallness of troupes, was at a more embryonic stage of development than acting itself, but it is plain from Cicero that pains were taken over the assignment of roles, and that a principal consideration was the actor's personality.[19] What emerges from this is that a *persona* is plastic without being set. He is, within limits, malleable. There are as many forms of him as there are actors to act him, and there are in addition actorless, imagined forms.

Such being the general nature of persons and *personae*, I now want to suggest that the frame of mind in which we watch plays, and that in which the Graeco-Roman public did so, and our and their theatrical experience of identity, are often misapprehended and misdescribed. For over a hundred and fifty years it has been commonly said or assumed that the theatrical experience is, and has always been, predicated upon "suspension of disbelief." The phrase is ultimately that of Coleridge, though the context in which he used it is generally forgotten. A thousand books about plays and the theatre have been written on the presupposition that the theatrical experience, both of action and identity, takes place within the confines of a voluntarily accepted illusion: the temporary taking as real, while we watch it on the stage or on a cinema or television screen, or read it in a playbook, of what we know to be unreal. In consequence anything which breaks the illusion tends to be regarded as intrusive; it is as far as possible ignored, or slurred over as "extra-dramatic," or at best cordoned off for separate attention.

No quarrel could be picked with this attitude if it did not overtly or tacitly claim to represent the whole, or at least the essence, of the theatrical experience. But in fact it is rather an attempted abstraction from it, and only one of several that are possible. The oddest thing about it is that of all possible abstractions it is the easiest to make without actually seeing the play. Given a play text and a little imagination we enter into this aspect of the experience without difficulty. It is very similar to the illusion we enter when reading any kind of fiction. Many books about drama, especially ancient drama, both find the reader at this point and leave him at it. One of the most popular of such books is entitled *Greek Tragedy: A Literary Study*.[20] Its author knew very well that he was making an abstraction, one of several possible, but this has been lost on most of his readers, who have regarded the last three words of the title as puzzlingly otiose and have assumed the author to be dealing with the whole, or at least the essence, of his subject. But if we are interested in estimating the quality of ancient theatrical experience and comparing it with modern, we should be prepared, if need be, to cut at right angles across the standard expository approach, based as it is upon the full acceptance of illusion, and to consider identity, both fictive and real, in the forms or aspects of it which have been examined above, as one of the furthest-reaching of theatrical facts.

It may be easier to do this if we remember, first, that Coleridge's "suspension of disbelief" has been popularly misunderstood. What has been read into his words is a Misgriff. When he used the phrase he was not really thinking of the theatre, or even of drama in book-form. He was referring to lyrical ballads (his own) containing "persons and characters supernatural," and setting them beside other lyrical ballads (Wordsworth's) in which the "subjects were to be chosen from ordinary life."

> It was agreed [he says] that my endeavours should be directed to persons and characters supernatural, or at least romantic; yet so as to transfer from our inward nature a human interest and a semblance of truth sufficient to procure for these shadows of imagination that willing suspension of disbelief for the moment, which constitutes poetic faith. Mr. Wordsworth, on the other hand, was to propose to himself as his object to give the charm of novelty to things of every day and to excite a feeling analogous to the supernatural, by awakening the mind's attention from the lethargy of custom and directing it to the loveliness and the wonders of the world before us. . . .[21]

The key words, about suspension of disbelief, could not have been so assiduously applied to drama unless they had considerable aptitude to it, but it will be noticed at once that, in making them apt, we are pressing upon "disbelief" a meaning which is palpably different from that intended by Coleridge. He writes on the assumption that the supernatural is of itself untrue and incredible; that we naturally disbelieve it; but that for the purpose of experiencing (enjoying) a poem in which it plays a part we may, at will and for the moment, pretend, or as it were agree, not to disbelieve.

Several things are salient here. In representing the supernatural as incredible he did not mean to include in this category the serious religious beliefs of, let us say, a man like himself. For the colophon towards which his whole book is moving is, when we get to it, THEOi MONOi DOXA, "Glory to God alone."[22] Moreover he is not implying that belief and disbelief are themselves under the control of the will. In common with many thinkers of his day, notably Shelley, he was inclined to hold that belief and disbelief are *not* matters of volition.[23] To him suspension of disbelief means consenting to act, or rather feel, for the time being, as if we did not disbelieve, although we really do. He takes it for granted that suspension of disbelief is quite different from actually believing (post-modernist theology is not so sure). What stands out most, however, is that the distinction he is making is not one between reception of fiction and that of fact. It is between reception of supernatural fiction on the one hand and fiction within the realm of the natural, and also fact, on the other. But when the theatrical experience is said to depend on willing suspension of disbelief, the distinction usually intended is that between fictive enactment on the stage (whether of things natural or supernatural) on the one hand, and offstage actuality on the other. Coleridge's authority therefore cannot be invoked to bolster the common version of the theatrical experience. How far his words might chance to be applicable in their proper sense, and to the ancient theatre, is another question.

It will be the theme of the remainder of this chapter that the species of illusion regularly proffered in Graeco-Roman theatres was simultaneously less pervasive and more pervasive than the quotidian sort to which regular parlance subscribes. It was less pervasive – and this applies also, in a different degree, to illusion in modern theatrical experience – because what the spectator habitually does is simultaneously to suspend *and maintain* his disbelief in what is being enacted. He stands, or rather sits, both inside and outside the illusion. He balances both attitudes in a scale. The more utter each is, and the better the balance, the more exquisite the experience. A hint that this is so lies in the fact that it has always been thought remarkable, and often funny, that any spectator should, whether by choice or willy-nilly, get the two requisite attitudes seriously out of balance with each other. At one extreme of the imbalance lies phlegmatic unimpressionability. At the other extreme lies incendiary over-impressionability. Theatrical like other anecdotes have to be used with care: often what is significant is not the positive action or event they narrate but the norm which that action or event contravenes. But there is a large number of stories which, properly taken, point towards a state of balance as the desirable norm, a state which I shall call the appreciative mean. Let us consider a few. It will be seen that corresponding to the appreciative mean for a spectator there is also a point of balance for the actor which we might call the agonistic mean, and for the great actor this would be where perfectly controlled artifice fuses with nature.

Already in the dawn of theatre both the equilibrium and its sideslips are notionally present. According to what may be the earliest theatrical anecdote in the world, Solon in old age went to see Thespis acting in one of his own pieces. Thespis would have a chorus, but there would of course be no other actor.

> After the show [*thea*] he went to speak to Thespis and asked him if he was not ashamed to tell all those lies in front of such a crowd of people. Thespis replied that there was no harm in talking and acting like this in play. Solon thumped his stick heavily on the ground. "Yes, but it won't be long," he said, "if we hold this sort of 'play' in such high esteem, before it rears its head in our contractual engagements too."[24]

Does this mean that Solon objected to acting *per se*, or to the substance of what was enacted? That is, did he in effect go to Thespis, penetrate his facial disguise, and say "Sir, you are a liar," or did he mean that the scene or story enacted was wholly or partly false and thus traduced its religious or mythological subject? Bizarre though it sounds, the first is nearer the truth. Solon, accustomed to purely choral celebrations, perhaps with sung or intoned antiphons between the chorus and a leader, rather like the end of the *Persae* (composed in the following century), was probably now hearing his first spoken prologue and set of *rheseis*, and was offended by the jump towards mimetic realism, which seemed to him like wilful deceit.[25] He keeps his stance in disbelief, outside the illusion, at or beyond the extreme of unimpressionability. At the other extreme, that of over-impressionability, are the audience as Solon thinks them liable to be, either nefariously imposed on or, if they reflect on it afterwards, taught to lie. The audience as they really are stand at the appreciative mean; Thespis stands at what in later days would be the agonistic mean, but as the story goes back to pre-agonistic days he is simply represented as at (the mean of) *paidia*, play or entertainment. Under his manipulation, the audience correctly both suspend and maintain their disbelief.

An audience may fail to suspend disbelief, and thus (unimpressionably) fail to reach the appreciative mean, for several different reasons. A distraction may peg them in unsuspendable disbelief, an actor or author may let them down, or individuals among them may be out of temper. The classical instances of distraction happened at the first and second showings of Terence's *Hecyra*; these were the tightrope-walker —

> ita populus studio stupidus in funambulo
> animum occuparat;

and the overpowering rumour that the play was to be followed by gladiators in the same showplace —

> populus convolat
> tumultuantur clamant pugnant de loco.[26]

When Augustus said of two pantomimes competing alternately, that one was a true *saltator* and the other no more than an interruption,[27] the setting was agonistic enough but the second performer failed to bring the emperor as a spectator to the appreciative mean. On another occasion the pantomime Pylades placed himself in the position of a spectator outside the illusion when he claimed to find his pupil and competitor Hylas, who was impersonating the blind Oedipus, too sure-footed and told him "You're seeing."[28] Once when Pylades himself disappointed a spectator of the appreciative mean, the man tried to hiss him offstage. The sibilation in turn dislodged Pylades from the agonistic mean and he included in his movements an impertinent gesture towards the man concerned. Besides nullifying the illusion for everyone, this in the emperor's judgment amounted to abridging the dignity of a citizen, and he for a time forbade Pylades, who was originally an immigrant from Cilicia, to let himself be seen within the confines of Italy.[29] Perhaps the most classical case of failure to reach the agonistic mean was the misadventure of Fufius acting as Iliona. In the first scene of Pacuvius' play so named, Iliona appeared lying asleep but was called to attention by the ghost of her murdered son. Having had too much to drink beforehand, Fufius, the moment his head touched the property couch, sank into the sleep of crapulence, from which it needed the many-throated shouts of the audience to awake him.[30] A famous modern instance of an auditor's unimpressionability happened in England in 1729 at the staging of James Thomson's *Sophonisba*. When the line

O, Sophonisba! Sophonisba, O!

was delivered, someone in the audience heckled

O, Jemmy Thomson! Jemmy Thomson, O!

As explained earlier, a *persona* is always a function of the author's personality (which is the fullest aspect of his identity), but if the latter ever becomes obtrusively banal, the appreciative mean is lost. It can also be lost for any member of an audience who is himself disgruntled, depressed, or too indrawn, in which case the *scaenae frons* remains precisely that, a backdrop a backdrop, a mask a mask, gesticulation gesticulation, and greasepaint greasepaint.

At the antipole, and defining the mean by their distance from the former cases, lie cases of over-impressionability, where the disbelief is inadequately maintained and the suspension of it shades into belief. Most, but not all, stories of this kind imply some small degree of physical or mental debility in the subjects of the imbalance, whereby they are betrayed beyond the appreciative mean. In what are perhaps the two paradigm instances, we see this happening to women and children. The faces and trappings which Aeschylus and his choregus supplied for the Furies, and which were meant to evoke the kind of frisson which finds its ultimate outlet in applause, were reputed to have caused children to faint and to have induced premature labour in more than one expectant mother;[31] while in imperial Italy the young could be equally unnerved by the chalky trumpet-mouthed mask of a character in exodiary farces —

> cum personae pallentis hiatum
> in gremio matris formidat rusticus infans.[32]

The phenomenon persists. Concerned people in our own century have telephoned the broadcasters of drama to communicate advice to *personae* in a dilemma, to offer sympathy when they are bereaved, to propose marriage on the strength of a female vocal modulation, and to enquire the best means of shelter from invading Martians. The paradigm case in the modern world is the widely told anecdote of a prairie farmer from the Canadian midwest, who went to see a touring company do *Othello* and who at the climax rose in his seat and shot Iago. This is, I think justly, said to be a canard on Canadians, but in its backhanded way it credits them with a warm acquaintance with the appreciative mean.

Actors correspondingly, as we shall see, are sometimes carried beyond the agonistic mean — while straddling the two means is the strange mixed-up personality of Sempronius Tuditanus, who was not an actor at all, but by a kind of *morbus histrionicus* fell into the delusion that he was, and procured enjoyment of both the glory and seeming abandon of stagefolk by parading in costume and flinging largesse to the people, no doubt with appropriate lordly gestus.[33] Among real actors the best instance of over-impressionable imbalance was a calamitous error of Clodius Aesopus. Plutarch introduces the affair with the verb *historousin*, which could mean anything from "the story goes" to "research discloses," but would not in general be used of anecdotes believed to be without foundation. The play in question seems to be either Ennius' *Thyestes* or more likely Accius' *Atreus*, and the tragic actor was so wrapped up in his portrayal of Atreus planning and foretasting murderous revenge on his brother that, when some underling suddenly ran before him, the play became more real than even the playwright intended. Workaday gestus became blurred in swingeing regality, and this in turn in the sickeningly actual. As his synagonist came within arm's reach, Aesop gave him a clout with his sceptre which felled him to the ground. The concussion was so severe that it proved mortal.[34]

The appreciative mean always includes a large element of the critical: this is what makes it a true correlative, for the audience, to the agonistic mean for the actor. In the Greek world, dramatic performances took place to a great extent on a competitive basis, and the audience in any such case are acutely interested in the question of who is to win. It was not the religious origins of drama which entailed this. Religious processions, pageants, and revels were, and are, by no means inevitably competitive. The cause was the *games concept*. The principle seems to have spread originally from such festivals as were celebrated by games, i.e., in the first instance, by athletics and racing. Many such festivals sooner or later had dramatic events incorporated into them, which were then naturally conducted on parallel lines with a view to determining the "winner." And the same spirit, from a very early date, entered festivals such as the Great Dionysia where *gymnastike* never played a part and all the principal events, other than the purely liturgical, were in the sphere of *mousike*. Now contests of gymnastic (and racing) and those of music (and drama) both required judges, but whereas in the former case the winner was determinable by fairly simple rules, in the latter case everything necessarily was, as we should say, "on points"; that is, the procedure had to be evaluative. A *krites* of drama and of actors had to be what his name implied, a discriminator, a critic, and the audience, as at a competitive music festival today, was always practising qualitative evaluation along with the judges, at the same time as it was surrendering to the dramatic illusion. This was the norm of theatrical experience, often enough underlined by appeals within the play for audience-support and a favourable verdict. It was the routine experience at the Great Dionysia for four or five hundred years, from the sixth to the second or first centuries B.C., and is traceable for shorter periods at other festivals. The principle was continued in the empire down to at least the second and third centuries A.D., when the proudest claim of a musician or actor, as also of an athlete, is that he is winner at a festival or at a whole circuit of festivals: that he is a *hiero-neikes*, a *periodo-neikes*, a *pleisto-neikes*, or a *paradoxo-neikes*.[35]

It is not to be doubted that the partly intellectual, extra-illusory, critical approach which this principle fostered in the audience was carried over from Greece into the cruder atmosphere of the Roman republican theatre also. It formed an element in theatrical experience there, even though one of the preconditions as it were — the proclivity towards elaborate physical competitions not involving bloodshed — was less in evidence at Rome, where ludi scaenici were only tangentially competitive, and the instinct for impressive show (as opposed to contest of skill) was greater. In the first half of the second century B.C., certainly, Plautus, Ambivius, and Terence had a struggle to educate their audience in the etiquette of viewing, and Polybius confesses embarrassment at the Roman reception of *tragoidoi* in 167;[36] but from the middle or later second century, the agonistic and appreciative means come to the surface, the latter including, as it must, acceptance of illusion and genuine interest in the *personae*, but also critical detachment — the detachment which at one moment foretells the ruin of Orestes by an actor's progressive hoarseness, at another claps off Aesop for a slight touch of the same fault, and at another finds excuses for Roscius when he is off his mettle.[37] Cicero, along with his lawcourt hearers, has clearly been appreciative, in the theatre, of the *personae* who subsequently figure in his speeches, but the strong, even preponderant, extra-illusory and critical element in his viewing is plain. It is evident from, for example, his comment on how *persona* X would behave to *persona* Y "if he were a normal man," as also from the tenor of his report on the scenic games in his well-known letter to Marcus Marius.[38] One of the less remarked effects of the Renaissance was to restore, among audiences of drama, the detached, objective element in the appreciative mean, the relative lack of which in mediaeval times, among the audiences of mysteries and moralities, has deprived us not only of factual information about authors and actors, but also of what might have been an illuminating body of contemporary criticism.

The sense of identity is, and was, constantly engaged by ancient drama, but the illusion generated by the *personae* is, and was, constantly criticized and analyzed. It is checked against the spectator's sense of personality in general, and it is analyzed and reinterpreted as a function of the personalities of author and actors. The checking has usually proceeded, ingenuously and innocently enough, from the dramatic form of the biographical fallacy, i.e. the supposition that the portrayal is of an individual or self in biographical terms, as it were, and is to be criticized accordingly. There thus began in antiquity, in the hands of Aristotle (despite his sense of praxis), Cicero, the scholiasts, Donatus, and many others, that long series of comments both on felicities and on seeming oddnesses, incongruities etc. in the characterization of the *personae* which was so vastly extended in the nineteenth and twentieth centuries in the work of such different scholars as Jebb, the elder Wilamowitz, and the latter's son. We have seen earlier the critical cycle which results when enthusiasts carry this practice too far.

Analysis of *personae* as a function of their author can perhaps be seen, though at a crude level, in the irritation apparently caused by some of the attitudes portrayed by the republican tragedian Accius. We cannot be certain that *personae* were involved here, but if they were, it seems that the dramatic attitudes were analyzed in terms of Accius by a mime actor (and author?), who then proceeded to defame Accius from the stage. The mimic *persona* involved was then himself analyzed as a function of the actor and the latter was taken to court for slander.[39] Aristophanes, so far as we know, never put himself by name, as a *persona*, into any of his plays, but this did not stop Cleon from motioning to impeach him for slanderous elements in his choral or other *personae*,[40] nor the poet from riposting in the *persona* of Dicaeopolis. The case of the Roman dramatist Naevius, imprisoned apparently for attacking the Metelli from the stage, is a further case in point, and many other similar examples will come to mind. The ideality in characterization which Sophocles claimed seems to have been linked, already in ancient times, with his own gentility and poise of temperament. The Greeks' treatment of his compeers at any rate implies this: in each case they apprehended a likeness between the style, by which in this context I mean the mode of portrayal, and the man. They saw in Sophocles' character-portraits a kind of reflection of himself — not so much in the substantive qualities of his characters as in their modality: for the famous *hoious dei*, by which he claimed ideality of characterization, refers more to a mode of portrayal than to the exclusion of depraved, cynical, or otherwise immoral characters.[41]

The palmary instance in the Greek world is the fifth-century modal reading of the whole range of Aeschylean and Euripidean *personae* as a function of their authors' personalities which finds expression in the *Frogs*. Scarcely any element in Aeschylus and Euripides as there portrayed seems to derive from common knowledge of their lives outside the theatre: their identities are read by modal analysis of their *personae*, as well as (of course) from other elements in their plays. Dionysus' punchline "It was my tongue that swore — but I'll choose Aeschylus,"[42] means, insofar as it is a parody, that there were provocative and questioning elements in Euripides which could be caricatured, and even courted caricature, as condonation of perjury; and that no such condonation was attributable to Aeschylus. This is part of the modern as well as the ancient experience and it is, so far as we can see, true. Of course the two *personae* themselves are modally (that is, apart from substantive qualities) in turn a function of the Aristophanic personality, and anyone watching is simultaneously conscious of this.

Ancient awareness that the actor, also, was applying his personality in his acting has been touched on already in the matter of care over casting: "semper Rupilius, quem ego memini, Antiopam, non saepe Aesopus Aiacem." The criterion of choice is: "suum quisque noscat ingenium."[43] The study of appropriateness in the self-casting of Demetrius and Stratocles at Rome in the first century A.D. is equally in point.[44] Such awareness has been seen also in the holding of an actor legally responsible for anything defamatory in his roles. For in this sense too, what he commits to the *persona* is himself. An actor's self was not obliterated by his roles. It was revealed, and was of interest, both apart from them and through them. Whether ordinarily masked or not, actors' real physiognomies were vividly present to the public mind, as witness, in the late republic, Spinther, after whom a Lentulus was nicknamed (compare Pamphilus-Metellus) because of resemblance.[45] The one thing known about the roles acted by Burbuleius is that they involved inordinate gesticulation, swaying, and teetering, all of which were functions of his identity.[46] An ironic climax is reached if you dress a slave in a trumpery crown and purple and let him act a king. Thus Seneca:

> Look at the actor who sweeps grandly across the stage and says with head thrown back, "Lo, I rule in Argos: my kingdom I have from Pelops. . . ." He is a slave; he gets his five measures of grain and five denarii. And look at the actor who with such pride and abandon and confidence in his power swellingly proclaims, "And if you hold not your peace, Menelaus, this right hand will fell you." He gets his daily wage and sleeps under a patch coat.

Seneca gives these as parallels of those who behave swellingly and with great show in real life: "In every case their felicity is put on like a mask. Denude them of it and you will despise them."[47] He is underlining the great gulf there may be between pretension (overt qualities) and actuality. But — even though servitude is a mere accident rather than a self-expressing feature of personality — what is implicit in his words is that he himself sees the gulf without needing to strip the mask off: he is aware already, in real life, of the mean truth behind the ballooning front and, in the theatre, of the modal hollowness of the trumpery king. Seneca, that is to say, keeps one foot outside the illusion.

Other extra-illusory aspects of the ancient attitude to *personae* could be described, but one will suffice. This is the readier and noisier responsiveness of Roman audiences to any topical applicability in the words spoken. Cases in point are the encores in 59 B.C. when Diphilus made the *persona* he was acting seem to refer to Pompey (Cic. *Att.* 2.19.3), and the similar hullabaloo in 56 B.C. when Aesop applied his role in behalf of the recall of Cicero (Cic. *Pro Sest.* 120 ff.). But it is needless to list examples: they are well known, and sometimes show the actors themselves stretching, ruckling, or otherwise playing fast and loose with the *persona* as he exists in his textual, uninterpreted guise, in order to serve topical ends. One way to express this would be to say that a *persona* may at any moment became a function of the political and social atmosphere of the day, and that a Roman audience regularly maintains the degree of detachment and, in a way, the feeling for ambiguity, necessary thus to interpret him.

In all the above ways an ancient audience refrained from wholly suspending its disbelief, and of course much of what has been said applies to modern theatrical experience too, from which some of the illustrations have been taken. The appreciative mean for the Graeco-Roman world has much in common with that for our own world. But this is only part of the story. Use of the critical sense, which contributes so much to the extra-illusory side of the theatrical experience, is very much a secular activity. Criticism is secular. Yet the Graeco-Roman theatre was not a secular institution. It was religious in origin and can be shown to have remained so in certain ways right down to the end of antiquity. Christians would not have fought so hard against it, or been so slow to introduce drama of their own, and under their own control, if the case had been otherwise. The fact that it was not otherwise puts the ancient audience, and the experience in which they partook, on a different footing from their modern counterparts. It was noted earlier that the Renaissance restored to play-watchers that critical element in the appreciative mean which had largely disappeared in mediaeval times. This is true, but the Renaissance simultaneously lost something which mediaeval audiences had in common with their ancient forebears. This was the magic interlock, guaranteed by religion, between the stage and life. Simultaneously with but separately from any critical activity, the ancient audience are drawn into the illusion, not merely by choosing to suspend disbelief in what they know to be mimesis, but because, at the profoundest level, they are concerned. They are by tradition, as their ancestors had been more palpably, necessary participants in a *dromenon*. They are not merely spectators but witnesses of what is done, and glorifiers of the gods by their presence. In their own proper degree they are, by tradition, as much *prattontes* as the stage-figures or the officiant in any liturgical preliminaries to the spectacle. In this sense the illusion was not less but more pervasive than any illusion we are invited to accept in the modern secular theatre. To many of those involved it was, in greater or less degree, a part of reality.

What matters here is the continuity of the thread running from the prehistory of drama down to the fall of the Roman empire. Its beginning is lost in anthropological speculation. To quote from a modern discussion:

> Ultimately, perhaps, the sacred drama of the Greeks is like
> much ritual activity of other times and places in that it seeks,
> through a carefully ordered repetitive mode, to secure
> favourable conditions for the past's return. There is nothing
> odd in setting about to recover the essential virtue of a time
> greater than the present, when men were heroically big and
> strong and beautiful, and the gods could be seen and
> touched. Even Christians have believed [something of the
> kind,] and they have been untroubled with questions of then
> and now and eternity, with the superstructure of sacramental
> theology, which a linear and inexorably progressive notion of
> time calls forth. I do not suppose the Greeks, for whom
> time's motion was cyclical, would have felt their rationality
> insulted by the suggestion that the Oedipus-mask, in the dim
> prehistory of their art, was at once the doer again of an
> aboriginally potent action, and the King himself returned.[48]

In the functional spectrum of myth this would seem to place
Oedipus about midway between the Prometheus-figure and the
Orestes-figure, and his "aboriginally potent action" would presumably have to be analyzed into the two phases of (a) his
parricide and incest and (b) his mysterious death and heroization.
We can assent to the concepts of origin-myth and re-enactment
without trying to make them a universal key or pressing the
matter in this particular instance.

The writer quoted above emerges self-confessedly on to more
open ground when he continues:

> A far cry, the distant object of such brooding, from the
> mature accomplishment of fifth-century Tragedy — remote
> and also powerfully linked. When we first encounter this
> literature it has moved into broad daylight, while language
> and physical setting and social context are still drenched in
> religion. Embedded in the plays, and especially in Aeschy-
> lus's, are forms of prayer and ritual cries and invocations with
> a religious significance which the audience must have taken
> immediately. The actors were sacred officers of the cult of

Dionysus; the priest of the cult occupied the seat of honour in the theatre; the god himself watched every play in the person of his statue; an altar to the same god commanded the dancing floor. For an Athenian citizen to undertake the expense of training and equipping a tragic chorus was a memorable act of piety; and performance, after months of preparation, fell within, and was dedicate to, a great religious festival. The catalogue is formidable, but still vitally incomplete until its items are ranged round an action of the kind handled over and over again by the older dramatists, their individual license extending no further than the adjustment of the story's details.[49]

In certain ways the religious dimension of drama persisted, rendering the audience part of the same illusion which the enactors (or re-enactors) before it were creating. Though concentrated in the theatre, it was an illusion which stretched out into large areas of their lives and faded by imperceptible degrees into ordinary daylight. We are again reminded of the mediaeval outlook. The Renaissance could ask rhetorically

What's Hecuba to him, or he to Hecuba?[50]

We do not find mediaeval drama asking

What's Abraham to him, or he to Abraham?

or

What's Solomon to him, or he to Solomon?

And if it had done so, the question would have been far from rhetorical. The Greek spectator of Euripides' *Hecuba* was nearer to the mediaeval attitude than to that of the Renaissance. As he was led by the poet through the *pathos* of the Trojan queen towards her final bestialization, he would not have found the question empty. If Hecuba's *pathos* meant nothing else to him it at least meant Kynossema, a visitable locality bearing witness in its name to her metamorphosis and death. The story was aetiological of the name. Hundreds of stories were aetiological — of names, species, of a variety of natural phenomena, and of institutions. The thing, which is here and now, joins with the illusion to certify the story, or at least to give it a special status and special claims. Together they appeal to the aboriginal potency of the event. Some reflection of such potency must have shone also in Pacuvius, Accius, and other Roman tragedians and handlers of myth. Even to Ovid, four hundred years after Euripides, this kind of aboriginal potency is not far below the surface.

Even when ancient drama was at its most secular, that is, in Greek New Comedy and Roman comedy, the theatrical experience was perceptibly different from any kind of private or secular entertainment. To be at the play was still to be on holiday: and this not privately, but because the whole town was on holiday. It was on holiday because of the festival. At Athens, holiday, festival, and play were all explicitly in honour of Dionysus. Down to at least 106 B.C. the Great Dionysia were preceded by the escorting of the god's image, after sacrifice and hymns, in torchlight procession from a point outside Athens to the theatre itself, and this was essentially a re-enactment of his original coming from Eleutherae. The festival included another solemn procession (to which Menander refers) called the *pompê*, headed by a bull to be slaughtered to the god, and there was also a *kômos*, which was either a revel-procession or one of the competitive events. One of the processions included the carrying of a phallus, as Plutarch attests.[51] As the audience watch New Comedy and hear it tell of the mischances of unchaperoned girls at the Dionysia and other festivals, they are themselves taking part in such a festival. Between the acts of the comedy a (symbolic?) revel-rout may appear with music in the *orchestra*, and the jollification, often a wedding-feast, with which the typical play ends seems to be itself a survivor of ancient revel-routs climaxed by fertility celebrations. The spectator can hardly forget that he is there to the glory of the god. He senses a command "let this claim your attention" – the command which the Romans, when at sacrifice, were later to express, perhaps were already expressing, in their blunt way, as *hoc age*.

The theatrical experience at Rome partook of the same character, though with reference to other deities. Gods operative within the plays themselves were identified by syncretism with their recognized Roman counterparts. Festivals were offered to gods of the Romans' own choosing. Scenic games had been introduced, according to tradition, to propitiate the gods.[52] The sense that performance is a rite is vividly expressed by the exclamation, which became proverbial, made originally by an audience returning after they had been temporarily called away by a moment of military emergency: *saltat senex, salva res est.*[53] Interruption of a play or similar event was tantamount to interruption of a religious ceremony. When it happened, *instauratio*, formal repetition, was requisite.[54] And the ritualistic origin of wedding or orgy at the end of a comedy may have been sensed by the Roman audience. Temporary and permanent theatres were erected within the prospect of temples, and therefore of particular gods; in many cases, from Pompey's theatre onward, a shrine was built as part of the theatre structure itself, so that both actors and audience were directly beneath the god's eye.[55] And the continuing intent to glorify the god, the fundamentally religious character of theatrical events — that is, in Christian eyes, their fundamentally pagan character — is emphasized and re-emphasized in patristic writings down to the end of antiquity. Where, asks St. Augustine, are scenic games to be found, except in religious contexts?[56] A man cannot be a Christian and remain an actor, because he is serving pagan gods, and the audience are his abettors.

Because of this religious character and, as part of it, the deeply buried sense of re-enactment, the illusion can at moments come right out of the play and assimilate, or drag forcibly into it, some event of the real world, of the here and now, which is akin to the emotive intensity, the shock, the aboriginal potency, of what is being dramatized. Two such moments in theatre history, where fictive arrogates real, concern the sorrows of Electra and the decapitation of Pentheus. Polus, acting the Sophoclean Electra, when at the lowest pitch of desolation she mourns over the supposed ashes of her brother, took into his arms no property urn of the theatre but that containing the ashes of his recently deceased son; "et ... opplevit omnia non simulacris neque imitamentis, sed luctu atque lamentis veris et spirantibus. Itaque cum agi fabula videretur, dolor actus est."[57] Gellius describes the outside of the event. But in its inner nature it is distantly related to the concept of "intention" at mass, the "particular end to which the celebrant prays that the fruits of the sacrifice may be applied, e.g. the repose of the soul of one lately dead."[58] Polus was not concerned with the repose of a soul; but in both cases the re-enactment (that of tragedy and that of the mass) assimilates the burden of the present, and the barrier between then and now is visibly removed. The fee-grief of Polus is momentarily taken up and made into an archetypal keening.

The other, and most classical, instance of fictive arrogating real is the macabre incident during victory celebrations in Armenia after the Parthian defeat of Crassus in 53 B.C. The occasion was not a regular or public festival, but the royal celebrations took on equally the character of a national rejoicing and thanksgiving, in which consciousness of the deity as strong and holy is at its height. The tale is best told in Plutarch's own words.

> When the head of Crassus was brought to the (king's) door, the tables had been moved aside and a tragic actor from Tralles, called Jason, was giving a rendering of the Agave episode from Euripides' *Bacchae*. During the applause Sillaces stood at the entrance of the hall and after making obeisance threw the head of Crassus in front of the company. Amid the clapping of the Parthians, who picked it up with shouts of joy, the king had his servants show Sillaces to a place on a banquet-couch. At the same time Jason handed his Pentheus costume to one of the chorus, seized the head of Crassus, and acting the frenzied bacchanal herself sang the famous lines as if the god were in him —
>> We bring from the mountain
>> a new-cut tendril to the palace,
>> a beatific quarry.
> Everyone was delighted; but as the next part was being chanted —
>> *Ch.* Who slew him?
>> *Ag.* Mine is the honour,
> Pomaxathres . . . jumped up and grasped the head, feeling it more appropriate for him than Jason to say this. . . . With such a finale, as in tragedy, the expedition of Crassus is said to have closed.[59]

Now Jason was no barbarian. It happens that something can be known of his background. Tralles, of which he was a citizen, shared some of its cultural traditions with Pergamum and, like that city, was from an actor's point of view within the province of the Ionian guild of the Artists of Dionysus. Twice in the recent past, when Mithridates held sway in the area, there had been a noted concurrence of the natural and supernatural worlds. For the guild's counterpart at Athens had claimed to recognize in Mithridates "our new Dionysus," as if he were an incarnation of the god;[60] and Mithridates himself, at Pergamum, in the city and theatre where Dionysus, surnamed *Kathegemon*, was especially revered, had been rebuked by a supernatural portent while trying to have himself crowned before a vast audience.[61] So now, at Tigranocerta, the two worlds again concur. The *sparagmos* (mangling) of Pentheus is re-enacted, and the aboriginal potency of the deed reaches a kind of epiphany in the hall of the Armenian king. The victim's head is real, and dead. The godhead lives. Jason is his votary. Illusion and present reality have become one.

Beginning from one of the apexes of a mandorla, the course of our argument has taken us first in one, and then in the other, of the two possible directions. Along one side of the figure we have found the illusory element in the ancient theatrical experience lessening in its pervasiveness, until amid the vociferous topical allusions of the Roman theatre it virtually disappears, as both the play and the identity of the *persona* are, by modern reckoning, pulled out of their true shape for the behoof of current political actuality. Along the other side of the figure we have seen the illusion maintain and extend its pervasiveness until both actors and audience are caught up as if in an epiphany. The extremes meet in Jason of Tralles, who stands at the further apex of the mandorla.

We come back to Coleridge and "that willing suspension of disbelief, for the moment, which constitutes poetic faith." We took as our point of departure the popular application, or rather misapplication, of his phrase as a description of the theatrical experience, disbelief being taken to mean disbelief in the reality of whatever is enacted onstage. Taken thus, the phrase is a kind of overstatement, in that, so long as the appreciative mean is maintained, the waking critical sense, which remains extra-illusory in its working, together with a genuine involvement with the actual personalities of the theatre, must always run parallel to, and accompany, acceptance of the illusion. But, as we saw, what Coleridge himself meant by disbelief was disbelief in the super-natural — not inclusively, but with reference to all those supernatural elements in imaginative poetry which his waking rational self would athetize as superstitious. Could willing suspension of disbelief in this sense serve as a valid *supplementary* description of the ancient theatrical experience? In this sense — a temporary acceptance of the irrational — it may approximate the truth for the sceptics among ancient spectators, who of course were many. But for the rest, perhaps the majority, the line between the rational and irrational was not so clear. They had all the inducements of tradition, upbringing, and public custom not so much to suspend disbelief as to hover on the brink of belief. It was as much upon what *they* would have called their waking, rational selves as upon the irrational in them that the carnival-religious atmosphere and the illusion of re-enactment, or of the *dromenon*, laid hold. And this applied not only to the worship of Dionysus in his theatre in the fifth century B.C. but also, even if in dwindling measure, throughout the history of the Graeco-Roman civilization, down to the licentious honours paid to the goddess Flora in the decline of the empire. Religions die slowly.

But to leave the matter thus would be to leave our underlying theme without a period. It has been argued that our appreciation of *personae* in all their variety, of the "characters" of "characters," and our sense (and enjoyment) of persons and personalities, are closely interrelated in the theatrical experience of identity, this including directly or mediately the identities of authors, actors, stage-figures, audience, and theatre personalities in general. And that in the Roman as in the Greek theatre, such experience of identity, and indeed the theatrical experience as a whole, includes both the tints of critical, and often also what posterity must call the shades of irrational, strands in its composition. I have also argued that the experience of identity is an important part of the whole theatrical experience, even if not fully capable of abstraction from it.

2. TERENCE'S ANTAGONIST: THE BACKGROUND

It has been the lot of the dramatist Luscius Lanuvinus to be known in the annals of the theatre mainly as a nuisance in someone else's life, as a thorn in the side of Terence throughout the latter playwright's brief career. He enters our ken through the prologue to Terence's first play. Thenceforward he is consistently old, malevolent, and anonymous. He is old while Terence is young, and malevolent while Terence is sympatique. The names of both playwrights were, at the time, well enough known to the public, but Terence in all his audience-relations consistently avoids mentioning the name of Luscius. And when Terence lays down his pen, Luscius disappears from life, and almost from history. But for the fact that someone fond of Terence, or of playbooks and the theatre, had cared enough, while living memory or written clues lasted, to note down the identity of this *vitupero*, this *subducti-supercili-carptor* (as Laevius the pre-neoteric might have called him), and the jackdaw activities of Roman scholarship had kept hold of that annotation for four or five hundred years and then expiringly got it into the hands of Donatus, who relayed it to ourselves, we should have been left in very tantalizing ignorance and reduced to the vagaries of *hominum doctorum probabiles coniecturae*.

In accordance with the slant which history has thus given to the matter, past discussions of Luscius have been mostly devoted to the nature and development of his quarrel with Terence, and also to his possible relevance in settling the order of Terence's plays.[1] These problems have perhaps been sufficiently aired in the present state of the evidence. My purpose is not primarily to shed light on the dates, career, and art of the younger dramatist, or on his critical presuppositions and the conduct of the polemics in which he became involved. It is the older man with whom I am concerned, and with some aspects of his cultural and professional background. His individual plays will be discussed in later chapters.

For a general impression of Luscius a present-day enquirer might most naturally turn to the pages of Duckworth or Beare in the first instance, and thereafter to Kroll in the *Real-Encyclopädie* and to Schanz-Hosius, who give some references to the earlier literature.[2] All four of these accounts are somewhat jejune. And to see what is left of Luscius' work in the context of other fragments of Roman drama we have still to refer to Ribbeck.[3] Most of the playwrights dealt with in Ribbeck's volume have since been formally re-edited by others, and the relevant advances in scholarship brought into view. But this is not precisely the case with Luscius.[4] The lack here is probably due to the exiguousness of the direct sources, which can be quickly enumerated. Kroll begins his article in the *Real-Encyclopädie* by saying that Luscius is known to us only from Terence's prologues. This is excusable shorthand. The ancient sources, besides Terence, are the Terentian commentaries by Donatus and Eugraphius,[5] the Bembine and other scholia,[6] and the ancient and mediaeval lives of Terence found in association with these works. Luscius is also mentioned in the so-called canon of Volcacius Sedigitus, dating from about 100 B.C.; he is there rated ninth among Roman comedians, somewhat below Terence, but even so above Ennius and (by implication) Livius Andronicus. Apart from this brief mention, however, any reader of the sources can see that Donatus and the rest were in possession of only three real pieces of information about Luscius beyond what Terence himself supplies. These commentators, or rather the best of them, knew (1) the name of Terence's antagonist, (2) part of the plot of one of his comedies (the *Thesaurus*), and (3), in the case of another comedy (the *Phasma*), an outline ostensibly of the source-play but more probably (in my opinion) of the copy. That is what Donatus knew; Eugraphius and the scholiasts knew even less. All the other remarks offered by these commentators are spun by *entechnos pistis*, that is, by argument without external clues, from the words of Terence himself. It is unlikely that any more direct evidence will come to light, but gains in our knowledge of later Greek comedy and of ancient theatre history in general are slowly clarifying our picture of Luscius' work and of the setting in which it was carried out.

I. *The Lanuvine Aspect*

As indicated above, the dating of Luscius is interlocked with that of Terence. Terentian chronology, however, at present wears the aspect of a perverse and horrid thicket, of which any attempt at clearance is apt to be regarded as a further inspissation. Yet so far the dates for Terence's career implied by the didascaliae have not been decisively disproved, and there is nothing faintly resembling a consensus of opinion in favour of any other proposed dates.[7] Provisionally therefore I shall accept the former, namely 166-160 B.C., and with them, so far as need arises, the traditional order of the plays, but without forgetting that a case has been put forward for setting Terence's whole career somewhat later, the latest at all plausible dates being 153 – 149/148.[8] If later dates of this kind were ever established, it would mean that our picture of Luscius must be brought down by about a decade, but this would not fundamentally change his background, and of course his connections with Terence and Ambivius would be unaltered. Now when the prologue to the *Andria* was spoken, Luscius was "old" (*Andr.* prol. 7); he was also "old" on the lips of Ambivius (*HT* prol. 22), and there is no reason to disagree with Donatus' impression that he was a *senex*.[9] Pending the discovery of better evidence, we must suppose that he was born about 226 B.C. His apparent decision to retire, indicated at *Eun.* prol. 15, provisionally 161, would then be taken at about the age of sixty-five, it being of course remembered that a man's alleged decision to retire need not be irrevocable and, even if it were, this need not damn the supposition that Luscius remained vocal after retiring. In fact Terence quite envisages that he may do so (*Eun.* prol. 18).

Luscius' praenomen is lost, and cannot be convincingly

guessed on the available evidence.[10] His nomen has never been in serious doubt. His third name, for a long time thought to be Lavinius, has in the twentieth century been re-established as Lanuvinus, with LANVINVS an acceptable alternative spelling in ancient times, and Lanivinus a less orthodox form.[11] Had the Latin alphabet contained a "w", it might well have been used in this name: Lanwinus. As things are, the spelling Lanuvinus correctly represents its derivation from a place-name ending in -u-vium, and LANVINVS probably approximates its pronunciation, as well as making quicker work for a chisel. The playwright's card of identity has had the misfortune, in mediaeval manuscripts and all through history, to be defaced by an uncommon virtuosity of misspellings, and even since the truth became generally known he has been called from time to time Luscius Lavinius (Allinson), Luscius Lanuvinus or Lavinius (*Oxford Classical Dictionary*), Luscus Lavinius (Edmonds), Lavinius Luscius (Edmonds), and even Luscus Lavinus (Ruck).[12]

He belonged to the gens Luscia, more probably by birth than by manumission.[13] Relatively little is known of this gens, and it cannot be traced back with certainty to a date earlier than his own appearance within it. The few republican Luscii who are known lived in three places forming the corners of a triangle in north-east Latium. Of the Luscii in two of these places we learn nothing but a few details of their private lives, gathered from gravestones. Rome is one corner of the triangle, and it provides a single gravestone mentioning three ex-slaves.[14] The co-presence and detail of their names suggest that most likely the owner who manumitted two of them was one and the same Titus Luscius; a Gaia who manumitted the third could have been his wife or sister; and all three on manumission took their nomen from the Luscian gens. The detail of the record, with the slave-names preserved after manumission as cognomina, suggests a date near the end of the republic, and it does not attest more than one generation of Luscii in Rome, or two at most. The second corner of the triangle is Praeneste, where three gravestones tell us of (1) a Lucius Luscius, son (less probably freedman) of Marcus, (2) a Marcus Luscius, son of Marcus, and (3) a Luscia, wife of Marcus.[15] There are no cognomina. These Luscii belong to two (not necessarily complete) generations and can be dated between about 250 and 82 B.C. They may therefore very easily have been contemporary with the playwright. But the best evidence of strictly contemporary Luscii outside his place of origin lies in his own cognomen. Away from there, in all probability, he acquired the name Lanuvinus to distinguish him from them.

Between Praenestine and Lanuvine households there most likely were ancient kinships, since about ten gentes are represented in both towns in republican times. But there was no direct road for such kinsfolk to visit each other. Fifteen miles of rugged country, including the Mons Artemisius, lay between, and neither place had the other on its horizon — which might in other circumstances have been possible as Lanuvium stands on a small eminence and Praeneste on a commanding one. It is interesting that about 205 B.C., in Luscius' early life, a comedy was put on at Rome in which one of the characters happens to mention that he has had visitors on the previous day from both Praeneste and Lanuvium, and is told that he should have entertained the former with nuts (they being notable nut-growers) and the latter with their own favorite dish — a nice boiling of tripe.[16] The play, like the terrain, hints that a family from either place would most naturally meet its relatives or friends from the other at the apex of the triangle, in Rome, to which both communities enjoyed access by good roads.

It was in Lanuvium that Luscius, or at least his family (I am assuming he was freeborn), had their roots. To speak of this place more particularly, it had formerly been a minor burg or fastness, but for over a century before Luscius was born a small peaceable market-town. It lay a little way off the Appian road, between the nineteenth and twentieth milestones as counted from the Capena gate. The buildings of the town were clustered round a hill-spur, looking towards the coast above Antium, and it was doubtless a freshening sea-breeze coming up before dawn which made, or was eventually to make, the place proverbial for coolness around cockcrow.[17] Its people, who might perhaps have numbered about a thousand all told,[18] were of ancient Latin descent. The townsmen had long held the Roman franchise, and their story had always been closely intertwined with that of Rome. As with other such communities, the Romans relied on their piety to report any extraordinary event of nature, in case it might prove interpretable as a message from their common gods, and we know of several dispatches of this kind which were duly posted up the Appian Way. The bond with Rome had been cemented in the fourth century, at the time when the divine patroness of Lanuvium, Juno Sospita, and her associated stretch of numinous woodland, had been officially shared with the Romans, and this entailed for the Lanuvines both privileges and responsibilities. It happened on one occasion in Luscius' lifetime that the town magistrate, while sacrificing at the festival of the Latins, inadvertently left the Roman people out of his prayer, and this was an event so clearly untoward for all concerned, that Rome pontifically required an instauration of the whole proceedings. Fresh farm animals were needed for the purpose, and Lanuvium, which had to supply them, found itself the poorer by so many prime head of stock.[19]

Luscius was in middle life at the time of this contretemps, and in its setting it usefully reminds us of his essential Latin-ness and his closeness to Rome, an affinity greater than that of Andronicus, Naevius, Plautus, Ennius, or Caecilius. This may partly explain why, grown old as an insider, it was a bitter day for him when some members of the Roman establishment who were rich enough to affect a cosmopolitan outlook, took up a young Tunisian — possibly of Italiot-Greek parentage or descent but said to be of dark pigmentation,[20] darker very likely than even the most shirtless of Lanuvine yokels — and (as Luscius believed) more or less marionetted him through the motions of playwriting, to their own gratification, applause in the theatre, and the short-changing of home talent in both festival time and emoluments. There is little to be said for the almost universal assumption that Luscius was concerned for his own sake. He was probably senior enough, and near enough to retirement, to be past that kind of envy. But there may well have been others who looked to him to protect their interests; and it is possible that what we are witnessing in the attack on Terence is the profession defending itself against the redoubtable backers of an imported near-prodigy who, by his own admission, did not feel confined to staging what was his own unaided work.

The digging of archaeologists at Lanuvium in the past eighty or ninety years has been rather desultory, and has led to an unsatisfactory state of affairs in which hundreds of objects have been "published" without adequate indication of their findspots or a systematic attempt at dating. A reliable history of the town in Roman times still waits to be written.[21] Here I shall merely point to one or two factors which help to show Luscius' cultural background and the general social milieu of a Lanuvine in the second century B.C. It is plain that the Lanuvines, like most of the Latins, included both Greek and Etruscan elements in their cultural inheritance. They claimed that the town's first founder had been a Greek of the heroic age,[22] but the thickset and tricellular temple on the hill brow was rather Etruscan in style.[23] Greece had nevertheless contributed to their art, and surviving red-figure vases and other objects datable before Luscius show us their familiarity with Greek cult and legend, including such personages as Dionysus, maenads, satyrs, and silens. An ornamental tile-end made in late Hellenistic times shows the mask of a slave from New Comedy.[24] This may be post-Luscian, but tragedy and comedy are both likely to have been known in the town, at least by repute, from early times, and certainly since 240 B.C. when they had begun to be acted in Rome. Whether there was any form of theatre — a *herbosum theatrum*, perhaps, such as Juvenal was later to describe[25] — is unknown; the existing theatre-remains there are of imperial date.

Literacy was well established. This is indicated by some early, though not precisely datable, Latin inscriptions, but of greater interest in the present enquiry is the finding of a number of stili, of which one, made of bronze, was buried with an unknown Lanuvine apparently of the late second century B.C. and was obviously a favorite personal possession of its owner during life.[26] It reminds us of the local Aelii. The earliest known of these, born hardly later than 174 B.C., became a crier. Whether the emphasis in his work fell on official proclamations or on auctioneering (both tasks were discharged by *praecones*) is unknown, but in either case he would be literate. And his son Lucius, born about 154, so often had a stilus in hand, and became so apt in the use of it, especially for writing speeches for other people to deliver in the

Roman lawcourts and elsewhere, that he acquired the surname Stilo, and is today commemorated in his home town by a Via Elio Stilone.[27] Belonging to a later generation than Luscius, he shared his interest in penmanship, and he also shared an absorption in playbooks, being one of the first to work on the Plautine canon. Luscius from this point of view is a perhaps not insignificant intermediary between the plays of Plautus, some of whose premières he probably saw, and Aelius Stilo's attempt, working with written texts, to distinguish those which were genuine from the tralaticious pseudo-Plautiana which had gathered round them by his own day. That is to say, memories handed on by Luscius could indirectly have helped his fellow-townsman in the work of identification. In a still younger *municeps* of Lanuvium, Quintus Roscius the actor, born about 132/131 B.C., the Plautine *personae*, by then grown classical, were to live again on the stage in the golden age of Roman acting.

No gens in Lanuvium, if we leave aside suspect cases, can be traced further back than the Luscii, and Luscius the playwright is thus the earliest Lanuvine known to us by name. As suggested above, his kinsfolk, and he himself in all probability (before going to Rome), were Luscii simply, without cognomen, just as were their *gentiles* in Praeneste. The Lanuvine branch of the gens, and in particular a family which came to be called Ocrea (Greave), proved a tenacious breed, among whose later representatives in the town, certainly or probably, we know of

(1) C. Luscius Ocrea, born perhaps c. 146 B.C. and mentioned as an aged senator about 76 B.C.[28]

(2) L. Luscius, also born in the second century, who became a centurion under Sulla.[29]

(3) L. Luscius Ocrea, known in the 70s of the first century A.D.[30]

(4) L. (Luscius?) Ocra (*sic*), a magistrate of the town in imperial times.[31]

(5) C. Luscius Summachus, a freedman, also of imperial times.[32]

It is entirely possible that the first four of these were direct or collateral descendants of the playwright. Among other gentes represented in the town as early as the second century B.C. we have already noticed the Aelii and Roscii. Others are the Licinii and Laberii, probably the Annii, Furii, Thorii, and Turullii, and perhaps the Caecilii and Velleii.[33] We can scarcely predicate more without reading first-century evidence back into the second century, which it is undesirable to do. As to activity in Roman politics, there is no Lanuvine family which we can trace in this connection, or call *nobilis*, as early as Luscius' time, though a *municeps* called L. Licinius Murena, who was probably in his youth when Luscius retired, went on to become praetor, not later than 147 B.C., and then to do government work in Greece. His descendants followed the example set — his son, grandson, and great-grandson likewise attaining the praetorship, the last-mentioned becoming also, in 62 B.C., the earliest-known consul drawn from a family in the town.

These cullings from municipal history make the town seem busier, more sophisticated, and more in the eye of Rome than it probably was. True, it was near, but it was also sequestered, and mainly the centre of a small farming community, the tenor of whose life was simple and depended more on the quiet rhythm of the seasons, on vintage and olive-gathering, on fattening the sow, huckstering in the market-place, keeping up religion, and providing for the winter, than on the doings of the world outside. Those few scions of Lanuvine stock who made their mark in Rome — a Luscius become *poeta* and known among the intelligentsia, a Licinius going on for senator and better — these were exceptions to the general rule. They doubtless featured in local gossip at crossways or by the hearthside, while invisible cicadas thrummed for ever in the leafage above garden walls, and the occasional lugubrious crowing of a rooster broke the long susurration of the fields. This at least is the impression received if one climbs the eminence in Lanuvio now known as St. Lawrence' hill and looks over the old clustering eaves to the seaward-sloping plain below.

2. *Luscius' Career*

As seen already, we ought tentatively to think of Luscius' adult life as extending from about 206 to 160 or later. The earlier years, say 206 to about 181, are those when he was a youth and a *vir iunior*, up to the age of forty-five; the later years, say 181 to 160 or later, are those in which he was a *vir senior* and a *senex*. We might think of the two periods as his juniority and seniority.

Luscius, Caecilius, and Ambivius were all much of an age, with Luscius possibly the oldest and Ambivius possibly the youngest. Caecilius, as an Insubrian, grew up in the Milan area; where Ambivius grew up is unknown. In 206 all would be in their youth, and in the next twenty-five years all reached maturity. All would be literate, probably from an early age, and at least the first two of them also learned Greek. There was no difficulty in doing this at Rome, where Greek speakers were plentiful. All were drawn to the theatre, which was coming to mean primarily the theatre of Plautus, and all familiarized themselves with playbooks in one or both languages.

No play by Luscius can be dated to his juniority, but Terence's phrase *vetus poeta* justifies us in assuming that already in his juniority he was a practising playwright though not necessarily a prolific one. As I have argued elsewhere, his rating as a minor dramatist, and the paucity of fragments and allusions in later authors are most easily explained if his total oeuvre was small, and by the age of forty-five he may have brought out the merest handful of plays. It is instructive, however, that he later charged Terence with taking up the craft *repente* (*HT* prol. 23), i.e., without due preparation. This implies that Luscius himself had taken time to learn it. We do not know whether he did this primarily by the reading and watching of plays, or by a more active participation in the theatre world. It has more than once been suggested[34] that he began as an actor, in which case he may also, after beginning to write, at first have managed the production of his own plays — a practice which Livy ascribes to the early dramatists in general.

The first twelve years or so of his seniority are again undocumented. His three or four known plays, the chronology of which will be discussed in later chapters, fall in the 160s or, to speak more guardedly, in the decade which ends with Terence's *Adelphoe*. We can however descry him emerging at the beginning of that decade as a man who has a recognized style and circle. It was no doubt the death of Caecilius, probably in 168, which gave him a senior standing, and it was at about the same time that he became aware of the existence, and of vexatious preparations for the staging, of Terence's *Andria* — with consequences which need not be further elaborated here.

We cannot trace, except conjecturally, Luscius' reactions to earlier events and problems in the theatre, but we can trace some of the general factors in his professional life and some of the developments to which he was reacting. These include the *studium* of the audience, the physical theatre, professional interest-groups, and the search for a formula.

3. *The* Studium *of the Audience*

Roman stage-shows as a carnival-religious phenomenon were already fairly old: regular theatre with important artistic and social values was a relatively new phenomenon. In neither form, however, was theatre available for many days in the year or in surroundings which a Greek would have considered worthy of the occasion, the state, and the gods. The audience during Luscius' working lifetime presents us with the picture of a majority pressing for more numerous and more uninhibited, boisterous, or spectacular shows, and an educated minority divided among themselves — having higher artistic standards, yet uncertain how authoritatively to inculcate them; uncertain how far to place any curb on popular demand, in the interests ultimately of law and order as understood by the establishment; and uncertain how far, in terms both of the performance and the setting of shows, to conciliate and pamper a rank and file on whose political support many of them were conscious of depending.

We notice, first, a pressure for the extension of ludi scaenici as a feature of religious festivals, The Plebeian games in November had been made scenic by 200 B.C.; the Megalensian in April became so by 194, and the Apollinarian by 179 or 169. The festival of Flora in April/May, at which stage-shows were traditional (though it is uncertain from when), began to be celebrated annually from 173, having previously been mounted less often. Thoroughly in keeping with these developments is the ready recourse to *instaurationes* indicated by Livy between 216 and 179. Estimates of the total number of performance-days around the time when Luscius would be at his floruit are based on evidence too frail to be worth much; as good a guess as we can make is that theatre days averaged something like one every two weeks throughout the year, though they would tend to come in small clusters rather than be evenly spaced out.[35]

The pressure for scenic games was part of an increasing demand for public entertainment in general. Moreover, in itself it was not synonymous with what we, using a modern and perhaps rather misleading phrase, should call a pressure for "serious theatre." What I intend by this latter phrase is drama in which the appreciative and agonistic means, as explained in the first chapter of this book, can normally be realized by the audience and the actors. As happens in most countries – Greece was an exception – serious theatre was probably a minority taste over which the multitude did not always wholly enthuse. In only one of the first three showings of the *Hecyra* was there sufficient *otium et silentium*[36] for the audience to reach the appreciative mean. In the other two the *populus studio stupidus*,[37] qua audience, disintegrated. The successive distractions of rumoured boxing-match and funambulist, and then of gladiators, are so familiar to us that we neglect to visualize them. How often is it observed that the arena for the gladiatorial show was expected to be (and doubtless was in fact to be) identical with the theatre where Ambivius was trying to get a hearing for the play? The inrush of people, the shouting and fighting for places, went on among the very ranks of the audience.[38] There could be no more ocular demonstration of the relative values attached by the average Roman to Terence's comedy, with its gentle Sostrata, and the hope of seeing physical prowess and bloodshed. Further, within the area of specifically scenic games, it looks as though mime – the short, unmasked piece or turn with strong audiovisual mass-appeal but negligible plot-development and as yet no pretensions to literary standing – was already, via the Floralia, beginning to stake its claim over against regular drama, which during the next century and a half was gradually to be ousted from pride of place. Playwrights had to choose between resisting this trend and meeting it half way.

Culture and politics cannot be kept separate. Another, and contrasting, instance of the demand that the theatre should reflect the realities of Roman taste and society is seen when, in 194 B.C., at the adding of scenic games to the Megalensia, the aediles, to the great chagrin of the people, carried out a resolution of the elder Scipio[39] to reserve special seats for the senatorial order, a thing which afterwards became normal practice. The seats were probably then, as later, those on the flat semicircle which formed the Roman orchestra, between the stage and the rising wooden tiers of the auditorium; it was only at special types of show that this area had to be kept clear for performers. The aediles' measure doubtless only legalized an existing effort of the upper class to pre-empt the best seats, and once the precedent was set, it would be natural for the next ranks of society to get as close to the senators as they could. Down to this time, however, the auditorium must often have looked like, and been, a motley omnium gatherum such as is portrayed in the prolgoue to Plautus' *Poenulus*. (This prologue, if appreciably later in date, is simply ignoring the front benches and concentrating for comic purposes on the promiscuity of the rest.) But from this point on, playwright and actor have a partially stratified audience with a tendency towards stratified tastes, and consequently a tension between the artistic desire for visible approval from a consensus of the best educated, and the need to interest, hold, and gratify the rest, without whose support a play could not *stare*, nor player nor playwright continue in business. Thus Luscius, from early in his juniority, had the most literate and sensitive part of the audience – and later of course also his rival's patrons – nearest the play. This was different from the atmosphere in which Plautine drama had matured. Its ultimate but logical sequel was the long-drawn and finally successful bid of the equestrian order, between Gracchan times and 68 or 67 B.C., to have the next fourteen rows of seats permanently reserved for itself. By the time of Pompey's theatre we can measure this as a fraction of the whole auditorium and it seems about a quarter.[40] The sequel of this in turn is the overt recognition, by an artiste, of the stratification of tastes:

> satis est equitem mihi plaudere, ut audax
> contemptis aliis explosa Arbuscula dixit.[41]

All that has been said touches on the *studium* of the audience only in its broadest aspects and most general differentiations. We can learn more about the tastes of Luscius' public, qualitatively regarded, and about the pressures being exerted, by considering the unsettled state of the physical theatre, tensions among writers and actors, and above all the search for a formula in play-adaptation which, it was doubtless always hoped, would put Roman drama on a par with Athenian.

4. *The Physical Theatre*

Another reality, though it included contradictions, was the pressure for improvement and aggrandizement of the theatre as a physical structure. Alongside admiration and envy of Greek, especially Hellenistic, theatre architectonics, of which one of the newest and nearest examples was the large theatre at Pompeii, completed about 200 B.C., there existed a fairly settled preference for the low stage, as opposed to the typical Hellenistic high one, though there is reason to believe that the playwrights, from Andronicus to Plautus and Ennius, were not unacquainted with the latter.[42] As mentioned above, this preference was accompanied by a firm superannuation of the orchestra as a scene of dramatically significant action, at any rate for tragedy and comedy. Alongside the desire, shared by some of the ruling class, for a stable, regular, and dignified theatre structure, there were, among others of the same class, fears of the moral and political consequences if such a structure should become permanently available to the people instead of being erected only when needed.

A few glimpses of the ebb and flow of sentiment emerge from notices in Livy and elsewhere. 179 and 174 were notable years for public works initiated by the censors.[43] Among the undertakings in 179 was a contract let by the censor M. Aemilius Lepidus for an auditorium and a stage to be built near the temple of Apollo.[44] As Livy does not record the ordinary erection and dismantling of the wooden theatres year by year, and as the other public works mentioned in this and similar contexts appear to be of a more durable nature, it looks as though something out of the ordinary (more permanent?) was here intended. We are left to speculate on the sequel. Either the building was, from the start, only meant as temporary, or some accident befell it, or some obstacle to the implementation of the contract arose, or some vacillation of sentiment caused the work to be later undone. At any rate we hear no more of it. If it was actually built it was fairly plainly intended for the Apollinarian festival which had either by now acquired, or was shortly to acquire, scenic games; and the most likely dramatist to have had plays performed there is Caecilius, whose floruit St. Jerome's *Chronicle* puts in this very year. The next censors, in 174 B.C., are also recorded as having let a contract for a stage to be used for the scenic games supervised by aediles and praetors.[45] We are not told where it was located, and much ink has been spent on discussion of the point. As in the previous case, no doubt a durable piece of work was intended, but I can see no reason why it should not also have been a movable one, for that is what would best have served the purpose indicated. It is interesting that the praetors in office this year probably included C. Cassius Longinus, who later as censor became a leading proponent of a permanent stone theatre.

The foregoing were intended for regular ludi scaenici. What arrangements were made for the staging of Pacuvius' *Paulus*, probably a *praetexta* (a serious play on a Roman subject) and acted in 167 as part of the triumph of Aemilius Paulus, we do not know, but we have a glimpse of exceptional arrangements in the bizarre show which took place in February of that year in connection with another triumph. This was the triumph of L. Anicius Gallus, who was destined to hold the consulship in the year of Terence's *Adelphoe*. The show was held in the Campus Martius, where, according to Polybius,[46] there were rigged up (besides what was probably a stage proper) a "very large *skene*," specially prepared for the occasion, and an orchestra to be used by dancers. Here we see an audience being offered something exotic. The *skene* probably was, or included, a painted *scaenae frons*, which has the same function as a modern backdrop. One reason for thinking so is the presence at Rome in the 160s — for certain in 164 — of one Demetrius from Alexandria, who was by profession a *topographos*. This term seems to mean a painter of large landscapes, townscapes, scenes with shrines, bowers, grottoes, etc.[47] There is evidence for both artistic and literary interest in such scenes in third- and second-century Alexandria, and for links between them and the theatre (at any rate links with Dionysus and satyr-plays). Demetrius may have been attracted to Rome by the chance of commissions such as Anicius and other *triumphatores* had to offer, but he or similar artists may also have carried thither illusionistic scene-painting for ordinary plays. This in turn inspired a fashion of decorating interior house-walls with eclectic adaptations of such scenes. Mature examples, of approximately Augustan date, survive from Boscoreale. They represent unpeopled scenes from tragedy, comedy, and satyr-play, and give us a good idea of the later republican *scaenae frons*.[48] It seems possible therefore that theatrical scene-painting of this kind began to become available to dramatists such as Luscius, Pacuvius, and Terence. Luscius and Terence in fact may have sent on their *senes*, parasites, etc. through some humbler and I suppose univalve predecessor of the ambitious bivalve doorway in the Boscoreale comedy scene. If this is so, it would be an amenity which Luscius only encountered late in life, whereas Terence could begin to think in these terms even as a novice.[49]

The baffled climax of the story is one which Ennius certainly, Terence almost certainly, and Luscius probably, did not live to see. This was when C. Cassius Longinus, who had probably been praetor in 174, rose to the censorship. He then (154 B.C.) with his colleague M. Valerius Messalla set vigorously afoot the building of a theatre of stone. The year is that of Pacuvius' floruit. The site is one which may have had reference to the temple of the Magna Mater and the Megalensian Games. The project got under way, with all the attendant engineering work and concentration of supplies, and was continued for three years. Not all censors, however, shared in Cassius' liberal aspiration. A very determined opponent was P. Scipio Nasica Corculum, whom Luscius and Terence had seen in office as aedile in 169, praetor four years later, and consul for a short time in 162. He attained the censorship in the year of Terence's death. He had plenty of experience of the Greek world and believed that too close an imitation of it, and especially anything that would facilitate a large, seated assembly, was fraught with danger to the Roman establishment. In 151 he used all his authority and eloquence as a distinguished *censorius* and consular to induce the senate to halt and undo the work. What had been built was pulled down, and the whole of the construction materials was auctioned off to private buyers. He even got a supplementary resolution carried banning all forms of seating at public games inside or within a mile of the city. The human physique, with its need for incumbition, soon got the better of this interdict, but about ninety years were to elapse before the Roman public saw the walls of a stone theatre going up again.[50]

5. *Professional Interest-Groups*

Before 200 B.C., and probably at the very beginning of Luscius' juniority, governmental recognition had been given to certain professional interest-groups by the assignment to them of the temple of Minerva on the Aventine as an official meeting-place, under the wardenship of Livius Andronicus, who was now nearing the end of his life. To judge from the notice of this event in Festus[51] (who had it from Verrius Flaccus writing in the first century B.C.), although the official award spoke simply of writers (*scribae*) and actors (*histriones*), there were in fact three interest-groups concerned since the term "writers" at that date included both poets or creative writers and government clerks or secretaries. We cannot tell for certain whether these parties had already for some time past been united into a guild, or whether (as seems to me more likely) the award in itself betokens the first formation of the guild.[52] In either case it seems probable that this Roman *collegium* was to some degree inspired by the Greek guilds of Artists of Dionysus, which had sprung up about the time when Andronicus was born. He in his early days (unless we accept the view that he was brought to Rome in childhood), may well have been a *technites* at Tarentum, and there is some evidence that Plautus also may at one stage of his life have worked among *technitai*. That many of the guild-members at Rome had foreign, and presumably Greek backgrounds is suggested by the phrase *dona ponere* in Festus, referring to the right now conferred of dedicating gifts in Minerva's temple; for both the right and the formula are known to have applied particularly to *peregrini*. One suggestion that has been made is that a private guild, honouring Dionysus, who had no temple at Rome, was being simultaneously recognized and romanized by deflection to Minerva, who was thoroughly Roman and yet at the same time sufficiently appropriate both as goddess of the intellect and cultural pursuits and as the Roman form of Athena, patroness of the home of drama.[53]

A sharp limit is put to speculation, however, by the fact that there is no certain later allusion to a guild of writers and actors as such. We cannot tell the exact terms of membership, though they were clearly not identical with those for the Greek guilds. We cannot tell how long the guild existed in its original form, and whether later allusions, especially to the *collegium poetarum*, are in reality a short-title for it or represent a metamorphosis of it or a successor to it. It has been argued[54] that Luscius was a leading member of the guild, but we cannot tell for certain whether he, or for that matter Plautus, Ennius, Caecilius, and Terence, ever held membership at all. We are in equal ignorance with regard to actors of the time, such as Publilius Pellio and Ambivius Turpio. The only attested member is Andronicus himself, in whose honour the award was made and who was, or had been, both a writer and an actor. What we can be sure of, however, is that the three interest-groups concerned, to one of which Luscius certainly did belong, continued in existence and continued to be interconnected. It seems apter to consider the groups themselves than to beat the air of conjecture about the guild.

The clerk-secretaries of the civil service, though of humble rank socially — often freedmen (as, it will be remembered, Andronicus himself probably was) — grew in numbers and importance and came eventually to form a respected order in the state. A continuing connection between them and creative writers is suggested by the career of Horace who, long after he ceased earning his living as a clerk-secretary and became an eminent poet, represents himself as still on call by the professional body when they wish to consult him *de re communi*.[55] A continuing link between the same group and actors, in the period of circa 90-70

B.C., is manifest from a little-heeded passage in Cicero, who implies that actors, whom he (tendentiously) refers to as *explosi*, may hope to graduate to the ranks of clerk-secretaries and thence perhaps even into the equestrian order.[56] And there is at least one imperial inscription linking together all three of the interest-groups under consideration.[57] What opened to these men the line of promotion suggested by Cicero was probably, in the first instance, their common asset of literacy, and it may have been this, as much as the interest in drama which many of them shared, which brought them together in the days when Luscius was young.

Luscius and his fellow-poets had cause to rejoice in the extension of scenic games and the pressure for improvement of the physical theatre. Such developments meant more festival-time and greater amenities in production, and these in turn meant a better livelihood and wider prestige. The poets, including Luscius, formed a recognized group within the intelligentsia, and play-writing was a recognized professional skill, to be preserved from the encroachments of unqualified amateurs. The more closed the poets could keep their shop, the better off they were. Hence, in the days of Luscius' seniority, the scornful complaint of an unqualified amateur against him and his kind:

faciuntne intellegendo ut nil intellegant?[58]

The economic picture was complicated by the randomness and, in a sense, the unfairness of patronage. It was not a formalized institution, but the *de facto* importance of patronage to those who received it was considerable. Terence, of course, received it (though not in the form of large and direct monetary gifts), and Ennius and Pacuvius seem to have had patrons off and on. There is no evidence that Naevius, Plautus, Caecilius, or Luscius had any; and when Andronicus had worked as a schoolmaster he had certainly done so in order to earn his living. In any case the run of early Roman poets were not well off. Terence, after six years of patronly support, finished up with twelve and a half acres freehold beside the Appian road,[59] which if he let it would yield a rent useful for keeping body and soul together, and even for buying books when in Greece; but I see no reason to share the almost universal doubt of the testimony that he did not own a house or leave any domestic establishment behind him in Rome when setting out on his Greek journey.[60] To professionals without a patron, the struggle for existence was real. Luscius in his prime was far from being Rome's most distinguished or popular writer, but after the death of Caecilius in or about 168 his age and experience gave him a senior standing; and it was probably in part as the spokesman of patronless professionals that he felt obliged, when faced with the phenomenon of Terentian comedy, to try to close the shop to it. Terence had his *Phormio* prologue-speaker put this in the baldest of economic terms:

> ille ad famem hunc a studio studuit reicere.[61]

Luscius' antipathy, which (as seen earlier) may have somewhat resented Terence as more of an outsider by nationality than any other of the leading poets, and again as not standing fully on his own feet as a writer, thus appears to have gained a sharper edge from a sense of the unfairness of his competition in the play-market. We cannot tell what precise degree of justification Luscius had. When Terence's work was chosen for exhibition at a festival, someone else's was probably rejected. A word in the ear of an aedile by a powerful patron might have been what tipped the scale.[62] I believe, however, that the antipathy cut still deeper. As we shall see, it cut right down to the bottom, to a narrow but crucial disagreement between the old man and the young over artistic principle and over the most desirable channelling of the *studium* of the public.

The third interest-group, the actors, had joint cause with the playwrights to rejoice in the growth of show business, and they were subject to some of the same tensions. Our sources of information are so circumscribed that almost the only actors who come into focus as persons are the ones whom it is customary to call the actor-managers. Luckily these were at the centre of the picture. We have of course to be on our guard against biased testimony. A large part of our knowledge comes from, or through, Ambivius Turpio — for it must be supposed that the drafting of Terence's prologues was done at least partly in concert with him, and it would be only human for him (and only natural for Terence as young and guidable to agree) to aggrandize somewhat the actor-manager's role as the kingpin of theatrical enterprises. Yet the fact remains that, making allowance for bias, we still have probably better documentation on actor-managers at this period than at any other in Roman stage history. The records, *in toto* scanty, tell us something of at least the following, in the half-century or so from the death of Naevius about 201 B.C. onward:

	Reference in Appendix I
(1) T. Publilius Pellio as producer for Plautus and/or in Plautine revivals	125
(2) Anon. Actor-manager (*Phorm.* prol. 10) as producer for Luscius	26
(3) L. Ambivius Turpio as producer for Caecilius	4
(4) L. Ambivius Turpio as producer or co-producer for all of Terence's plays	4
(5) L. Atilius Praenestinus as producer or co-producer for Terence	55
(6) L. Sergius (Turpio?) as producer or co-producer for Terence	141
(7) L. Minucius Prot(h)ymus as producer or co-producer for Terence and (seemingly) also producer of tragedy	112
(8) Cincius Faliscus (probably of this period) as (seemingly) producer of comedy	66

Although I have called them actor-managers, they should rather be thought of as actor-manager-producers, since they united all three functions. The contemporary name for such a man was *actor*,[63] though the Latin of the day far preferred to allude to his work by some part of the verb *agere*, such as "*egit* so-and-so." The expression *dominus gregis* is now sufficiently discredited as a figment of scholarship:[64] it would imply ownership of the troupe, which is a quite different concept from *agere*. The composition of a *grex* was in fact midway between stable and fluid: a free actor could no doubt hire himself out to one, just as a slave-actor could be hired out to one by his real *dominus*, for (naturally) varying periods. The actor-manager, besides his evident right of hiring and firing the *gregales*, was responsible for the techniques of production, had a vested interest in revivals, could in some cases acquire proprietary rights over manuscripts, and doubtless had the chief say in those divergences and optional variations which, almost throughout theatre history, have distinguished "actors' copies" from official texts. What concerns us most, however, is the entente between actor-manager and dramatist.

The function of the actor-manager was one originally performed by the dramatist himself. Now it is quite clear that Ambivius had never been a dramatist and regarded playwriting as out of his province, but his memory, like that of the two dramatists Caecilius and Luscius (but not Terence) stretched back into a different age — into the lifetime of Andronicus and Naevius, under whom the older arrangement was presumably normal. Indeed Caecilius and Luscius may themselves have begun as actors and then become actor-producers of comedies of their own before handing over, as we find them doing, to professional producers. The changeover from writer-cum-actor-manager to a differentiation of these roles would in practice be gradual and was perhaps never quite complete, for as fast as tragedy, to take the paradigm case, passed into the hands of professional writers, and then of gentlemen dilettantes, another kind of writer-cum-actor-manager and performance were to come along and break the surface of literature, namely, Publilius Syrus and his handling of the mime. In Luscius' day, while comedy and tragedy, like the Latin language, are green and growing, before any Roman plays have achieved unquestionable status as classics, before anyone thinks of them as literature to be taken away and read, the key fact about the actor-manager is that he works necessarily as interpreter and champion of a living dramatist, in whose success or failure he has a considerable stake. As much as the dramatist, he aims to indulge, but also to mould, the *studium* of the audience by the quality of the play. The interlocking of the two interest-groups was fully as strong, if not stronger, when Luscius had his known plays produced in the 160s, than was the union between writers and actors at the founding of the *collegium* forty years earlier, symbolized by their common privilege of dedicating gifts to Roman Minerva in her Aventine temple.

The general history of drama from 240 B.C. has been summed up as "the hellenizing of the Roman stage."[65] The vital first forty or fifty years had been a time of healthy rankness, with an audience blessedly ignorant of rules and schools. The exuberance of the stage, as Luscius was making his first steps towards it, rose to the moving hyperbole in which Naevius wrote, before finally laying down his pen:

> If spirit may mourn for flesh
> then mourn, Poem, for your poet.
> He lies in death's hoard of silence
> and living men are bereft of words.[66]

If that was not by Naevius, it was by someone with a brilliant sense of his identity. But the ensuing years, and in particular the years of Luscius' seniority, were critical in a different way. For it was then that the questions first arose: how many varieties of hellenizing are there? What are the tolerable limits to which hellenizing can or should go? These fundamentally cultural questions had to be settled empirically, and the actor-managers were as deeply committed to their solution as the penmen. The tradition that Minucius and Cincius had something to do with turning into a Roman *placitum* the Greek dogma of masked acting[67] testifies, even if the facts are unproved, to a belief in the cultural, and one might almost say anthropological, involvement of these second-century figures in Roman evolution.

The actor-managers were thus caught up in a twofold tension — that between the writer and the *studium* of the public, and that between one writer and another. The most regrettable gap in our records is that we know virtually nothing of who, during Luscius' juniority, rode out the double tension and carried Plautine drama at its most mature to what must be regarded as the greatest all-round success in the history of Roman comedy. However, for certain other events of that time, and for the next phase — the period of Luscius' seniority — the darkness lifts a little. In three cases an actor-manager is seen labouring to commend what was originally a minority *studium* to either a playwright or the audience or both. The initial rise and temporary failure of Caecilius Status must be put between about 194 and 185/180. It would be towards the end of that time that Ambivius came to his aid (Ambivius states that he was *adulescentior* than when, turned sixty, he carried the *Hecyra* to eventual success). The struggle was not decided in a moment. The audience was not content to hear out and praise or condemn but sometimes condemned a play, in ignorance and prejudice, before it got well started:

> partim sum earum exactu', partim vix steti.[68]

But Ambivius persevered with the Caecilian programme and succeeded.

> perfeci ut spectarentur: ubi sunt cognitae
> placitae sunt.[69]

There is nothing wrong with the tradition which places Caecilius' floruit in 179.[70] From thereabouts, as we have seen, Luscius enters upon senior status, and needs an actor-manager to champion his own programme. He found one. We catch one direct glimpse, a glimpse of how matters stood in the 160s when his play (of unknown title) about a young lover with protective wish-fulfilment hallucinations was put on. The pejorative report represents this comedy,

> quom stetit olim nova,
> actoris opera mage stetisse quam sua.[71]

Once again the actor-manager is trying to convert the audience to a view not its own. But he is simultaneously contending against another author and manager within the profession. For the third case is, of course, the return of Ambivius to the picture to champion Terence both against majority *studium* and against Luscius and those for whom he spoke. This part of the story is well known. All that need be remarked here is that Ambivius was not working alone: as co-producers or successors he had at different times Lucius Atilius from Praeneste and probably Lucius Sergius and Lucius Minucius. We shall see that what lay behind all these histrionic negotiations with the public was the search of playwrights for a formula.

There are other, related interest-groups, but they lie more on the fringe of Luscius' experience. There were the imported *technitai* who came and went home again. In the 180s they were on exhibition at Rome for at least two ten-day periods.[72] They had a point of view, and notes to compare with Roman actors. It has been remarked, for instance, that they "were all used to performing on the Greek high stage."[73] This is likely to be so even if they were not *tragoidoi* and *komoidoi*. In 167 some more came over, for Anicius' triumph, and this time it is certain that *tragoidoi* were included. Roman actors had to watch out for their own interests, but they may still have sympathized as these foreign Artists ran the gauntlet of the Roman crowd. Earlier I described the show that now took place as bizarre. What seems to have happened is that the Greeks were prepared to offer a series of stage acts forming something like a pageant-cum-ballet-cum-boxing-match, which the Romans watched with a slightly xeno-phobic mixture of admiration and contempt and with an itch to turn it into horseplay. Roman dissatisfaction, expressed by Anicius himself, who perhaps prudently but still unworthily sided with majority *studium* in finding the proceedings too aesthetic, converted the show into so confused a melee that Polybius blushingly draws a veil over the end and blots from the record what the *tragoidoi* themselves were reduced to.[74] The public appetite for horseplay was not more regretted by Polybius than it would be, in principle, by the more sensitive among Roman observers, or by Terence if present. Theatrical riot was apt to go off in spontaneous combustion, and there is no need to attribute to Luscius, or to *maligni* within the profession, the disappoint-ments caused to Terence and Ambivius a few years later over the *Hecyra*.

The crossing of Greek with Latin impulse is seen in a last group, surprising at this early date, namely, the hardy carriers of Latin talent into the heart of the Greek festival-world. We know very little about these men, or what their ethnic connections were, but some kind of Roman-style or Latin-language entertainment, possibly sub-dramatic but still acceptable to a Greek audience, was put on at Delos by an Agathodoros in 172 and perhaps by an Antipatros the previous year.[75] And shortly before 155 we find a Novius, perhaps of Campanian stock, writing drama in Greek and competing successfully with Greek comic poets at the Lenaean festival in Athens itself.[76]

6. *The Search for a Formula*

Luscius was probably over fifty, and perhaps over sixty, when he first heard of Terence. Despite the unhappy way in which history has slanted things, he still deserves to have the tenor of his working life, if at all possible, understood. This would entail trying to form some estimate, however slenderly based, of what he stood for prior to that sour day in the calendar on which it became known that some *libertus* of a senator – a young alien with a dark skin and surprisingly smooth Latin – had done an adaptation of Menander's *Andria* and got it accepted by the aediles for the next festival. There are two choices before a writer for the stage: he may come to terms with his public, or he may proudly fail. Each choice resolves itself into a series of others. As we have seen, not Luscius only but all contemporary writers for the stage – of whom there may have been about a dozen in the effective running – faced serious cultural questions about varieties of hellenizing and about the tolerable limits to which the hellenizing of the Roman theatre could or should be carried. Luscius saw this problem, but, while mulling it over, what he and a few others had the curiosity to go on and do was to stand the last question on its head and ask what are the tolerable limits to which a Greek play can or should be romanized. The signs are that those few, of whom Luscius was prepared to act as spokesman, had been attempting the formation of a responsible body of opinion on this subject long before Terence was out of puberty.

In speaking of the search for a formula I shall not try to review synoptically the whole field of Roman comic play-adaptation but shall merely comment in brief on some aspects of it where the evidence suggests comparability of Caecilius and Luscius with each other and with Plautus and Terence. There is no harm, however, in beginning from a single-sentence summary of Plautus:

> Plautus was an original artist whose technique developed and matured in his later work; he made the Greek plots more farcical and the characters more laughable and grotesque; he gradually increased the amount of song and dance, making

the plays almost musical comedies with gay and festal conclusions: he added Roman references and did not hesitate to break the dramatic illusion; he increased the quantity and vulgarity of his jests; and, by eliminating a certain amount of exposition and repetition of information, he sought to introduce more suspense and surprise into his plays.[77]

The Plautine formula had not been a static one. Like any beginner, Plautus had possibly at first been – one cannot say overawed by the Greek, but given in some degree to a gingerly handling of it which might have passed for respect. As he attained to a more penetrating knowledge of the mass of his audience and a better grasp of his medium, he moved in the direction of greater freedom from his sources: not so much, however, in terms of plot-structure as in technique and tone. He did indeed hold himself free to graft scenes from one source-play into another, but the direct evidence of his so doing is minimal, and we cannot establish a trend one way or the other. He used his freedom particularly for the remoulding of Greek trimeter dialogue and monologue into longer lines, both iambic and trochaic and having a more accentuated swing than the originals. He also, and still more strikingly, used it for developing spoken ideas in the Greek into polymetric song, no doubt accompanied by heightened gesticulation and by dance. Both these changes are now beyond reasonable doubt, and the first of them has lately been reillustrated by a piecing together of the Greek source of *Bacchides* 494-562, where the original is all in trimeters but the larger part of the Latin in trochaic septenarii.[78] In view of such versatility, no wonder that at his death "all his measures beyond measure wept for him."[79] Another part of the Plautine formula which evolved gradually was the dispensing with careful preparation of the audience for events to come. Foreshadowing was a Greek dramatic technique about three centuries old, but in Plautus it lessens in the later plays. Elements which tend to increase, besides song and dance, include verbal embellishment of many kinds, grotesquerie in characters, robustness of humour, and farce. His *neglegentia*, if we are to call it such, grows with time, and he experiments more readily in crossing New Comedy with what have been called the "pre-literary dramatic forms of central and southern Italy."[80]

These ultimately themselves had partly Greek origins, but origins earlier than New Comedy. Compared with the latter they were either more directly based on music and movement, or else were dramatic extravaganzas, the aspect in which they were weakest being argumentum or plot.

The trend of Plautus' art, as it develops, is thus away from such things as the Menandrean structural finesse, urbanity, sense of identity, sentiment, everyday realism, and avoidance of the extravagant and far-fetched. The spirit is altered. There was no such thing as native Roman comedy, but Plautus romanized Greek in the direction of the nearest native equivalents, and his actors doubtless acted out his intentions. He was not in a strict sense trying to carry New Comedy over into Latin, and he recognized no such duty to his sources as this would have entailed. The hellenism of his plays, if we are to speak of it at all, is residual. It is distantly comparable to what is residual in some types of modern musical — the residual Shavianism, for example, which manages to invest the perfectly genuine art by which *Pygmalion* is turned into *My Fair Lady*. Plautus' mood and his fashion of publicity are reflected in his handling of titles, among which, if we take account of the lost plays, some eleven may be reckoned as transliterated Greek names and some seven as transliterations of other Greek words, but some forty-four (including eight -*aria* titles) as whole-hog romanizations.

The vulgate view of Caecilius, which happens to be right as far as it goes, is that, as temporally, so artistically, he was intermediate between Plautus and Terence, the chief contention being between those who place him nearer the one, and those who approximate him more to the other.[81] How I think the Caecilian formula was arrived at is like this. At the time of Plautus' death, when Luscius was probably in his forties, the general increase of traffic between Rome on the one hand and Athens, Alexandria, and the cities of Asia on the other, the greater familiarity of the Greek theatre, and especially the visits of *technitai* to Rome, began to impress on the more sensitive the discrepancy between the dramas of the two nations. The *studium* of the audience began to develop a minority pole desiderating positive, rather than residual, transference of the content and spirit of Greek plays. As often happens, this became a vogue demand, satisfiable in the case of the majority by a limited number of hellenizing features which would leave the texture of the drama to an appreciable degree in the Plautine mould. The continuing popularity of Plautus' own formula is proved both by revivals and by the welter of plays in circulation, or in the *capsulae* of actor-managers, falsely claiming his name.

Plautus and Caecilius both came from what modern geography would call the northernmost third of Italy: the area least imbued with Greek traditions and cultural ideals. What they had of these they had had to acquire in Rome or further south. Caecilius is really much nearer to Plautus than to Terence. He seems to have all of Plautus' comic vigour and Latin wit, and as great if not greater cleverness. The Greek element in the Caecilian formula is best described as a *nominal* hellenizing. Among play-titles the balance tips to the Greek side: about thirty-four (including thirteen proper-name titles) as against eleven Roman titles or subtitles, the only -*aria* formation being *Rastraria*, an alternative title for the *Hypobolimaeus*. Ancient mention of his skill *in argumentis* and his *gravitas*[82] probably means that he tinkered less with the plots. In this respect he no doubt went further than Plautus in giving people the "straight" play. We happen not to find him scene-grafting or inserting Roman allusions, and much has been built on this, but the evidence is not sufficient to show his real attitude. At the same time we catch him at least once drastically refashioning Greek trimeter speech into the Plautine type of polymetric canticum.[83] As far as tone and spirit were concerned, he satisfied the majority, at any rate in due course, without troubling about duty to his originals. He romanized as Plautus had done, and in certain ways went further. The pressure which made the Floralia annual in 173 was the same pressure which made Caecilian comedy mimic or mimelike, as two ancient authors attest that it was.[84] Mime was as un-Menandrean as the comic stage could get.

Here are two *senes* talking. I shall first try to render the Greek original:

A.   And my wife's an heiress and a positive fright of one.
      I've told you that before, haven't I? Eh, haven't I? . . .
      House in her name, and so's the land and every blessed

> thing. To deal with she's as awkward as they come. And
> she's got it in for everyone, not just me . . . for her son
> . . . and for her daughter worse than ever.
> B. Sounds as though you just can't win.
> A. Don't I know.[85]

By the application of Caecilius' formula it comes out something
like this:

> B. But that wife of yours: sour-tempered would you say?
> A. Ask me another.
> B. I mean, in what sort of way?
> A. Oh, it wears me down talking about it. Her. No sooner
> have I got home and drawn up a chair than she gives me a
> hunger-honed sniff of a kiss (*savium dat ieiuna ani-*
> *ma*). . . .
> B. Quite right too. Wants you to throw up all you've been
> drinking while out.[86]

This adequately shows us his tone and colour, the independence or
cavalier spirit of his adaptation, the nominality of his hellenizing.
Let it also, however, vindicate him in part from the charge of
going out of his way to depict "the physical unpleasantness of the
rich wife,"[87] the charge of coarseness and of meeting "the grosser
demands of the Roman public."[88] The fragments are not coarse; in
the case of another fragment it happens to be Menander, not
Caecilius, who makes the suffering husband refer to his wedding-
night; and in the present fragment, on which, above all, the charge
is based, *ieiuna anima* has been leading many critics astray. Nonius
glossed it partly as *odor*, whence a confused note in the most
popular modern edition explains it as "breath that makes you
want to vomit," "nauseous breath."[89] *Ieiuna anima*, fasting
breath, here means inhalation which has been deliberately sensi-
tized by hunger in order to detect the least suspicion of alcohol.
This is not exactly coarse, and in any case it is not the wife but the
husband's confidant who here introduces such physical unpleasantness as there is.

    The Caecilian formula, like the Plautine, was not static. Some
aspects of it, at the level of production if not of basic

composition, had been developed, after initial failure, by the help of Ambivius. It is hard to be sure which aspects these were: the likeliest guess, on the evidence, is that the Insubrian had originally modelled himself on Plautus, and then on hints from Ambivius gone further to meet the growing minority taste for something nearer Menander and its vogue counterpart, the demand for superficial hellenizing. In any case Luscius, who may have attended some of Plautus' premières and who lived through the whole Caecilian experiment, rejected some of the fundamental propositions of both the other two poets. In doing so he also forfeited their very visible success. The way in which he and a like-minded group (the *isti* of *Andr.* prol. 21) set out to stem the tide of romanizing will emerge, I hope, from the following chapters, but here is a curt preview. Luscius had no quarrel with the type of sources chosen nor with their vigour of action and their colourful characters. We shall find in his own plays the *servus currens* — a form of the *servus callidus* which Plautus had made a staple of his own drama — and two or three examples of the *insanus adulescens* on whose passion the typical plot in this art-form depends for its mainspring. We shall find the *avarus senex* and the *pater severus*. He uses motifs already established in Plautus such as the treasure-trove and the hearing before an arbiter. He adheres to the festal conclusion. But his quest for a superior formula led him to reject both romanizing and nominal hellenizing and to fix his eye on Athenian standards. The two titles of his that are known to us he left in their original form apart from transliterating.[90] This would count for little in itself: it counts for more when we remember that both titles had probably suggested themselves earlier in Roman theatre history, and both had been discarded as too Greek. It is a first indication of his sense of duty to a source-play. In principle he rejected plot-tinkering, what Terence was to call *neglegentia*.[91] He rejected scene-grafting absolutely. He gave the play more "straight" than Caecilius, and free of his mimery. He believed that the first qualities required in an adapter are care and devotion, what Terence was to call *diligentia*.[92] It seems likely that the Luscian formula called for as exact adherence as possible to the line of the Greek dialogue, a matter in which he was totally at odds with the two earlier poets.

He stuck to this even if it led to allusions, and even locutions, which were outside the normal idiom of the Roman audience: a practice which Terence calls *obscura*.[93] And we shall find reason to believe that he wanted to recreate not only the Athenian theatrical experience in general, but also the experience of a specific contemporary occasion, an event at the Dionysia of 167 B.C.[94]

This was the programme, and as in the earlier cases, it no doubt took years to evolve. It would not be unfair to call it a programme of *academic*, perhaps even *dogmatic*, hellenizing. Besides the obvious requirement of a perfect understanding of the originals, its success depended on three things. First, a gifted fluency and élan in the writing of Latin. The signs are that the Luscian school of thought did not possess this beyond possibility of cavil. Second, a genuine desire in the mass of the audience to be taken in the footsteps of Menander. When it came to the point, almost the only Romans who had such a desire in an unqualified form were those who could read or see the plays in the original. Third, it depended on the absence of any acceptable compromise between the Caecilian and the Luscian formulae. But the lack of such a compromise came to an end at the Megalensian Games of 166, when the public was given its first glimpse of what the world has subsequently agreed to regard as *enlightened* hellenization, scene-grafting and all. The Luscian formula did not succeed in second-century Rome. At the very time when Luscius could most have hoped for the plays of his circle to meet with fullest understanding and for himself, perhaps, to sit back as the doyen of the profession, his programme was undercut by Terence and the enlightened philhellenists who were his backers. Terence's star rose, at first shakily, later decisively. Copies of Luscius' plays were known and used for at least fifty or sixty years: how much longer they survived we cannot say, probably not long. But let us not forget that at the present day, as for a long time past, the principle we most expect to see applied if we go to watch Euripides, or Molière, or Goldoni – or for that matter Menander himself – in English dress is not the "enlightened" Terentian principle. It is the principle of Luscius of Lanuvium.

3. LUSCIUS: THE *THESAURUS*

As the recovery of later Greek comedy goes on, it is interesting to return from time to time to areas of Roman comedy believed lost beyond recall and check the appearance of the site and any traces left upon it of what was formerly there. What we cannot rebuild we may yet be able to visualize in a better perspective or a sharper focus.[1] Among the comedies of Luscius Lanuvinus only two are known to us by name:[2] the *Phasma*, based on Menander's play of the same title, and the *Thesaurus*. These are known from the prologue to Terence's *Eunuchus* and from the Terentian commentators and scholia. The texts of the two plays probably dropped out of sight at an early date, for they seem not to be quoted or referred to by any other authors, commentators, scholiasts, grammarians, glossators, or deipnosophists. Terence, after criticizing Luscius' work in general terms, goes on to speak of these two plays in the following words:

> idem Menandri Phasma nunc nuper dedit,
> atque in Thesauro scripsit causam dicere
> prius unde petitur, aurum qua re sit suom,
> quam illic qui petit, unde is sit thensaurus sibi
> aut unde in patrium monumentum pervenerit.[3]

With the aid of the fragments of its Menandrean original, and related archaeological evidence, Luscius' *Phasma* is becoming the clearer and the less imponderable of the two plays, but it is to the more difficult one, the *Thesaurus*, that the present discussion will be devoted.

A partial outline of the plot is given by Donatus. From this it appears that a young man who has squandered his inheritance on evil living sends a slave to his father's tomb, which the old man during his lifetime prepared on an expensive scale. The slave is to open it and take in a repast which the father arranged should be brought to him on the tenth anniversary of his death. Now the land where the tomb is situated has been purchased from the young man by a *senex avarus*. The slave obtains this old man's help in opening the tomb and finds inside a treasure, accompanied by a letter. The old man keeps the treasure, alleging that he buried it there himself in time of national emergency, and claims it as his own. The young man *capit iudicem*, and the old man who is keeping the gold addresses the *iudex* first and states his case thus: "The war which took place between Athens and Rhodes there is no need for me to tell you about, it being something within your knowledge." – That is as far as the summary goes.

The actual words in Donatus' commentary are:

> Adulescens, qui rem familiarem ad nequitiam prodegerat, servulum mittit ad patris monumentum, quod senex sibi vivus magnis opibus apparaverat, ut id aperiret illaturus epulas, quas pater post annum decimum caverat inferri sibi. Sed eum agrum, in quo monumentum erat, senex quidam avarus ab adulescente emerat. Servus ad aperiendum monumentum auxilio usus senis, thesaurum cum epistula ibidem repperit. Senex thesaurum tamquam a se per tumultum hostilem illic defossum retinet et sibi vindicat. Adulescens iudicem capit, apud quem prior senex, qui aurum retinet, causam suam sic agit: "Atheniense bellum, cum Rhodiensibus quod fuerit, quid ego hic praedicem, quod tu scias?" etc.[4]

Donatus immediately adds that Terence is stigmatizing these proceedings as contrary to what is natural and to ordinary judicial practice, the more desirable order of events being that the young man who is presented as the complainant should put his case first. The outline and comment thus serve to explain the title of Luscius' play and the particular feature of the play which Terence is criticizing. Donatus' further remarks and our other sources on Luscius add nothing of substance, though one of the Bembine scholia speaks of the *senex* as the "possessor or finder" (*possessorem vel repertorem*) of the treasure, which gives a different emphasis and may come from an independent source.[5]

As it seems highly doubtful whether the plays of Luscius survived till the time of Donatus, the latter must have drawn his information directly or indirectly from an earlier commentator who was able to consult them; for the sentence beginning *Atheniense bellum* ... has long been recognized as a quotation from Luscius himself. The earlier commentator presumably also provided the partial plot-summary, which Donatus has borrowed. And it seems likely that this summary was either itself derived from a versified *argumentum* of the play, or at least was influenced by the style and rhythm of such compositions, for there are fairly evident echoes of epitomating *senarii* in Donatus' prose version.[6] Be that as it may, however, we cannot blame Donatus for not telling us more about Luscius' play. What he might have done, and has failed to do, is to settle a point which Terence leaves unclear, i.e. to identify the Greek source-play upon which Luscius drew. And this is a question on which certainty has eluded us ever since, though reasonable guesses can be made and it may not be long now before one or other of them is confirmed by papyrological finds.

Luscius' title almost certainly implies a Greek *Thesauros* as source-play. "The Treasure," with its wish-fulfilment associations and the dramatic irony to be developed from attendant anxieties, was an obvious title and theme for comedy, and it has been known since the time of Meineke that at least six or seven Greek comedians chose it. The list may be set out thus:

(1) Krates
(2) Anaxandrides
(3) Archedikos
(4) Dioxippos
(5) Philemon
(6) Diphilos
(7) Menander

The chances are that Luscius drew from one of these. But two of them can be quickly eliminated. (1) The Suda lists two poets of the Old Comedy named Krates.[7] One is well-known, but it is the other to whom a *Thesauros* is there attributed — an obscure figure whose date and indeed whose very existence is doubtful. If the evidence of the Suda is accepted this Krates can be ruled out. So can (5) Philemon, since his play was the original of Plautus' *Trinummus*,[8] and the latter bears no resemblance to what we know of Luscius' plot. But in the present state of our knowledge it does not seem to me that any of the remaining five can be absolutely excluded. Neither content nor form is decisive against any of the fragments, and with one small exception these are all in the same meter, that is, the iambic trimeter.

(2) Anaxandrides, a major poet of what is usually called Middle Comedy, is said to have been the first to make dramatic use of amours and seductions, i.e. the kind of use which was to become so characteristic in later comedy. There are extant only two fragments of his *Thesauros*. In one of them we find somebody defending money in preference to beauty as the next most desirable thing after health; this could be a forerunner of the *parasitos* of New Comedy, but it could equally well be an old bawd schooling a refractory pupil, or anyone. In the second fragment somebody says "I picked up a reed-pipe and played the wedding song."[9] Of uncertain date, but probably of the same period, is (3) Archedikos, from whose play we likewise have two fragments. One is apparently spoken by a cook, professionally querulous about the high price of victuals, which he is apt to get the blame for; the other fragment is another cook-speech, this time professionally boastful but no doubt attributable to the same character.[10] (4) Dioxippos may again belong to Middle Comedy. All we know of his play is that at some point a character who has just come onstage from a house or other building, with a secret on his mind, feels a sudden alarm in case someone has heard him. With allusion to a figure proverbial for ill-intentioned listening he says, "I hope the Corycaean didn't hear me." Someone else immediately responds "Well, I did hear you: I followed you out."[11] Obviously any of these incidents could in themselves have formed part of Luscius' play, and Roman playwrights may well have drawn on Middle Comedy when they felt inclined; but as no Roman playwright shows the least sign of being attracted to any

of these Greek writers, who have no réclame whatever in the Roman world, it may well be that Luscius was not attracted either.

The foregoing requires one, perhaps important, qualification. Chronologically speaking, Dioxippos has been a will-o'-the-wisp. He has been conjecturally dated both to the fourth century and to the second. The later date depended on a piece of epigraphic evidence which suggested that one of his comedies was produced at the Athenian Dionysia as a new play in (probably) 181 B.C. and took second place in the competition.[12] It has recently been claimed however that one extra consonant can be discerned on the inscription, which would, if certain, eliminate the supposed reference to Dioxippos' play. If Dioxippos had indeed been at work about 181 B.C. he would be an actual contemporary of Luscius, and if the source-play were his, Luscius would then be highlighted as enabling the Romans to share in a relatively current Athenian theatrical experience. We later find Luscius doing precisely this, though in another way, in the *Phasma*. Dioxippos is probably of the mid-fourth century, but it is perhaps desirable not to close one's mind against the possibility of a second-century date, at least until agreement is reached about the inscriptional evidence.

There remain the indubitable poets of New Comedy. From (6) Diphilos' play we have only one two-line fragment which says "I regard the lie told for safety's sake as a quite straightforward thing to avail oneself of."[13] The accessibility of texts of Diphilos at Rome and the success of his plays with Roman audiences are attested by Plautus' use of his work for the *Rudens, Casina, Commorientes,* and perhaps the *Vidularia,* and the fact that Terence was later to draw upon Diphilos for a scene of the *Aldelphoe.* Other things being equal, Luscius might very well choose to adapt Diphilos' *Thesauros.*

Lastly we come to (7) Menander. Three of the five fragments[14] extant from his play have to do with Eros. In one a speaker says —

Surely then Eros is the greatest of the gods, and the one who has far the most homage paid him. There is no one in the world so parsimonious or by temperament such a strict reckoner but pays a portion of what he has to this god. Now where Eros has gentle dealings, he levies this payment from people while they are still young, but the ones who put it off till old age are charged interest in addition for the time they have waited.

Again —

But when you rob a lover of his courage, he is done for, can be written down in the book of Waly-Waly.

That is said of a faintheart. And

To many music is love's firelighter ⟨— it gives it the start⟩ .

The mention of *mousikê* (really much broader than our term "music") in this play need not mean that there was any episode centred on it: someone could be going through a list of possible incitements to love. Another fragment is the saying "blacker than a beetle," while the remaining one refers hyperbolically to an ordeal of "going seven months without food, and with no water either, not the squeeze of a drop."[15] It is obvious that these fragments are insufficient to enable us to guess the plot-outline. They do however suggest certain *personae* or at least character-elements, namely:

(1) an old man who is parsimonious (*pheidôlos*): in Roman terms, a *parcus senex*;

(2) an old man who has fallen victim to Eros or is in danger of doing so: in Roman terms, a *senex amator;*

(3) a person who comments on the ways of Eros;

(4) the beloved object: in Roman terms, a *virgo* or *meretrix*;

(5) someone presented as the sufferer of a hyperbolically described ordeal.

True, the first fragment quoted above does not guarantee the existence of a *parcus senex* and a *senex amator*, but it becomes much more pointed if they exist, as it can then apply directly to them. These two may of course be one and the same person, in which case (3) is a fairly neutral personage, perhaps a friend or neighbour who is turned to as a confidant. On the other hand the *parcus senex* and the *senex amator* could be separate, but the latter identical with (3) and trying to explain and justify himself to the *parcus senex*. Both of these situations are possible within the conventions of New Comedy.[16]

Among the scholars who have touched on this problem in the last hundred years and more, it has been argued by some, and assumed by others, that the Greek playbook which Luscius took in hand was indeed Menander's *Thesauros*.[17] In terms of known content, Menander's play is neither significantly more, nor significantly less, compatible with what we know of Luscius' plot than any of the other like-named plays considered above. The most cogent reason for favouring Menander is that Terence, who certainly knew the facts, mentions Luscius' adaptation of Menander's *Phasma* and then the present play (*Thesaurus*) in the same breath. Such a phrasing and sequence would be most natural if Menander was the author of both source-plays and not of the first only, and if the audience could be expected to know this. Other considerations include the general popularity of Menander and the fact that none of the other plays called *Thesauros* seems to have been at all well known, except Philemon's, which has already been eliminated. The *Phasma* and *Thesauros* did in fact fall into the group of Menander's best-known plays, and are more than once mentioned in close proximity by ancient writers. Thus a certain Fronto wrote an epigram based on a series of puns on Menandrean titles, in which these two particular plays occur in successive lines.[18] They also occur close together in a papyrus text of the third or fourth century A.D. in which Menandrean titles are arranged in a suitable order for practising shorthand.[19] Here the proximity might seem, from the literary point of view, utterly random, but it proves that both titles, like the author himself, were familiar and respected enough to seem suitable material for a quite unrelated purpose in the educational world of late antiquity. The conclusion would be that since Luscius was interested in one of these plays he is more likely to have been interested in the other one as well, than in any namesake of the latter written by a different playwright.

Cutting right across this belief, however, is an idea which has been long canvassed, that Menander's *Thesauros* is the original of

Plautus' *Aulularia*. If this is so, Luscius must have drawn his own play from some other source, since the two plots are very unlike, and anyway if Luscius were repeating Plautus he would be living in such a glass house that he would have no business throwing stones at Terence for alleged rehashing of Plautine material. This theory about Plautus' play falls into three parts. First, it can be shown that the *Aulularia* is in a number of different ways convincingly Menandrean; the whole strategy of the play attests kinship to the *Dyskolos*, and a verbal parallelism is traceable between lines 91-97 and actual fragments of Menander.[20] The supposed original has come to be known as Fabula Incerta VIII. Second, Choricius refers to a Menandrean Smikrines who is *philargyros* (money-loving) and "afraid that the hearth-smoke might have gone off with a bit of his household stuff,"[21] and this seems to be reproduced at *Aulularia* 301, where the slave says that Euclio cries out to heaven and earth that he is being robbed and brought to ruin

de suo tigillo fumus si qua exit foras.[22]

The play to which Smikrines belongs seems therefore to be identical with Fabula Incerta VIII. Third, if we seek to identify the latter, that is, if we look among the known plays of Menander for one which indubitably contains a treasure (as in the *Aulularia*) and most clearly has room for an old *philargyros*, the choice appears to fall on the *Thesauros*, the fragments of which could, with a little exercise of imagination, be fitted into the story outline.[23]

Against this it has been argued that, although the *Aulularia* is pretty certainly Menandrean, and although the correspondence of Euclio to Smikrines may be accepted, the lack of positive and close agreement between the *Thesauros* fragments and anything in the *Aulularia* unseats the conclusion drawn above, and there are other known or imaginable plays of Menander in which we could find a likely original for Euclio. Menander wrote more plays than are attested by extant titles. He may have written a second *Thesauros*. He may have written a *Philargyros* with Smikrines in the leading role: the words of Choricius might well be taken to suggest this. Or there is the known *Apistos*, which is aptly enough named for Euclio the arch-mistruster, and of which the single known fragment could fit into a "Euclio-Megadorus" scene. It has also of course been argued, by what is from the present point of view a *petitio principii*, that since in all likelihood the *Thesauros* is the play adapted by Luscius, it cannot have been the play used by Plautus.[24] Clearly, the most that can be legitimately inferred from these arguments for our purpose is that the *Aulularia* is not necessarily based on Menander's known *Thesauros*, and therefore that the latter is not excluded as a source-play for Luscius. Future papyrological discoveries, which it is not over-sanguine to hope for, may settle the question. For the present, all we can do is leave the possibilities open. All in all, it seems to me that the *Thesauros* of Menander or that of Diphilos is the likeliest source for Luscius to have used. The others are less likely, with the qualification that Dioxippos would become a most interesting possibility if he should prove after all to be Luscius' own contemporary.

Luscius, then, took this phantasmagorically elusive Greek playbook in hand and read it. He may also of course have seen the Greek play acted somewhere or heard reports of it. He found it suitable for his purpose and went to work. From all that we know of him, we may surely infer both that it had not previously been offered in Latin to a Roman audience, and that, if he made any structural changes he at least did not, in furtherance of this purpose, "contaminate" any otherwise as yet untranslated play, that is, any *integra fabula*. He retained the Greek title, merely latinizing its spelling. A table of *personae* formed in his mind, of which we can reconstruct the following elements:

- ADVLESCENS (the prodigal)
- SENEX (*avarus*, and not related to the *adulescens*)
- SERVVS (servant and helper of the *adulescens*; perhaps young, since Donatus calls him *servulus*)
? - SENEX (who acted as *iudex* in the dispute)

That the adjudicant was probably a *senex* will be shown later by the analogy of other plays. The ubiquitousness of the love-motif in comedy suggests a *virgo* or *meretrix* as the likeliest addition to the above list. For the rest, we can only go by the possible source-plays. If Menander is the source, the *senex avarus* in Luscius will no doubt be the same as the *pheidôlos*, and may then also be the *senex amator*, though this latter could be a separate character. There is further the person presented as the sufferer of a hyperbolically described ordeal. If Diphilos or Dioxippos were the source, we cannot identify any additional *personae*. If Archedikos were the source we should have at least a cook, and if Anaxandrides, possibly a parasite.

The scene of the action, to judge by the allusion to Athens' war with Rhodes, is very possibly Athens or Attica, and the play takes place at the tenth anniversary of the death of the young man's father. Whether this means ten years after the event, or (by inclusive reckoning) only nine years, it does not seem possible to determine absolutely.[25] Donatus' phrase *post annum decimum* suggests the former, but a ritualistic analogy between the repast now to be offered to the deceased and the Roman *cena novendialis* may have led Luscius to think rather in terms of nine years. Everything that precedes this anniversary chronologically must have been among the antecedents to the action proper.

What scenes can be determined? It has been claimed that the only certain one is the adjudication scene.[26] It seems to me that two earlier scenes can be inferred with some confidence, viz. (1) an exposition scene, and (2) a scene immediately after the treasure has been found in the tomb. The exposition of time, place, setting (including what the *scaenae frons* represented), and antecedents (including the past behaviour of the young man as a wastrel) may have occurred in an initial or deferred prologue. That Luscius used prologues of some kind is overwhelmingly likely in the light of comic tradition. It has often been assumed that he used them as Terence did, for extra-dramatic purposes – indeed for the purpose of attacking Terence – but there is no evidence on this point; his attacks on Terence could have taken many other forms.[27] However if he did make his prologues the vehicle for hostile criticism, at least some part of the exposition may have had to be managed, as in Terence, more or less dramatically within the play.

As to the discovery scene and the quarrel which followed it, we have, it is true, to allow for the possibility that all this was merely narrated afterwards, at the adjudication. But all that we know of the dynamics of comedy suggests that the playwright would do his utmost to heighten the interest of the adjudication by building up tension beforehand instead of merely relying on the speeches of the parties in the dispute to do this. If he could not show the actual discovery, which took place inside the tomb-building, he would take pains to dramatize (besides the moment of entrance), possibly the exultation, and certainly the friction, which form its immediate sequel. The *Rudens* affords a close comparison. Plautus could not show Gripus in the act of fishing the travelling-hamper out of the sea, but he spends some 150 lines (*Rud.* 906 ff.), first to show Gripus cock-a-hoop over his luck, and then on the ensuing brawl with Trachalio, which leads up to the adjudication. Corresponding developments for the *Thesaurus* would fall neatly into place if we can assume that the tomb entrance was close at hand or even actually visible on the stage. Donatus' indication that it was on the *ager*, probably a piece of farmland, need not exclude its being visible. A visible piece of *ager* seems to abut on the houses in Terence's *Heauton Timorumenos*, and there is an onstage tomb in Euripides' *Helen*. Donatus speaks of the present tomb as one which the father *magnis opibus apparaverat*. This would be a somewhat otiose remark if its sole purpose was to indicate that the old man was rich, though it incidentally does this. It seems at least possible that the phrase originates because the expensively built tomb-entrance was visible as a sort of doorway in the *scaenae frons*, and Luscius felt it fitting to explain this in words. Hence the emphasis on the point in Donatus, which no doubt goes back to a senarius

> quod vivus magnis opibus apparaverat.

That line, if not Luscius' own, must have been inspired in a versified argumentum by what he did in fact say and show. Of course at least one ordinary house-door would be visible on the *scaenae frons* also. The latter, in fact, may have looked something like a combination of the comedy and satyr-play (countryside) scenes from the Boscoreale cubiculum, though less grand.

All this is amplified by Donatus' touches of generosity over detail. The slave used the help of the *senex avarus* to obtain entrance to the tomb and found a letter (inconsequential in Donatus) along with the treasure. The Bembine scholium[28] indicating the *senex* as finder of the treasure falls perfectly into place if we imagine the slave coming quickly back into view the moment he lights on the letter, followed later by the *senex* with the treasure. The slave will have been trying to read the letter, and may have pushed it quickly out of sight as the *senex* comes up.[29] Its contents are probably not fully disclosed until the adjudication takes place, and a scene of wrangling between *adulescens* and *senex* may well have intervened.

In regard to the adjudication itself, two questions of paramount interest are (1) what form did it take? and (2) why did Luscius expose himself to the charge of "making the defendant speak before the plaintiff"? The latter phraseology is somewhat misleading — a fact for which Terence and his commentators are largely to blame — but I leave it for the moment as it stands. Both questions can be answered. Indeed the second one was answered in principle long since, though in publications which are now rather inaccessible; while the first question merits a franker consideration than it has yet received.

Comedy could and did, when it wished, make use of lawsuits, lawcourt hearings, and various kinds of adjudication as part of the comic plot, and one way of doing this was to have the business transacted offstage and briefly reported, with only the antecedents and/or aftermath enacted. Thus for example Phormio, in the play named after him, acting in connivance with Antipho, brings a suit against the latter to compel him to marry a girl alleged to be a destitute kinswoman. The hearing is offstage, but we see it planned (125 ff., 129 *ad iudices veniemus*) and hear the aftermath (214 *lege, iudicio*, 231 ff., 236 *lex coegit*, 229 *iudex*, 282 *ad iudices*). Two mild and incidental ironies in this play — a play which Terence had in writing close to the time when he was animadverting on the *Thesaurus* — are (a) in re Phormio vs. Antipho, that the man who is a parasite and Antipho's helper should appear in court as his resolute adversary; and (b), in re Terence vs. Luscius, that Terence, so far from making defendant speak after plaintiff, did not let the defendant speak at all (237). An earlier and equally amusing court action which was similarly dramatized in absentia in Roman comedy was the suit of Plesidippus vs. Labrax in the *Rudens* for breach of contract. Here we are shown the odious Labrax being frogmarched off to court

(859 *in ius rapiam*, 866 *in iure causam dicito*). We gather that he enjoys the services of an *advocatus* (890), but he comes back cast in his suit and proportionately bitter and twisted (1281 ff.) On this occasion Plautus, with more structural sense than he is sometimes given credit for, seized the chance his Greek exemplar offered of using the very interim to present another adjudication, one of greater human importance and very properly conducted onstage. It is an arbitration scene (1035 ff. *eius arbitratu* etc.), but such a thing in the Roman mind was by no means to be disjoined from, and seen as adversative to, the notion of a *iudicium* (cf. 1039 *abiudicabit*). This is true despite the fact that the case here, Trachalio vs. Gripus, is conducted as a quickfire brouhaha on which we lack the benefit of Terence's procedural comments. As far as offstage lawsuits are concerned, however, it would be unusual for the onstage report of them to contain speeches in extenso, or anything more than an outline — apart from other considerations, comedy does not usually have the space. Now from Luscius' play there survives, as we have seen, what is clearly the opening sentence of the speech of one of the parties. If, as seems certain, the play contained both speeches verbatim, this is probably not an offstage and reported lawsuit. We may say provisionally that it is part of an adjudication which was enacted live.

And yet a widespread impression has remained that these were, none the less, legal proceedings, with the corollary that Luscius is often vaguely thought of as having staged a genuine lawcourt scene. Beare, for example, tells us that the young man "brought an action,"[30] and Webster, in an unguarded moment, speaks of "the trial scene"[31] — phrases which cannot but suggest a lawcourt, even if they are not meant to. It is indeed natural that we should think in these terms, and I do not exclude the possibility that Luscius half desired such a thought to simmer in his audience's mind. Translators of the lines in Terence from which we began speak of the "defendant" and "plaintiff." Donatus has *petitor* and also *iudex*. But what has cooked the goose in this case is that the scribe of some archetype of the Donatus manuscripts, either from supine inattention or with touching up aforethought, altered the wording of the old miser's exordium to make it fully forensic. This corrupt text of Donatus was the only one available to Ribbeck, and as his *Comicorum Romanorum Fragmenta*, reprinted in 1962, has not been formally superseded as an edition of the fragments of such playwrights as Luscius, we to this day are liable to hear the "defendant" addressing a real jury:

Athenienses, bellum cum Rhodiensibus
quod fuerit quid ego hic praedicem?..[32]

The end of the second line, represented by dots in Ribbeck, is corrupt in all the manuscripts except one (*F*, of the fifteenth century), and the vocative *Athenienses* (or *-is*) in the first line is the reading of all. The same corrupt and defective text appears in Kock under the head of Menander's *Thesauros*, and it is only partially rectified in Edmonds.[33] No wonder the mind's eye sees a court in session.

Approaching the problem from the other end, it would, I think, be agreed that the conventions voluntarily accepted by later Greek and by Roman comedy would normally preclude a formal lawcourt scene. A dramatist writing in this mode asked for certain concessions from the audience and structured his plays upon them with marvellous ingenuity in return, but his mimesis did not carry to the length of full-dress court scenes and settling issues of law on the stage. Not only would the number of supers have caused choregic embarrassment, but the accepted locale of comedy – the outside of private houses, farms, temples, grottoes, and the like – is quite unsuitable for the insertion of a court scene. The actual Athenian courts are never shown, and whenever an agora, which to a Roman is the forum, is mentioned, it is indicated as being offstage. In formal terms the most a comedian can contemplate showing is a private arbitration, in which only an issue of equity, and not an issue of law, is involved. "Arbitration" is a suitable term insofar as the characters have to plead equity, but "adjudication" would sometimes be a better one, as where the issue comes to be practically one of title to the property in dispute, or where, equity notwithstanding, there are cogent reasons why the property should not, or cannot, be divided. And that the "defendant" in the *Thesaurus* is not in fact addressing a jury in a lawcourt, or any kind of plural audience, becomes plain as soon as we consult the corrected text of his opening sentence.

> Atheniense bellum, cum Rhodiensibus
> quod fuerit, quid ego hic praedicem, quod tu scias?

The last three words, which have manuscript authority and are indubitably genuine, show that the whole speech is addressed to a single person. The dramatist, of course, can and does go a long way to suggest the atmosphere of a court, in which in real life such settlements would often take place. He is helped by the fact that both Attic and Roman legal processes encouraged attempts at agreed settlements, where possible, at an early stage, indeed as an early stage, in real lawsuits. Comedy therefore, though staging a private arbitration, may well seek to capture the excitement of a formal public hearing or court scene, and of course utilizes the audience as a means to this end.

There is, however, one point in all this on which we cannot be absolute. Though, as argued above, the evidence that the play presented the two pleas in extenso gives us a fair warrant for supposing that they were originally delivered onstage and not merely reported, recently discovered fragments of Menander's *Sikyonioi* preclude certainty. In the *Sikyonioi* it is now known that a messenger brings a lively report, extending over 103 lines, about the proceedings of a quasi-judicial gathering at Eleusis, where a claim is made that a girl who is being sold as a slave is of free Athenian birth and should have an appropriate guardian appointed for her. One of the reported speeches, that of Stratophanes, extends – though not without interruption – over at least twenty-one lines (see 235-257 Kassel). If reporting on this scale is possible in one play, its possibility cannot be excluded in another. There is, however, a significant difference between the two plays. In the *Sikyonioi* Menander is reporting a crowd scene, deliberately recalling the one reported in Euripides' *Orestes* (866 ff.), whereas the speech in the *Thesaurus*, addressed to a single person, suggests the opposite of a crowd scene. Moreover, there is not a syllable in Terence or Donatus to suggest that the adjudication in Luscius' play does take place offstage, and it has been the unanimous impression of critics that it was enacted live.

The new discovery must introduce an element of doubt, but the odds still seem to be substantially in favour of the traditional view.

Two of the best-known comic adjudications onstage are the one mentioned earlier, on the issue between Trachalio and Gripus in the *Rudens*, and that in the *Epitrepontes* on the issue between Daos and the character called Syriskos or Syros. In both cases the adjudicant is a person senior in age, respected in status, and acceptable to both parties before the case is heard. The same may be assumed of Luscius' play, i.e. the adjudicant was most likely a *senex*. And while the passage in the *Rudens* has little in the way of legal language, that in the Greek play goes some distance in toying with it.[34] It may however be objected that these other cases are not really parallel to the *Thesaurus* because in them (1) all four disputing parties are of servile or near-servile status, which deprives these episodes of the dignity and the formal element appropriate to a binding arbitration between citizens; and (2) that in the *Rudens* the adjudicant, Daemones, is nowhere actually called a *iudex*. It remains therefore to show (1) that the concept of such a private adjudication or arbitration as between citizens really was familiar and was acceptable comic material to the theatre audience, and (2) that the Roman public in Luscius' time would think of the adjudicant in such cases as a *iudex*.

We need go no further than an episode in the *Mercator*. There the *senex* Lysimachus is caught by his wife in having given domicile to a courtesan, and has to explain her presence in the house as something entirely innocent. In a very tight corner he tries to think fast, and finally blurts out: *De istac sum iudex captus* (733). He wants his wife to believe that the courtesan, a slave, was disputed property between two self-alleged owners (therefore persons of free status), and that he, doubtless as a stranger,[35] was *captus iudex*, i.e. they had recourse to him as an adjudicator or arbitrant to settle the case, the disputed property (that is, the courtesan) being lodged with him, according to normal practice, until his decision is given. It is of course desperate and very funny, but the procedure implied is plainly familiar to the audience, as is also the name *iudex* for the adjudicant. In Luscius' play events must have taken a similar course. The young man *iudicem capit*, his adversary must have agreed to the choice, and the treasure itself would be held by the *iudex* while the case was heard. That the parties are addressing a single man becomes clear as soon as we look at a correct text of the fragment in Donatus: this we have already seen. But the desired legal colouring is increased for us, as it was perhaps already then for the second-century audience, by familiarity with the phrase *iudex arbiterve* in Roman jurisprudence.

What is misleading in the English terms "plaintiff," "defendant," and "judge" is that we tend to take them not for atmosphere or colouring but for the substance of the scene. We would not be misled if the play were intact and we could see it all happening there in front of the tomb or of the adjacent house (for there is no *change* of scene), but in default of that we need to bear in mind the lay or private nature of the adjudication. Terence of course wanted to formalize it wholly; the more formal the "action" or "suit," the more regular it would be for the plaintiff to speak first, and the greater therefore is Luscius' divagation from normality. And perhaps it was Terence's noble friends, steeped in their forensic duties or tirocinia, who supplied him with this criticism. In private adjudications the procedure would in fact be less fastened with tape, and though it is most natural and convenient to hear a complaint before hearing the answer to it, dramatic instances suggest that it was not felt grossly invalid for the arbitrant to listen to the answer first or, in other words, to conduct the enquiry as he thought fit. However, Luscius' best vindication – and this is the real reason for the way he arranged things – is that art is not life, nor drama a slice of it. Leo maintained that the charge against Luscius was that of reversing and spoiling the order of speeches in the Greek original;[36] indeed at one time he unhappily cited the *Epitrepontes* to show that Menander at any rate got this kind of thing right. This opinion was fairly exploded by Fraenkel, who in a little-known paper has pointed out that in that very instance Menander himself made the "defendant" speak first, and the same must have applied to the original of the *Thesaurus*, to which Luscius has almost certainly been faithful.[37] Indeed it was, as Fraenkel claims, a general rule of comic technique, and necessary for the proper heightening of tension and the climax, that the party destined to be defeated should speak first, and this rule takes precedence over judicial verisimilitude. Now since the *senex* is avaricious and unsympathetic, and since comedy destines the young man, as we may guess, to obtain the treasure, both so that he may recoup his fortunes and in furtherance of a love affair, in dramaturgical terms Luscius had no choice about the order of the speeches.

The *senex* accordingly begins, and says that he takes for granted the adjudicant's awareness of certain late hostilities between Athens and Rhodes. Whether this allusion to a war comes unaltered from the source-play, whether it refers to a historical event, and if so, to which — these points cannot at present be settled, though guesses have been made. We can however reject the suggestion[38] that the *senex* himself may be inventing a war which never happened. He must, for the sake of plausibility, be citing a war or national emergency which for the purpose of the play really did happen. Either therefore it is historical or the playwright invented it as a fact recognized by *all* the characters: it cannot be merely a fiction of the *senex*. He alleges, then, that in the crisis he hid his gold in the tomb on land which he had bought from the young man after the death and burial of the latter's father; and that the slave, coming on an ostensibly unconnected errand, tried to claim it as his own.

After this speech the adjudicant calls on the young man. Fraenkel thought it possible that the young man might have a parasite speak for him.[39] This seems to arise from the notion of a court scene. In an actual lawsuit it might well happen, and in later days Horace gives us a momentary glimpse of a would-be posthumous parasite, a legacy-hunter, behaving just so, becoming his patron's *cognitor* and acting for him in court (*Sat.* 2.5.38). But we have no reason to suppose any deputizing in the play. The young man no doubt produces his father's letter in furtherance of his case.[40] This letter cannot, of course, say anything specific about the *senex avarus*, whom we are to think of as not coming on the scene at all until he bought the land after the father's death. What the letter can do is to indicate beyond doubt that the treasure is intended for the son. Whether the authenticity of the letter is challenged we do not know; if it is, some plausible reason is found for the *iudex* to uphold it. If he is an elderly man, as I have supposed, he may turn out to have known the youth's father personally and so can recognize his handwriting or seal. This will come out in the adjudication speech, and as we have seen already, dramaturgical practice entitles us to assume that the *iudex* gives his verdict in the young man's favour, the elderly adversary being worsted.

The further developments of the story are at present obscure. We should not press Donatus' phrase *senex avarus* to the point of assuming that this character has a history of miserliness and that this is a leitmotif of the drama. Doubtless he is stingily-inclined (compare, perhaps, the word *pheidôlos* in Menander), but there is no reason to suppose that he hoards other valuables or that his graspingness is exhibited otherwise than in wanting to keep the treasure he found in the tomb. Almost certainly, however, there is a love element in the plot. And the father's letter, at the same time as it ensures the treasure for the son, may introduce stipulations about the use of the money which complicate the amour (or in some other way thicken the plot). Alternatively, the letter may clarify someone's status or relationship so as to assist the unravelling. If Menander is the source, there seems to be a *senex amator* who may be the same as the rival in the adjudication. He could indeed be a rival in the young man's love affair. If Diphilos is the source, somewhere a lie is told "for safety's sake." All that we can assume at present is that just as youth triumphs before the *iudex*, so youth and love triumph in the dénouement. For the rest, we must wait till the sands of Egypt disclose the truth.

It would be foolhardy to attempt to characterize a dramatist of whose work perhaps no more than two lines survive. Luscius had great faults, which Terence and time between them have amply punished. Even if we had his whole oeuvre we would have to characterize it not so much in terms of his creativity as in terms of the choices he made from his source material. Yet one turns away from the dry work of plot reconstruction with a half-formed wish that he could be better known to us. Indeed if we add to his handiwork in the *Thesaurus* the other hints left by Terence and his commentators, with which I have not been concerned in this discussion, possibly distinctive predilections begin to appear. They are of a kind which suggest that a crackbrained mediaeval clerk may have been psychologically, though not literally, near the truth when he said that Luscius Lanuvinus and his friends brought some *bears* to the theatre for the purpose of incommoding Terence by the sensation that would be caused.[41] The glimpses we have of his work — of a running slave, that is, a sort of Dromio scene; of youth defeating crabbed age in the judgment we have studied; his dramatic use of a tomb here, and of a *Vision* elsewhere; and his one surviving poetic image — the image of a hunt, the dogs, the hind, the moment of pity and terror, the plea of a wild creature to a human being to preserve it from a cruel death — this image and Luscius' attempt by it to enact simultaneously the outward fact of a girl's peril and the inward drama of her lover's mind's disorder — all these things, even if carried over from Greek sources, entitle Luscius to a niche in theatre history which his public half begrudged him and which his young competitor failed to understand, but to which Virgil, Seneca, and the Elizabethans would have given a nod of recognition.

4. LUSCIUS IN THE STEPS OF MENANDER: THE *PHASMA*

The other play by Luscius to which we can give a name is the *Phasma*.[1] To see what it was like will bring both his personality and his art into clearer focus. Our only direct knowledge of the play comes from a line of Terence (*Eun.* prol. 9) already quoted:

idem Menandri Phasma nunc nuper dedit.

nunc nuper dedit *codd.* nuper perdidit *Bothe*

The ancient commentators and scholiasts seem to know nothing more about the play itself, though they do discuss Terence's reason for passing no explicit judgment on it, and they offer information about its Greek model. Luscius brought the play out *nunc nuper*. How recent a time is that? The phrase can hardly refer to a date more than a year past, and probably implies that Luscius' play was staged during the most recent celebration of scenic games before the *Eunuchus*, i.e. the most recent before the Megalensia of 161 B.C. if we accept the Terentian didascalia. Donatus and Eugraphius rightly stress that the play was fresh in the audience's memory — somewhat more so, evidently, than the *Thesaurus*, to which Terence turns in the next line of his prologue. The enterprise of creating a Latin *Phasma* could have been germinating in Luscius' mind any time in the later 160s.

Can we point to anything that may have influenced him to write it? In general, a vision, apparition, or ghost is palmary thematic material for drama. The conventions within which both Menander and Luscius worked, however, tended to impose two important qualifications on its use: (1) that the handling of the motif should centre upon the human response to the eeriness of the supernatural, rather than upon the working of the supernatural itself; and (2) that the best concentration is achieved by linking the effects of the supernatural to the human intrigue element, i.e. by introducing a pseudo-vision or pseudo-apparition instead of a "real" one, so that its activities can be humanly manipulated.[2] Sometime during Luscius' juniority, Plautus had handled the apparition-motif in the *Mostellaria*. He had observed the two provisos mentioned above, and the play had been successful — at least sufficiently for copies of it to be permanently in circulation. Plautus appears to have drawn upon a Greek *Phasma*, apparently that of Philemon. He had left Menander's like-named play untouched, and had latinized his own play-title. In Menander's *Phasma*, therefore, Luscius found a play that was technically *integra*, had an excellent theme, and bore a title which could be acceptably transliterated without suggesting work that had been plagiarized locally or was déjà vu.

There is, however, another, quite different factor which may have prompted his choice. This was the interest recently taken in Menander's play at Athens, where an audience which probably numbered at least several thousands had attended Monimos' production of it in 167. In the 170s the play was nearing, if it had not reached, its sesquicentenary, but neither the Greek nor the Roman theatre paid much attention to such anniversaries, and we do not know whether the Athenian authorities had any special reason for selecting it on this occasion. Nor do we know how far the circumstances and merits of the production were reported at Rome by travellers. All that can be said is that the theatre of Dionysus, where Monimos produced the play, held about 16,000 people; that to personal memories there was added a permanently available official record in the Athenian theatre archives; and that the arrival in Rome of reports about the play seems very likely when we recall the amount of traffic between the two cities and indeed the known presence at Rome, in the year and probably the very month of this performance, of a number of Greek *technitai*.[3] They and their successors would spread word about what was currently being chosen, or rehearsed, or performed, in the most famous of Greek theatres.

A few particulars relating to the Monimos production are known. At this period the performance of comedies at the festival of Dionysus took place, on average, every other year. As it happens, the performances of 167 are the latest of which we know for certain before Luscius produced his own play at Rome. An Athenian acting team consisted of a principal, two other qualified actors, and some supers. The practice at the Dionysia was for one such team to stage the revival of a classic, this being followed by a competition among new plays, up to about six in number. The same team could participate in more than one play. An award of honour was made to the victorious author and another, independently, to the leader of whichever team acted best. In due course a record of the results was cut in stone in the hexagonal archive building. The whole proceedings were characterized by a respect for the playwrights and for the acting profession which had no real counterpart at Rome, where it seems safe to say that Luscius and the actor-manager of his *Phasma* received no inscriptional acclaim unless they cut their own.

At Athens, Monimos had been principal of his acting team for some time past, two or three years at the least, and was experienced though not invincible. The previous performance year for comedies at the Dionysia had been 169, when he had produced a new play called *Chorêgon* by a certain Paramonos. It is a coincidence that the names of author and producer somewhat resemble each other, and both suggest "steadfastness" or "staying power." As things turned out, neither of them won on that occasion, and shortly afterwards Paramonos died. However, the account was not closed. Paramonos had left in manuscript an as yet unperformed play which was accepted as an entry among the new plays for 167, was produced by another actor, and won. This is not to be construed as a reflection on Monimos: his own standing is shown by the fact that this time he was given a double charge, namely, production of a new *Aitôlos*, and also of the classic, Menander's *Phasma*. The *Aitôlos* may have had a topical interest because of recent Roman military operations in Aetolia and northern Greece generally, and because of the ensuing visit to Athens of the Roman commander-in-chief Aemilius Paullus, with whose family the name of Terence was soon to be, and perhaps was already beginning to be, intimately linked. It is precisely news of this kind which, along with reports of the *Phasma*, may have percolated to the ear of Luscius. The *Phasma* was put into rehearsal, and Monimos produced it upon the appointed day.[4] He himself in all probability took the parts which fell to the protagonist (we cannot at present determine which these were); his two qualified subordinates would be deuteragonist and tritagonist. The Greek text of the play, as set out in actors' copies, would not require more than three speaking parts in any one scene. As however the table of the *dramatos prosôpa* contained many more than three characters, roles would be doubled, Monimos and the other two changing mask and costume offstage as necessary. Mute parts, if any, would be taken by the supers. It may be noted that Monimos' troupe, who were all male and probably all citizens of good standing, had not only to double parts but had, at need, to take on the roles of women, slaves, and in one case, it seems, a semi-divine figure or deified abstraction. The play was probably done in five short acts, with entr'actes consisting of music, dance, or other entertainment not specified in copies of the text. The content of the play will be considered below. No other details of the performance are preserved, but we know that it was carried through and honourable record of it was later duly added with hammer and chisel to one of the walls in the archival hexagon.

The working copy of the play which Luscius procured was a contemporary of the acting text used by Monimos. These are, of course, both lost, though what Menander on papyrus looked like at that time can be seen from surviving fragments of a copy of the *Sikyonioi*, made probably during Luscius' early life, or from the Menander extracts in the papyrus Didotiana, written out as a lesson or exercise by some students in Egypt in the same decade as Luscius' own play.[5] The Roman adapter's task was to assimilate the Greek text and then realize it in Latin. He had to realize it, moreover, in a form suitable for a stackaway timber-joisted auditorium with vigorous but raw traditions and an audience suckled on *Plautinisches* though preening itself latterly on the nominal hellenizing of Caecilius Statius. Beside Menander and the theatre and craftsmen of Dionysus, the whole Roman ambience was a come-down in sophistication. But sophistication is a relative thing: judged by the simple rhythm of life in Lanuvium, where Luscius had his roots, or in the not-far-off and still quieter Solon's Field, where there may have stood even at this moment an unassuming farmstead among whose folk, a generation later, Quintus Roscius was to be born — judged by the tenor of life in such backwaters as these, the task which Luscius set himself was sophisticated and metropolitan enough.

For anyone wishing to see what can be known about the content of Luscius' play, the usual work of reference is still Ribbeck's *Comicorum Romanorum Fragmenta*, of which the second edition (1873) was reissued in 1962. But the information there given is woefully curtailed. Ribbeck was using an inferior text of Donatus to that now available (this does not matter for the couple of sentences he quotes), and he almost unbelievably stops short where Donatus says that *Phasma* was the title of Menander's play, instead of proceeding to give us the synopsis which immediately follows.[6] Indeed Ribbeck says nothing more about Menander at all, beyond noting that mention of his name by Terence was appropriate to avoid confusion with the other, like-named plays by Philemon and Theognetos.

We must turn our attention to the plot summary. It runs to the following effect. A certain young man had a stepmother. Before being introduced into the family, the stepmother had had a child as a result of an irregular union. The child, a daughter, she had had brought up in secret. She was now keeping her daughter in hiding with the next-door neighbour, and contrived a way of seeing her daughter regularly without anyone's knowledge. Between her husband's house and that of the neighbour was a parti-wall. She had an aperture made in the wall in such a fashion that at the actual point of transit she could pretend there was a shrine, hanging it about with wreaths of flowers and festive greenery and frequently performing religious rites there. Thus she could call the girl to her. When the young man became aware of this phenomenon, at his first glimpse of the beautiful girl he was violently startled and took her for a vision (or spirit), whence the name of the play, *Phasma*. As time went on, however, he found out the truth and fell so deeply in love with her that nothing short of marriage could assuage his passion. The outcome is that to the satisfaction of mother and daughter, in answer to the prayers of the lover, and with the agreement of the father, a wedding is celebrated and so the play ends.

Donatus' actual words are:

> Phasma autem nomen fabulae Menandri est, in qua noverca superducta adulescenti virginem, quam ex vitio quondam [*Kassel*; ex vicino (vitĩo, vicio) quodam *codd.*][7] conceperat, furtim eductam, cum haberet in latebris apud vicinum proximum, hoc modo secum habebat assidue nullo conscio: parietem, qui medius inter domum mariti ac vicini fuerat, ita perfodit, ut ipso transitu sacrum locum esse simularet eumque transitum intenderet sertis ac fronde felici rem divinam saepe faciens et vocaret ad se virginem. Quod cum animadvertisset adulescens, primo aspectu pulchrae virginis velut numinis visu perculsus exhorruit, unde fabulae Phasma nomen est; deinde paulatim re cognita exarsit in amorem puellae ita, ut remedium tantae cupiditatis nisi ex nuptiis non reperiretur. Itaque ex commodo matris ac virginis et ex voto amatoris consensuque patris nuptiarum celebritate finem accipit fabula.

As mentioned above, we are not told of any changes introduced by Luscius into the plot. It would seem that the only means of getting closer to his play is to reconstruct its model.

A little of the act-structure can be divined from the summary. It has been supposed by some[8] that the "vision" which startled the young man, whether or not actually shown, occurred in the middle of the play or was in some other sense central or climactic to it. True, it comes far on in the summary, but that is only because the antecedents of the plot have to be explained first. It is much more likely that the "vision" came in the first act, since the young man learned the truth and fell in love only by stages, and the whole action, including the happy ending, has to be compressed within the limits of a "stage" day. This play is, in fact, one of several which draw their titles from a prominent antecedent or early episode or character, such as Menander's *Perikeiromenê* and *Dêmiourgos* (an obvious exception is the *Rudens* of Plautus, who may, however, have tampered with his unknown original on this point). On the other hand, the wedding and, prior to it, the consent of the father, would come in the fifth act. It has been debated whether the *pater* mentioned is the young man's or the girl's.[9] The run of Donatus' Latin strongly suggests that he meant the former, whose consent would be much more imperatively required than that of the illegitimate girl's father (if known), though the consent of the latter may also have featured in the action. Before the young man's father can give his consent he must have learned the facts, and it may be surmised that the discovery upsets him greatly, (a) because his present wife turns out to have had an illegitimate daughter, (b) because of the interference with his house and the deception practised against him, (c) because his son wants to marry someone so unsuitable (and dowerless?), and (d), possibly, because he had another match in mind. A natural consequence would be for him to oppose the marriage at first and try to prevent further contact between his son and the girl. The happy ending implies reconcilement at that stage with his wife, and there was never much plausibility in the suggestion,[10] based partly on forcing the sense of Donatus and partly on the phrase "the woman who is going to get married," in one of the fragments, that perhaps the father dies and his wife marries the girl's father, thus providing a double wedding as finale. The young man's falling in love and his father's discovery and (probable) opposition, with complications not yet apparent, would occur mainly in acts 2 − 4.

A welcome fixed point in this sequence of events came to light in 1961 among the Menander mosaics discovered in the villa at Chorapha, Mytilene. They belong to later antiquity and allowance must be made for this. They probably date from the second half of the third century A.D., perhaps from about A.D. 270, some eighty years before Donatus was writing and the same length of time, or a little more, after Julius Pollux was ingesting into his *Onomasticon* the probably Hellenistic catalogue of dramatic masks which appears there. Among these mosaics the fourth one in the portico or corridor shows a scene specified as being from *me(ros)*B, that is, the second act, of the *Phasma*.[11] The detailed interpretation of the mosaic is in some ways problematic, but its main features are fairly clear. On the left a girl stands framed in a rectangular aperture in the form of a doorway. A figure of paternal aspect, wearing an old man's mask and carrying the short staff or wand typical of such characters, moves towards her — rather dramatically, as shown by the backward swing of the skirts of his clothing. Behind or beside him (on the right of the mosaic) stands another figure in a disconcerted posture — a young man who seems, judging by a gesture of the right hand, to wish to restrain the old one. From this it would appear that the second act of the play contains an encounter, probably the first and obviously a critical one, between the young man's father and the girl, and this presumably takes place in the presence of the son, who is unhappy about the incendiary situation.

Does the aperture represent the shrine? Its narrow double doors are opened inward, and the girl stands far enough forward for the sleeves of her dress to be set in relief against them, though we cannot be sure that the artist would not have stationed her further back had the space not been so cramped. The rest of the girl's background is black, presumably representing darkness. That the girl is standing still, and not walking, is shown by her posture and the outward splay of her feet. There is no sign of altar, festive chaplets, or auspicious greenery, but mosaicists habitually, and understandably, simplify and stylize scenic surroundings, or omit them altogether, and it therefore seems probable that the present artist meant to suggest more than he shows. That is to say, if ordinary doorways are usually omitted in mosaic, a doorlike aperture which is carefully portrayed may represent something much more unusual. Of all the scenes shown or described in the *Phasma*, a mosaic artist, or any graphic artist, would be likely to feel the attraction of the shrine-scene most. If then the aperture represents the shrine, as it seems to do, the girl must be taken unawares, as she would not voluntarily have risked such an encounter. How much the father learns at this point we cannot say, except that his demeanour on the mosaic is that of a person angry or suspicious.

The masks depicted, and doubtless the costumes also, would be those worn by the characters concerned not only during this scene but throughout the play. Comparison with other mosaics in the same building helps to elucidate various details of mask and dress which would otherwise be obscure, though the late date entails some post-classical features, especially in dress-ornamentation. The girl's mask has a clear complexion, pink to off-white and with no sign of wrinkles. Her eyebrows have not been delineated. Whether her hair is parted or not is debatable, and so is the intended colour, part of it being black and part, especially the braided tresses, being reddish-brown. It has been proposed[12] to identify her with the Maiden, who is number 33 in Pollux' list, but as in this case the mask should have an off-white to yellowish rather than pink complexion, together with straight black eyebrows, the likeness cannot be pressed. Her appearance as a whole is by no means calculatedly phantasmal: on the contrary it is very human and natural. She is dressed mainly in yellow, though the sleeves of a whitish inner garment, marked with a lozenge pattern and ending in a cuff of two red bands, is visible from elbow to wrist, and this or another garment has a white fringe visible at foot-level. Her yellow outer apparel has elbow-length sleeves and two vertical red stripes (*clavi*) running from the shoulder. Her mantle also is yellow, with two small red decorations. This and the garment it covers seem to me separate, though some wish to regard them as a single, rather full, *himation*. The artist's attempt to outline the feet in beige suggests lightweight footwear.

The father's mask has a yellow complexion with clearly marked wrinkles, evenly-curved eyebrows, and hair and beard in off-white, shading into grey-blue or beige. It has been proposed[13] to identify him with the Wavy-haired Old Man, number 4 in Pollux' list, who, besides having wavy hair, is full-bearded, easy-going in aspect, and does not have emphatically raised eyebrows. Again the likeness cannot be pressed. The father's attire is typical of such father-figures. He has an inner garment with sleeves and cuffs rather similar to the girl's, and this or another white garment is decorated with a red neckline and a small cinquefoil pectoral ornament in white and red. Over this he wears a very full mantle of unbleached stuff, handsomely draped from his left shoulder and leaving his right arm free. It is expensively bordered at the lower hem with a red band and fringing, and is also decorated just below his knee by two pieces of red material shaped like hour-glasses or diabolos. He is shod in black and carries like a mace the thin black crook stick which is a symbol of his age and status. As for the young man, his mask shows him as clean shaven and of fresh pink complexion. He has black hair which falls in long locks down to chest level. Visible in front of his left ear and across his forehead, is what has been taken for a row of short curls, though it is perhaps rather a wreath or *tainia*. From all that we know of this character, and especially his original shock and evidence in the fragments of the play about his health, we should have supposed him to be the Delicate Youth, who is number 13 in Pollux' list, but then his complexion should be pallid, not bright pink. It has been proposed[14] to identify him with the Curly-haired Youth, number 12 in Pollux, whose complexion is of a reddish tinge. In this case as in the others a neophyte in mask-interpretation can only reserve judgment. By the time when the mosaic was made, there may have been more, or other, subtypes of mask in existence than the source used by Pollux recognizes, and anyway the mosaicist may have seen fit to deviate from the rule-book in certain particulars. Like his father and the girl, the young man has an inner garment of which the lower sleeve is visible, patterned again in lozenge and with cuffs as before. This may be the same as, or different from, a long white inner tunic fastened by a girdle of red, yellow, and grey, of which the ends hang down. Over this comes his outer garb: a much shorter red overtunic having elbow-length sleeves and decorated with two vertical stripes (*clavi*) of blue; and, probably a separate garment, a red mantle decorated with two blue V-shaped or gamma-shaped motifs of a type associated with later antiquity and called *gammadia*. He too is shod in black. In the case of all three figures experts are divided as to the exact number of visible garments, but all three figures seem to me to wear more than the classical *chiton* and *himation*, and this elaboration is undoubtedly due to the relatively late date of the mosaic. We must think some of it away if we are to get a true picture of the *Phasma* in its first hundred and fifty years of existence.

It is within such a narrative and visual framework that the extant fragments of the play have to be fitted. They are six in number — the first two, on a parchment, known since the nineteenth century, and the other four, on papyrus, first published in 1971. They may be listed as follows:

(1) "Petr. 1a" Leningrad parchment recto, 27 fragmentary trimeters (supplemented from a literary source to a total of 31): dialogue between a young man called Pheidias and a dependant (servant) of his.

(2) "Petr. 1b" Leningrad parchment verso, 25 fragmentary trimeters: mainly exposition-speech, though first 8 lines may be part of a dialogue.

(3) "A" Papyrus A, 16 fragmentary trimeters: interrogation and confession scene between a wife and her husband, with or without others present (or possibly the *planning* of such an interrogation).

(4) "B" Papyrus B, composite:

    col. i 18 fragmentary trimeters: talk involving a cook, a slave (called Syros), and a master, with or without others present. This leads into

    col. ii 18 fragmentary lines, of which at least the last 14 are trochaic tetrameters: dialogue in which a slave describes to a master the petting of a young couple whom apparently the slave has seen but not the master.

    col. iii 6 fragmentary lines, trochaic tetrameters, continuation from col. ii but after a gap of 12 lines: subject uncertain, but with possible mention of the name Chaireas.

(5) "C" Papyrus C, traces of 5 lines, metre uncertain:
may contain a greeting to a neighbour-deity of the home.

(6) "D" Papyrus D, slight traces of 4 lines, meter and subject unknown.[15]

The right supplementation and ordering of the fragments is still at many points uncertain. Possible personal relationships and a possible thread of events were worked out by Turner, who at the same time reserved judgment on many points. Since our present purpose is to guess how the play may have looked to the eye of Luscius as he read it over, all that I shall attempt is to present the episodes with as little dislocation as may be; that is to say, cutting the interstitial reasoning to a minimum, while frankly acknowledging that the result is tentative.

    It is at the beginning that reasoning is most necessary. Petr. 1a and 1b are both, in a way, expository or preparatory, and will come early in the play. Turner demonstrated, contrary to all previous opinion, that there is no codicological bar to taking them in that order, and that in terms of content it is the preferable order, since 1a ends with advice to the troubled young man Pheidias to get himself ritually exorcized by "the women" — presumably the women of the household since no others are indicated — and 1b goes on with what could be a sequel to it. That is to say, 1b begins with what could be (by a guess of Turner's) advice from a stepmother to her son. The stepmother may be speaking directly or (as is perhaps more likely) the son may be repeating, in soliloquy, what she has said to him within. The speaker (or quoted speaker) seems to talk to her interlocutor about being discreet or "sane," seems to think of him as the "bridegroom" and also mentions "the mother of the young lady" (i.e. presumably of the bride, but not of the "vision," since, as will be shown, this latter mother-daughter relationship cannot yet be disclosed). The speaker then seems to urge the listener not to shake people's confidence in him or give them an excuse (for calling the wedding off?).

Passage 1b continues with what is an exposition-speech in a more formal sense, addressed to the audience (cf. line 19). Its key-statement, if we accept a likely supplement, is, "However, she is not a vision, but a real girl":

$$\ddot{\eta} \ \delta' \ o\dot{v}\chi\dot{\iota} \ \phi\acute{a}\sigma\mu'] \ \ddot{e}\sigma\tau,' \ \dot{a}\lambda\lambda\grave{a} \ \pi\alpha\hat{\iota}\varsigma \ \dot{a}\lambda\eta\theta\iota\nu\acute{\eta}.$$

It would follow that up to now the audience have thought of the vision as a vision, and therefore that the vision's mother, who at the outset alone knows the secret, cannot yet have explained it to anyone within the play. Therefore, whatever advice she may have given her stepson, she has not undeceived him: he does not yet know that the vision is a real girl, still less that she is his stepmother's natural daughter.

The exposition-speech goes on to explain where and how this daughter lives in secret. We know from Donatus that she lives next door, but she is here (line 10) described as

$$]\underset{.}{a}\theta\epsilon\iota\sigma\alpha \ \tau\hat{\eta}\varsigma \ \gamma\alpha\mu\upsilon\mu\acute{e}\nu\eta\varsigma.$$

The first visible letter is uncertain. Turner argued that this must either locate her in the house of the bride-to-be, or at least show their relationship. The sense of the line might be "having been received into the house (or by the mother) of the bride-to-be." Thus not only the "vision" but also the bride-to-be appear to live next door. In certain circumstances, the speaker apparently goes on to say, the girl is kept guarded (concealed?), but for the rest of the time (there is need of?) less guarding. The device of the pseudo-shrine is then explained, with possible mention of some object (an altar?) "within, belonging to the goddess." It seems likely that the man of the house, Pheidias' father, is at this moment away. Since he can hardly go abroad or come home from abroad more than once in the course of a "stage" day, and since the mosaic shows him home in the second act, he must be away at the beginning of the first, and must in the second have recently returned.[16] His return may not be wholly unexpected (especially if, as appears, this is intended to be his son's wedding-day), yet something about it is so, since we see him on the mosaic evidently surprising his son and the "vision" at the "shrine." A further implication of this speech, which refers to the shrine as ἔνδον (line 20), may be that the mosaic boldly takes us into the house and shows us something which Menander only describes. Among theatrical mosaics this would be an unparalleled innovation, and scholars of our time have in consequence been fiercely divided, some espousing the alternative view that it is Menander himself who takes us in, surrealistically bringing the *phasma* into view in what is physically a stage doorway and making her visible to a person who is physically onstage and thus for all other purposes outside the house.[17] Such surrealism seems to me unlikely.

Putting all these clues together, we find the play opening somewhat as follows. The principal young man, the one of whom Donatus speaks, is Pheidias. From an opening scene the audience learn that this is to be his wedding-day and that he is to marry the daughter of the household next door. This may be dramatized by having servants and/or hired caterers begin to prepare a wedding feast.[18] Suddenly Pheidias, who has the character though not technically the complexion of a Delicate Youth, catches a glimpse of the *phasma* in the shrine and confronts the audience in a state of daze and possibly collapse. If he tells others of what he has seen they can't make any sense of him. He passes into a state of mooning, says he is sick, yet at the same time begins to dream his way into some big airy inference about his powers or fortune. The only conclusion that can be drawn is that he is mentally ill, and consequently at this point (as seems to me most likely from the sequel), the wedding has to be provisionally called off. If there are caterers about they take their paraphernalia away for the time being.

As Pheidias continues to moon, some kind of male dependant (perhaps a freedman, and possibly a *paidogôgos*), who from long observation of the young man believes that he is predisposed to psychological trouble by his slack and enervating environment, comes to have a word with him. This is Petr. 1a, which after a ragged beginning, goes on:[19]

Servant: What's the [market price of] wheat?

Pheidias: What do I care about that?

Serv. Nothing. [It was just words. But I] used [them, I guess,] in order to get at the truth. If wheat's dear, you ought to feel a literal pinch on my account [...] – I'm a poor man. The thing to get hold of is that you [...] are just a member of the human race yourself, no more and no less than [a man with nothing to his name]. Then you won't go hankering on after [things] above your head. You tell us you can't sleep. Well, if you [study] the [way you live], you'll understand the reason. Your way of going on is to stroll around [the market and] then come in straight away the moment [your legs] feel tired. You'll go for a luxurious bath, then [come] back up again [and eat] to your heart's content. Your [life] itself is slumber. Conclusion: there's nothing the matter with you, and [your illness] that you went on about – I'm going to use a vulgar [expression], Master Pheidias, [you'll] excuse me, won't you – it's what they mean when they say you're so piled around with luxuries you don't know where to turn to [have a sh–]. That's it, believe me.

Pheid. Oh, go [to blazes].

Serv.   I'm telling you the truth, my word I am. That's all your complaint amounts to.

Pheid. Oh, [I feel so weak — I do feel] off colour — [horribly] weighed down.

Serv.   A [natural] lack of brain-power: it always makes for weakliness.

Pheid. All right. So [you seem to have got] this all [reasoned out. So what's] your advice?

Serv.   My [advice? Here's what. If] there was anything genuinely the matter with you, Pheidias, you'd have to be looking for a genuine prescription for it. But there isn't: then find an imaginary prescription for your imaginary illness. Imagine that something is doing you good. Get the womenfolk to stand in a ring around — give you a rub-a-dub round in a ring around — then burn sulfur round in a ring around — then take water from three fountains — in goes salt and in goes lentils — then go sprinkle, round in a ring around.[20]

The woeful vulgarism in the middle is certified by, of all people, Marcus Aurelius. In the twenty lines or so which may have intervened between this fragment and the verso of the parchment, it is possible that Pheidias, though not, I think, taking the servant very seriously, goes to look for the womenfolk of the house, and in particular his stepmother. It has been supposed[21] that he may now see the *phasma* again and learn part of the truth. But, apart from lack of space, this seems ruled out by the exposition-speech that follows. Rather it looks as though he has some serious words about his mental state with his stepmother, whose anxieties are of course raised on her own account as well as because the wedding has been jeopardized. Indeed the two concerns interlock. At the beginning of Petr. 1b (the verso), then, it appears that we have some words of the stepmother, whether directly spoken or merely reported, apparently pressing for the wedding preparations to go on, telling the young man to be sensible, and urging him to avoid talking about his experience to one person in particular.

$$\begin{aligned}
&]\nu\upsilon\sigma\iota\omega\nu \ldots \\
&] \ \grave{\epsilon}\pi\iota\tau\epsilon\lambda\epsilon\tilde{\iota}\nu \ \sigma\upsilon\lambda\lambda\alpha\mu\beta\acute{\alpha}\nu\eta\iota\varsigma \\
&]\nu \ \nu\upsilon\mu\phi\acute{\iota}o\nu \ \sigma\alpha\upsilon\tau\grave{o}\nu \ \phi\rho o\nu\epsilon\tilde{\iota}\nu \\
&\tau\tilde{\eta}]\varsigma \ \pi\alpha\rho\theta\acute{\epsilon}\nu o\upsilon \ \tau\grave{\eta}\nu \ \mu\eta\tau\acute{\epsilon}\rho\alpha
\end{aligned}$$

5
$$\begin{aligned}
&]\epsilon\rho\omega\iota \ \tauo\tilde{\upsilon}\theta' \ \grave{o}\mu o\mu\eta\tau\rho\acute{\iota}\omega\iota \ \tau\iota\nu\grave{\iota} \\
&] \ \mu\grave{\eta} \ \pi\alpha\rho\alpha\delta\tilde{\omega}\varsigma, \pi\rho\grave{o}\varsigma \ \tau\tilde{\omega}\nu \ \theta\epsilon\tilde{\omega}\nu, \\
&]\alpha \ \sigma\alpha\upsilon\tauo\tilde{\upsilon} \ \mu\eta\delta\epsilon\mu\acute{\iota}\alpha\nu. \ o\breve{\upsilon}\tau\omega \ \pi\acute{o}\epsilon\iota'. \\
&\tau]o\tilde{\upsilon}\tauo \cdot \tau\acute{\iota} \ \gamma\grave{\alpha}\rho \ \breve{\alpha}\nu \ \tau\iota\varsigma \ \pi\acute{\alpha}\theta o\iota;^{22}
\end{aligned}$$

The first word could conceivably be $\theta\upsilon\sigma\iota\tilde{\omega}\nu$ and the reference to sacrifical offerings made on a wedding day, $\theta\upsilon\sigma\acute{\iota}\alpha\iota \ \gamma\alpha\mu\acute{\eta}\lambda\iota\alpha\iota$. The speaker could be saying that the wedding must be called on again, and everything will be all right if (or Pheidias must make his appearance so that) "[while the sacrifice is being offered,] you'll take part in the due performance of it. [Show] yourself [as] bridegroom [willing] to be in your [right] mind. [Conciliate] the young lady's mother [and never talk about] this ("vision") to any other child of hers; don't in heaven's name give them [any pretext against] you. Well, that's what to do." "[Very well,] that['s what I'll do] – I might as well."

A long uncertainty has prevailed as to the identity indicated by *homomêtrios*, that is, a "child of the same mother," in line 5. The word has generally been taken to imply a stepbrother of Pheidias, i.e. a son born to his father and his stepmother, and even Turner, who divines the correct answer, thinks that possibility still open. But the reference cannot be to such a stepbrother of Pheidias if it is the latter's stepmother whose words we are hearing. For (1) she cannot mean a son of her marriage who is homometric to Pheidias: that makes nonsense – the word cannot refer to relationship through a stepmother and would lose its whole raison d'être if it did. Pheidias and a child born to his father and his stepmother could only be called homopatric. But (2) neither can she mean by *homomêtrios* a child of her marriage who is homometric to her natural daughter. She could not mean this without disclosing who the "vision" is, and, as we have seen, she cannot make that disclosure because Menander is reserving it till a few lines further on, where the audience are let in to the mother's secret. The person meant, then, can only be one who is homometric to the bride-to-be, i.e. her brother or stepbrother, and indeed μητέρα in the previous line opposes any other interpretation. We thus have in the adjoining house a man (known from Donatus), a woman who is doubtless his wife, at least one son and one daughter (siblings or half-siblings) and, living with them, the girl who is the *phasma*. And where the son of that house is concerned, Pheidias seems to have been warned to tread with special care. As for line 8, where, probably, Pheidias says he might as well do his stepmother's bidding, the brevity of this conclusion inclines me to suspect that the stepmother's speech was really made earlier inside the house, and has here been repeated outside the house by Pheidias in soliloquy, for the audience's benefit.[23] It is a little like the situation in Terence's *Hecyra* (see lines 352-402) where young Pamphilus repeats onstage a plea of some length which has just been made to him within by his mother-in-law, and then in a single line indicates his assent. At any rate the stepmother in the *Phasma*, if she is there, goes in at this point, and it would seem that Pheidias half-heartedly prepares (directly or indirectly) to have the wedding called on again. The stage is left clear.

At this point (still on Petr. 1b) occurs the formal exposition-speech. Its purpose is to possess the audience of the stepmother's secret, and analogy suggests that this is done by a semi-divine figure or deified abstraction, delivering what it would be proper to call a deferred prologue. We do not know who the speaker is, or even of what sex.[24] The disclosure begins thus:

>] ἔστ᾽ ἀλλὰ παῖς ἀληθινὴ
> 10   ]αθεισα τῆς γαμουμένης
>] μήτηρ πρὶν ἐλθεῖν ἐνθάδε
>] ταύτην δίδωσί τ᾽ ἐκτρέφειν
>]υν ἐστὶν ἐν τῶν γ⟨ε⟩ιτόνων
>]ενη καὶ φυλαττομένη κόρη. . . .[25]

"[However,] she is [not a vision] but a real girl, who was [taken in at the house where lives] the bride-to-be. Her mother [had been violated and as a result] gave birth to her, before coming to live here. She gave her [to another woman] to bring up, [with whom she now] is, next door, being [brought up secretly] and kept watch over in her girlhood — ." In line 12 Turner has shown that Koerte's supplement, ἐκ γείτονος, will not do: the word most needed seems to me βεβιασμένη or some equivalent. Koerte also proposed τίτθη as the first word of line 13, but it would be rash thus to introduce an extra character (a nurse) into the play for whom there is not a shred of evidence elsewhere.[26]

The rest of the speech, though textually unsettled, is less controversial in content. With possible supplements as indicated, it runs: " — in her girlhood, [at any time when her mother's husband comes] here; whilst for the rest of the time, [when he is abroad and there is]n't [need] of so much guarding, [she does leave] the house [where it is her lot to live]. — How then does the girl make her mysterious appearances? This too you would no doubt like [to learn from me. Indoors,] her mother has [opened up a wall so as to make] a way through. [This is in a particular room where she can] watch over all that goes on. [The way through] is [well] concealed with festive chaplets, [to stop any busybody from] coming along and finding out. [There is also,] in there, an [altar] of the goddess — ." At this point the parchment gives out. The "way through" the wall has usually been described as a "passage" and there has even been speculation about its "other end." I think it is nearer to being two-dimensional, like a doorway, and we may if we wish imagine the altar (assuming there is one) to be free-standing, either beside or in front of it. As to what we are told of the father's presences and absences — if we are told anything at all about them — it is surely now evident that this announcement would not be in place *after* his return home (shown in the mosaic) and therefore that at the moment he is to be regarded as away.

Two ironically opposed developments are now set in train. On the one hand it seems that, though considerable doubts are still felt about Pheidias' mental health, preparations for the marriage begin to be resumed, and perhaps for the moment he acquiesces in them. As he said, he "might as well," though the conventions of comedy, which are as stern toward approved matches as they are lax toward others, require that he shall never before marriage have been alone with his intended bride, and perhaps hardly even have seen her. On the other hand, the heart and instinct are wayward things, and he finds himself drawn contrariwise back on a private visit to his stepmother's chapel-room, as he supposes it to be, where, amid the chaplets and (if Donatus is to be believed) auspicious greenery, he is rewarded with another sight of the "vision," whom no doubt a like instinct has called there, though it is not a moment of liturgical obligation. This time they speak; he divines that she is real, and the adumbration is presently confirmed by sense of touch. They fall in love, and are entertained by the prospect of a series of further meetings, à deux — provided of course that the marriage continues to be "off." Pheidias resolves that the more definitely his marriage is "off," the better, and he seems to come to the conclusion that the best way to achieve this is to manifest continuing mental instability,[27] and have fits. Or rather, it is less likely that he resolves upon this himself than that it is put into his head by some servile confidant. That would be the normal convention, and we have here a hint that there is a *servus callidus* in the play.

The people next door are no doubt upset by the morning's turn of events, or rather by such part as they are aware of. Menander perhaps did not say much of the bride's feelings (though one of the characters makes a guess at them later), and very likely she does not come onstage. The greatest indignation seems to be felt by her brother (possibly called Chaereas, cf. fragment B col. iii), at the slight done to his sister and family by the behaviour of Pheidias, who, over and above being something of a milksop by nature, must needs go off his head a few hours before the wedding ceremony and then subside into a mooning melancholy varied by some kind of supercilious daydreams, as well as by fits, with the result that nobody can tell whether the marriage is off or on.

According to the scheme which I have elected to follow out, however, the bride's brother has a further reason for disquiet. We have hardly yet considered the position of the *phasma* in the house where she lives. Someone in that house is a party to the secret of the opening in the wall. It has often been supposed that this person is what in Roman drama is called a *nutrix* (and what K-T call an *anicula*). More likely, I think, the bride's mother herself. To the rest of the household where she lives, the *phasma* is simply a foster-daughter and foster-sister, peculiar only in that she is kept strictly indoors whenever the head of the neighbouring family is home from abroad. She happens to be attractive (*pulchrae virginis*, Donatus) and, since a foster-sister does not come within the prohibited degrees, she arouses the interest of the son of the house, that is, the brother of the bride. Should he now form a suspicion — we cannot tell how it comes about — that there is something going on between her and Pheidias, and that her heart inclines in that direction, annoyance over the slight to his sister is likely to be aggravated by jealousy (unless, of course, something happens to turn his thoughts elsewhere). We recall the apparent warning given to Pheidias about him (Petr. 1b, line 5): the dramatist was preparing the audience for the rivalry. The climax of this seems to be that a slave reports to him what is happening. This is in the chief papyrus fragment (see below). Turner suggests that he even sets the slave to spy and report on Pheidias' behaviour.

We are left with the papyrus fragments and the mosaic. Fragment D, which consists of only a few letters, we cannot place. The natural order of the others is probably not that in which they have been printed,[28] but C, then A, with the mosaic between them. The major fragment B possibly precedes C, and if not, it probably follows the mosaic. We thus have two potential orders:

First hypothesis	Second hypothesis
B	C
C	mosaic
mosaic	B
A	A

It will be best to look at B, then see how the rest verge towards a dénouement.

B is in lively dialogue. We become aware of the presence on stage, or at least within talking distance, of (a) a cook, (b) a slave Syros, and (c) a master, who is probably the bride's brother and who seems to be receiving a report on certain events indoors. The two ironically opposed developments mentioned earlier have here reached an extreme. On the one hand the presence of the cook implies that a serious attempt is being made to renew the wedding preparations and prepare a feast. On the other hand, mixed up with this is the oral report, seemingly made to the bride's brother and describing a love scene between Pheidias and the *phasma* which has taken place inside.[29] In B col. i the translatable words are as follows (a dicolon — that is, an empty pair of brackets — indicates change of speaker).[30]

> ... [previously] he was touched with melancholia ... now in better health ... and marrying again ... matters inside are ... ( ) Syros! ... to ... ( ) is marrying again ... sister. ( ) I'm done for now. [The thing's as plain] as I am seeing you now. ( )? [Well,] I can see [fire, to go by? everything befogged from?] the smoke ... one clean [dish?] ... is lost. ( ) Near at hand ... you, sir: tell me ... [neither?] of the two. ( ) You hear ... for ... is going after... call [him] from the very spot ... Syros, confound you! ... to me ... give a further indication if the paraphernalia in readiness is clean and nicely got up.

B col. ii is the immediate continuation of this, but little survives of the first four lines except παντοδ[απ- and νῦν ὄντων. The passage runs:

	... all manner of ... now being ...
( ) *(brother speaking?)*	I'm done for now.
( ) *(slave speaking?)*	the girl ...
	... himself. [He's no] Embāros, [this one]. I was right [then] to suspect him from the outset. ... all manner of ...
( ) *(brother speaking?)*	Nothing [was he ashamed of?] ...
( ) *(slave?)*	... right-mindedly enough ... got to grips.
( ) *(brother?)*	He seems to me to have got the thing thought out [all right].
( ) *(slave?)*	Then he went into another clinch ...
( ) *(brother?)*	I'm out of it, where Aphrodite is concerned!

( ) (*slave*)	Oh no, sir — you belong to the family that is actually giving for ... the girl who has been kept caged. If the fit comes on him, he'll eat off [the] girl's [nose maybe?], in his malady.
( ) (*brother*)	No, no, in heaven's name!
( ) (*slave*)	Yes he will, or her lip and all, with kissing.
( ) (*brother*)	What!
( ) (*slave*)	And maybe that's for the best, for you'll stop being in love just like that, if [you see] her then.
( ) (*brother*)	Aren't you making game of me?
( ) (*slave*)	I making game of you? Before heaven I'm not.
( ) (*brother*)	I shall go in to my sister and [learn it all] plainly. She must be in low spirits, I fancy, at [the] wedding that is [under way].

In the papyrus, the last two lines above read thus:

> ( ) εἰσιὼν πρὸς τὴν ἀδελφὴν πα[. . .]σομαι σαφῶς·
> οἴομαι δ᾽ αὐτὴν ἀθυμεῖν [τῶι πο]ουμένωι γάμωι.

The phrase πάντ᾽ ἀκούσομαι or πάντα πεύσομαι, "I will learn all," has been proposed for the first gap. This introduces the assumption that the bride-to-be knows more of what is really happening than her brother, and further that he is aware of this fact. If so, the betrothed girl may have learned something from her foster-sister, the *phasma*, and it is not impossible that Menander arranged an entente between the two girls, in order to avoid pain when the betrothal is finally dissolved. A simpler supplement, in terms of sense, would be "I will *relate* all," but it is very difficult to say this in convincingly Menandrean Greek in the space available on the papyrus. The words "you'll stop being in love," a little above, are an interesting dramaturgical hint to the audience that the brother is destined not to win the hand of the foster-sister.

At this point there is a break until the lower part of B col. iii.

What is left of this column yields little beyond the words " . . . the door (?) . . . it is strange(?) . . . to fight(?) . . . through the one not(?) . . . Chaerea (?) . . . ." χαιρεαν, if a name, is probably a young man's name, as elsewhere in Menander, and may be the name of the brother. We cannot follow the plot here.

Where exactly this series of events (the whole of B) fits into the plot, we cannot be certain. But let us consider the remainder of our evidence. Pheidias' father comes home from abroad; we may assume this to be in the second act. The small fragment C, as restored,[31] may give us this moment, with his greeting to a statue of Apollo beside his house:

$$\ldots \; \text{"}Απολλον \; \grave{ω} \; π]άροικ' \; ἄναξ.$$

The next line appears to contain the word "to see," which is appropriate enough. The father probably knows it is his son's wedding day, and indeed may have arranged the betrothal before he last went abroad. In the house, though they may have known he was likely to come, it seems that he was not expected at this moment, and presently he approaches the chapel-room and catches his son in the company of the *phasma*. This, in my view, is what the mosaic shows, and what it specifies as being in the second act. The relative position of the figures is perfectly acceptable if we think of the natural impulse the father would have to thrust himself *between* his son and the *phasma*.

We cannot of course affirm that all details which the mosaic shows of the father's golden-coloured dress, with its decorative hour-glass panels, and the red mantle over a white tunic worn by his son, go back by genuine tradition to Menandrean or Roman republican times; but the richness of the father's dress certainly tallies with what we heard of the pampered life of his son. In a difficult medium, the artist has conveyed a good deal of the psychology of the discovery-scene — the father's angry surprise, the face of the *phasma* staring fearfully leftward at him out of her dark, box-like background, and an air of dismay in the bearing of the culprit, whose joy in secret converse with the "vision" is thus brought to a rude halt. We do not know exactly how much the father finds out. Not, I think, the whole story, but enough to make him (a) angry with both his son and his wife, (b) insistent that the wall be blocked up at once, (c) resolved (at first) to prevent further contact between the two young lovers, (d) bent on getting the marriage definitely "called on" again if he can,[32] and (e) probably suspicious of what further revelations may be in store for him about his wife. It does not follow, of course, that all his wishes will take effect.

Now, as to the placing of B in the temporal sequence, this will chiefly depend on whether the reported love scene took place in the actual "shrine" or not. If it did, the shrine cannot yet have been blocked up, nor indeed the father be aware of its existence. In that case our first hypothesis above (p. 112) represents the probable order, and the spying slave very likely spied from inside the house where the *phasma* lives, the slave and his master having discovered the "way through." But it is also possible that, at the time of the love scene, the wall has already been blocked up, and the lovers have found some other way to meet; in which case the slave may even have gained entry to the other house and spied there. This sequence is the second hypothesis (p. 112). The attraction of it is that the words γαμεῖ πάλιν and the apparent bustling activity of the cook in B col. i then become more dramatic as the direct consequence of the father's return: that is to say, it would be by reason of his vigorous intervention that the marriage is "on again."

This may have carried us about half-way through the play, but as we saw, much less is known of the second half. There does, however, remain fragment A, which is both fascinating and tantalizing in the way it supplements what Donatus tells us of the dénouement. He tells us that eventually "the father" gives his consent to a marriage between Pheidias and the *phasma*, and it was seen above (p. 99) that, in the context, the father in question is more likely to be the father of Pheidias than that of the *phasma* — though of course we cannot exclude the possibility that these two fathers are one and the same person. Whether the play actually settles the paternity of the *phasma* we cannot be sure; on the whole it ought to, but in any case it will be revealed to Pheidias' father that she is the natural daughter of his wife, and there must be a scene of disclosure to effect this. On the other hand there may equally well be a disclosure scene between the husband and wife next door, as we have been given two or three slight hints that their family history, too, has its complications. For (1) though they agreed to bring up the *phasma* as their foster-daughter, we don't know exactly what they believed about her parentage – most likely they believed different things. There has been some secrecy in that house about the aperture in the wall, so there could be divergent impressions on this other matter as well. (2) Again, the first time, to our knowledge, that their son is mentioned, he is not described, as would be most natural in the context, as the brother (*adelphos*) of the betrothed girl, but as her *homomêtrios* (Petr. 1b, line 5). The most natural inference is that the speaker believes they have different fathers, though she *might* merely be emphasizing the importance of their mother in the story. (3) Thirdly, the manuscripts of Donatus do, as they stand, say that the head of that household is the father of the *phasma* too, and although the tradition is probably corrupt at this point (above, p. 98), the corruption may possibly have been prompted by a disclosure to the same effect late in the play. It follows that Menander's dénouement may entail a disclosure or confession scene in either household, or in both.[33]

Now in fragment A we may have such an interrogation and confession scene, in which a husband, a wife, and possibly others are present. This at least is the interpretation that I shall elect to follow, though, as noted earlier, it could also be the *planning* of such an interrogation, in which case the dénouement becomes more ramified. It seems then that a wife is trying to tell someone that, before marriage, she lost her virginity as a result of an escapade during a night festival, and it can be assumed, though the fragment does not go far enough to say so, that a pregnancy resulted and that she gave birth to a child whose identity is now being made plain. The surprising thing is that the person addressed, instead of paying the close attention we should expect, seems to be only half listening, and for the rest is absorbed in puzzling thoughts of his own, which involve (a) the prospective testimony of a different woman, and (b) a different festival from that which has been mentioned. We can perhaps go beyond the immediate inference that the testimonies envisaged must disagree on the festival concerned. The most likely reason why they disagree is that there have been two different escapades at two different festivals, each speaker being involved in one and having become a parent in consequence.³⁴ The fragment begins as follows:

> . . .].υ τίς ἐστι; τίς καταισχ[ύνει ∪ −;
> . . .]θεν οὐκ οἶδ' · οὖσα γὰρ [
> παν]νυχίδος οὔσης καὶ χο[ρῶν
> . .μ]ανθάνεις γάρ; τὴν οδ[
> 5 . . .]ελέγξεις, ἡ δ' ἐρεῖ Βρ[αυρωνίοις
> . . .]ωνίοις σύ · πηνίκ' οὐ π[
> . . .]η πλανηθεῖσ' ἡ τάλαι[να

.. [The man responsible for this,] who is he? Who brings shame on ...? ... [He has remained undetected,] I do not know. For being [an unwed girl at that time,] there was an all-night festival and dances ... surely you understand? The ... you will question [her], and she will say it was at the Brauronia, whereas you [say it was] at the [Ad?] onia. When ... not [present?] ... wandering [by myself], luckless girl that I was, [I met calamity] ...³⁵

The festival at which the wife lost her virginity may have been that of Adonis,³⁶ at which her interlocutor seems to say he was never present.³⁷ The inference would be that he is thinking of another episode and another woman who, if questioned, will name the festival of Artemis of Brauron. His own involvement becomes clearer in what follows:

> . . .] ( ) ἐρωτήσεις τὰ προ[
> . . .πλ]εῖστον εἶτα θαυ[μα-
> 10   ]ον · ποῦ ποτ' ὢν λ[◡ − ◡ −
> ◡ φιλ']άνερ, γνώριμον τ[
>].ς γάρ ποτ' ἐν Βραυ[ρωνι −
>]αιδ' ἐνθαδὶ τὰ π[−◡−
>]αντι τῶν γεγ[

( ) You will enquire about events [before our marriage?] ... then the greatest astonishment ... Wherever [are you wandering in your talk? Do be understanding,] husband [dear,] it's known to happen, [this sort of thing] ... [Yes, it

is,] for once, at the Brau[ronia I happened to have got drunk
and . . . to have been done] there [everything you say?] . . .
in consideration of what [has happened?] . . .[38]

Thus the papyrus leaves us with a handful of inconclusive
threads. If the wife who speaks is Pheidias' stepmother, she is
certainly describing what led up to the birth of her natural
daughter, and to this moment she does not know who the father
was (though she may have tokens by which he is later identified).
The husband's replies suggest that it is not he, but that he did
become father, before marriage, to someone else in the play. On
the other hand, if the wife who speaks is the one next door, we do
not know which child she gave birth to in consequence of the
misadventure, except that it was not Pheidias or the *phasma*.
Neither do we know what child resulted from her husband's act,
except that in his case paternity of the *phasma* is a possibility.

It seems then that at least one husband has had to admit to his
wife an indiscretion comparable to her own, and this disclosure,
directly or indirectly, will have the effect of reducing opposition
to the wedding, which we know takes place in the end, between
Pheidias and the girl after whom the play is named. The removal
of obstacles will also quit Pheidias of his melancholy. The other
threads give out before we can see where they are leading. Of the
young people in the next house, the girl has lost her proposed
bridegroom and the young man has lost the girl he admired.
Menander is unlikely to have left both of them quite solitary at
the end. Yet, however we reconstruct the premarital adventures of
the elders in the story, it seems difficult, especially in view of the
word *homomêtrios* (in Petr. 1b), to give these two young people
the minimal requirement of different mothers, so that they could
marry each other. This difficulty applies in equal measure both to
what would be the most sentimental solution in the other
household, namely, for Pheidias' father to turn out to be also the
father of the *phasma* (in which case, however, he could hardly be
the male speaker in the confession scene), and to the most
astringent, wacky, and Menandrean solution, namely, for each
husband to turn out to have been responsible for a premarital
pregnancy of the other one's wife. In any case, even if the
originally intended bride and the young man jealous of Pheidias

turn out not to be brother and sister, or at least not to be uterine siblings, and thus could, legally speaking, marry each other, the psychological readjustment which this would require, both for the couple themselves and for the audience, would surely strain the framework of the comedy beyond what is reasonable. New Comedy readily uses the sudden discovery of consanguinity to block a proposed marriage, but it seems unlikely that the sudden discovery of non-consanguinity could precipitate a marriage otherwise quite uncontemplated. In the *Phasma*, perhaps one, if not two, other potential spouses have been among the *personae* throughout, or are produced out of a hat at the end. If not these, perhaps the next most likely thing is the presence of a courtesan. This uncertainty underlines the incompleteness of the story as we have it, and the hypothetical nature of the reconstruction attempted. We know something of acts one, two, and five; but much in act five, and the whole of acts three and four, remain very indistinct.[39] Yet, whatever other characters there may have been, and however precisely the later part of the action was laid out, we cannot doubt in the light of Donatus' summary from which we began, that the principal young man in the play is Pheidias, and the principal love affair is his.

Pheidias marries his Vision, and hereby also the poet tells us, under a similitude, that he sees his bride not simply in the light of common day, as others see her, and as brides in parentally arranged marriages must be seen, but as radiant with a shimmer of mystery and romance: he sees her as a being whose first nearness, never to be forgotten, had made him physically start and tremble, from seeming to have about it somewhat of the aura of the divine.

This then was the story to be told, and when Luscius lifted his eyes from the colophon, or whatever terminated the last column in the Greek, there stretched before him an exacting task. It was primarily a task in communication. It would culminate in the word — or at any rate the sentiment — *plaudite*. This injunction to the *populus Romanus* was the end to which the playwright first, and after him his actor-manager, must strive. The essence of the task was to hear the Menandrean personages speaking the Roman mother-tongue, and speaking moreover a Latin decorous to their ages and characters. The challenge was to recreate what a later Roman called "that simple and delightful effect of Menander's, which is so true to nature and is taken from the very heart of human life."[40] And perhaps one should add that the beginning of the task was to be young in spirit, as Menander had always been, and Plautus after him, and as Quintus Roscius from his own district was to be also in a later day, keeping alive the genius of this art-form after the supply of playwrights to renew it began to fail. Luscius was now past middle-age. If he had ever thought, felt, and spoken like Pheidias it was at a time now thirty or forty years in the past. Terence had the advantage of him here. But though we can see the nature of his task, and make some estimate of it as a whole, we cannot closely follow his steps or judge of his success, for lack of explicit testimony as to how he proceeded. I shall therefore not trash the reader through many quires of speculation. It will suffice to adhere to reasonable inference and to what is nodal.

We know that he kept the title unchanged and claimed to be presenting what was, in substance, Menander's play. The -*aria* titles which had been given to a number of Plautine comedies had sprung from a wish, on the part of Plautus or others, to designate, perhaps to advertise, each comedy as a *fabula*, that is, a stage-piece with a connected plot, thus reminding us how close Rome still was to the plotless predecessors of comedy proper. But the practice had been outgrown, as indeed it was bound to be, thanks in part to the sheer awkwardness of fangling the multiplicity of denominative adjectives required, such as *aulularius* and *mostellarius*. As New Comedy became more familiar, the cachet of the original Greek titles (adapted to Latin orthography) increased, and after Caecilius' use of *synaristosae* (which Plautus had changed to *cistellaria*) and *exhautuhestos* as titles, the two we have from Luscius seem modest, familiar, and euphonious. The word *phasma* probably conveyed to the Roman ear about as much as it does to our own: a phantasmal phenomenon of a supernatural but otherwise unspecified kind. It could of course mean the ghost of a dead man, whether appearing to the waking sight or in sleep. It had apparently meant this in Philemon's play so named, but it was by no means limited to such a connotation. It could equally suggest the vision of a divinity, and this possibility is clearly left open in the title of Luscius' play. I do not think the deferred prologue was spoken by the goddess whose suppositious shrine was in the house, but the revelation given to Pheidias there, if interpreted in any way at all, may very well have been connected by him with that goddess or with some associated divine being. At least he would not exclude the chance of its being a vision in our sense, and Donatus faithfully reflects this in his phrase *numinis visu*. It seems wrong then, to translate the title as *The Ghost*, as is often done. Luscius was relying on the wider acceptation which the word enjoyed, and if part had to be sacrificed, would probably have sacrificed "ghost" rather than "vision."[41]

His play would be set in Athens or at least in Attica. That this was the setting of the original was until very recently tentatively supposed on the ground that it appeared to mention the Dionysia (Petr. 1b, line 1, Jern's supplement), and though other cities had festivals of the same name, that of Athens was always foremost in the mind of Menander and his audience. The conjecture *Dionusiôn*, however, has proved unwarrantable, and this would have left the locale of the play completely uncertain but for the fact that, as we have seen, it is now known to have hinged partly on an episode at the festival of Artemis at Brauron, which was purely Attic. Now since Athens or Attica is the favoured setting in Roman comedy generally, and since Luscius himself had very likely used it in the *Thesaurus*, there is no reason to think that he would go out of his way to change it in the *Phasma*.

If his inclination to be faithful to the Greek kept him from altering the name of Pheidias beyond necessary latinization of the spelling, we can reconstruct as follows a substantial part of his table of *personae*:

PROLOGVS	(*dea vel deus, ut videtur*)
PHIDIA	ADVLESCENS
	MATRONA(*Phidiae noverca*)
	SENEX (*vicinus proximus*)
	MATRONA (*uxor senis vicini*)
CHAEREA(?)	ADVLESCENS (*filius senis vicini vel certe uxoris eius*)
	SENEX (*pater Phidiae*)

SERVVS *vel* LIBERTVS (*Phidiae fortasse paedagogus*)
?   SERVVS (*servus callidus*)
            SERVVS
            COCVS
?   VIRGO (*phasma*)

The *nutrix* assumed by Webster[42] and most others should be omitted. The nicest question is whether either of the two *virgines* in the story appeared onstage, or whether their actions and feelings were merely reported by others. Menander had reason to keep his list of *prosôpa* short, and probably took the latter alternative. Luscius, with more actors at his disposal and probably certain minor structural alterations to make, may have brought on the girl who gives the play its name. We cannot see precisely how the recognition or recognitions at the end are handled, but in certain circumstances her presence could be particularly desirable here. The presence of the other girl onstage is more doubtful.

Did Luscius modify the plot? Not, I think, fundamentally. The apparent silence of Donatus on this point, though suggestive, might be thought inconclusive since he may not have had the text of the Latin play to refer to; but the witness of Terence (*Eun.* prol. 9), who either saw the play acted or knew people who had done so, proves that it both claimed to be, and recognizably was, the Menandrean story. Besides, Terence, in the same context and in the previous line, credits Luscius with *bene vortendo*, and this confirms his faithfulness to the outline of the original. The widespread modern impression that Luscius "ruined" Menander will be considered below.

I believe, however, that we can come substantially nearer to proof that the plot-summary in Donatus is valid in its entirety for Luscius' play. He says, of course, — and he has been taken at his word on this by everyone, including myself up to this point — that he is summarizing Menander's play, though if questioned he would probably have said that it made no difference which play one had in mind, and that it is a fussy point to quibble over. By and large, this is probably true, but how can we be sure? The only way of testing the supposition, for Menander, is to check the summary against the fragments and the archaeological evidence. We have done this as we went along, and not found any jarring discordancy. On close inspection, however, it is a little curious that where Menander described the aperture in the wall merely as veiled by chaplets (ταινίαις, Petr. 1b, line 23), Donatus has the fuller phrase

sertis ac fronde felici.

This does not look like the work of an epitomator of Menander. It is much more suggestive of an argumentum originally written in Latin senarii and drawing upon an actual Latin playtext for the words quoted, though their order may have been changed round. Now it was shown by Leo in 1883[43] that Donatus' summary of Luscius' other known play, the *Thesaurus*, is indeed based upon such a versified argumentum. Neither Leo nor anyone else, so far as I know, suspected the same possibility in the case of the *Phasma*, precisely because Donatus here claims to be summarizing the Greek text, of which there is small likelihood that he (or his source) could draw upon a "hypothesis" already turned into Latin verse. But the more closely his wording is examined, the clearer it becomes that his source really was in senarii. Keeping not only to his choice of words, but even to his inflexions, except where indicated, we arrive at the following:

noverca, supérducta ádulescenti, virginem,
quam ex vĭtio quódam[44] ⟨péper⟩erat, furtim educ⟨at⟩.
habe⟨t⟩ in latébris apud vicĭnum proximum,
habe⟨tque⟩ secum assĭdue nullo conscio.
inter dom⟨os⟩ qui médius fúerat, parietem
perfodit ut ĭpso transitu sacrum locum
esse simul⟨et átque⟩ fronde felici ⟨obtegit⟩
sertis⟨que⟩, rem divinam saepe ⟨illic⟩faci⟨t⟩.
aduléscens ánimadverti⟨t⟩, pulchrae virginis
aspectu primo exhórruĭt: re cognita
in amórem exársit, út tantae cupidi⟨nis⟩
remédium ⟨núllum⟩ réperi⟨at⟩ nisi nuptiis;
ex voto ama⟨ntis atque⟩ cónsensu patris
fabula celebr⟨átis⟩ nupti⟨is⟩ finem accipit.

It seems to me that the source upon which Donatus drew must have been something very like this, and that the verse was originally composed as an argumentum not for Menander's play but for that of Luscius himself. Whoever made it, of course, had read the text of Luscius, and seems quite likely to have incorporated one or two actual expressions from it, of which *fronde felici* is the most patent.

This puts us on more satisfactory ground in investigating the structure of Luscius' play. We can be sure the outline is correct. We can also guess from Terence that he was reluctant to romanize the manners of the play, and we can see at least one point where the play itself resisted romanizing. This is the moment when Pheidias' father returns from abroad. Roman custom in such a case was to send a slave a little ahead to announce the arrival to the household. Terence, hellenist though he was, has been thought to have introduced a Roman element into the *Hecyra* (line 314) on this account. But Luscius, when showing the return of Pheidias' father, clearly had to retain the surprise element, and therefore could not romanize even if he wished. There are, however, four heads under which it is proper to ask whether he is likely to have introduced structural modifications. These heads are: (1) the problem of consanguinity, (2) *contaminatio*, (3) the prologue, and (4) the entr'actes. Let us examine these.

(1) The play ended with at least one, and perhaps two, pairings off. If the respective partners were not consanguineous, no structural problem would arise. If they were, it may be taken for granted that the Greek and Roman playwrights carefully avoided matching any couple who were within the prohibited degrees, as understood by their respective audiences. But the Greek and Roman definitions of what constitutes a prohibited degree were not the same. To a Greek, for example, marriage between half-siblings of the same paternity did not break any incest taboo, and therefore the possibility of it cannot be excluded from the Menandrean finale. Neither (in our present state of knowledge) can the possibility of some other blood-tie between the marriage-partners. The detailed differences between Greek and Roman viewpoints are somewhat obscure, but the inhibition of the Roman is summed up by Plutarch when he informs his Greek

readers that Romans used not to marry their συγγενίδες, which expression he proceeds to paraphrase by αἱ ἀφ᾽ αἵματος.[45] We cannot be sure, then, that Luscius adhered exactly to the kinships given in his model. This would particularly affect the anagnorisis but may also have modified certain presuppositions throughout the play. The danger of such alterations is a weakening of the tight logic on which a Greek plot of this kind tends to be built.[46]

(2) In regard to *contaminatio* we can see the lie of the land more clearly. Luscius took over the *Phasma* as whole as he could, and would hereby be recognized by at least some of the play-writing fraternity (Terence's *isti* and *pauci*[47]) as pre-empting it. At the same time he did not "contaminate," i.e. interfere with the *integritas* of, any additional Greek play by borrowing scenes or characters from it for insertion in his own work. If he had done so, Terence, while the matter was still fresh, would not have overlooked so flagrant an anomaly between his practice and his preaching. We may take it that Luscius fully observed the then etiquette of "translation rights," and equally, and for the same reason, that he did not pilfer from his Roman forerunners. How far professional principle restrained him from free invention is a different question, but it would be consistent with Terence's *bene vortendo* to suppose that he limited this kind of rewriting to what the circumstances of his theatre and audience necessitated.

(3) Short of rewriting the whole first act, he would need to keep the deferred prologue, though he may have changed the identity of the speaker from one deity or deified abstraction to another, as Plautus did in the *Aulularia*. There is indirect evidence (Ter. *Phorm.* prol. 13-15) suggesting that his plays in general had prologues, and it has often been assumed that he made these the vehicle for his attacks on Terence. But this latter supposition is an unproved guess: the passage on which it is based could as easily, or more easily, mean the opposite, namely, that Terence himself is the innovator in this respect. We in fact do not know that the attacks of Luscius were made from the stage at all.[48] In the case of the *Phasma*, it would be impossible for a deferred, expository prologue to enter into polemics. There could have been some other, additional introductory speech, à la Ambivius, but since a double prologue might calamitously strain the audience's patience,

Luscius probably began the play with some kind of dialogue, as Menander had done in the *Heros* and Plautus in the *Cistellaria*.

(4) What did necessitate structural alteration, and free invention, was the elimination of the entr'actes. Greek practice required (at least) four pauses in the action, with an empty stage and a nominally choric interlude. All the evidence of extant Roman comedy confirms the statement of Donatus that the Romans avoided this and made the play continuous; and Donatus may well be correct in the reason he gives, that an interlude meant too great a risk of losing one's audience. The five acts of a Greek play, Donatus says,

> retinendi causa inconditi spectatoris, minine distinguunt Latini comici, metuentes scilicet, ne quis fastidiosus finito actu velut admonitus abeundi reliquae comoediae fiat contemptor et surgat.[49]

This does not mean that the stage was never empty during a Roman play, only that there was no formal entr'acte or intermission. The restructuring thus necessitated need not be large — an inserted speech of fifteen lines or so onstage could correspond to a much longer lapse of time in supposed offstage developments, though the best solution would sometimes be to bring onstage episodes which the Greek original merely reported. To this extent, then, Luscius was committed to restructuring, and this is another reason why he may have chosen to enlarge the visible cast.

Metrically the fragments of the original consist of iambic trimeters and trochaic tetrameters. We know from a grammarian[50] that, among lyric and quasi-lyric metres, it included the ithyphallic sequence $(- \cup - \cup - -)$. The first two of these metres it would be most natural for Luscius to reproduce as senarii and septenarii. In the deployment and polymetry of cantica he was probably nearer to Terentian restraint than Plautine exuberance. As for ithyphallics, which were probably rare enough in Menander to begin with, they are very rare indeed in Plautus and not found at all in Terence or in what we have of other Roman comedians. Luscius probably found some less exotic substitute.

It remains to ask what was the impression created by the play as a whole. On this we have three possible pieces of evidence, namely, (1) the line in Terence which mentions it (*Eun.* prol. 9), (2) the context of that line, especially what precedes, and (3) Terence's general charge at *Andr.* prol. 21 that Luscius and his associates practise an *obscura diligentia* which Terence disdains. (1) We have already noted that the line

> idem Menandri Phasma nunc nuper dedit

contains no explicit comment. The feeling of a need for comment led Bothe to his conjecture *nuper perdidit.*[51] It has long since been shown that the change is unwarranted.[52] Terence, as is well known, often subordinates natural sense-content or thought-sequence to the pull of sentence structure, as the beginning of this very prologue shows. He had nothing specific to say of the *Phasma*, and mentioned it partly (as Donatus notes) to identify his adversary more clearly, and probably also, in a vague way, to suggest that it exhibited a general fault which he has attacked just before. But the irresistible pull, first of a *qui – idem,* and then of an *idem – atque* sequence, led to the present unsatisfactory articulation. It is Terence, not some copyist, who is at fault. (2) The two preceding lines are

> qui bene vortendo et easdem scribendo male
> ex Graecis bonis Latinas fecit non bonas.

Again the lure of a structural effect (antithesis) has led to something unsatisfactory, the opposition of *vortendo* to *scribendo,* of "translating" to "writing" what one translates. If a thing is badly written we would not normally say that it was good translation, unless the original was also bad. However, doubtless the common view is correct that Terence refers to translation which is faithful to the word of the original but insufficiently natural and convincing. This is supported by (3) his earlier charge of *obscura diligentia.* As was remarked much later in antiquity, an over-close translation "sensus operit."[53] Of course, the work of Luscius cannot have been a literal rendering. Verse translation never is. But it may have been somewhat stilted and overscrupulous for the needs of the theatre. One wonders how clear "Brauronia" would have been to the Roman plebs, or the allusion to

"Embaros" (the Greek Simple Simon) if Luscius kept these. There is probably something in Terence's implied criticism of the *Phasma.*

It comes down in the end to the question how far a duty to one's audience entails a duty to one's source. We can see more clearly in the case of Luscius than in that of any other Roman playwright that he recognized a definite duty to the text of the source-play. This duty is so familiar to us that we take translation as the norm and free adaptation as exceptional. But in a society which had far different standards and conventions, Luscius should not be denied the credit of his principle, of trying a stricter method, even if it was too academic to achieve great popular réclame. In the last analysis, he showed good critical sense in his choice of original, and his version was one which the aediles examined and approved, and which held the stage, shall we say, better at least than the *Hecyra.* Nor should we forget that the critic Volcacius rated him above Ennius as a comedian and, by implication, above Livius Andronicus. Among the miserable relics which form his memorial today, we may single out three words by which I think it might not displease him to be remembered. While Terence proudly pasted what art historians call a "detail" from one play into another, and Plautus transmogrified some original to produce "the play of the pot,"[54] Luscius may have been content to do what his very young critic declared he had done: "Menandri Phasma dedit."

5. LUSCIUS: THE UNNAMED PLAYS

We have reason to suppose that the *vetus poeta* from Lanuvium wrote more than the two plays whose titles are preserved. In the present short discussion I propose to consider what can be known of Luscius' work apart from the *Thesaurus* and the *Phasma*. That is to say, the enquiry will concern what have been called his *incertae fabulae*, which at first sight are two in number. In the course of examining the deducible scenes we may succeed in filling out a little our general picture of Luscius' dramaturgy. We shall also find reason to question the number of plays involved.

First Unnamed Play

When Terence's *Heauton Timorumenos* had its premiére, Ambivius Turpio in the prologue (31-32) appealed to the audience for a chance in return for a chance (*copiam . . . copiam*). The chance he requested was for writers such as Terence — a modest plural — to go on writing and advance in their profession, instead of being unfairly debarred. The chance he offered was that of seeing new plays free from bungling. This plea for playwrights, he said, must not be understood by Luscius as embracing himself: he had recently staged a scene which was egregiously bungled.

> Ne ille pro se dictum existumet
> qui nuper fecit servo currenti in via
> decesse populum: quor insano serviat?

... Because there's someone who should realize that my plea doesn't include him: the writer who recently had a slave come running along the street and the people make way for him: why is he represented as slave to a madman?

It appears, then, that the play in which Luscius did this was enacted "recently" before the delivery of the *HT* prologue: that is to say, if we go by the didascalic dating, "recently" before the Megalensia of 163 B.C.[1]

Could this scene of the running slave have appeared in the *Phasma*? In content, yes, easily: it would be quite in tone for a slave of the melancholic young hero, for example, at some point to burst on or off the stage in the manner described. But in date, seemingly not: the *HT* preceded the *Eunuchus* by about two years, and a play enacted *nuper* before the former could hardly be identified with one enacted *nunc nuper* before the latter. We cannot on chronological grounds be quite so sure that the scene in question did not come from the *Thesaurus*, which is the earlier of the two named plays. But I suggest we assume this as a hypothesis unless and until some link can be established: it will be shown presently that the evidence of content is against such a link. A slight token, at the outset, is that whereas Terence's complaint about the slave scene is really a criticism of detail, his complaint about the order of speeches in the *Thesaurus* (*Eun.* prol. 9 ff.) is, if taken at its face value, more serious because it relates to structure; and it is hard to see why, if the two episodes occurred in the same play, he was not struck by the major point straight away. Provisionally, then, this unnamed play seems earlier than the *Phasma* and different from the *Thesaurus*, though we cannot establish its temporal relationship to the latter.

The original of this first unnamed play is unknown. We cannot closely connect this episode of the running slave, for whom the people make way, with any specific moment in Greek comedy, and Leo conceived it to be of Luscius' own invention. Fraenkel argued against this that it comes from the source-play. He held that *all* of Terence's criticisms are of Luscius' failure to maintain a free hand in adaptation, so as to eliminate, in the present scene, something un-Roman and not in keeping with social practice, just as in other cases he failed to eliminate things that were in other ways indecorous to the genre in which he was writing.[2] The real fault here may be Terence's, for having too narrow an idea of what is decorous. As to Luscius, it is likely enough that he followed his source, but as things are, we cannot be sure.

There is one way, however, to learn a little more about Luscius' play, and that is to settle more exactly what are the points of detail which Terence is impugning. It is generally believed that there are two *vitia*; namely, (1) giving prominence to a noisy *servus currens*, by contrast with Terence's own quieter type of comedy, and (2) the impropriety of showing free men – the *populus* – make way for a slave, and of showing a slave who expects that they should do so. And in pursuance of this latter item, it has sometimes been thought that Terence in his final question is asking, why should it (the people) be subservient to one who is out of his senses (the slave)? Much has been written on the *servus currens*.[3] The phrase occurs often enough for it to rank as a quasi-technical term, though such a slave seems not to have been an established type, among those inherited from Greek comedy, in the sense of having one definite mask, and he does not correspond to any one entry in Pollux' list of masks. He was quite likely to be a Leading Slave, but was not always so. Formally, his main function is to deliver a message, and sooner or later he does so. Since, however, such a slave appears five times in Terence – oftener, relatively, than in Plautus[4] – Terence cannot be objecting to him in principle. It is true that Terence used the slave more for comic irony (the audience knowing his message in advance) than for suspense kept up by prevenient horseplay, but if his objection to Luscius is based on this, could he have expected the audience to guess the distinction he was drawing? We must surely conclude that what he objects to is not the character nor his function but the event specified, namely, the slave having the people step aside to make room for him.

But let us visualize the scene. At once it is apparent that Luscius could not *show* "the people" stepping aside, any more than, in the *Thesaurus*, he could show a court and jury in session. He might of course show two or three of the other characters in the play stepping aside, but to the audience these are A, B, and C:

how can it equate them with the *populus*? The fact is that the audience has to imagine "the people" stepping aside, and it can only do this if given a plain enough hint. The hint must be provided by the slave himself, running along and shouting something like "Decedite omnes!" It is this, rather than any *populus* onstage, which lies behind Terence's criticism. And the words must have come in a very prominent place for Terence's own audience to recollect the allusion.

What then of the remaining words, "quor insano serviat?" Eugraphius, in his otherwise rather puling commentary, is certainly right in taking the slave, not the people, as the subject of *serviat*.[5] The verb in this context must refer back to the noun *servus*. But what link does Terence intend between the people stepping aside and the slave serving a madman? A causal link, says Eugraphius: they step aside *because* he is slave to a madman. But how do they know that? On this point Eugraphius is silent. The answer must be, as before, that the slave tells them. As he runs, he cries something like

Decedite omnes: domino insano servio.[6]

And this at once gives a heightened appropriateness to Terence's subjunctive *serviat*. It is not a direct deliberative, but the oblique interrogative form of a factual statement, "he serves a madman" becoming "why does he, on his own allegation, serve a madman?" I suspect that Terence's objection, on which (just as when he based his criticism of the *Thesaurus* on lawcourt procedure) he may have received advice from his aristocratic patrons, is that under Roman law a slave was not obliged to be in bondage to a madman. This was one of the very few protections a slave had, though of course he had it merely by virtue of being a piece of property. The law was willing to protect property even from its owner if he became insane. If a man is mad, "he has not *intellectus* (or *affectio*) *possidentis*";[7] he himself, with his property, passes under the charge of a sane *curator*.[8] This then is Terence's complaint: he clearly means that servitude to a madman is strange to the law, and he clearly bases the complaint on what Luscius' slave himself said. It is a line in Luscius' play, such as I have indicated, which gives logical cohesion to the whole situation. And it must have been prominent enough to be remembered verbatim from its first utterance, for few if any of the audience would know the play from a written text.

In theory, Luscius' slave could be either bursting off or bursting on. His line could be the pay-off line at the end of a scene in which he has been charged with some errand by a master whom he believes insane. But the analogy of the *servus currens* elsewhere suggests rather that it is an entry-line, marking the beginning of a scene or even of the whole play. In the latter case, the interview with the master is of course merely narrated as an antecedent. And though it suits Terence's purpose to take the insanity heavily au pied de la lettre, the likeliest state of affairs is that the "madman" is a young man in difficulties in his love affair and driven thereby to a real or feigned distraction — a situation which has a certain amount in common with the mental instability of the youth in the *Phasma.*

We can thus discern among the *personae* of the lost play (1) a *servus* who may perhaps be a Leading Slave, (2) his master who appears to be demented and is probably an *adulescens* in love, and (3), in the background, no doubt a *virgo* or *meretrix.* We have adumbrated the scene which Terence has in mind, as well as its background and an approximation to what is probably its opening line.

Second Unnamed Play

Luscius, who must have been among the better-qualified men in Rome to express an opinion, said repeatedly that in his judgment Terence's stuff was *tenuis* and *levis.* The criticism has become famous in a slightly fuller form — "that the speaking was thin and the writing lacked weight." That is:

tenui esse oratione et scriptura levi.

We cannot be sure whether it is Luscius or Terence who is responsible for the pseudo-antithesis: certainly there are other examples of it in Terence. That it is a pseudo-antithesis I am fully convinced: *oratio* should not be wrenched into meaning "content," and Eugraphius' determination to extract this sense from one or other of the two nouns should be resisted. Luscius at different times made further allegations, but the present one does not seem to us particularly defamatory. We recognize it at once as merely an unsympathetic reaction to Terence's *elegantia* and atticizing. Since drama is so largely verbal, it may also refer more generally to his lack of high dramatic colouring and the limitations of his comic power.

When the *Phormio* was staged, the actor-manager Ambivius appears to have followed the normal practice of entrusting the prologue to a younger member of the troupe.[9] Terence rather surprisingly had this actor refer to the criticism in his first sentence, where Luscius' behaviour is described as "abuse" and "intimidation." Terence tried to counter it by irony. Luscius lays this charge, the actor said, presumably because our author never ventured on the critic's own little extravaganza:

> quia nusquam insanum scripsit adulescentulum
> cervam videre fugere et sectari canes
> et eam plorare, orare ut subveniat sibi.
> quod si intellegeret, quom stetit olim nova,
> actoris opera mage stetisse quam sua,
> minu' multo audacter quam nunc laedit laederet.
> (prol. 6-11)

... Because he has never said in a play that a demented youth sees a hunted doe on the run with hounds in full chase, and the doe come and implore and beg for his help. If he only knew that when the play had its première a while back and got a hearing, it was more thanks to the producer than the author, he would be a good deal less brazen in his nasty remarks than he actually is.

Terence has answered general with particular. He has cited one episode from Luscius' work of which he would not himself be proud. As we are not told the title of the play in question, let us assign the episode to a second unnamed play. This play, then, antedates the *Phormio* prologue, which, if we accept the didascalia, belongs to the ludi Romani of 161.[10] More than this, it was produced *olim*, and although this word can signify "on the occasion," "at the time which I mean," with more of a demonstrative than a temporally distancing reference, yet it has the latter for its commoner and more natural function, and this would put the unknown comedy some way back in time, though probably not before Terence began writing. We shall not go far wrong if we think of it as produced during the first three or four years of Terence's career.

As with the first unnamed play, the Greek original of this comedy is unknown, for again we cannot closely connect this episode of a "mad" youth, whose protection is begged by a hunted doe, with any specific moment in Greek comedy. Again Leo held the episode to be of Luscius' own invention, and again we find Fraenkel convinced that it comes from the source-play.[11] Donatus and Eugraphius both rightly point out that Terence's complaint is of a breach of comic decorum, the subject-matter of the episode being (they say) more appropriate to tragedy. But since there is abundant evidence of the incorporation of tragic motifs into later Greek comedy, both on a serious level and also by way of parody, it seems to be Luscius here who is nearer the norm, and Terence who again is overcramping the acceptable limits of the genre. We must not forget that this overcramping is one of the crucial reasons why, in the hundred years after Terence, palliata gradually ceased to be viable. It was indeed still destined to reach an apogee of glory on the stage, by the help of Roscius, but when the stay of his genius was withdrawn, the art-form dwindled and died.

The scene in Luscius' play does not of course presuppose that any hunt takes place. It was narrated as a figment of the youth's imagination. The description of him as "mad" merely means that he is in love, and in difficulties over his love affair, to the point of distraction. The hunted doe is a psychic image for the girl he loves, who is in some way endangered. Such psychic images are most familiar as the manifest content of dreams (ultimately representing wish fulfilment), and it was long ago suggested that the scene in the play showed the youth recounting a dream.[12] Plautus had dramatized at least two such accounts of dream-situations, where in one case a beautiful she-goat (*formosam capram, Merc.* 229) and in the other a pair of swallows (*hirundines, Rud.* 604) correspond to girls who are in what the dreamer regards as jeopardy. The first of these dreams probably derives from Philemon,[13] and the motif in general can be traced back to tragic and other literature, and even to life itself. But could Terence reasonably have objected to the mere narration of such a dream?

Dramatically speaking, the irruption of unconscious wishes, reshaped by the ego, to form a manifest dream is most effective if the dream is recounted by someone in a normal state of self-possession, that is, by someone sane. We then see it in a double perspective. If, however, the subject is not sane, it makes better theatre for the irruption to take place whilst he is awake, that is to say, for him visibly to take the stimuli he receives as external sensory stimuli and act the hallucination accordingly. Theatrically speaking, it is better for the sane Orestes or Pentheus to have a significant dream, but for the mad one to have a hallucination. There is a good parody of this latter situation in the *Menaechmi* (835 ff.). Indeed, the subject's madness is in a sense wasted if the dramatist sidetracks it by the further mechanism of a dream; wasted, too, are the rich opportunities for gestus, in which actors revelled, to body forth the hallunication. And as we are told that in Luscius' play the youth "sees" (*videre*) the events happening, we cannot really doubt that it was a hallucination. Nor is it the words only, but the words quasi-dramatized as part of the youth's experience, with the extravagant gestus involved – something akin to the tragic pantomime of the empire – it is this that Terence found so alien to his own concept of the decorum of palliata.[14]

That, then, is the scene; and the *personae* of the play, so far as we can recover them, are: the *adulescens* (*insanus*), a *virgo* or *meretrix* (= *cerva*) – this need not be a speaking part –, and certain other characters represented by the *canes*, i.e. the entourage of a rival claimant, a leno, a *senex amator*, or whatever. As to the value of the dramatized image of the hunt, it would be interesting if we could have the opinions of Virgil and Seneca, to set beside the rather naive dismissal of it by Terence. That is about as far as we can go on present evidence.

It will not have escaped notice, however, that we now appear to have *three* plays by Luscius, all turning, at least in part, on mental instability, and at least two of the three on the mental instability of a young man. For the youthful hero of the *Phasma* is and/or feigns to be malancholic to the point of unbalance, and both the unnamed plays contain an *insanus* who is in one case probably, and in the other certainly, an *adulescens*. Did Luscius really overwork the dementia-motif to this degree? It seems to me more likely that there is some overlap of identity among these plays. We have seen that chronology tells to some extent against identifying the first unnamed play with the *Phasma*, but nothing tells against identifying it with the second unnamed play. Terence's repetition of the same word *insanus* from the one case to the other could be a hint of the truth. On this hypothesis the order of scenes in the unnamed play would be: first, the *servus currens* announcing that his young master is mad, and then ocular proof of the fact by a staging of the hallucination.

It would follow that our knowledge of Luscius' plays is limited to three all told. It seems possible that although he lived much longer than Terence and could claim greater experience, he may not have been much more productive. If his total oeuvre was, let us say, nine or ten plays, this would help to explain his rating by Volcacius as a minor dramatist, a rating which Terence is in danger of sharing with him in the canon. It would also help to explain the apparently early loss of his works, with the consequence that except for two lines they seem not to be quoted verbatim by any grammarian, lexicographer, or scholiast.

6. THE THEATRICAL INTERESTS OF SULLA

The secret springs of the mind are often revealed by the way a man quotes. When Sulla's men brought to him the head of his last enemy, he knew that it was a moment of some importance. In Sulla's boyhood, when the first seditious blood had been shed, Scipio Aemilianus had been heard to say in Greek,

And so perish any other beside, who doth such deeds.

That was fifty years back; it was twenty years since Sulla had taken the measure of Marius, and now he was looking at the head of Marius' son and would-be successor. What he said to this young opponent was,

First learn to row before you try to steer.

He marked the moment, as Scipio had done, by choosing Greek words, old words, words of a poet. But whereas Scipio's thoughts had turned to epic, Sulla's turned to the theatre, and what is more, the Aristophanic theatre. Among statesmen and rulers of Rome he is the only one to our knowledge who may have shared Augustus' possible fondness[1] for Aristophanes. It was on this note of sardonic humour that he left the head exhibited in mid-forum before the rostra, where new fashion on both sides had begun to hang up the heads of political criminals. He spoke as he did because the theatre was always present as an undercurrent in his mind, though fortunately not always in such a grim context.

Two of the watchwords in recent historiography of this period are "background" and "process." Mere personality is falling into disfavour even with biographers.[2] We are certainly indebted to this practice of looking before and after, but there is still perhaps a time to judge men as individuals, and Sulla's interest in theatrical matters was of a highly individual kind. The tradition about it, though slight and neglected as frippery in many modern books, deserves some attention and some confidence. What we learn ultimately from Sulla himself is not self-glorificatory; what comes from his friends is not adulatory; what comes from his enemies is thrown in by the way as their mind was on other things.[3] Unlike the emperors he had no aura of majesty for wits and peddlers of dirt to enjoy themselves transmogrifying. I would therefore like to sketch the picture in outline, taking account of the sort of man he was, the sides of his character for which the theatrical world had peculiar appeal, and the ways in which he contributed to this aspect of the culture of his times, both Roman and Greek.

When Sulla was forming his tastes and ambitions, there were two older senators whose demeanour, though unlike his own, he could hardly help noticing. One was Aemilius Scaurus. He was a man who, when he spoke, had about him the look and manner of authority.[4] He was shrewd, optimate, and calmly persuasive, and in his late forties was chosen as princeps of the senate. (Seen through inimical eyes he was a grabber at power, place, and money.) Between him and the next generation there was something of a shift in taste and manners. He was old enough to be in tune, as it seems, with the old, frowning attitude towards stagefolk, and in fact his consulship coincided with an attempt at governmental repression of them;[5] yet he left at his death a son who became interested enough in shows and the theatre to find ways of promoting their attractions. He also left a young widow, and Sulla married her. Much-married opportunist though he might be, he found in Caecilia Metella a wife who, in as daunting a situation as any woman of republican days encountered,[6] nevertheless gave him her love and secured his, and it was his most bitter grief when he finally lost her.

The other senator, likewise father of a son who served the theatre well, was a rather easier man, Catulus. Sulla turned to Catulus as a likely political ally when he first fell out with Marius, but in a friendship and cooperation of at least fifteen years he became acquainted with his private life too. In private life Catulus, without being necessarily the centre of a literary circle,[7] was at least the centre of a very literate family. He indulged in light verse, as Sulla did after him. He happened, too, to have a genial attitude to the theatre, which could see tragedy through the eyes of comedy and not make too heavy weather of the delicate social problems involved. He was the kind of man who brought snatches of plays into his conversation. His old and much revered mother could remember back to the days of Terence. His stepbrother, an early literary dilettante, wrote tragedies, handicapped only by their author's excessive amiability, on such subjects as Adrastus and Tecmessa. The Catulan household was some time augmented by the presence of a slave whom they called Amphio or Amphion, and though various men gave such names to their slaves, in principle it must have been like calling one's office-boy Rosencranz or one's Scotch terrier Tamburlaine. On the social side it is as well that Catulus was not easily ruffled. The man he married his daughter to turned out to have a mad uncle, who took to mounting the rostra in stage clobber and throwing pennies to the people. The fact that this was an embarrassing memory forty years later indicates that it must have been very trying at the time. For his own part Catulus had his eye on a young comedy actor from Lanuvium, which was a day's journey down the Appian Way, and recording an encounter of theirs he wrote, a great deal more significantly than he realized, "Roscius exoritur."[8] I do not suggest that these two senators greatly influenced Sulla, but they are a useful foil against which to look at him.

Sulla, whenever he could, made a sharp division between business and leisure, but he could not do this altogether in regard to public games. To him they could be good entertainment but they were also an instrument of power, and needed time, money, care, and ingenuity. When Scaurus had been aedile he had been too busy and perhaps too high-minded to do much about games,[9] and the omission was remembered against him. Not everyone learned the lesson of this: for example, Mamercus Aemilius Lepidus did not,[10] and Sulla learned it only by experience. After his work in Africa he had really wanted to jump being aedile and go straight on to the praetorship. By his own account, however, the people did not want to miss seeing what, with his African connections, he could do in the way of games, and therefore voted him down and tried to push him towards the aedileship first. It needed a pledge of praetorian games, not to mention a good deal of ready money, for him to get himself elected praetor the following year.[11] From this moment he developed the games actively (culminating in his own ludi Victoriae Sullanae), at one time or another devising mass lion-hunts, importing athletes and all sorts of other performers, patronizing the increasingly popular gladiators, and bettering their bloody jousts by an infusion (so it is believed) of shield-and-dagger "Thracians." In Greece, too — and here more humanely, as will be seen — he supplied means for improving the festival at Oropus, its contests being made cultural as well as physical. A central optimate view of Roman games was that they were worth doing well provided one eliminated the risk of moral and political subversion. Scaurus' group had been sensitive about this subversion. Accius, a fellow-traveller of theirs, had hard things to say of the "mob" and "rascally men of the people," and the censors who promoted Scaurus were men who also severely clipped the wings of what is nowadays called "show business."[12] Sulla, once he was firmly in the saddle, could be in certain ways more liberal without running more risks. Private spending during games was limited by law, but he seems to have let people have greater latitude in this respect than they had previously been granted. He said about his own games that the masses needed a respite and recreation after all they had gone through,[13] and it may have been he who let the people into the front seats of the theatre to stop them from being monopolized by the knights.[14] At the same time everyone knew who was master. After Sulla was dead, an actor in tragedy could say of Pompey from the stage:

Nostra miseria tu es magnus

(and Magnus was the name that Sulla had given him). But to have said of Sulla in corresponding circumstances

Nostra miseria tu es felix

would have been courting liquidation. It is doubtful, however, whether an actor, or audience, would have wished to participate in this hypothetical provocation. The actors of that day owed too much to Sulla to wish to take sides against him or satirize him,[15] and the people appreciated the entertainment they derived from the actors. Both these circumstances were very likely the fruits of policy on his part.

Pompey, as a matter of fact, was not there to hear the obtrectation of himself, and Sulla would probably not have been either. Tragedy and dictators do not go well together, and it has been suggested that both he and Julius Caesar favoured mime, as against tragedy, to lessen the risk of any parallelizing by agitators between the tyrants of fiction and those of fact.[16] But the choices of a public figure are sometimes more due to character, and to taste as affected by circumstances, than they are to policy. Sulla's mind was big enough to have comprehended the primacy of tragedy among dramatic arts, and if (as is possible) Hermodorus of Oropus told him that the Oropians, thanks to his benefaction, were henceforward going to stage tragedy in their festival,[17] which they did, Sulla would have congratulated him frankly. All the same, tragedy was not his first liking. The only *tragoidia* he is recorded to have seen was the real-life tragedy which ensued when he told Scaurus' daughter to marry Pompey and bring him into the family.[18] This is an accident of the record, but it gives us a truth about him. It does not mean that he never saw such plays, nor that tragic acting was then in low water. Aesopus was in full career, not to mention Cimber and Rupilius. But none of these three names is ever linked by ancient writers with that of Sulla. The cardboard horrors of tragedy seem simply to have lacked appeal for him. After he became the arch-proscriber this is not surprising, but even in the days when his strong emotional and responsive side was unspoiled he had never been able to settle to heroics. His taste for living was heightened by any smack of the convivial, the comic, or the absurd. Gripped in the vice of power, he naturally became sardonic, but some who knew him well knew him as fond of laughter and jesting from his early years.[19] Myth and heroics he was inclined to belittle, if not actually to parody,[20] and when the Mithridatic quislings in Athens, unable to hold out under siege, sent a deputation to remind him that the city he was attacking had been in her day the home of Theseus, the beneficiary of Eumolpus, the scourge of the Mede, and other such things, he replied that he had not come to study the classics but to crush rebellion. The only lodgement their appeal found in his mind transpired after Athens had gone down in blood and rapine. When giving orders to stop the killing, he "premised a few words in praise of classical Athens and said that he forgave a few for the sake of many, and the living for the sake of the dead." Some five years later, in days of peace, the pro-Roman party seems (if conjecture is correct) to have tried a different psychological tack by renaming their festival of Theseus the Sylleia.[21]

And yet he was fascinated by the stage and stagefolk, and at some period he tried his hand at writing Latin sketches. They seem to have been atellans, a form which sometimes in the past had provided a vent for the histrionic high spirits of the ruling classes. Hitherto they had mostly been quite unstudied or at any rate unpublished, but in Sulla's time literati began to take them up and make something better of them. Current opinion about Sulla's is that they parodied mythology,[22] partly because they are described as *satyrikai* and partly because other literary atellans occasionally did this, as did also the older Graeco-Italian farces which had helped to launch atellans in the first place. What we have seen of Sulla's attitude to heroics is quite in keeping with this view. But it seems to me equally likely that what he wrote was the commoner sort of atellan, the vigorous, earthy farce of market-town or country life, full of Maccus Copo (= *caupo*) and Pappus Agricola, rather resembling in theme the vigorous and wily Karaghiosis plays in present-day Corfu. What possible contact, it may be asked, can there be between a statesman's mind and such barnyard material? In our own day the head of the Russian government, on getting rid of an eminent colleague and his following said, to the best of my recollection, "We took the mangy sheep by the tail and slung them out of the flock." Here is what Sulla said on a very similar occasion: "A farmer was busy ploughing when he felt lice biting him under his clothes. Twice he let go of the plough and shook them out of his shirt. But they bit him again, and that time he burned his shirt to stop the interruption."[23] The interest of this is that here we are listening to Sulla on himself. It is *Sulla* busy ploughing and being interrupted. Such a man may have had plenty to say about some Maccus Agricola.

Rather less familiar as yet in Latin, but well known through Greek performances and urgently craving to be watched, was the mime. This was to be seen at Rome throughout Sulla's life, and in his later years it was fast overhauling the palliata, which had written itself out by 100 B.C. though its popularity and prestige in the theatre were still great. Among other drawbacks, the palliata was regularly masked, it did not allow actresses, and it never treated the fascinating triangular situation which arises through adultery. The mime, in some of its forms, put all these things right. It was maskless, acted by both sexes, and adulterous — rather like our own theatre in those respects, though it seems also to have resembled the Renaissance novella and at other times to have used myth. There was plenty of dancing and miming in the modern sense, and the mime-actresses included very young girls. Eucharis (who may be of this date) had already "danced at the games of the *nobiles*" apparently before she was fourteen, and someone in the gens Galeria pushed on a child called Copiola to make her début in 82 at the age of twelve.[24] Sulla knew several of the mime-actresses, but the person he most respected was a team or troupe-master called Sorix, who came to be very close to him. Prosopography can do little for Sorix (unless he got his name from being beaky or shrew-like), but one seems to catch track of Campanian associations. Sulla was often seen talking to him in that last phase when he sent his nephew to colonize Pompeii and then decided to retire to the same part of the country himself. At any rate the thousands of demobilized ex-servicemen settled at Pompeii helped to stimulate a more flourishing theatrical life than the town had ever seen. And the name Sorix was remembered there; the children or grandchildren of Sulla's men saw it revived by a new Sorix and put up monuments to his popularity. The extant bronze head accompanied by inscriptions can hardly refer to the original Sorix, but the spirit, the simmering comedy, can still be seen in its features.[25] It is also possible that Sorix's mimes were watched by two kindred spirits with ideas for naturalizing or otherwise improving the libretto.[26] One was twenty-five-year-old Decimus Laberius. The other, who may have seen them either at

Rome or Pompeii, was a young Antiochene. He had originally been found standing on a gantry, his feet smeared with whiting or chalk-powder to show that he was for sale,[27] and his purchaser, with that unfocused attention to identity which we reserve for marginal people, had called him simply Syrus. Learning Latin was to him as creative an experience as it had been to Terence, and he afterwards made his name with mimes that could be read as well as acted, and which epitomized the situation step by step with what the Romans so loved, a perfectly expressed thinking-point. The mimes are gone but the morals remain, and with their accreted progeny have run into more than 277 printed editions. It is mildly interesting that Publilius Syrus may have first seen Italian mime in the heyday of Sorix.

On the more dissolute fringes of the world of mime were the performers called lysis-singers, specialists in sex-appeal and in some form of male-female impersonation which research has not yet succeeded in visualizing. They were mostly immigrants from Greece or further east. A friend of Catulus' knew one, Antiodemis, who had set out for Rome from Paphos in Cyprus before Sulla was born, or in his earliest years, and wrote about her soft, melting eyes, her intoxicating manner, the liquid movement of her arms, and her body as boneless as cream cheese.[28] Among her successors was an effeminate young man whom Sulla knew personally. His real name, Metrobius, had certain comedy overtones, and he kept it. Sulla knew him from his early years, liked him a great deal, would do anything for him, and was seen to have fallen under his spell.

Tragedy, atellan, and mime, together with comedy (which I hold over) had at that time mostly to be watched from wooden seating erected near temples and perhaps in circus or forum. On the question of whether to build a permanent stone theatre there was a conflict in the mind of the governing class, who suspected, as such a class is liable to do, that concessions in a spirit of liberalism would tend to corrupt society, as well as providing an unnecessary arena for political meetings.[29] What the smaller Italian towns did was their own concern — in the event they led the way — but at Rome puritanical suspicion of Greek practices was still strong, and previous attempts to get a theatre built had been thwarted.[30]

Public opinion was not yet ripe, but we can gather from theatrical developments under Sulla that it was steadily ripening. Though an encourager of building enterprises, he — for whatever reason — did not try to build a theatre in the capital. But under his impulse Pompeii quickly had its old theatre renovated, as well as acquiring a new one and the first of the amphitheatres. The men to whom he gave control of Praeneste soon restored to use that remarkably theatre-like building, the temple of Fortune, and his rule created a propitious climate for Roman theatre-building elsewhere, particularly at Alba Fucens (deep inland beyond Tibur), where there are known to have been pro-Sullan sympathies.[31] Of all Italian stage-types the atellan, in which Sulla had a creative interest, had been making the deepest imprint on Roman theatre structure.[32] Perhaps his surest mark, however, can be seen in Pompey, who is sometimes called his "heir" and whom he had once wanted to make his son-in-law. The son of Scaurus and the son of Catulus both worked in the direction of greater comfort and splendour at theatricals, but it was Pompey who made Rome finally take the moral plunge. He built his theatre on the Campus Martius where Sulla's monument was; he gave it some of the features of Alba Fucens; he dedicated it to Venus Victrix, a very Sullan choice; he included a shrine of Felicitas; and for the opening celebration he called in several actors of Sulla's day, one of them having to be specially brought out of retirement.[33]

Nevertheless, if some metahistorian of this field of enterprise, some Toynbee of the stage, were to analyze theatrical evolution into three conceptual phases — a phase of the dramatist, a phase of the actor, and a phase of the building — Sulla would undoubtedly belong to the second phase. Actors, for him, were at the centre of something which must be shared in, rather as the prima donna or concert pianist is felt to be in modern times. We can trace this not only in his life at Rome, but also on several occasions during his four-year campaign east of the Adriatic. Here the world of the stage was dominated by a few large and well-organized guilds, the Artists of Dionysus as they called themselves.[34] Three of the best-known of these guilds — that of Athens, that of Ionia and Hellespont, and that of the Isthmus and Nemea, who between them controlled all the highest grades of dramatic and musical performers in the Aegaean area — severally engaged Sulla's attention in the intervals of his fighting. As Sulla found them, all three guilds had already had their corporate existence recognized by the Roman government, and thus, besides whatever stimulus of private interest and goodwill he felt, he had good ground for respecting in his official capacity the privileges they had won for themselves over the years, such as immunity from military call-up and from the distraints and impositions which war commonly brings on the civilian population.

The guild of Athens, it is true, was in no very good position to benefit by this amiability. Artists of Dionysus sometimes entangled themselves in affairs of state; they openly claimed to have a public polity, and the Athenian guild had made a serious political blunder. As Sulla probably knew, the year before his arrival on the scene they had openly allied themselves with the anti-Roman party in the city. They had joined enthusiastically in the welcome given to its leader Aristion (or Athenion), when he returned from Mithridates' court and set about making Athens a satellite of Pontus with himself as puppet ruler. They invited him as guest of honour to ceremonies in their guild-hall and sacred precinct, with much palaver including advance notice, conveyed by a herald, of the pledges to be solemnized — for all the world like a state within a state. Their invitation had been addressed with a theatrical flourish to "the harbinger of our new Dionysus." All this, to the Roman observer, cohered as close as sin with the bloody attempt of that new Dionysus, namely Mithridates, to liquidate the whole Roman name in Asia. The extinction of the anti-Roman party at Athens was one of Sulla's principal aims in Greece. When he achieved it, it is not surprising if the Athenian guild of Artists found themselves under a cloud. It is not known what action was taken against them, but we find half a century's busy and vocal activity on their part henceforward shrunken to mere parochial concerns.[35]

There had of course been widespread damage and destruction in Athens, besieged, stormed, and partly sacked as it had been by Sulla's troops. Sulla was nothing if not a military realist, and it is among his few disservices to the world of theatre that, over and above the human casualties, certain buildings and monuments connected with drama, in this its home, should have suffered in the fighting. The Odeon or Odeum (as Sulla would call it), built by Pericles, was over 350 years old. It was a large, square, roofed hall standing next to the theatre of Dionysus, and in it there had traditionally taken place — we do not know how long the practice continued — the ceremonial prologue to the Great Dionysia, a prologue in which each competing poet mounted the platform with his actors, all in diadems, and told the people what story his play would enact. Here the aged Sophocles, on learning of the death of Euripides, had stood in tribute, himself in the garb of mourning, his actors and chorus all uncrowned. This building suffered heavy damage in the course of the struggle, each side tending afterwards to blame the troops of the other.[36] The ruin of private buildings would interfere with many kinds of business, including no doubt the manufacture of those small terracotta figurines which were so prized as ornaments and among which actors in mask and costume were such favourite subjects.[37] Another place affected was a sanctuary of Demeter and Kore, where Artists of Dionysus used to go and provide the hymns when the mysteries were celebrated. Restoration of the precinct and its altar, which had been "destroyed in the national emergency," was among the parochial activities of the Athenian guild in the next decade, their president Philemon meeting the cost.[38] It has often been believed[39] that Sulla's men played havoc with the theatre of Dionysus itself, but no irrefragable proof has been brought, and we must leave the verdict open. The truth may be that here the conqueror stayed his hand.

The guild of Ionia and Hellespont fared better than that of Athens. Thanks to a partially successful amalgamation with the Pergamene Artists, it had for some seventy-five years past been organized like an erratic binary star, one of its centres being at Teos, except at times when it fell foul of the Teians and was driven elsewhere, the other at Pergamum, where its particular patron god was Dionysus with the surname Kathegemon.[40] The Artists here had had to exist cheek by jowl with Mithridates, but partly by good luck and partly by good management they avoided compromising themselves in any unforgivable way. Their noble theatre, built or rebuilt during the previous century, was chosen by Mithridates in 87 as the setting for a royal pageant, doubtless involving the Artists but with himself as the cynosure. The audience was on eighty rows of seats, the topmost rising 180 feet above the orchestra. Unknown to him, his pageant more or less coincided with the day when Sulla with his army was putting out from Brundisium to bring the aggressor to book. Mithridates was concurrently being dogged by evil omens, and the tale has often been told how on this occasion a theatrical winch was ceremonially lowering towards his head a statue of Victory holding a crown, when Victory broke to pieces and the crown went tumbling into the body of the theatre.[41] It was on all hands a superb omen, and became even more so when viewed retrospectively from 84, by which time the day of reckoning had arrived. The Artists doubtless made what capital they could out of this and anything else they could find to gratify the conqueror with, as well as out of their traditional non-combatant status, in order to escape the reparations which he was imposing on the area as a whole. They did, in the event, fare better than the civic authorities. The reparations which Sulla imposed on the pro-Mithridatic towns were of such an order that they had to scrape up loans on their largest public buildings to pay them. The upshot was that some of the actors presently found themselves acting in mortgaged theatres.[42] When however, the Artists' own case came up before the imperator's council he decided, all things considered, to show them the favour of renewing their earlier privileges, and he addressed an official letter to the guild, in which he said that he was acting "in order that you may continue in possession of the same, and be exempt as formerly from every class of public undertaking chargeable to private means, and from military service; may not be required to pay any imperial tax or charges; be not pressed by any person for provision of necessities or lodging; and be not obliged to provide any person with a billet." The wording was doubtless supplied by draughtsmen from the guild itself. The favour was subject to formal confirmation by the Roman Senate, and Sulla later arranged for a suitably worded motion to go through. In or shortly after 81 the guild picked one of its leading members, a lyrist from Laodicea called Alexander, to go to Rome and request authority to put up on the island of Cos, and perhaps also in other places, a record on stone stating exactly what the privileges were. Permission was given. The record at Cos is still extant and it includes the text of Sulla's letter.[43]

Before he returned to Rome, however, Sulla formed a more intimate contact with another group of Artists belonging apparently to the third of the guilds, that of the Isthmus and Nemea. This had a number of affiliated groups spread over a wide area, including an off-and-on connection at Thebes and branches in Euboea. Sulla may already have supplied the Theban group with a professional commission when in 86 he staged festivities in honour of his victory at Chaeronea and required the performers, presumably local, to compete in artistic celebration. Normally they would have been judged by some of the city fathers, but Sulla's anger lay too heavy on Thebes for that, and they had had to perform before imported judges.[44] Now, in 84, Thebes was no place for the vacation which Sulla, on his way home, found that he needed to take for health reasons, instead of sailing with his army round the Peloponnese. Athens was likewise unsuitable for a rest-cure, and he considered Euboea. There was a branch of the Artists at Chalcis, and another, it seems, at Aedepsus. This latter place was a spa, and was the resort of "invalids, tourists, artists and intellectuals."[45] Sulla fixed his choice upon it. After four strenuous years his stay gave him a chance to indulge his favourite recreation, and he duly sought out the Dionysiac Artists, spending much time in their company and following their day-to-day activities with lively interest. It was only after this refreshment that he set out again for Italy, to win his last battle at the Colline Gate and establish himself as dictator.

Meantime something else that he had done was coming to fruition. It was his consistent policy, while punishing the enemies of Rome if they were also his own enemies, to reward in an equally exemplary manner all who had remained loyal. Loyalty was scarce in and around Attica, but it had been shown by Hermodorus, priest of the great shrine of Amphiaraus on the Attica-Boeotia frontier, and Sulla was also under the impression that a bargain which he had mentally struck with Amphiaraus himself, the demigod, had been accepted and had materially contributed either to his bodily health (which needed divine aid) or to his victory. By contrast therefore with his spoliation of other shrines he awarded to the Amphiareum both the land round the temple, to be inviolable in perpetuity, and in addition the revenues of the township, harbours, and district, the property of Hermodorus alone to be exempt from any liability. His announcement, datable to the years 86-84, ratified by the senate in 80, and reconfirmed in 73, said that the revenues were to be applied "to the contests and sacrifices which the people of Oropus offer to the god Amphiaraus, and likewise to those which they shall offer hereafter in regard of the victory and hegemony of the Roman people,"[46] It is not certain whether the "hereafter" clause was in the first instance an idea of Sulla's or whether the Oropians proposed it to please him, but its effect was to turn the Amphiaraia, which had been celebrated as far back as the fourth century if not earlier, henceforward into a Festival of Amphiaraus and Rome. The monies helped to finance the various classes of contest, both musical and gymnastic. It is part of the psychology of the picture that the classes include satyr-play, tragedy, and comedy. If these particular classes existed already (of which there is no evidence), they would help to explain Sulla's interest and favour: if they were now newly instituted, which seems more likely, the intention was to stimulate his continuing regard.

Portions of the festival archives, dating from soon after the war, are extant, though they have not so far as I know been translated into English. To give the relevant entries will show Sulla's benefaction more clearly at work. The opening formulae specified the various officials in office for the year and referred to the festival by its new name; underneath came the list of classes and results, usually headed by the words "Winners were as follows." In one year we read (preserving the Greek spelling):

Author, satyr-drama:
Kalippos, son of Kallon, citizen of Thebes.
Author, tragedies:
Lysistratos, son of Mnaseas, citizen of Chalcis.
His (leading) actor:
Glaukias, son of Zosandros, citizen of Thebes.
Author, comedies:
Ariston, son of Chionos, citizen of Thebes.

His (leading) actor:
Kallistratos, son of Exakestos, citizen of Thebes.
New tragedy:
... citizen of ...[47]

For another year we read:

Author, satyr-drama:
Herakleides, son of Herakleides, citizen of Athens.
(Leading) actor in tragedy:
Epinikos, son of Alexandros, citizen of Athens.
(Leading) actor in comedy:
Iranos, son of Phrynides, citizen of Tanagra.
Author of tragedy:
Hermokrates, son of Alexandros, citizen of Miletos.
His (leading) actor: Charias,
son of Charias, citizen of Athens.
Author of comedy:
Ariston, son of Posês, citizen of Athens.
His (leading) actor: Straton,
son of Isidotos, citizen of Athens.[48]

And for a later year:

Author, satyr-drama:
Philoxenides, son of Philippos, citizen of Oropos.
(Leading) actor of old tragedy:
Philokrates, son of Theophantos, citizen of Thebes.
(Leading) actor of old comedy:
Zoilos, son of Zoilos, citizen of Syracuse.
Author of new tragedy:
Protarchos, son of Antimenes, citizen of Thebes.
His (leading) actor:
Philokrates, son of Theophantos, citizen of Thebes.
Author of new comedy:
Chionnes, son of Diogeitondas, citizen of Thebes.
His (leading) actor:
Polyxenos, son of Andrytas, citizen of Opous.[49]

Sulla very likely saw in this festival a healthy politico-cultural influence and perhaps a kind of sidetracking of the home activities of the guild of Artists at Athens and of the festival judges and administrators at Thebes.

The Greek guild-system had penetrated to Sicily and southern Italy, and perhaps to Campania. Whether it had yet established itself in Rome is obscure. Artists of Dionysus had been brought in on special occasions, but the censors' act of 115, attempting to ban from the capital almost the whole *ars ludicra,*[50] may reflect the Artists' difficulty, in the face of old anti-Greek feeling, in getting a firm footing there; and there seems to be no record of any dealings of Sulla at Rome with an actors' union as such. His contact with actors here was personal rather than official, and in any case extended beyond the social limits set for themselves by the *technitai.* The latter excluded from guild-membership whole classes of stage-performers — mime-actors, women, and slaves — but Sulla in his personal relations had no such exclusiveness. Over and above all elements of policy, all insurance against being satirized in the theatre, he turned to stagefolk because they were stagefolk and because they were convivial. To do so was something between a solace and a passion. And the proclivity was lifelong. Even making allowance for the vagueness and exaggeration of rumour, the picture is remarkably persistent. Of his early life we are told, "he would pass his time with mime-actors and comedians, joining in all their gay abandon." Of his later years and dictatorship, "he used to keep company with mime-actresses, female string-players, and theatrical artists in general, and would be drinking with them . . . from the morning hours." We are told that he was a very good singer himself: an unlikely-sounding report, but one which takes on more colour in the present context. Again, "he would regularly gather round him the pick of gaytime stage and theatre folk and spar with them at jesting-matches." And again, "to mimetic singers and dancers he used to behave like a *tamed* creature; they found him amenable and compliant towards their every request." These characteristics were to reappear in a later head of state: we find them noted, in almost the same words, of the Lanuvine emperor Commodus.[51] More than once Sulla gave actors large sums of money, and even made over to them, as Mark Antony was to do, tracts of state-owned land. If there were political and social consequences, they ensued because private life inevitably impinges upon public, as when Plutarch reports the gossip "that he not only misbecame his high office but also neglected a great deal that required attention."[52]

The bad side of such behaviour was picked up by two of his younger associates, Verres and Catiline,[53] and copied in the next generation by Mark Antony, but there was perhaps a good side, in that we find high society henceforth unbending a little, in a manner that in Scaurus' day would have seemed out of place. There is an amusing side-light on this, connected with the sporadic Roman practice of nicknaming various highborn folk after members of the riffraff who happened to resemble them. One of Sulla's senior officers, the C. Scribonius Curio who was praetor by 80 and consul in 76, had a distracting way of bending and swaying his body as he talked. Curio "thrashing about" and teetering "like someone trying to make a speech from a little boat" became a byword; added to his bad memory, the habit seems on occasion to have cost him his entire audience. Evidently the theatre too had one of these contortionists, called Burbuleius, and Curio presently acquired the nickname Burbuleius.[54] This seems to have promoted a fashion. Two of Sulla's own relations,[55] at present young men, were later teased with actors' names because of a supposed resemblance, and two other twenty-year-olds, likewise making for the *cursus honorum*, found when they reached the top that in the eyes of the world they were not so much Nepos and Lentulus as Pamphilus and Spinther, because they looked like these actors. In Lentulus' case the name stuck and was passed on to the next generation. Thirty years after Sulla's death one of the Scipio family was nicknamed or surnamed Salvit(t)o, after a mime, and we are told that this was done *ad opprobrium*. After that the practice seems to flag. Can we be sure, it may be asked, that it was not in vogue earlier? It is not found. As for the cognomen of Ambivius Turpio, which one would have thought so tempting as a potential sobriquet, it does occur here and there, but not by intentional transference from the actor. In this capacity it lies low for centuries until a resourceful church father hurls it at a Pelagian, incidentally baffling later scholarship which wanted to emend the text to *Turpilius*.[56]

We have seen that the staging of Greek comedy and satyr-plays at Oropus was felt to be, in principle, to Sulla's liking. We have yet to consider the dictator's increment from Roman comedy – *Plautinisches im Sulla.* When his penetrating gaze[57] met the squint of Roscius, there took place more than a meeting of eyes. Roscius obviously could communicate with him, sharing the inflexions of his language and inward sense in a way that immigrant stagefolk, many of them servile, could not. Whether Sulla first met him through Catulus or in some other way, and how far the acquaintance was voluntary on Roscius' part, we do not know. Roscius was some years the younger and reached about fifty by the time of the dictatorship, when they were often together. Both men had kept their hair,[58] both had collected certain compliments on the way they carried themselves; both were in the limelight and were currently being written of in other men's books. Roscius had prospered in his career. He probably now managed his own company of actors, and he had property in the country as well as his ordinary house. The dates of his performances are lost, and inferences drawn from them can only be of a general kind. What is not in doubt is Sulla's appreciation of him. He had two histrionic gifts, gifts which were no doubt grounded in his nature, though they required intense practice as well. First, he could universalize human impulses and predicaments in a way that made thousands of people feel simultaneously "This is *right*." Yet at the same time he could lift up and transmute the portrayal into something for which the only word was "enchanting."[59] Therefore his audience was no mere random crowd on the wooden tiering. It was, as a friend once hinted in proud phrase, the *populus Romanus* itself. In examining the testimonia of hundreds of Roman actors over the centuries, one can find very few others who inspired this national feeling.[60]

But now Sulla had him at his table for the sake of his company, and Roscius became *carissimus*[61] to him. What were the two characters like in convivial contact? The tantalizingly brief records of their friendship[62] suggest talk of food, drink, women, money, and probably health and entertainment. From hints elsewhere we might add art and religion.

Sulla on food was worth hearing, especially à propos of

something which happened during his stay at Aedepsus. As he was going for a walk along the shore of the Euripus certain individuals approached and offered him some very tempting fish. He asked these men where they came from and they mentioned a place which he thought he had blotted off the face of the earth. What does etiquette prescribe for such a moment? He was in fact startled into an exclamatory question which they in turn were too terrified to answer; but then, recovering, he looked at the men and looked at the fish, offered smiling indulgence, and said, "You have brought no mean or despicable intercessors." It would be agreeable to suppose, though we are not entitled to do so, that there was a memory of this in his mind when, after returning home, he sponsored a measure to lower the price of fish so that people could enjoy it more often.[63] Roscius of course understood the comic side of food as well as he understood anything, because he so often had to convey it to others. Procuring their next meal was for the lower classes a familiar enough problem to give food-allusions a piquancy in ancient comedy which they have largely lost in our own society. In one role, between his first entry and exit, Roscius had verbally to give his audience the taste, or glimpse, of no fewer than twelve succulent comestibles and drinks — with "wheat galore" and "a whole year's groceries" thrown in for good measure. In regard to drinks, it appears that on the same occasion one of the troupe had to copy him with a mellifluous "myrrh-wine and raisin-wine, decocted must and honeydew."[64] With Sulla, even on this subject, the sardonic touch was never far away, and it is well known that when he celebrated his final victory, he did so by broaching a Gracchan vintage.

Roscius, though personally abstemious as far as our reports go,[65] was a shrewd and whimsical observer of sexual behaviour, and sex to Sulla was a perennially interesting subject. For his Greek official correspondence he devised for himself the name Epaphroditos, and amid all that historians have written on this, I do not know that it has ever been asked what his actress friends from the demi-monde thought about it. If quips were to be bandied, as we are given to understand they were, this one must have been hard to resist. Detractors of course put about inflated stories of his sex-life and said it ruined his health; undeniable were the long house-parties, the expensive gifts to beautiful women, and his memories of the strumpet Nicopolis. If salaciousness was required at these parties, the lysis-singers could doubtless readily supply it. Not that Roscius wished to deny to life, or the theatre, its bawdy element, but he seems to have been apt at expressing simultaneously the pathos and humour of man's dealings with woman. We find him coming on to the stage in a play which may have been written when he and Sulla were both young. He came on, if as a young man, then in a role rather like the hero of *The Catcher in the Rye*; if as an old man, then in the role of an admonitory father recollecting his own wild oats; and he spoke of:

> A woman, a wench, who came to know,
> To know me for her livelihood . . .

As the reed-pipe player started the musical section "By chance but now," Roscius built up his gestures to a climactic pun:

> *Ita — me — destituit — NUDUM!*

"Meministi Roscium?" wrote one spectator to another, long years afterwards. They were discussing how much it is possible to get away with.[66] Sulla, although in other ways strongly heterosexual, had succumbed to an erotic relationship with Metrobius. It began years back; he found that it answered to a need in him, and he clung to it long after the lysis-singer was past his first bloom. When his friends mentioned the subject he simply said that he loved him. Roscius was in a position to understand this, and to see how it looked from the younger man's point of view. For he had been semi-beloved once, too, and that was by Catulus. Now Catulus in all likelihood did not feel like this except for literary purposes, but he had written a poem comparing Roscius to the divine Aurora:

> . . . A human he,
> A goddess she,
> And he for beauty her outshone.

Can one be beautiful with a strabismus? I quote from the author of *The Catcher in the Rye*. "His eyes . . . were slightly crossed," we read, " . . . and . . . one might have thought long and seriously before wishing them straighter, or deeper, or browner, or wider set. His face, just as it was, carried the impact, however oblique and slow travelling, of real beauty."[67]

Perhaps the best symbol for the Sulla-Roscius friendship would be the leather bottlebag, of which the largest variety, made from a whole oxhide, was called the *culleus*. We are near enough to the Romans on the grape-vine of European languages to catch something of their feeling for this word *culleus*, for we have the word "cowl," which carries a similar direct suggestion of bulging, capacious fabric. The verbal root has the same kind of instant propriety as the words "cow" or "balloon." Roscius had occasion to know bottlebags well, because it seems that at least the largest kind were manufactured at Lanuvium (*cullei Lanuvini*). They were evidently made from local hides – perhaps smaller ones were made of goatskin too – and sent up to Rome; and possibly one reason why the Lanuvines were so attached to their goddess Juno Sospita was that she always carried a goatskin round her neck and wore leather bootees. Such bottles, whether artifacts or whole skins, ranged from mere flasks to the *culleus* itself, and they were in principle a serious and useful domestic article. But when plumped up they looked rather funny, and they had gathered associations, associations of drink, sex, and doom.[68] Who better fitted than Roscius to express all this? In his famous horror-comic role of bawdy-house keeper to the bourgeoisie, which he played many times, he stood on the stage glowering at a dubious *meretricula* and saying:

> I'll see thee haled in a bottlebag (*culleus*)
> Into the common stew –

(i.e. the *demotic* bower of venery.) *Improbissimus*, was the verdict on the whole business.[69] It was a case where Roscius could be *improbior* than Sulla. But could he be more sardonic? Sulla had a memory of how he had turned the screw tighter and tighter on the hungry and doomed Athenians. He had them stewing weeds. He had them boiling their boots. He had them gnawing strips of bottlebag. And then he struck.

Sulla also found in Roscius one who could appreciate as he did the meaning and colour of personal names. Such an interest often begins as no more than a joke, but to some men it can expand to become a symbol, and then an omen, and then a veritable covenant with Providence. Roscius professionally had to make the names of comedy dramatically effective to the whole vast concourse in the theatre. On a quite trivial plane, for instance, he had to stand holding a leather strap and say to a slave-girl, "I'll tan your hide scarlet, Scarlet!" — and carry it off.[70] He had to bring out the savour of other courtesan-names such as Hedytium and Aeschrodora. In real life actors well knew the experience of adapting name to identity or identity to name, an experience shared in modern times by such artistes as, for example, Mr. Elvis Presley, Miss Ursula Andress or Miss Eartha Kitt. Roscius' own name (which was pronounced Rōscius) was sensible enough, but — to say nothing of Hilarus the "merry," Eucharis the "graceful," and "heart's desire" Eros, the dates of whose débuts are a moot point — here was Sorix, carrying about permanently in his appellation the engaging nosiness of a shrew, and here was twelve-year-old Copiola, trying to be Copiola, trying to be "little Miss Modicum" — with plenty of time to succeed in, as it happened, for she lived to be over a hundred. Most of these names were cheerful and auspicious, but one did meet the occasional provocative exception such as, in later times, Bulimio or Avidius Fatalis. Roscius in his spare time had once coached an actor called Panurgus. Was it perhaps tempting Providence to have a name like that? Panurgus at all events had come to a very bad end.

If in this connection Sulla and Roscius looked round their past and present friends, it certainly provided food for thought. A noble house or a noble mien can dignify an otherwise somewhat absurd name, but there is something about it which remains a standing temptation. Catulus was as noble a name as, say, the Italian name Guelph, but at the same time it was totally homophonous with "whelp," which made it a sheer gift to the heckler. Scaurus was as noble a name as Rosencranz or Fortinbras, but to a Roman ear it sounded like nothing so much as "swollen-hock." That was precisely the impact of these names on the young Cicero, who knew Roscius well by 81, and he is on record as saying, in the next quinquennium, that if men with names like Gwelp and Swollenhock could do so well, it should be possible for him, with a name distantly like Vetchman, to do even better.[71]

Sulla's feelings about name and identity seem to have run the whole gamut. His name has been doubtfully explained as a colloquial form of *sura*, so that it would mean "neat-calf." Evidently a physical connotation was there and was felt, and *surula* expresses probably enough the Roman feeling about it. As a name it would have been grander, and Sulla's family may have claimed an etymological connection with *sibylla*.[72] The truth is that one's name is like one's face, it becomes entangled with one's amour-propre, and up to a point one is prepared to stand by it. As in the trench badinage of 1914-18, so in the siege of Athens, daredevils had gone up on the walls to boo the enemy commander. They booed his name, his face, and his wife. They did not know enough Latin to ask how Metella enjoyed her aesthetic promotion from Scaurus to Surula, but one of the things they shouted sounded like

Syllabub, syllabub, mulberry crumble![73]

Athens paid for this, because Sulla really did have a blotch-and-barley-flour complexion, and was annoyed. But then came the great victories, Chaeronea and Orchomenus, and one can see the triumphant selfhood emerging in his response to the Mithridatic peace-feelers. "Do you, Archelaus, . . . dare propose treachery to me, who am a Roman commander and *Sulla*?" "O Pythian Apollo," he prayed once, "now that through so many struggles you have raised *the fortunate Cornelius Sulla* to glory and greatness, have you brought him to the gates of his native city only to cast him down?"[74] He had people at Rome talking of the "Games of Sulla's Victory" as, at Athens, they talked of the "Sylleia." He saw the name Sulla go up everywhere in inscriptions and graffiti: even today it is legible on some thirty of them for the seven years 84-78. An extension of this feeling is his use of names to ally himself and his family permanently with the dispensations of Fortuna: his adoption of "Faustus," first for himself and then for his son, of "Fausta" for his daughter, and then, after the episode of young Marius' head, his claim to be in truth Sulla "Felix." "Dictator, . . . I, too, wish to partake a little in your felicity," said a young woman, judging her moment. They were watching gladiators, but in what Plutarch calls a *theatron*, and she became his last wife.

Even convivial conversation can wax metaphysical. Sulla, as he wrote his memoirs, had much in mind the various providences which had enlivened the course of his wars, and some of them sound well adapted for the ear of Roscius. I have already mentioned the débâcle in the theatre at Pergamum, where the suspended crown crashed past Mithridates just as his future conqueror was setting sail from Brundisium. Sulla always capitalized on omens, and he employed a reliable diviner, Postumius, to do the same. One incident that he is known to have been writing up (and we have Cicero's testimony both to the event and its inclusion in the book) was what happened once in camp at Nola. Sulla was sacrificing in front of the praetorium when a highly ambiguous snake came slithering from underneath the altar. They made it out to mean *action* — and the ensuing battle was won.[75] Roscius may well have been favoured with this excerpt, for he often used to say that his own success in life originated from just such a snake. It had got into his cradle, probably in the house where he was born, and had confronted the religious authorities at Lanuvium with a similar dilemma. To welcome or not to welcome? Now it happened that Lanuvium possessed a very holy snake. It lived on the demesne of Juno Sospita, and contributed not a little to the fame of the district. This, I imagine, may have influenced the soothsayers' decision. They divined that the omen meant *glory*: and now Roscius was achieving it.

Sulla decided to make him a knight. He raised him formally to the equestrian order, making sure at the same time that he was well within the equestrian census, and burking possible objections about the civil disabilities of actors.[76] Making a knight cannot have been exceptional for Sulla in itself, amid all the promotions and decapitations of those times, but there are two interesting things about this event. It is the first time, to our knowledge, that the person so honoured is drawn from the acting profession, and it is the first time we hear of the bestowal of the gold ring. Some people dismiss "bestowal of the ring" here as a merely symbolic phrase, or as an error and anachronism, but Sulla seems to have believed in a peculiar fitness about this choice of ornament compared with others that a man might choose. He had had a ring made for himself, a very personal gold *sphragis*, with a story attached. He might have commemorated the story in a hundred ways, but he chose this way. He wore his own ring often, and when he made his will, a year or two after the present event, he happens to be mentioned to us as *sphragisamenos.*[77] He may well have wanted Roscius to have a gold ring too, though their use as marks of rank was not yet common. By this time he had begun to lean on him a little (as he did also on his mime friends) partly perhaps as a relief from the mad world of politics, and partly because his health was giving way.

To Roscius the promotion, which may have included gifts in money or estate, meant social and probably financial betterment beyond an actor's hopes, and also as much leisure as he liked. He lived to qualify, at least in theory, for the office of *iudex*, if he wanted it, and what came nearer home — since he often watched other actors[78] — to qualify in old age for one of the reserved front seats in the theatre, which the knights had by then recovered.[79] Moreover for five or six years now he was on an even social footing with Cicero, his friendship with whom was to constitute a new phase in his life.

There were repercussions in theatrical history. Julius Caesar at this time was still young, but he was old enough to know Sulla. He in due course developed an interest of his own in Syrus, the mime writer and producer, and the two of them, with the knight Decimus Laberius, were to have a memorable appointment in the theatre some thirty-six years on. Soon afterwards in the provinces another actor was honoured as Roscius had been and led to the front seats of his own theatre. Familiar contact between stagefolk and the Roman head of state became the rule rather than the exception. As one of them put it to Caesar's great-nephew, "Just you leave the people to busy their minds on us." By Domitian's time people were claiming that it was not the emperor but Paris the actor who chose the recipients of the golden ring. And by the early third century another figure from the stage world was appointed to check the qualifications of both knights and senators and given supervision over the morals of youth.[80]

Sulla died at Puteoli, and his body was brought back, in solemn cortège, up the Appian Way, past the turning to Lanuvium, through the Capena gate and the Forum, and on to the Campus Martius.[81] Among those who escorted him out from the Forum on the last stage of his journey was the Roman knighthood in full and grand array. Clopping in wind-blown regalia behind the processing ranks of the senate, they watched the billowing smoke of the funeral pyre, and then went home — in the rain.

Sulla did not lack a morality, though it was of a pre-Socratic kind, and he appears to have given thought to a summation of it to be incised on his monument. Greater good, so the sense ran, was done him by no friend on earth than that friend received, and greater evil by no enemy than that enemy received. There was no such epigraph cut on stone since Darius, king of the Medes and Persians, was laid to rest in Persepolis. The expression was a little different in the two cases: the naked ethic and the assurance of excelling in it were the same.

But when all is said, it remains that, culturally speaking, the theatre did much for Sulla, and Sulla did much for the theatre of his time. He developed the games at Rome in many directions and showed them more plainly to the people, besides endowing the festival, including the dramatic competitions, at Oropus. He stimulated by his interest the Artists of Dionysus, and continued the Roman government's recognition and support of their guild-organization, thereby paving the way for the world-guild which was to begin under Augustus. His generosity enriched, and his strength protected, many individual actors in Italy who might otherwise have been destitute or, what is worse, trapped in political cross-currents. By contrast with the following century, we hear of no actor in Sulla's day who suffered whipping, imprisonment, banishment, or death for reasons of politics or pique. Actors could not avoid jeopardy — no man then in the limelight could do so — but it did not, to our knowledge, destroy them. Nor was there any debility in his judgment of histrionic merit. He needed no one to tell him that comedy is a serious business; in the supreme case, at any rate, Cicero, who was so different in all else, saw eye to eye with him. We have seen Sulla's manifold involvement, direct and indirect, with comedy, satyr-play, mime, atellan, lysis-song, and even tragedy. When he turned the bright and bitter vitality of his eyes upon them, they lived in his regard:

for this he could, far rightlier than his Pontic foe, have been termed a "new Dionysus." And if the rampaging troops who made a wreck of Pericles' Odeum were his (we do not know that they were), it may without any implausibility be imagined in compensation that he sometimes talked with the young Pompey about the theatre which Rome deserved to have, and which Sulla did not live to see.

Sulla desired it to be remembered that he had done good to his friends. We may leave his account with Roscius at that. But I should like finally to ask what all this had meant to the greatest actor of the ancient world. There is much that we can never know, but the story itself prompts three reflections. "All Sulla's friends were being put to death," says Appian of the year 87,[82] and on any reckoning, Roscius had lived through times of immense danger, from which he had somehow emerged unscathed. Second, he could look back on interchange, willing or loth, with the caesious-eyed humorist, often no doubt matching in tone the rude emblem of the leather bag. Third, he had met with the luck of unprecedented professional advancement, foretold in his infancy by the omen of the snake. This was the picture, in retrospect.

Every good theatrical story should end with an aetiology. I do not have any to give. But once I was looking at some trinkets on sale in Somerset, England, when I noticed a small silver coin, priced at forty-five shillings, and bought it. It was a denarius, of a kind which came into circulation probably late in Sulla's life, and was still fresh enough to be interesting later, about the time when the twelve-month official period of mourning for his death ended and the world could breathe freely again. The coin I was looking at might have passed through Sulla's hands. It might, with greater likelihood, have passed through the hands of Roscius. And if it, or any coin of the same minting, passed through Roscius' hands in those days and months after the gusting smoke of the funeral had blown away, we may wonder with what feelings the actor studied it. For the Roman mint had evolved a new design, showing Juno the Safeguarder,[83] of Lanuvium, in her full panoply, and curling beside her leather boots, a visibly exultant snake.

7. HOW ROSCIUS ACTED BALLIO

One of the least-read speeches of Cicero is that in which he appeared in court on behalf of the actor Roscius. The details of the case are somewhat anfractuous, but the gist of the matter is that the plaintiff, a certain Fannius Chaerea, had many years before gone partner with Roscius in a project connected with show business, and was now alleging that Roscius had overreached him. The speech as it has come down to us is hard to read because by the fifteenth century it had lost both beginning and end, and Cicero's pertinacious discussion of how accounts stood monetarily between his client and the plaintiff had become obtusely garbled. The speech was in this state when Bishop Andrea first printed it in 1471, along with Cicero's other orations, and its obtruncated condition and opacity as a document may account for the singular fact that when the contents page of the bishop's volume was being compiled, the presence of this speech within was completely overlooked.

There does however survive, with vivid exactitude, a passage[1] where, in the course of rebutting the aspersions cast upon his client, Cicero improved on the occasion by briefly comparing the appearance and character of Fannius the plaintiff to one of Roscius' roles in the theatre, namely that of a man who lived on immoral earnings. This role, from the *Pseudolus* of Plautus, is the only complete, extant role known for certain to have been acted by Roscius, and but for these few precious sentences in Cicero, which alone give the vital information, we could scarcely attempt to visualize in action the greatest actor of the ancient world. Can we attempt it even now? To help us we have Cicero, the text of the play, and various kinds of literary, historical, and archaeological background knowledge. My object is to show, not everything, but the sort of thing, which can be inferred about the Roscian performance.

I might have said "performances," for there were a number. Cicero tells us that Roscius has become accustomed, *consuevit*, to act this role, and implies that he still does so, *agit*. The date of the speech appears to be about 76 B.C. There is no demonstrable reason why Roscius should not have been acting the role, on and off, over the previous fifteen or twenty years, including the recent two-year period of Cicero's absence in Greece and the Aegean area; but as we cannot pinpoint any precisely dated performance, let us choose the nearest, which must have taken place within a year or two before the time of speaking, for Cicero to be able to appeal to it as current knowledge. In what circumstances, and in what spirit, did Roscius betake himself to the boards to do his act?

He was now in middle age and at the height of his fame. A few years previously Sulla during his dictatorship had formally created him a knight;[2] but Roscius insisted on continuing to act, and this may have compromised his social status. Cicero never refers to him as a knight; he is content to cite the opposing counsel's description of him as a *vir primarius*,[3] and it seems possible that the knighthood may have been for practical purposes in abeyance. More likely, however, Roscius found he could satisfy the social obligations of knighthood by merely taking no fee for his performances. We know that he had in fact taken no fee for his acting since the age of forty-five or thereabouts,[4] and the aim of this, fairly plainly, was to increase his respectability.

He acted in the usual kind of small troupe (we hear of his *gregales*)[5], and judging from his status, experience, and the wealth he had earned before ceasing to be a paid entertainer, it is possible that he was the troupe's leader or manager. The fact that he was in demand as a teacher of acting would fit in with this. He did not, however, when acting in the play with which we are concerned, choose the title role, that of the leading slave Pseudolus. This role, which is longer than the one he did choose, must have gone to the other principal actor. It is this kind of situation, where two actors star together, which more than eighty years earlier, at the staging of Terence's *Hecyra* and *Adelphoe*, may have led to the presence, in the production records, of a pair of names in each case — that of Lucius Ambivius with Lucius Sergius in the former play, and that of Lucius Ambivius with Lucius Atilius of Praeneste in the latter. There may be other explanations for the seeming Roman departure, in those cases, from the Greek rule of naming only one principal, but this — the sharing of kudos between co-stars — is the simplest. However, no production record survives to give us the name of Roscius' fellow-principal in their joint revival of the *Pseudolus*, and we do not know the name of any other of the *gregales* unless, which is possible, they included Eros. This Eros was a failed comedian whom Roscius had recently retrained and made a success of, admitting him *in domum, disciplinam, patrocinium, nomen.*[6] Admission to his teacher's *patrocinium* and *nomen* suggests that the regenerate Eros was currently known as Eros Roscianus or perhaps even Q. Roscius Eros.

Why did Roscius not play the title-role? Terracotta figurines and other monuments of New and Roman comedy confirm statistically our impression that the leading slave was normally the chief role, and in the Greek world, where festival time and emoluments were so much a peculiar of the Artists of Dionysus, who were free men without exception, it must have been entirely regular for a free man to take the leading slave's part or indeed any other slave-role. The practice in fact antedated the guilds of the Artists and was independent of them. In the middle of the fourth century B.C. a comic actor at Athens known as Olynthian Satyros, who was famed for his acting of such slave-roles as a Karion or a Xanthias, was none the less a free man, *persona grata* with Alexander, and held in honour because of his nobility of temperament. And in the time of the guilds, but somewhat later than Roscius, another actor at Athens, a free citizen called Alexandros of the deme Sphettos, was adept enough at the role of leading slave for those who mourned him when he died to have an appropriate mask cut on the piece of marble from Hymettus which they were preparing for his gravestone. But Greece, it may be said, is one place, Rome another. Yet at Rome also one or two actors are known by name who, though apparently free in private life, specialized in slave-roles among others: in the first century A.D. cunning slaves were a speciality of Stratocles and honest slaves of Demetrius. These were, of course, men of Greek origin, though where their names occur they are spelled in a Roman way; but Publilius Pellio, who in Plautus' time seems to have repeatedly acted the leading slave Epidicus in the comedy of that name, was manifestly a Roman citizen, whether free or a freedman, and was the actor-manager of his troupe. Nor can it be doubted, to come to Roscius' own day, that Q. Pomponius Musa, when serving as a moneyer in about 67 B.C., would have refrained from depicting on some of his denarii the Muse of Comedy with a leading slave's mask in her hand — that same mask which we find on the tombstone of Alexandros — if the enacting of such roles was regarded at Rome as essentially a servile employment.[7]

We therefore cannot assume that Roscius would avoid the slave's role on the ground that it was unbefitting a person of free status, though naturally the higher his personal rank in Roman society, the more delicate — perhaps also the more piquant — such a situation would become. Nor can we argue that he was influenced by artistic decorum, feeling unsuited in age to act Pseudolus, who is a young man's confidant. The leading slave, though not as a rule senescent, is commonly older than his young master, and is regarded as a perverse kind of *paedagogus* or *magister* to him, and a *veterator* in trickery.[8] Roscius could have chosen the role of Pseudolus but did not. And the principal reason is that from the beginning he was attracted by the sheer pulsation of life in the role he did choose — the disreputable, horror-comic figure of the leno. A Frenchman seeing Garrick in one of his low roles exclaimed, "Comment! je ne le crois pas. Ce n'est pas Monsieur Garrick, ce grand homme!"[9] Englishmen, who understood Garrick better, were less incredulous. The slave Pseudolus appears in fifteen scenes by the modern reckoning, the leno in only seven. But Roscius had long fixed his choice on the latter role because he saw in it the finest of all lenos — the apotheosis of what a leno stands for.

When Roscius put his mind to a role, he searched to the heart of it. Existence for him became aesthetic, and the moral elements which colour everyday experience were rigorously subsumed, as in Nabokov's *Lolita*, into a dynamic of Affekt and of subjective truth. That is, however Other a character might be to the audience, he got inside the part, conveyed unmistakably what it felt like, and so to speak justified it in its own eyes. The phallus, which had disappeared from the Greek stage about the time when stage shows were beginning to feature in Roman festivals, was, if known at all in the period when Roman comedy developed, known mainly from books and folk-art as an anthropological curio, a bygone appendage to the Greek actor's costume. It was not used in Roman comedy. But its presence persisted in men's minds as a powerful image or symbol for the importunity of the sex drive, and it was no less powerful when left only semi-explicit or unexplicit. It filled the consciousness of young men on their way to a bordello, and (human nature being what it is) they could not dissociate it from the price there to be paid. Both to them and to their elders and betters it underwent a kind of displacement or transference and became odiously projected on to the exacter of the price in question, the *pornoboskos* or leno. At the level of the emblematic, decorum made a phallus the imaginary and invisible emblem of the leno as surely as, among ourselves, a barber is associated with a real and visible striped pole or a pawnbroker with three golden balls. But beyond this, it became identified with the man himself, and some genius unknown — perhaps the writer of the Greek original of the *Pseudolus* — had taken a variant of the root *phall-* and formed from it a name to epitomize such a character for ever: the name Ballio. There is abundant evidence both that the derivation is true and that it was conscious. The betacized form of the root can be traced back at least to the fifth century, where Aristophanes has his "Triballoi" side by side with his "Triphales."[10] It thus became incumbent on Roscius, before all else, to symbolize "phallus" with all its overtones — things ranging from the immoral earnings which the leno lived on to the ultimate genius of comedy itself and the ritual perpetrations from which it began. He had to do this, even though Roman comedy itself had never been phallic in the technical sense and was seldom overtly indecent in its language. All was a matter of suggestion. And Roscius did not jib or blench at the phallic moment in drama. This much is evident from another role of his in a different play. It there fell to his lot to reflect bitterly on a fairweather harlot to whom he had given much, and how she forsook him on a rainy day, and what his plight had been in consequence. "Ita," he said with fitting gesture, "me destituit nudum."[11] So now his first task was to walk about the stage with a kind of upstanding baldness (*phalakrotês* to a Greek) and to have within easy reach — clutched in fact by a pathic menial of a boy — that important stage-property his money-bag (Greek *ballantion*), full, as every young man knew, of costly exacted prices. The lore of such word-associations as these might not be fully patent to a Roman audience, but even when not understood it had gone to the making of the leno tradition — the same tradition, no doubt, which long afterward contributed *ballio* as a term of obscure meaning to the vocabulary of imperial soldiers, turning up as it does in a barrack-room schedule of fatigues or other turns of duty, drawn up in Egypt in A.D. 90. The small promontory called Viriballum in Corsica seems to confirm that this word-root was not slow to convey its meaning to the Latin consciousness.[12] It was into this tradition that Roscius entered.

A question which may be raised here is whether Ballio was Roscius' sole concern in the play, or whether he doubled this role with any other. Examination of the text shows that there are only two roles which can be doubled with that of Ballio, unless the troupe was also prepared to split a role among two or more actors. For such splitting there seems to be no ancient evidence. We know, moreover, that the Ballio role was not split: if it had been, Cicero could not have given Roscius sole credit for it. And it is intrinsically unlikely that that of Pseudolus was split, since the play hinges on him as the leading slave, and in a parallel case, namely, repeated performances during the previous century of the corresponding role in the *Epidicus*, we know that a single actor, Pellio, was for better or worse held responsible. Thus any splitting done in the *Pseudolus* is likely to have been of minor importance. This apart, the two roles which can be doubled with that of Ballio are Charinus, coeval and friend of the leading youth in the play, and Callipho, coeval and neighbour of the leading youth's father. These two personages have one scene apiece. But the fact that Charinus is less than half the then age of Roscius tends to eliminate him, leaving Callipho as the only really likely role to be doubled with that of the leno.[13] Thus for practical purposes it was above all else the leno's eye-view which concerned Roscius in this play. The other principal actor, who plays the title-role, naturally sees the comedy as the triumphant escapades of Pseudolus, but from Roscius' viewpoint the drama might well have had a subtitle, and that subtitle would be *The Brothel-Keeper's Birthday*.

In the distich which does duty for a prologue, and which in Roscius' time was both already tralaticious and apt enough for the occasion so long as the play happened not to come first on the morning's agenda, the audience have been invited to stretch their legs. Let us assume that they have done so, and are ready to pick up the story. In a purlieu of Athens, so they are given to understand, there was a certain house of ill repute. After coming in from the city-gate, one happened upon a street containing six moderately respectable houses apparently separated by passage-ways (critics wrangle over the imprecise topography) and then, towards one end of the stage, a seventh house, the bordello. This is the home of a bevy of courtesans, a posse of male domestics who may or may not be mixed up in the same business, and their common owner and master the leno. Among the girls pent in this harsh durance is fair Phoenicium, the mute prize round whom the play revolves. She is being sold to a military man from Macedon and she has written in despair to her true love here in Athens, who is now unfortunately penniless.

The doorway of the house is prominent on the stylized and perhaps somewhat elaborate painted wooden stage-set. The door in question, whether univalve or bivalve, was probably something like the one on the imaginary stage-set which was painted in a Vesuvian villa (in the village now called Boscoreale) about twenty years after Roscius' death and reflects practice current in his lifetime.[14] Another suggestive door is that in the comedy scene shown on a well-known relief from Pompeii, of the first century A.D.[15] This would not be too elaborate for theatrical pretension of the late republic but is possibly too architectural for the painted woodwork then in use. The *Pseudolus* can be acted with only one other house-door in view, and if it was, one of the three doors customary on the painted woodwork could be veiled by a drape, as is shown on another part of the Pompeii relief.

Roscius waits behind the stage-set, and in the second scene of the play,[16] when he receives his first cue, a loud commotion is made backstage, and the door crashes open. Plautus has left it to the producer to decide who leads on — slave or master — but the most effective entry would be for one of the male slaves to come hurtling on, ruefully rubbing some part of his anatomy and looking for somewhere to hide. Hot on his heels comes a second likewise, then another and another, until there are five or six, including the young boy-slave mentioned above, clutching his master's money-bag. Finally, armed with rawhide whip, and with his voice roaring menaces before we see him, enter Roscius as master of the house. Even from outside a theatre, as we may infer from Cicero in the *Brutus*,[17] a passerby could tell by audience-reaction when Roscius was onstage: by the rapt silence, he means, leading up to thunderous reverberations of applause.

Roscius opens his lips in trochaics — the octonarius, next of kin to the tetrameter, which is the oldest and most elemental rhythm in all drama:

Exite, ágite exíte, ignávi, mále habiti ét male cónciliáti,
quórum numquam quĭcquam quoĭquam vénit in méntem ut
    récte fáciant,
quibu', nisi ad hoc exémplum expérior, nón potest úsura
    úsurpári.
(133-135)

Out, get out, you idle rascals, rotten to own, rotten to have laid out money on . . . never a day's work do I get out of them, unless I mete them out this treatment!

He beats them round the stage.

Leaving aside the roaring and flogging for a moment, what are the qualities incident to lenocinium, what is the heart and essence of the leno's nature, and what ought he to look like? In the decent Latin of a doctoral thesis printed at Darmstadt in 1920,[18] we find the qualities incident to lenocinium (as conceived by Plautus) set forth. They include, among others, the following fifteen:

Arrogance
Avarice
Braggadocio
Expressiveness
Ferocity
Fraudulence
Impiety
Impudicity
Inhumanity
Perfidy
Quickwittedness
Self-confidence
Superstition
Suspiciousness
Unscrupulousness.

For every one of these Ballio is convincingly cited in evidence. But his heart and centre, as a leno, is surely the phallic atrociousness of his trade. It is that, owning female slaves, he purveys sex as a commodity, with all the moral bluntness or distortion which this entails. This is the manner of the leno, and his appearance should reflect his nature. A loose and rather milder adaptation of Roscius' role cropped up in a twentieth-century musical, which was played first in Washington, then on Broadway, then in London, and later filmed. It was called *A Funny Thing Happened on the Way to the Forum.*[19] In the London production the actor Jon Pertwee, who played the leno, conveyed moral distortion and negritude by thick, lank, black hair, a sunken, pouchy, pasty skin, and a twisting of the lips. He wore a dark, long-skirted coat, and when bent on custom adopted an insidious, fawning gait and an oily clasping of the palms.

Roscius naturally interpreted his role within the limits of ancient comic convention for the procurer-type. These laid down that a procurer should be one of the older generation and bearded — in order to appear a more plausible object of hatred to the young men. He should like other free persons wear the normal tunic and pallium, though these were made parti-coloured, probably in order to abridge his dignity, and the wardrobe assistant is invited by the text of the *Pseudolus* to transmogrify them in whatever way he thinks will most drastically betoken criminality. The leno's mask, as we may judge partly from Pollux' description[20] and partly from artistic representations which Pollux has enabled us to identify, was bearded, rather snub-nosed, sometimes ruddy-complexioned and sometimes sallow. It should combine a business smile about the mouth with something severe or disgruntled about the eyebrows, these latter being either knit in a frown or raised in a high arch. And it should be bald: either bald at the front with a grizzled, curly fringe at back and ears, or bald without mitigation.

There are extant in the form of terracotta statuettes, orna-mental masks, and so forth, probably about forty[21] represen-tations of the comic *pornoboskos* or leno, together with fifteen mediaeval portrayals of him among the miniatures in five manuscripts of Terence. The mediaeval pictures are unreliable for mask and costume. Of the ancient portrayals hardly more than one or two belong to republican Rome, and some are rather unhelpful visually. Such word-pictures as I may base on them are of still more modest utility, but they may serve to give a notion of the *materia lenonia* among dramatic monuments.

On a piece of pot handle, dated third century B.C., from Haliartos in Boeotia there is to be seen a face with the full beard, an almost V-shaped mouth, snub nose, and firm, arching brows, but the forehead merges into a piece of decoration, and it is an enviable expertise which can with confidence identify the por-trayal as a *pornoboskos*.[22] A glass plaque from Egypt, of the first century A.D., gives us a clearer specimen: he is red-faced and has an unexpressive mouth, snub nose (identifiable from the front because slightly upturned, revealing the nostrils), and eyebrows which are knit or at any rate markedly − in Pollux' phrase − "drawn together." He has a bald head under an ivy wreath, of which the significance will appear presently, and a tidily crimped beard which seems markedly detachable, in more or less the same way as spectacles are. As a whole, however, the face looks too vacant to make a good Ballio.[23] Another handle-mask, from Priene near Miletus, and interesting because contemporary with Roscius, gives us a bald head or sinciput, knit brows, a spade-shaped beard, and something of the air of a *pornoboskos*, though the sides of the head fail to show for certain whether the ears are human or those of a *papposilenos*.[24] Of unknown origin, but possibly from late republican Rome itself, comes a carved gem or cameo of a procurer, with a skull-like bald head, high, arching eyebrows, again a carefully cultivated beard, this time formed in rows of parallel curls, and a very large mouth with the ghost of a smile about it. To one side is a crook stick, a common attribute of older men.[25] From Rome of the second century B.C. comes another tiny mask with appropriate beard and bushy, knitted brows, the dome of the head seeming to show the remains of a substantial headband or wreath.[26] This was dug up among the remains of the temple of the Magna Mater, and could have been inspired by comedies performed at the Megalensian games. Topographically, this is about as near as we can come to Roscius.

But it is a mosaic mask from Delos which seems to bring us closest to the performance we are thinking of. It is either contemporary with the *Pseudolus* or falls between that and the birth of Roscius. Republican Rome was very much nearer to Delian cultural life than geography would suggest. Intercourse between the two places was frequent. From the times of Plautus on, men with Roman names are found performing in Delian festivals, and there was a permanent colony of Roman and Italian traders on Delos, including some of the Laberii, a gens which may have centred on Roscius' own town of Lanuvium. This need be no unfamiliar mask, then, to a Roman audience. It has a high, bald dome, eyebrows that swing out and up, a sallow complexion, and a beard which is long but considerably less trim than some of the others — less of a beard to preen oneself on.[27]

Do we know that Roscius looked even remotely like this? Do we know that he wore a mask at all? The answer is a fairly confident yes to both questions. That he was bearded is vouched for by the text of the play.[28] As for his head, the reason why the plaintiff in the lawsuit could be compared to the Roscian version of Ballio was that the plaintiff, for some peculiar reason of comfort, health, hygiene, or inverse vanity, always kept his head completely shaved.[29] Now Roscius in real life evidently had a good head of hair, and this must have been sheathed over in the play by a completely bald covering. The plaintiff in the lawsuit used to shave his eyebrows too, and this may also have been included in the Ballio *persona*, unless the eyebrowless plaintiff simply somehow reminded people of those high, arching brows which are one of the options for a leno. Cosmetic art sometimes achieves the reverse illusion in smart women of about forty-five: expensively delineated, high, arching brows producing an effect of resolute depilation and calvity. The complexion of the plaintiff, and of Ballio, is unknown. Now although Roscius could have been given all these features merely by greasepaint, a false beard, and a headpiece, it is known that he began to wear masks early in his career,[30] and the overwhelming likelihood is that he did so for Ballio, especially as the convention was by now thoroughly established and maskless acting was associated with the mime and with social inferiority and civil degradation.

The baldness, supplemented by a goatlike beard, gave Roscius one of his chief clues for the interpretation of the part. Although the Greek and Roman *physiognomonici* did not know, in so many words, that baldness is the concomitant of an excess of male sex hormone or androgen, they knew at least that eunuchs tend to keep their hair; baldness was associated with unhusked and phallic thoughts, and therefore, as in the case of a silen, with dissipation, risibility, and sex run riot. Had Bishop Synesius, who in later days undertook a jocular encomium of baldness, been cognisant of this tradition, he might perhaps have abandoned his brief. But Ballio's baldness had another aspect. It suggested also, especially to penniless young clients, that which is unsympathetic, impervious to appeal, and queerly Other. With the penniless young client in this play, as with the wily and ubiquitous slave after whom the play is named, the spectator's fancy can for the nonce identify itself; but Roscius is the great embodiment of Otherness, against whom these two characters have to pit their wits. It is one of the paradoxes of comedy that the leno should have this function at the same time as he is in certain ways an established figure of society and a kind of father-surrogate.[31] The explanation of course lies in the fact that for comic purposes insiders tend to become outsiders and vice versa. All these things contributed to the decorum of the Ballio role, and Roscius was a master of theatrical decorum. Besides decorum, his other most famous attribute as an actor was said to be *venustas*. There is little obvious outlet for *venustas* in Ballio, but there was ample outlet for the poise and vitality and even (as Roscius began to live the role) for empathy; and these – poise, vitality, and empathy – were undoubtedly constituents of the Roscian *venustas* elsewhere.

We left him beating his slaves around the stage with his rawhide whip (*terginum*), amid picturesque denunciations of their greed, their idleness, their forgetfulness. "Wearers-out of whip-ends . . . whenever you get the chance, lift, filch, hug, loot, swig, gorge, run!" Eventually he whips them into a line and proceeds to remind them of their orders for preparing a party, the aim of which is to attract potential clients. For today is his birthday: "nam mi hodie natalis dies est." It would be a stroke of comic genius to combine the whip of chastisement in his hand with a garland of jollification on his bald pate. The play does not specify a garland, but surely implies it. Any procurer who entertained clients might wear a wreath, and a number of the surviving figurines and other representations show the *pornoboskos* duly begarlanded. It may even be that in a statuette from Myrina, south of Pergamum, made in the second century B.C. though perhaps copying an earlier, Attic model, we have the actual procurer of the lost Greek original of the *Pseudolus*. A high authority has indeed described this figurine, looking at it with the eye of a reasonable faith, as "thong in hand."[32] Orders given, Roscius puts his strap away and announces that he himself is going to the forum to hire a cook and buy some fish. He savours the word "fish" as he says it. It was part of his job to make all food terms piquant to the groundlings, the range of fare with which he hereabouts titillates the listener running from salad and oil to fish and ham; from sow's udder and chines to lamb chitterlings and crackling; and from sweetbreads to water, nuts, and wine.

The audience are poised to clap him as, accompanied by the boy with the money-bag, he walks off with Ballio-gait toward the right of the stage, when, no doubt with a carefully meditated gesture, he stops short saying, "No, wait! – a little matter indoors – I almost forgot." Back he comes and throws open again the door of the bawdy-house. "*Auditin? . . . mulieres!*" Here follows the famous scene, unique in Roman comedy, of the hetaeraparade. This is a miming part for four members (junior members?) of the troupe, dressed up as *meretriculae*. Many representations of stage courtesans are known, of assorted date, provenance, and charms. Their lot, in real life, was a hard one, but fortune has made them a gentle recompense in giving them some of the least distorted and most natural girlish or womanly faces in the whole of ancient prosopopoeia.

Without saying a word the girls have to react in dumbshow whilst Roscius, walking up and down, delivers a forty-seven line harangue — punctuated by remarks from two unseen eavesdroppers. He lays down what will be the special duties of these girls for this his birthday. Under his tutelage, he says with a preposterous kind of glowering unction, theirs has always been a most easy lot, they have had a most select clientele — *summi viri* — respectable tradesman, farmers, and so forth. "Make sure I see your lovers' gifts come showering in on me this day. For unless a year's supplies accrue today, *cras populo prostituam vos.*" He reminds each one in turn of her own field of operations, naming the girls by their names. And here we see Roscius' duty to bring out something in which Roman audiences at that time were a good deal interested, the significance and flavour of personal names. He names Hedytium (Sweetie-pie), Aeschrodora (the antonym, incidentally, of the young man in the play, Calidorus), Xytilis or Xystilis (the right form is uncertain: Xytilis might mean Smoothie, and Xystilis perhaps Mlle Sweeptrain), and lastly Phoenicium, whom Calidorus loves, her name suggesting something like Scarlet.

When talking to Xytilis Roscius had an opportunity to mention something probably familiar to him from his home town of Lanuvium — the bottlebag. As I have explained elsewhere, bottlebags, which came in many sizes, had varying associations — of drink, sex, and doom — and comedians exploited them. But they were an important article in the ancient economy, as can be seen in an oxcart full of them represented in a late mosaic. The largest kind of all, made from a whole cowhide, was called the *culleus* and could be mounted in a wooden frame on two wheels or even on four. Lanuvium, if we may trust a textually controverted passage in Cicero,[33] is one of the two townships in Italy recorded as producing *cullei*. "Xytilis," says Lanuvine

Roscius, " . . . your admirers are the oil-merchants: if I don't soon have oil delivered here by the *culleus*, tomorrow I'll see you haled in a *culleus* over to the common stew!" Lastly it is the turn of Phoenicium. Though the balance of the purchase money for her is expected in at any moment from Macedon, she is not excused present duties any more than the rest. "If you don't earn a year's keep today, tomorrow I'll tan your hide scarlet, Scarlet, and have *you* bundled over to the stew." Ballio is always careful to emphasize the selectness and superiority of his own house of assignation as compared with a common brothel, to the service of which it was of course within his power to hire out his female slaves at will. The nearest modern equivalent, if we leave aside exotic imaginings, is "being put on the streets." Phoenicium is thus caught in a crossfire between three kinds of loving: that to be expected in the stew, that promised by her Macedonian fancier, and that despairingly hoped for from her true love Calidorus. Ballio is not above taking offers for a fourth kind of loving also, as explained by his pathic boy-slave at a later point in the play.[34]

A second time Roscius prepares to quit the stage. A second time his exit is delayed. The two eavesdroppers, the *adulescens* Calidorus and his slave Pseudolus, outraged at Phoenicium's present treatment and promised fate, penniless and helpless as they are, step out of hiding. They can only try the power of words — to change Ballio's mind, rescind the sale, gain a respite, anything. This is the only time in the play that Roscius is on stage together with the young man and, more important, it is the only scene which he shares with the other principal actor of the troupe, the actor who plays Pseudolus. We are told by Valerius Maximus that Roscius never made a gesture on stage which he had not previously thought out and rehearsed at home. Indeed he was at one time engaged on a book comparing the expressiveness of gesture to that of speech, and he used as a recreation to pit the expressiveness of his own gestures against that of Cicero's eloquence, the two men playing a game to see which could express a given emotion or idea in more ways.[35] The present scene is one of the rapidest in Plautus, with a gesture required for almost every other word. To begin with, Roscius must react to Pseudolus prancing round him and crying "Birthday baby, hello, birthday baby — *hodie nate, heus, hodie nate!*" A few lines later the keynote is struck for the scene:

Bal.   Iuppiter te
          perdat, quisquis es.
Ps.   te volo.
Bal.   at vos ego ambos.
                                                      (250-251)

In the twentieth-century adaptation mentioned above, Pseudolus has the upper hand; while the young man stays in the background, the leno is duped, smells a bargain, begins to fawn for custom. But in Plautus the slave and his master have at the moment nothing to back their words with, and these are totally impotent against Ballio's dexterous parrying and counterfire.

Some distant echoes of the gesturing leno of Roman comedy, when in animated conversation with slave or *adulescens,* have come down in the miniatures of the Terence manuscripts. One of them shows the leno with shoulders thrown back, giving a piece of his mind to a slave, to the accompaniment of a bit of admonitory shoulder-tapping and hem-plucking.[36] Another shows him with an expressive sweep of the right arm sustaining his monetary claims before an *adulescens.*[37] This particular gesture has come down with amusing variations, from the single original, to each of the four scribes or miniaturists who draw it.[38] In one case the young cleric whom we may surmise to be responsible has so far departed from the costume of palliata that he seems to be confusing the leno with his bishop.[39] However, not too much should be read into this as he draws many of his characters like bishops. The original of these miniatures may date only from late antiquity, but erroneous or anachronistic ideas then current about theatrical mask and costume prove nothing about the gestures depicted. The gestures were an old and carefully nurtured art, which some have wished to trace back to Quintilian's time, arguing that Quintilian inherited them from the tradition of Roscius.[40] There seems the glimmer of a chance that this may be true.

The irate badinage continues. "If you were really in love," says Roscius to young Calidorus, "you would have found some way to borrow, gone to a moneylender, paid his bit of interest . . . rooked your father. . . . " "Rooked my father! Me? A tight-fisted old blighter like him? Besides . . . *pietas prohibet*." "In that case," replies Roscius, "It is *pietas* you had best cuddle at night instead of Phoenicium." Matters come to a point where, under Plautine manipulation, there is nothing left for youth and slave but to resort to that ancient remedy of Italian Volksjustiz, the *flagitatio*. This was an act of loud and sustained public defamation, by the aggrieved, of a rascal whom for any reason the law cannot or will not touch.[41] It was aimed at the destruction of any credit he might still possess in the eyes of the world, at robbing him of any further presumption upon its tolerance, at hounding him, if possible, out of his place in the framework of society. It was, in short, a verbal thrashing — best administered in the market-place, but failing that in any confrontation on the open street or, if the man was lying low, in the form of a barrage directed at his front door. As with some kinds of salesmanship, it was found to reach highest pressure and be most telling when delivered by a group, or alternation, or succession, of different voices. This made it both raucous and ritualistic: the solemn bawling of anathemas.

Here youth and slave have the leno cornered, as they think, though he is practically on his own doorstep. They stand on either side of the unconscionable figure and, in alternation, exhaust their vocabulary of abuse upon him, Roscius inclining his brazen visage to each in turn. It is excellently set out in the Loeb edition, with the lines broken into staggered pieces to suggest the blows of the bastinado.[42] One of the things yelled at Roscius during this exchange is *sociofraude*, "partner-swindler." On the stage this is comically gratuitous and barrel-scraping, as Ballio does not have any partner to swindle. But offstage and in private life it happens to be the exact offence of which Roscius was currently being accused in his lawsuit. It was thus all the more skilful and ingenious on Cicero's part to twist the Ballio role round upon the plaintiff. In the present scene of the play the *flagitatio* is unavailing, but finally Roscius does go off, saying, " 'M — I have much on my hands just now, *negoti nunc sum plenus*," and the actor who plays Pseudolus turns to the audience gazing after their hero, and adds with exhilarating ambiguity, "*Paulo post — magis.*"

After this tour de force in ethopoeia, Plautus proceeds to

inspissate the plot, but the entanglements need not long detain us. Machinations are set afoot, and Ballio, in the absurd flush of his birthday, lays a wager that Pseudolus will never cheat him of Phoenicium or of selling her to the man from Macedon – a sale which he hopes to conclude during the day. He is in fact awaiting the Macedonian's servant, Harpax, who is to bring the balance of the sale price. Still in ascendancy of spirits, Ballio reappears, bringing a cook back from the forum. The cook will perhaps be dressed for the road, with cloak and basket on the lines of a well-known maison-cook figurine from Megara,[43] made about ten years before the *Pseudolus* was written; but he is soon to be girt for action like the equally well-known see-how-it's done chef from Myrina,[44] made probably some time between the premiére of the *Pseudolus* and the present performance.

This is in further preparation for the proposed birthday party. Cooks and their assistants were notorious pocketers of what they regarded as justifiable perquisites, and over and above giving the strictest orders that this cook be watched, Ballio goes in through the door himself, both to keep a personal eye on him and at the same time to warn the household to beware of Pseudolus. Pseudolus is well to the fore, lurking in readiness, not with Harpax, the Macedonian's servant, but with a member of the troupe who has been doubly bedizened to act as a pseudo-Harpax. The door creaks and begins to open for Roscius' next entry. "The *aedes,*" Pseudolus observes, "must be feeling sick: *ipsum lenonem evomunt.*" But something unexpected happens. Instead of being "vomited forth," Ballio, we are told, enters crabwise, *transversus . . . quasi cancer.* We have no ancient illustration of this, but Varro, who had at least as good opportunities as Cicero to see Roscius do it, indicates that what Ballio has to do is to emerge through the door, which is apparently just pushed ajar, and then shuffle a few steps sideways close to the house wall, peering back along his shoulder through the doorway so that he can still keep an eye on what the cook is doing within.[45] The action gives him an amusing flash of kinship with the Plautine Euclio and with Molière's Harpagon.

The pseudo-Harpax confronts him. "Hey, you with the *hirquina barba,* the billy-goat beard, . . . are you Ballio?" Lenos' beards vary, as do those of goats, and no one who has looked at the extant leno masks or scrutinized goats on a goat-farm will suppose that *hirquina barba* must necessarily imply the spruce modern goatee. It is as likely to mean a shaggy tuft of a beard, or one that is wispy and unkempt; the mosaic mask from Delos mentioned above[46] shows a tolerably wispy and unkempt specimen. We have been waiting a long time for a goat-image to complement Ballio's phallicity of name and underline his vicarious promotion of lechery, and in this allusion to a *hircus* Plautus supplies the want. The pseudo-Harpax attempts to finger Roscius' tunic and pallium, which must have been the wardrobe's pièce de résistance. "Because, the way you're dressed," he explains, "you look as though your trade is burgling of houses." Roscius takes this in his stride. "Yes," he says, "and I daresay if you met me in the dark you'd keep your hands off me." This recalls a broken mask from Priene, made perhaps about the time when the *Pseudolus* was written, which with its contorted brow and mephistophelean glower shows us just how nasty a *pornoboskos* could look.[47] In the ensuing dialogue the trap is sprung. Pseudo-Harpax departs safely with Phoenicium, and Roscius is left rubbing his hands in a fool's paradise, confident that the girl is now disposed of according to his intention and beyond Pseudolus' reach for ever.

Ballio's sense of triumph at having finally wiped Pseudolus' nose for him is coupled with the stimulus of appetizing savours now presumably being wafted through from his kitchen. If Roscius did not wear a festal wreath in his opening scene, surely he does so at his next entry. He reappears with an exclamation which, if our manuscript collations are to be trusted, occurs nowhere else in Plautus in quite so crowing and hubristic a form. "Hahae! " he cries, " . . . *now* tell that arch-trickster Pseudolus to come and do me out of the wench." *Hahae* marks the apex before his peripeteia, and as the dénouement proceeds, Roscius, who has hitherto acted the mercenary, unprincipled bully, has to portray the growing realization that he has not only been done out of the wench, but must repay the large cash advance made on her by the man from Macedon, as well as losing her entire value over again in the bet he has made that things could never turn out like this.

Roscius throughout has acted the non-sympathetic character. He is Otherness, the *improbissimum et periurissimum lenonem*, as Cicero aptly said in court, *persona illa lutulenta, impura, invisa*.[48] And Plautus, in a tragi-comic speech of unparalleled power – the soliloquy of the pansy-boy manqué in the very middle of the play – has taken care to etch in the sulphurous darkness of the leno's soul.[49] But Ballio none the less reminds us distantly of Malvolio and Shylock as, in finally departing for the forum to see his banker and draw the excruciating sum necessary for paying his debts, he plays his last card, which is to put on the air of a man more wronged than wronging. "What I'll do," he growls, "I'll keep my birthday from now on as my death-and-damnation day, *certum est mi hunc emortualem facere ex natali die*."

Thalia's mill has ground slowly but fine. The audience watch him as, his last gesture over, and expressing his defeat now only by his carriage and gait, he slowly leaves the stage for the last time. The play has two more scenes to run. "An actor," wrote one of Roscius' friends about eighteen years after his death, "need not remain on stage until the close of the play: he only needs to win applause in his own particular scenes. It is like life itself. There, too, a man who knows need not stay on till the last word and the clapping. Even a short role gives you time enough to show skill and virtue in your performance."[50] Roscius behind scenes will be changing back into the garb of a Roman citizen, in which, in his proper dignity, as in the moral character of his private life, it seems that he might well have passed for a member of the senate,[51] just as could that other actor, if actor he was – the *parasitus Apollinis* whose togaed, magisterial image is preserved to us from the following century.[52] But perhaps Roscius waits first, to take his bow. While he waits his chief fellow-actor superintends the remaining scenes, which culminate in a beanfeast for the winning side. Finally, on behalf of Roscius and the whole troupe, this other principal doffs his mask and requests applause for *hunc gregem et fabulam*.

8. THE BACKGROUND TO THE *PERSONAE* OF SENECA

Writing in the 1920s, Léon Hermann declared that the whole effort in Seneca's plays is directed toward the psychology of the characters, and he invited his readers' admiration for the depth and accuracy of portrayal in Medea and Phaedra and for the sculptural impressiveness of figures like Atreus, Thyestes, and Deianira. It was not for nothing, he held, that these were models for Corneille, Racine, and Shakespeare.[1] Characterization of such an order ought not, in Herrmann's day any more than subsequently, to have been neglected; but in the bibliography with which *Le théâtre de Sénèque* was provided and which covered every conceivable aspect of *Senecastudien*, ranging from a dissertation on Seneca's use of *in* with the accusative to an enquiry into his influence on the discovery of America, out of more than three hundred tracts and treatises not one devotes itself to this side of the playwright's art. What should we make of the apparent silence? Seventeen years later, Mendell, with the air of one giving a reason upon compulsion, used the following words to describe Oedipus:

> He comes on without any reason: he goes off without any reason. He is a device for arousing horror, and he is only that. We do not see the normal man — if such existed in Seneca's mind; we do not really find a man at all, only the mouthpiece of horror, an eloquent and even a moving exponent of dread, but not a sympathetic hero.[2]

And the characters have been trounced worse than this.

Estimates of their influence on Elizabethan tragedy have been whittled down to right and left — "merely verbal material," they have been called, "rhetorical cannon-fodder"[3] — and the first edition of the *Oxford Classical Dictionary*, obliged for reasons of space to deliver its opinion in narrow compass, awarded to Senecan character and psychology the solitary epithet "crude."

There is thus the paradox of an art of characterization which has somehow contrived both to stimulate and to bore, to matter greatly and not to matter at all. I wish in the present discussion to suggest that there are two causes for this contrariety of judgments and that, if they are disentangled, one cause is seen to be, in a sense, accidental and the other serious and important.

What I would call the accidental side of the matter is the shift in methods of character criticism which has been going on since the turn of the present century and which has concerned, among other things, the tragic novel, Shakespeare and other post-Renaissance drama, Greek tragedy, and Seneca. The effect of it was first to unseat former assumptions about character portrayal and then, after a period of disillusion, to reinstate the characters on a sounder footing. The key part of this development took place, roughly speaking, between the First and the Second World War; and it is conceivable that the history of those years had something to do with the phase of disillusion.

Centred about the turn of the century, and extending with greater or less lustre over the twenty-five years preceding and the twenty-five years following, was what might be described as the golden period, in which it is assumed that the characters are an element which can be abstracted, criticized in abstraction, and speculated about — a period which produced some of the most treasured of Shakespeare studies and which may be represented for Greek tragedy by the prefaces and commentaries in Jebb's edition of Sophocles. It is a feature of this criticism to find a personal motive for everything that is said or done and to fill in the personal background, if need be, by speculation. If Antigone, in the presence of Creon, bitingly ranges her sister on Creon's side, Jebb explains to us (as Sophocles does not) that she has a secret motive, a wish to save Ismene's life. A reader coming freshly to the tragedies of Seneca today could be forgiven for doubting whether it was ever thought possible or desirable to treat Seneca in this manner. Herrmann's book, however, goes part of the way toward resolving the doubt, inasmuch as he achieves a series of no fewer than seventy-two character sketches, one for every person in Seneca, including the anonymous, the mute, and at least one man whose separate existence he admits to be highly questionable. In these sketches the leading term of praise is *vraisemblable*, and the fault most noticeably complained of is that some characters are too given to a rhetorical manner of speaking. There is even a little speculation; at any rate, it is suggested that the Messenger in the *Medea*, whose part is very short and comes to an abrupt stop, probably leaves the stage "at a run."

But the appetite for this kind of sketching waned. It waned in the criticism of classical drama partly because it was turning a blind eye to obvious limitations and recurrences in the character-ization and partly because it was realized that motive-guessing and suchlike, by becoming oversubjective, were liable to be carried beyond what was either profitable or honest. Hence, first, an occasional preference for typology. According to Drexler, Euri-pides' people are all types;[4] and of the two best-known books on Seneca in English, neither dwells particularly on the personality of the heroes but one contains a chapter on Stock Characters. Types, however, are not the stuff of which tragedy is really made, and this form of character criticism lies to one side of the main development.

What sets in is a fit of disintegration.[5] Abstracting of characters is felt to lead to so many absurdities that serious character unity comes to be despaired of altogether. And the disintegration applies to more than character, so that sometimes we find even unity of action regarded as outside the dramatist's probable aims. This began in Shakespearian criticism even before 1914, when a searching finger was pointed at the Elizabethan audiences as tempting the dramatist by their hunger for strongly flavoured effects.[6] For Greek tragedy it was of course the younger Wilamowitz who took the lead, demolishing character unity in Sophocles for the better appreciation of dramatic technique, scene by scene. Presently Seneca comes under the same influence; and we find scholars about 1930 breaking up the plays and characters in the belief that the emotion and psychology which matter are those of individual scenes and dialogues, and that this explains and justifies all those blanks and ruckles in character which used, on the earlier view, to put an interpreter so busily about. One result of this is the attempt to drive a wedge between psychology and characterization, as when Electra in Euripides is said to be motivated "psychologically but not characterologically."[7] The wedge is driven between the mere psychology, which is all that we seem to find in whatever plays happen to be under scrutiny, and characterization proper, which we assume is still operative elsewhere. The student of Seneca refers us, for genuine, unified characters, to Euripides; the student of Euripides refers us to Sophocles; the student of Sophocles refers us to Shakespeare. If it comes to that, Shakespeare's people, according to Tolstoy, are certainly not characters, because they all speak alike. This is forcing a meaning upon dramatic characterization which it ought not to bear.

It became evident that some better account must be given of, say, the Sophoclean Ajax or the Senecan Medea; that is, an account must be given in more appropriate terms than had been customary hitherto. Character is simply the whole impression which a *persona* makes, and how he makes it depends on the play. Of the vast number of suggestions put forward for dealing with the second episode of the *Ajax* perhaps one of the soundest was that of Schadewaldt, who, noting both the extreme difficulty of studying Ajax' mind and motives at that point and at the same time the tragic necessity here for this kind of event, came to the conclusion that the speech is a λόγος ἐσχηματισμένος, a falsehood told through Ajax rather than by him.[8] This could not be done with a real person, and to talk about a strain of mendacity is to miss the mark. But Ajax is very far from being a law to himself. Seneca's Medea declares her plan of vengeance about half way through the play (549):

> sic natos amat?
> bene est, tenetur, vulneri patuit locus.

Yet long before, in her tempestuous prologue, she has cried out, "It is already born, my vengeance is born! I have borne children!"

"It is the art of the poet," commented Gronovius in 1661, "causing her, before she realizes what she forebodes, to presage and utter confusedly what sorts with her future plans."[9] One could hold Medea's prologue, then, to be another λόγος 'εσχηματισμένος. But the truth is that something of this kind applies to tragic character in general. The person, whether more or less visualized, is a complex of language which has to and does mould itself about the dramatic centre and is conditioned by the shape of that. It can have a truth and a unity, but they apply within the context of one play and are not best seen (and may be seriously damaged) by abstracting. There is no "normal man" to argue about.

Jason says in his first speech, "I am sure that she cares more about our children than about her conjugal rights." And his last words to Medea are: "Go, and bear witness, where you ride, that there are no gods." The complex of rhetorical utterance in Senecan tragedy is spun, like this, round centres that are plain and for the most part given beforehand. And if the centre of an Oedipus play is the shattering hand of fate, the criterion for judging Oedipus is less whether he is *vraisemblable* than whether he is a character so made as to bring home the drama. Criticism since the 1940s, such as the unity studies of Steidle and Müller,[10] has been in a better position to deal with these characters insofar as it has been willing to respond to the whole *persona* rather than the part, yet without wishing to go back to the study of character *in vacuo*. And this is a truer, if a less obvious, kind of vision.

But there remains the serious and important cause of the conflicting pronouncements quoted at the beginning of this present discussion. This is that the texture of Senecan characterization is itself ambivalent. It is simultaneously positive and negative, attractive and repellent. Before the attempt is made to account for these stiff, imposing, lurid, and sometimes fine and pathetic figures, let them, in a pair of random passages, speak a moment for themselves. In what we have of the *Phoenissae*, the banished Oedipus, while his sons are taking up internecine arms, wants nothing but to die. Antigone talks to him to dissuade him, putting a longdrawn series of dissuasive questions. To the last of these, "*quem, genitor, fugis?*" her father returns this answer:

Me fugio, fugio conscium scelerum omnium
pectus, manumque hanc fugio et hoc caelum et deos,
et dira fugio scelera quae feci innocens.
(216-218)

Myself I flee. I flee the consciousness of all my crimes;
And I flee this hand, and this sky, and the gods,
And I flee the *appalling* crimes which I have committed —
innocently.

In the *Troades*, the Messenger has been telling Andromache how
the young boy Astyanax jumped of his own accord from the
top of the tower before his executioners could throw him
down. The mother speaks:

Quis Colchus hoc, quis sedis incertae Scytha
commisit, aut quae Caspium tangens mare
gens iuris expers ausa? non Busiridis
puerilis aras sanguis aspersit feri,
nec parva gregibus membra Diomedes suis
epulanda posuit. quis tuos artus leget
tumuloque tradet?
(1104-1110)

Who even in the land of Colchis, what nomad Scythian
Ever committed such an act? What uncivilized tribe
Beside the Caspian dared it? The inhuman Busiris' altars
Were not stained with blood of children, nor did Diomede
Serve baby limbs to his herds to feast upon.
Who will take up your body and give it burial?

The ground was steep there, she is told: what body is left? The
marks which showed that it was a prince's body, his face and the
striking nobility he had from his father, have been disfigured. His
neck and skull are broken and his brains dashed out, and now he
lies there, a corpse robbed of its own form. The climax is a sigh
from Andromache:

Sic quoque est similis patri.

Thus also is he like his father.

The visualizing power of a dramatist or narrator, unless it is very great, may be able to meet only one of two important claims upon it. These are: seeing what the characters and relationships in the artistic framework should be like, or "were" like, and seeing into the mind of those addressed, to know the diverse ways in which it can be worked upon. Augustan and Silver Age literary orthodoxy, influenced so much by the idea of orator and audience, steadily guided the inspiration of writers into the second channel. In such an event it is possible for the shaping of characters to be a matter of rule or tradition; but they will also be affected by what is, from their point of view, an oblique rather than a direct use of their maker's imagination.

Had Seneca any rule? If the prose works may be taken as evidence in this connection, his interest in *ethos* from the purely theoretic point of view was nil. He had, of course, felt the power of *ethos* in Greek dramaturgy, as is apparent to begin with from the famous "Medea superest," where, in answer to the Nurse, Medea opposes her own spirit as the sole and sufficient resource against a sea of troubles: and this is only one of half a dozen places where a person summons up the consciousness of all that he or she has stood for. In the *Troades*, before Astyanax died, Andromache had kissed him and wept over him and given him some of her torn hair, saying: "Now hasten, *plenus mei*, to your father." And when the Messenger arrived to tell how the boy died, it was Hecuba sho spoke to him first, conscious of herself as the central character in this great *pathos* of the Trojan women:

mihi cuncta pereunt: quisquis est, Hecubae est, miser.

For theory and criticism, however, we have to look elsewhere than in Seneca. Cicero, for example, had felt a warm interest in the subject. He not only roughed out the decorum theory, later to be crystallized by Horace, but made a study of dramatic moods, and he even proffers a little genial realist criticism. There was a scene in a tragedy between Patroclus and the wounded Eurypylus. Cicero remarks that one would naturally expect Patroclus to take him along and let him lie down on a bed and then bandage up his wound. "At least he would do so if he were a normal man (*si quidem homo esset*), but I have never seen anything less like one." Instead, Cicero tells us, Patroclus put Eurypylus to the question and extracted from him there and then, all in pain as he was, a dramatic account of the battle.[11] Alive as Seneca in his prose writings is to the theatre and tragedians, his interest seems nowhere to take a form comparable to this. It can, of course, be claimed that he was using part of the decorum rules in preserving to heroes their traditional and historical *ethos*, though he pays scant attention to the doctrine otherwise; he is much less anxious, for example, than are some modern productions of Greek plays to equip every old man with hoary tresses, bowed shoulders, and palpitating knees. But the *Moral Letters* and other prose works suggest that what interested him first and foremost in the plays he heard or read was language, style, and thought.

> Quam multi poetae dicunt, quae philosophis aut dicta sunt aut dicenda! non adtingam tragicos nec togatas nostras ... quantum disertissimorum versuum inter mimos iacet![12]

> What a multitude of poets there are who say things which either have been, or are worthy to be, said by philosophers! I need not touch upon the tragic poets or upon our own historical plays ... what an abundance of lines that are triumphs of thought and expression are to be found embedded in our very mimes!

The dramatist, it seems, who can produce ideas and express them trenchantly is one whom Seneca would always be very pleased to shake hands with.

But if Senecan characterization is not the result of a doctrinaire approach, it does bear the marks of a complicated past. Tragedy in its long decline had modified itself in several ways affecting the characters. "Nobody," wrote Demetrius, probably in Seneca's own lifetime, "could imagine tragedy indulging in a jest,"[13] and the cleavage between the genres was felt to be well-nigh absolute. But comedy, beneath the surface, had been impinging upon even the most austere tragic purism: as may be seen in epitome in the fact that, whereas, to allow entrance of characters, Sophoclean and Euripidean doors *open*, by the time of Accius and in Seneca there is a fair chance that they will *creak* in doing so. Comedy stimulated interest in domestic drama, the love theme, the confidant; and while it helped to drain the vitality out of the chorus, the assurance of its typology was bound to affect such recurrent tragic figures as the tyrant and the nurse. Superimpose this tendency on an aim of arousing pity and horror, and we have one cause of the stiffening of texture previously noticed. Second, loss of faith in the Olympian religion alters the meaning of the tragic myths. The pain and evil in much of Greek tragedy is that of a broken order; Senecan tragic character, at its most vivid, is seen to grow and to become more iron in a world of final disorder. Thyestes, victim of the horrific banquet, cries to heaven for Atreus' punishment. "And yours," replies Atreus (they are the last words of the play), "I leave to *your children*!" The loss of a true sense of the numinous and the enthronement of Fortuna as supreme goddess modify the substance of both fear and hope. When narrating fearful experience, a *persona* emphasizes the lurid and the weird; and in a paraenetic role (since the issue of character is not now between ὕβρις and τὸ σωφρονεῖν, but between self-disturbance and securing the mind's own peace) he will seek to restore hope by counselling some form of ataraxia. The verbal philosophizing in Seneca, however, does not go much deeper than a thought colouring. He seems to be original in making it more or less consistently Stoic, but he only half captures the new dimension which it could have added to character; and unlike the nonchalant Pacuvius, who brought in jarring words like *philosophus* and *physicus*, Seneca never allows philosophy to be discussed overtly.

The characters, particularly when in love, draw also from outside the dramatic heritage. A Phaedra portrayed after the *Heroides* loves more passionately and more articulately. Seneca did well to leave to Phaedra some of the inward struggle and self-disgust which Ovid dispensed with, but he did equally well to allow her the Ovidian heroine's sensuous appreciation of physical manhood. Or perhaps better, for whereas in Ovid she details to Hippolytus his own attractions, in Seneca she relates to him those of Theseus in days of youth, ending with the declaration, "And his features were like those of your Phoebe or my Phoebus — or rather, were your own." To a tragedian, of course, Ovid is something between a hindrance and a help, and Seneca's Agamemnon (to speculate for a moment) appears through what should be the tensest part of the tragedy to be hankering for a love scene with Cassandra. Virgil, characteristically, lends less in tone and treatment than in phrase and association. The Senecan Deianira gains a depth by association which Sophocles could hardly have given her when she exclaims, "Let the sword, deep driven, go through my body: *sic, sic agendum est.*"[14]

In making his characters thus allusive Seneca was merely extending a special property which they had from the beginning by reason of their literary-minded audience, an audience indifferent to the mechanics of getting Oedipus on and off but discerningly aware of this Oedipus as a variation on a theme. Whereas in republican days a tragedy was meant to be received per se, Seneca is writing for fellow *literati* who have Sophocles and Euripides full in mind, and he often sets the *persona* in a sort of counterpoint to its Greek original. Instead of the anticipation of uncertainty, this Oedipus embodies the anticipation of suspense.[15] This Clytemnestra is one who can still waver in her course, and in this Medea love and care for Jason are not yet extinct.

With such an endowment from without, the characterization passes into the orbit of Seneca's own literary training. T. S. Eliot protested in one of his essays against the use of the word "rhetorical" as a synonym for bad writing; and indeed, since Aristotle declared that beginners among playwrights spoke like rhetoricians, and since his contemporary Theodectes incurred censure for this very thing, the word has been so regularly used in a wide pejorative sense that it has almost ceased to signify. To a man brought up as Seneca was, rhetoric is the whole formal art of composition: it guides the intelligence and controls the imagination at every stage. It taught how to construct, how to handle emotion, and how to prove or persuade, as well as how to write a "received" style. And Seneca, in his characterizing, whatever faults the orthodox training begets, is able also to break some new ground by each of these avenues.

Rhetoric taught structure; and since dramatic structure is the framework on which character is spun, a sound structure (as in the *Troades*) helps the portrayal, and an aberrant structure (as in the *Oedipus*) has the opposite effect. Robbed of its religious import, the *Agamemnon* of Aeschylus falls slack. Seneca aimed to restore the tension by portraying the minds of Clytemnestra and Aegisthus before the deed. Hence, in the first episode, a pair of "private" scenes. First, Clytemnestra is in a fury of jealousy, hatred, shame, and desperation born of the feeling that "returning were as tedious as go o'er." But her Nurse calms her; and in the next scene it is precisely a craving for return, return to innocence, that Aegisthus has to combat in her. This is pure pain, and of course she despises him. Not only the altered dramatic scheme, however, but the characterization in the episode itself is something of a formal construct. Clytemnestra is hesitating about the murderous plan: the strands which go to motivate the subsequent action are almost schematically presented, and then the decision is ratified.[16] In another respect Seneca paved the way for something new. A drama substituting the merely supernatural for the numinous incorporated in its structure an increasing number of ghost scenes and ghosts appearing in sleep. Seneca carries this to the very threshold of what it was to be for the Elizabethans, hallucination as the drama of a mind's disorder. He might well have crossed the threshold. "*Adestne . . . Creo*," he makes Oedipus ask,

> an aeger animus falsa pro veris videt?
> (203-204)

And once, perhaps, he does cross it, when Andromache (*Tro.* 442) relates her grim vision of Hector during sleep:

> si somnus ille est mentis attonitae stupor.

The formalized study of emotion had gained some ground in psychology but paid the penalty of system. An orator has the emotions categorized and sets out to realize them by a technique which, over against its merits, on the one hand lacks flexibility and on the other may easily be overdone. In Seneca, accordingly, contrasts of mood between *personae* are set pieces, and Clytemnestra moves but jerkily from her scene with the Nurse to the scene with Aegisthus. Since Euripides' *Medea* there had been a fascination about conflicting emotions within a single person, and Seneca elaborates a kind of emotional decorum of inward conflict for use not only in Medea but in Andromache, Clytemnestra, Phaedra, and others. The *Medea* appealed to him more than any other Greek play, and the drama of μὴ δῆτα, θυμέ is expanded into many varieties of self-address. "Aude, anime," murmurs Phaedra in Hippolytus' arms, "tempta, perage mandatum tuum."

A third deeply ingrained habit of mind was that of persuasion or proof. Speakers with a case to make out had a choice of method: given the basic facts, there was *entechnos pistis,* or artificial proof, a demonstration based on principles and probability and deduced out of the orator's own head, and *atechnos pistis,* proof got by collecting factual evidence from outside, that is, a form of research. Cicero in defending Caelius chose to rely mainly on *entechnos pistis;* in the *actio secunda* of the Verrines it is to a larger degree *atechnos.* Seneca, by habit of mind rather than design, clandestinely carries over such demonstration into drama. The experience of the man who witnessed Hippolytus' death is of a thicker, less articulated cast than in Euripides and is painted over with what at first sight looks almost like fantasy. The destroying monster which he has seen and which he describes to us had a blue neck and a green forehead and eyes of changing aspect, now flame-coloured, now blue; on breast and dewlap it was green with moss, and its sides were dappled with red seaweed. There is no adjective of colour in the source passage in Euripides, but what here at first sight resembles Spenserian fancy is really a piece of demonstrating. The monster is the bull of Neptune (Poseidon) from the sea, and Seneca deduces the blue and green, the flame, the moss and red seaweed, in effect, by *entechnos pistis.* Proof by evidence is chiefly carried out by mythological research. The hints in Euripides that the tragic plight of Phaedra and Hippolytus is partly the outcome of heredity and family background, notably the "Cretan infirmity" influencing Phaedra, these Seneca extends with resource and determination. Phaedra on her side (698) recognizes the *fata domus,* and Theseus on his side (905) asks: "unde ista venit generis infandi lues?" Seneca takes account of the relation to the present calamity of Phaedra's ancestors Jupiter and Phoebus, her father Minos, her mother Pasiphae, her so-called *frater* the Minotaur, her sister Ariadne, and her two young sons. In portraying Hippolytus he takes account of his ancestor Neptune, his grandfather Aegeus, his father's stepmother Medea, and above all of his mother Antiope. Amazons shun the male sex and hate love; yet Antiope loved — "elle a pourtant aimé," as Racine echoed from Seneca — and Hippolytus is the only male offspring of that unbalanced race who was cared for and reared. In consequence:

> solamen unum matris amissae fero,
> odisse quod iam feminas omnes licet.
> (578-579)

> I count it the single consolation for the loss of my mother
> That now I may hate all womankind.

Much of Seneca's characterization derives from these practices of inference, extension, exaggeration. The strength of the method lies in giving body and circumstance to an *ethos*, and psychological depth; the weaknesses are that it too easily runs out of hand, but still more, that it always remains the putting of a case.

Texture in characters is also determined by the author's expression in the narrower sense. The Senecan *persona* is distinguished here from his Euripidean counterpart (who has likewise often been called rhetorical) by the contrasting qualities of precision and rant. His argument, if narrow in range, is lucid and to the point. Euripides' Ion may lose his *ethos* in digressing, his Orestes may run aground in insecure generalizing about birth, riches, and merit; but Seneca, though he frequently pays the penalty of digression in narrative, rarely does so in argument. As for generalizing, the true and apt sententia can add powerfully to the home thrust of a character: it is not for nothing that some 2,700 different sententiae and maxims are found in the plays of Shakespeare. Greek tragic characters seldom rant; and it has been customary to regret Senecan inflated speech, that of Medea for example, when she says:

> non rapidus amnis, non procellosum mare
> Pontusve Coro saevus aut vis ignium
> adiuta flatu possit imitari impetum
> irasque nostras.
> (411-414)

Not raging river, not tempestuous sea,
Nor Pontus savage under the north-west gale, nor violence
Of fire in the wind's blast could imitate
The onrush of my anger.

But heroic character was enriched, not impoverished, by the faculty of ranting. Where much is attempted something is likely to be achieved. Rant lends volume and a vague, looming quality to character, and bombast no less than *gracilitas* has been one of the avenues to the sublime. It needed five preceding lines in true "Ercles' vein" to bring Hercules to the thought, "Though the whole ocean should stream along my hands, deep will the wicked blot cling" (*HF* 1328-1329).

We may then reject the view that the contribution of these characters to later drama was due solely to the chance which destroyed or so long kept hidden the rest of classical tragedy. Seneca lacked the realizing vision of the individual which has been the glory of the modern stage, and his achievement was often a by-product of concentration on some other end. But in his unique context of time, place, and circumstance he was able in a number of ways to extend the tragedian's means of characterization. Nothing would have surprised him more than to be told that these enlargements set up a tension in the tragic figure which was destined to split it into two. For his art can be felt to stand at a parting of the ways. Along one path, passionate intensity under a formalized control was to be handed down to the French classical stage, while a disorderly residue in dramatic character — the gaunt, the lurid, the weird, rant, revenge, and repartee — awaited its own renaissance in Tamburlaine and Hieronimo and the Globe.

9. THE ROSCIAD IDEA

The *Rosciads* today are collector's pieces. They are, with one exception, so rare that anyone proposing to read them in their entirety must either go court hayfever in a museum or chafe the epithelium of his fingers by scrabbling with xeroxes. Even then he would be lucky to set eye on them all. There are some that the British Museum — and they are a British invention — seems never to have owned. Some have sunk and left only a ripple on the surface of learned enquiry. But the idea behind them, in a period stretching almost from the death of Swift to the birth of Shaw, busied the bookish and the theatre-minded on some twenty different occasions over the years. It provided a tilting-ground on which classicist, poet, and theatre-critic could meet, and although it would perhaps be going beyond the truth to say that, in the infighting which resulted, friendships, careers, and fortunes were made and broken, they were certainly affected, and the social consequences were not altogether negligible.[1]

It is not however the social effects that I wish to dwell on, nor the jumble of personalia from which socio-literary induction must begin, but rather the origins and progress of the idea itself, and also something done long before, in antiquity, which in good time supplied the idea with needful impetus. This something done in antiquity was not the creation of the genre. For antiquity did not create it, though of course stray comment on actors and acting is as old as the theatre itself, and Greeks and Romans readily admitted it to their occasional literature. Some of them even organized their thoughts of the subject into essay-form. English poets in the eighteenth century cannot be supposed to have known or cared that the sophist Aristides, back in the second, had penned a lost invective against heroic pantomime, of which the substance is to be gleaned from a replication by Libanius. Few can have dipped into the writings of Aristides' contemporary Lucian, whose surviving defence of the same art incorporates many laughs at individual performers, mostly unnamed, who debase it by bad acting. It was not this, but rather the occasional comments in authors more widely read, that the eighteenth century was apt to imbibe, such as Cicero's remarks in his letters about what goes on at the Games, and how Aesop the doyen in tragedy is justly superannuated, since his voice cracked in the recitation of an oath and he could not finish his part. Odd lines on actors and buffoons came down in the farrago of satire, too, and were the better digested for their Lucilian smack. If English writers did not meet the line of Lucilius himself, where he tells of

Orestes hoarser, ever hoarser, till the player wrecks the play,[2]

they met those of Horace on extempore burlesquing:

bade him dance Polyphemus since he had
capital mug-mask, buskins natural;[3]

or of Persius on scenes of tragedy:

Procne's or Thyestes' boiling pot —
ham for ham-actor Glyco;[4]

or Juvenalian bawdry on a comedian so adept as wife, maid, or mistress that

you'd swear he has, not acts, a female part.[5]

These are only scraps of predisposing atmosphere. And they are fairly remote, even though several of the English writers grace, or attempt to grace, their title-page with snippets from Terence, Cicero, Phaedrus, and classical satire.

France, too, had a desultory actors' literature, including seventeenth-century works such as Bruscambille's defence of the profession, or the Abbé d'Aubignac's *Pratique du Théâtre*, both of which had incidentally held up the best of Roman acting as an example to the modern world. Not that anybody much in England read these books, but they were straws in the wind. And in the following century the French theatre, like French culture generally, attracted greater and greater interest even when it annoyed. A new Gallic foppishness on the stage, by seducing a certain amount of English histrionic talent, gave the English poet-critics positive fuel; but the greatest of them, Charles Churchill, lies in his grave at Dover to testify that France, where his last days were spent, could still speak very softly to the English mind.

A more native root was the concept expressed in England by the word "histriomastix," which literally means "whip of players." In the eighteenth century the word itself seems to slumber. It is bypassed by Dr. Johnson (just as it was later to be bypassed by the *Oxford English Dictionary*), but the concept ripens without the name and cries out, as it were, for the name to be clapped on to it. One can feel the idea pass through four shapes. Around 1600, actors are metaphorically whipped merely as one corrupt element in a generally corrupt society. A second position is reached in puritan times, when actors and the stage are singled out as the one egregious canker from which a fundamentally moral society must be preserved. Towards the end of the seventeenth century we find the whipping now being carried out upon a set of individual actors, and carried out for two joint and barely distinguished reasons – that they are vicious in private character to an exemplary degree, *and also* that they are bunglers at their art. Then finally, in the eighteenth century, both society and the stage are assumed to be morally acceptable or neutral, and private character more or less irrelevant, and the actors who are whipped are primarily those who fail artistically. The first phase is represented by the *Histriomastix* in which John Marston had a hand – a play of alienation begun about 1596, revised a few years later, and finally printed in 1610. The second phase appears in 1632, in the big homonymous work in prose by William Prynne, in which he ransacks the Church Fathers for anti-histrionic matter. It was in demand, and several times reprinted, down to 1670, but then not again until the nineteenth century. The third phase appears in *A Satyr on the Players*. This is in verse, anonymous and undated, but I think must belong to the 1680s. It is written by a very vigorous and profane histriomastix who flails about him in scurrilous defamation. Except for his scurrility and the lack of a stabilizing classical element, he might be reckoned an anticipator of the poet-critics who were to arise in the eighteenth century, though it is unlikely that they knew the *Satyr*, which remained in manuscript till 1928.[6] These poet-critics themselves represent the fourth and final stage, and among them Charles Churchill (1731-1764) is the most notable flagellant, but he seems to have missed his right name when alive, and it is not until 1953 that we find a biographer calling him "the Scourge of the Players."[7]

Going back a step, it may be said that by the late seventeenth or early eighteenth century there existed in English literature, in lean configuration, the idea of an entertaining commentary or critique or polemic, possibly in verse, on individual contemporary actors. But to become effective and attain any rank, it needed the enrichment in form and style which would come of being drawn into the mainstream of English poetry, and it needed one of those great validating touches which evoke the warm recognition of the polite world. The mainstream, at that epoch, meant many things. It meant the heaving wake of Milton. It meant the ease and thrust of Dryden and the prosody of *Hudibras*. It meant Swift and Pope, with the poetry of criticism, neo-classic satire, and the mock-heroic. Many changes could be rung on these elements, and we do in fact find the future poems on actors ringing them: mock-heroic, for instance, not necessarily in the couplet of Pope but in blank verse, and trailing the aura of *Paradise Lost*. Neo-classic satire was important partly as showing how to combine freedom with discipline, but more because it gave living air to Horace and Juvenal. In it they breathed again, as they rarely did in the dog-eared duodecimos and the slow, myopic plod of the school-room.

Among all these exemplars, Pope and in particular the *Dunciad* held a special place. The *Dunciad*, which is thought to have been the most widely read poem of the eighteenth century, set circling in men's minds a bevy of principles as to how literary attack should be ordered: that limits should be observed in some degree corresponding to those set today by the laws against obscenity and libel; that style should be crisp, and polemic witty rather than vulgar; and that, given sufficient address, a beaming kinship could be claimed, not only with ancient satire, but (by way of epic machinery) with Milton and Virgil, and the whole be brought under the ultimate broad aegis of Homer. Pope was not himself especially a man of the theatre, or interested in the world of actors and their rivalries, but to those who were, he offered three further usable notions. In the *Dunciad* as a whole, and especially in the Variorum version and commentary, he teaches by example the neat pillory of named and recognizable individuals, men well known in town, with any amount of personalia to gratify the curious. Then, in his second book, he works out a new form of *agon*-motif, borrowed from the physical contests of ancient epic and transferred to the sphere of literature and the arts. And third, in the original form of the poem, the prime target of his satire had been Colley Cibber, and though Pope's main concern had been with Cibber as an author, his writings were inseparable from his career as an actor-manager, in which capacity he was equally in the eye of the public. When the *Dunciad* was revised, Cibber was displaced from its centre, but still attacked; and the theatrical connections of the poem are maintained by a prognostication that Covent Garden and Drury Lane will become increasingly bleak houses, since (to quote the Argument) "the nation shall be overrun with farces, operas, shows; and the throne of Dulness advanced over both the Theatres."

There was one more thing which the *Dunciad* did: it established the ending *-iad* for poetry of a mock-heroic kind. Pope excogitated his title by jumping from the form *Iliad* to another Homeric poem, the lost *Margites*, named from its hero, Margites the dunce. There was a long history in Greek and Latin literature of poems whose titles ended in similar phonemes — *Iliad, Thebaid, Theseid*, and the rest — but they were characteristically heroic, not mock-heroic, in nature. It may be added that they were, as a rule, formed from proper names. The *Poetics* tells us, however, that there once existed a *De(i)liad*, which by etymology should mean either an epic of the island of Delos or a poem that treated of cowards, and we have in this phenomenon both an ancient mock-heroic poem — it is confirmed by the context to have been such — and an *-iad* title which may be derived not from a proper name but from a common noun or adjective.[8] Pope apparently had the *Poetics* before his eye when working on the *Dunciad*, for he quotes a nearby part of it in his Scriblerus preface, and *De(i)liad*, whatever precisely he made of it, may have helped to nudge him towards the right name for his own poem.

But that is by the way. Although serious *-iads* had been written in England and France before this time, the *Dunciad* prompted a far-reaching new vogue of them, adopting all manner of themes and forms, but henceforward predominantly mock-heroic or satiric. Most were in verse, a few in prose. Most titles were formed from proper names, a few otherwise. Many years ago Professor Richmond P. Bond collected over two hundred examples. "But after about 1810," he remarks, "*-iads* decreased in number, until today we regard it as a bygone mode."[9] That was written in 1929. In my own schooldays, about 1941, I recall that on the subject of poetry our allegiance was divided between classical and romantic, and one of my classmates who was an authority on taste produced a *Herculiad* in twelve cantos, one for each of his hero's labours. Thus does adolescence recapitulate evolution.

Again going back a step, we must remember that what later became a welter was in the 1740s still a novelty, and also that the employment, by many, of names as trivial and lacklustre as the writing they inspired, did not preclude the use, by someone with insight, of real name-magic, the use of a name to conjure with. The right name authorizes; it validates like a heraldic blazon. All the needful elements were now assembled — the inchoate notion, that is, of a critique or polemic on contemporary actors, preferably in verse and drawn into the mainstream of contemporary poetry. It should be, in greater or less degree, mock-heroic or satirical, with epic machinery and an *agon* or contest-element, and should form as *-iad* in the manner of the *Dunciad*. But it still needed validation, and in 1750 someone whose identity will probably never be known suddenly effected this by drawing all the incohate elements into contact with the Roscian Tradition. To express it another way, the idea had been hitherto blunt-edged, and now it was suddenly sharpened.

A tradition can be looked at from two ends. It can be seen

teleologically, and it can be seen in terms of its origin. That is, it can be seen as moving towards the final bolting together of a constructional toy, a kind of meccano which successive generations have played with, working towards an end which satisfies their psychological need; or it can be seen as, by causal chains, the gradual but real consequence of that temporal event, whatever it may have been, from which the tradition began. Often the end is more important than the beginning. But when, as in the case of the Roscian Tradition, the causal chains derive from some uncommon human achievement, and when there is reason to think that the operation of those chains was in some measure planned or intended from the beginning, history is as much concerned with that beginning as with the ultimate outcome.

The achievement of Quintus Roscius was something more signal than even the rosciadists conceived. They took it for granted, and they never fully represented to their imagination the odds against which he contended. To come, as he did, from a place called Solon's Field, which is as good as saying, from nowhere, from very close to the earth and the slow rhythm of crops and seasons; to inherit genes which, probably by the sixth week of infancy, made it certain that his eyes would never track together; to learn to know himself as a Lanuvine, and to regard Lanuvium — "Woolerton" — as home, a negligible town on the last spur of the Alban hills, which some courses of prehistoric stones kept from crumbling into the plain below; to see through slanting vision that market-place with farm-carts, pig-smells, and big cowhide bags which townsfolk made for the carriage of latin wine; to look up, perhaps, at some scouting raven, or hearth-smoke issuing from a smoke-hole, or at the temple on the hill brow, where under a baking sun the only sign of activity might be the sudden skelter of a small green lizard across the travertine; to know this much of metaphysics, and know it viscerally, that Juno the Safeguarder guarded her people; to study the swart, chaffering faces of these, their movements and postures; to begin to mime them, and be insensibly led on to mime the business of life itself; to be and do this, and then from such a background go up the Appian road to Rome and scratch a mark on the tensile, elongating glass of time, which it would carry for ever — this was the degree of his merit.

He was to become the prime representer of Old Western Man to himself. Of course, the beginning was neither so fortuitous, nor the conclusion so foregone, as first appearances would suggest. Lanuvium had heard of stage-plays. Silen and slave-mask stared down here and there from ornamental tile-ends along the eaves, and the town might claim as a son that Luscius who in bygone years had gotten hold of some Greek playbooks and done *The Treasure, The Vision,* and other pieces into his mother-tongue. These may have been, to Roscius, symbolic prompters. It is likely enough, too, that before he received his first engagement in Rome, boyhood and adolescence had already seen him there many times, craning forward at shows to pick up the actor's business. Nor need we think of him as wholly self-taught; he may have had at some point a Roman (or Romanized Greek) teacher, and this could be why Horace calls him *doctus.*[10] Again, histrionic ambition did not lack a fairway. Though to act was no high calling, such acting as his could not be ignored. His rewards and fame, in life, were solid, and I know of no other actor, among hundreds, who could be – and was – pointed out for his "services to the Roman People."[11]

That, however, was one thing: to achieve immortality was another, and was by no means a corollary. Until recent times, an actor's glory, along with that of singer, dancer, and instrumentalist, has been of the most ephemeral kind. How could *multa pars mei* go down to posterity? Visually and aurally it could not. In 1760 the simple pathos of this fact was beautifully expressed by a young man called Robert Lloyd, who stands very close to the rosciadists though not actually of their number. He concludes his poem *The Actor* with these words:

> Yet, hapless artist! though thy skill can raise
> The bursting peal of universal praise,
> Though at thy beck Applause delighted stands,
> And lifts, Briareus like, her hundred hands,
> Know, Fame awards thee but a partial breath:
> Not all thy talents brave the stroke of Death!
> Poets to ages yet unborn appeal,
> And latest times th' eternal nature feel.
> Though blended here the praise of bard and play'r,
> While more than half becomes the actor's share,

Relentless Death untwists the mingled fame,
And sinks the player in the poet's name.
The pliant muscles of the various face,
The mien that gave each sentence strength and grace,
The tuneful voice, the eye that spoke the mind,
Are gone, nor leave a single trace behind.

Plautus could survive, but how could Roscius? All his aptness, strength, and grace had to die with him, or soon after. The youngest who could remember him died themselves in the reign of Augustus. Yet, given luck and determination, something could survive, and reading between the lines of such scraps of evidence as have come down, we trace, or seem to trace, three bids made by Roscius and his friends and well-wishers, to perpetuate his memory.

First, backed by the people of Lanuvium, he furbished and put about the story (doubtless true) of how one night in his infancy a snake had managed to enter the house and sly into his cradle for warmth. No harm had resulted, and the thing had been interpreted by the religious authorities as an omen of fame to come. This story, perhaps in the form of a commission, reached the ears of Pasiteles the embosser, a man of uncommon toreutic skill, who took a silver dish or panel and beat out a depiction of the incident upon its surface. But permanence was denied to this precious memorial. Though some Greek and Roman silverware of that age survives, the sweep of time has tumbled Pasiteles and all his works into oblivion. There was, too, a short Greek poem on the same event, by the poet Archias, but this has likewise gone. The poem might have lived if Archias had been a more powerful writer, and in what looks like another bid for survival Roscius decided to turn his hand to literary composition. Actors' biographies and auto-biographies were a genre not yet invented; instead he wrote a monograph comparing actor and orator in their power to portray such things as feeling, impulse, and predicament, the actor by gesture, the orator by the spoken word. The treatise did not run to great length — one book-roll, the length of an article or couple of articles in a modern journal — and it is not quite certain that it was ever finished. This bid likewise failed. The muses who so blessed his acting did not smile equally upon his authorship, and the monograph is lost — so wholly lost that even to Professor Henry Bardon of Poitiers, who has written a large work on "la littérature latine inconnue" — we find it to be "inconnu" even to him.

There remained his personal character. By a happy stroke, this commended him to the special regard of a younger man who knew the secrets of literary style. Roscius embraced the friendship. He was old enough to have been Cicero's father, but from the time when he put in the young publicist's way his first important brief in a lawcourt, Cicero and he remained fast friends, and Cicero was able to confer on him the gift of lasting survival, which so many prayed for in vain. For there can be little doubt that Cicero was, if not the originator, at least the most conscious and effective foster-parent of the Roscian Tradition, though he would not have admitted to being so, nor did the Tradition take the exact form which he intended. He speaks of Roscius in nine or ten of his books, and also in a letter — always with admiration and affection. "He was an old man when he died," Cicero said, "but so fine was the mastery and grace of his acting that one felt he should have been exempted altogether from mortality."[12] On another occasion he wrote:

> We might thus set a standard for successful public speaking parallel to what this actor has done. Do you notice how there is nothing he does which falls short of perfection, or fails to enchant? Everything in fact proves exactly right, speaking straight to the feelings and delighting us all. For this reason it has long stood to his achievement that the most outstanding practitioner in any artistically creative field should be called, in his own line, a Roscius.[13]

There was doubtless an element of truth in this, but there is also design, and design of a subtly self-effacing kind. Cicero does not make the claim directly. The words are part of a fictive dialogue supposed to have taken place thirty-six years before the time of writing. They are represented as said, not by Cicero, but by Crassus, a leading orator of the previous generation. And they suggest the existence of the Tradition not merely at the time when the fictive words were spoken, but "long" before. If "long" is more than ten years, it would take us back to a time when Roscius was still in his twenties. Is Cicero embroidering the truth? Certainly, whatever may have been the truth at that early time, in most of the interim Cicero as youth and man had done all he could to nurse the Tradition along. It is possible that in this passage his enthusiasm leads him into well-meaning hyperbole. At least posterity, in the course of time, has judged so and made a tacit correction.

For it will be noticed that the claim put forward is in no way limited to acting. The claim is that it stands to Roscius' achievement that the most skilled practitioner in any field of artistry should be called a Roscius. And elsewhere Cicero emphasizes the illustration of this claim nearest his own heart, namely that a master of oratory may fitly be recognized as a Roscius.[14] The generalizing claim was repeated in reference books of other centuries as a certified truth, and sometimes as a still operative truth: by Festus in the late second century, by Paul the Deacon in Carolingian times, by Erasmus in his *Adagia*, where he teaches that a good pleader may indeed be called a Roscius, and by Charles Estienne in his historical dictionary, which led a very long life beginning in 1553. As we approach the time of the rosciadists, Robert Ainsworth writes that "such as excelled in any art were called Roscii," and another lexicographer says in the present tense that "if any excel in any Art, we call him a Roscius in his Art."[15] This is probably what Cicero hoped would happen, but it is not the form in which the Tradition actually took root. I doubt if the *proverbium* (as Erasmus calls it) is ever honorifically used of men in other professions. The living fact is different. Posterity accepted the spirit but not the letter of Cicero's intention and awarded his friend's name to one sort of man only, those who achieved mastery in the field of acting. The only exceptions have been actor-playwrights and actor-managers, and these are merely such as prove the rule.

There was a long delay before this happened. It happened only after the classics had become classical, and even then not until theatre life burgeoned again. It is a curious fact that neither in the last years of the Roman republic nor under the empire is there any certain or probable instance of Roscius' name bestowed honorifically. If it was so bestowed, the record is lost; but we must remember that it and its feminine counterpart "Roscia" continued in quite ordinary use down to at least the fifth century, when a certain Roscia, daughter of a bishop in Gaul, provides the last clearly dated example.[16] In the largely theatre-less centuries which followed, memory of the actor survived by a slender thread. Paul the Deacon, whom I have mentioned above, seems to have thought of him as "Roscus,"[17] and in the ninth century a glossator of Horace, probably Heiric of Auxerre, got the name right but threw out the puzzled suggestion that it stood for "some moneylender," *usurarius quidam.*[18] It was from such a nadir that recovery had to be made.

In and after the Renaissance, however, the handing on of the memory bears the marks of a living tradition, at least of that mixed kind which is partly shaped by the contemporary world and partly by smatterings of learning picked up in school. In England the pronunciation of the name had been gradually anglicized: the long Roman "o" was shortened and the hard Roman "c" softened, giving a sound like "rossius" or "roshus," which is the way Shakespeare pronounced it and the way many people still do. When "Rosciad" came on the scene it was pronounced "rossiad," and "rosciadist," coined in 1764 (with a capital letter), was pronounced "rossiadist." The cardinal point, the connection with primacy in acting, was reiterated through grammar school doses of Cicero and thence diffused to a wider public. In general the Tradition existed alongside the progress of true scholarship without taking any notice of it. For instance one or two apocryphal stories, the products of sham learning or the beginning of legend, gathered round the actor's name, such as a story about his often dining with Cato. It is just possible that Roscius did dine with Cato, but ancient record does not attest it and the chronology is awkward. Historical imagination was poor, and for this reason also the age-gap between Roscius and Cicero was seen very hazily, with Roscius sometimes thought of as the same age or even (as in a drawing of 1644) Cicero's junior. Scholarship knew him as one who might occasionally have acted in tragedy but who was far more characteristically a *comoedus.* So too, to some extent, did popular repute, as when in 1589 he was called "the best histrien [sic] or buffon that was in his days to be found."[19]

But the qualities and interests of men to whom his name was given rubbed off on him. If they were tragedians, so was he, and as in Elizabethan times serious acting meant predominantly tragedy, he is mostly thought of as Roscius the tragedian. Through the sixteenth and seventeenth centuries, with intervals, men of the theatre glimpsed him in the styles of successive masters, and what they were, he became. Small, proud comparisons dot the literature of the time. Burbage was "England's great Roscius," Alleyn was "the Roscius of our age," Ostler "the Roscius of these Times," Lacy "the famous Roscius, or comedian." An epitaph for Tarlton records that

> hic Roscius Britannicus sepultus est,

and at the funeral of Betterton in Westminster Abbey, Sir Richard Steele found his mind dwelling on the same theme.[20]

Now the Tradition had hitherto nearly always appeared in more or less serious surroundings, and it had at first no obvious place outside of them. The satirical poetry of Dryden and Pope shows no interest in it, and anyone who gauged national habit from them alone would judge that, at the same time as satire grew to be a major genre in England, the Tradition was in a state of suspense. Their immediate followers and imitators in the first half of the eighteenth century give the same impression. Indeed, after the funeral of Betterton in 1710 there seems to have been a real lull, an intermission which lasted for thirty years, in course of which the only transaction which would have pleased the *manes* of Roscius was that Pope intervened to set right the spelling of his name in Shakespeare's *Henry VI*, which the original printers had printed exactly as the actors pronounced it, with "s" for "c," an error which theatrical indifference to scholarship had tolerated for a century and a quarter.[21] Meantime another kind of adjustment was going on. If the pulse of literary fashion was to continue beating loud in satire, satire must ramify, and must find a place for (though not necessarily attack) many things which had customarily belonged in more serious contexts. Correlatively, if the Roscian Tradition should be renewed, the chances were that satire would now take notice.

The decade in which everything converged was 1740-1750. We

have already seen pointers in the literature of acting and the vogue and character of *-iad* poems. Now there had always been in the Roscian Tradition a subordinate figure, Aesop or Aesopus the player in tragedy, whose name was sometimes linked to that of Roscius in the actor-talk of posterity, just as it had been in life. It shared in tributes and comparisons and in the tone of voice adopted. But in 1740 some nameless penman used it to salt a pasquinade, a mock-life of the actor-playwright Colley Cibber bearing as caption *The Life, Manners, and Opinions of Aesopus the Tragedian.* Here we see the Tradition becoming reoriented. This shift of attitude happened just two years before the rise of David Garrick and the triumphant realization that in him Roscius was come again. It was Dubliners who first proclaimed the discovery. Garrick, then twenty-five, had gone to Ireland for the summer season of 1742. He was already known to be good, but Dublin, which bred many actors of its own and was well able to tell a hawk from a handsaw, found him superlative. Amid the excitement a eulogium was composed, attempting to salute at once his technique, his gay appeal, and his cultivated mind — with a very Irsih pickle of images as the result: "Roscius! Paris of the stage,/ Born to please a learned age. . . . " How squarely he kept his repute in Ireland appears indirectly from an incident during his next visit there in 1745, when a young actress, piqued in a squabble over parts, played a trick on him, and later recorded her pleasure at having given "the immortal Roscius his first humiliation."[22] In the next five years England endorsed his primacy by bestowing on him the same title, and his recent biographer Carola Oman, looking over that chapter of his career, heads it with the single word "Roscius," finding in this the most applicable rubric.[23] 1750 saw the dawn of the *Rosciads.*

The essence of the idea, to which the individual *Rosciads* approximate, though with great variations of detail and emphasis, is a critique of contemporary actors or of one contemporary actor, usually but not always in verse, usually but not always mock-heroic or satirical in tone, with an explicit or implied appeal to the standard of excellence originally set by Roscius and the consequent notion of a primacy passing to someone claimed as his greatest living successor. The rosciadists begin from the assumption that every actor aspires to be a Roscius or, in the case of actresses, his feminine counterpart (whom nineteenth-century advertisers sometimes call a Roscia). Antiquarian detail, had they wanted it, could have been obtained from a classical dictionary, though it must be confessed that Robert Ainsworth's, which was probably the most accessible (second edition 1746, third edition 1751), would not have helped them much. It says simply

> Roscius,-i. m. An excellent actor in the scenes, Cicero's master in pronunciation and action. So perfect was he in his way, that such as excelled in any art were called Roscii

— with a couple of references. Across the Channel, there had long been entries in the dictionary of Moréri and in those of the Estienne brothers, all of which had been frequently reprinted, the latter two even existing in London editions. Further east, Zedler's *Universal-Lexikon* reached its thirty-second volume, with a column on Roscius, in 1742. Moreover in 1717 a full-dress paper on the actor's life had been read to one of the French Academies by the scholar-abbot Fraguier, and this was published (after a trifling publication-gap of twenty-nine years) in the Academy's *Mémoires.*[24] But I do not believe the rosciadists ever consulted any of these books: this is not how a tradition works. They remembered what they had picked up about the actor at school or college or by chance elsewhere — usually only the one central fact — and built upon this. All that the reference books and Fraguier's researches did was to spread the name wider and improve the climate of interest.

To write, or read, a commentary on the *Rosciads* as a whole would take a long time and lead into many bypaths. It would also require a keen relish for prosopography. Scholarship — and idle curiosity — need a better register of English Augustan and Regency actors than they have yet got, though the painstaking work of recent elucidators of Churchill provides a partial vade mecum. Here I shall only follow the thread of the central idea through its four phases, showing how it forms in its time the chief embodiment of the Roscian Tradition and offering a few adversaria on things that stand out.[25]

To the first phase belong the two earliest *Rosciads* and

Churchill's. We may call it the first Garrician period, 1750-1761. It is a striking fact that even the most recent and learned editors of Churchill, and his best biographer,[26] have omitted to notice the earlier *Rosciads*, though they are titular precedents, and may well have been sources, for his own poem. The 1750 *Rosciad*, beginner of the series, is a blank verse poem of 573 lines by a hand unknown. The author is well-read and not a bad classicist, though on his title-page some ill-printed lines of Calpurnius Siculus are unhappily ascribed to Juvenal. It is a mock-heroic but partly serious poem, closely modelled on the style of *Paradise Lost*, with epic machinery from the same source, perhaps via the *Dunciad*. Melpomene, muse of tragedy, and Thalia, muse of comedy, visit London and institute a tribunal of which the aim is, by rewarding merit, to arrest what the author considers to be the decline of the British stage into poor taste and "exodiary mimes." Attendant on the two muses sit the playwrights, chief among them Shakespeare and Ben Jonson. Melpomene, in a preamble to the hearing, outlines the history of the theatre to show how the present state of affairs came about and then calls on "the contending heroes of the stage" to put their case. Three leading actors come forward, each claiming the primacy by expatiating on his plays, roles, and histrionic merits. These men are not named in the poem, but marginal glosses show them to be Mr. Q—, who I suppose is James Quin, now aged fifty-seven, Mr. G—, who will be Garrick, and Mr. B—, who will be the tall spendthrift Irishman known as Spranger Barry. One of the author's minor problems was how to refer in adequately epic tone to the fact that Garrick was raised in Litchfield. He solved it by discovering, perhaps from some eighteenth-century map of Roman Britain, that the town fell within the area anciently inhabited by an obscure tribe called the Cornavii or Cornovii. Garrick is thus introduced:

> Now the Cornavian Roscius with an air
> Vivacious, gay as young Lothario, came
> To pay obeisance: though no martial port,
> No stride majestic, and no front august,
> His person grac'd; yet Nature in his eye
> Roll'd beauteous, on his visage stampt the seal
> Of rich perfection dignify'd by Art,

And from his soul beamed forth the brightest ray
That with meridian lustre e'er illumed
The muses consecrated dome: he bow'd
With decency respectful; and, with voice
Harmonious as the soaring lark, began.

After the main contenders, a ruck of lesser actors press forward, but Melpomene dismisses them. Her adjudication dwells on the merits of naturalness and propriety (with particular abhorrence of French foppery), and declares Quin and Garrick the winners, with Garrick, it is implied, narrowly in the lead; Barry may hold the stage when the other two are not by. The poem has its faults. Making the actors present their own case involves making them boast, and this reveals less about them than objective criticism might do. But the main fault is a structural lack of tension, with Garrick lodged awkwardly between the other two candidates and a verdict which is clumsy instead of clear-cut. Again, to call Garrick Roscius at the very moment when he is introduced makes the tribunal all but superfluous, and the new-coined word "Rosciad" is limited to the rather slack meaning of a mock-heroic poem in which an actor already nicknamed Roscius vindicates his superiority to the rest.

Three years later there seems to have come out an *Ancient Rosciad*, which is now lost or latent.[27] This is tantalizing, because the title suggests that it was called into being by the stimulus of the earlier poem and that it dealt in some way with ancient actors and the original Roscius, possibly using these as a cloak for comment on the contemporary stage. It cannot have been very striking, but might have opened a window for us on the Roscian Tradition in 1753.

We now come to a real histriomastix. For behind the deadpan face of Charles Churchill (twenty-nine and the Reverend) as he sat in the front row close to the pit-spikes, watching play after play through the winter of 1760-1761, a more mordant conception was forming. Although on the title page of his *Rosciad*, which came out in March 1761 and remained anonymous till the second edition, he placed a quatrain professing the poem to be an unbiased critique, and although his modern biographer defends the impartiality of his intentions,[28] in execution his work was a satire more witty and stinging than anything seen in England since the *Dunciad*. Churchill's discrimination does leave a small number of actors, on balance, secure, and he is fairly chivalrous to actresses, but the consternation of his far more numerous victims, and the pother of written rejoinders, were to fill the theatrical and literary air for some time to come. His indebtedness in a general way to earlier theatrical pamphleteering, and in a more personal way to his old classmate Robert Lloyd, whose gentler poem *The Actor* was written the previous year, is known: far less known is his relationship to the rosciadist of 1750. Their two poems agree in title. Both describe a tribunal for settling the primacy among actors. In each poem are lengthy preliminaries, including, in the earlier one, a review of theatre history, and in the later a contribution to the "ancients versus moderns" controversy. Shakespeare and Ben Jonson are prominent in both poems – in the one, as assessors, more or less, to the muse, and in the other as actual judges. Both poems deal with Barry, Quin, and Garrick and place them, relatively to each other, in the same order of merit (with Barry and Quin less tenderly handled in the later poem). Churchill was never the man to be a slavish copier, and if he had a conscious model it was rather the *Dunciad*, whence the demi-goddess Dulness flits through his pages; but he has certainly got something, even if only by unconscious rumination based on hearsay, from the poem of 1750.

His technical improvements, however, are striking: the heroic couplet for the sake of mordancy; more actors and a less tawdry scenario; human judges instead of Melpomene, and judges who are chosen on the recommendation of Robert Lloyd, not imposed by arbitrary fiat; actors, moreover, spindled by their name in the text, and presented in thumbnail sketch or brief self-disclosure, not in long-winded "monology." Above all, the poem does not go off at half-cock. It begins:

> Roscius deceased, each high aspiring player
> Push'd all his interest for the vacant chair.

The tribunal is not pre-judged; it is not skewed in the mind of the ordinary reader by a premature revelation. A proper structural tension is maintained (though Churchill later weakened this through the interpolation of additamenta). Garrick is nowhere called Roscius; he is kept till last among all the actors described; and the verdict, pronounced by Shakespeare, reserves its nub till the final sentence:

Garrick! take the chair,
Nor quit it − till thou place an equal there.

Churchill uses the Tradition to excite, not disperse, interest, and he imparts to it something new. For this is, so far as I know, the first appearance in literature of Roscius' Chair. In his lifetime no such mark of honour existed for Roman actors, and Cicero, who recognizes the chairs of kings, magistrates, and schoolmasters, never supplies one for Roscius even in a trope. But henceforward the Chair becomes tralaticious.

A second Garrician period runs from 1761 to 1779, when Garrick died. He keeps his primacy, though he has enemies and is sometimes objurgated. The *Rosciad* idea is prolific: it recurs in the pattern already established but also takes on new forms. It may be applied to the theatre in a wider sense than before, or it may centre on a particular theatre or class of actors. London remains the hub, but the idea springs up elsewhere in England, and even outside it. Besides the heroic couplet, it may take the form of Hudibrastic verse, prose treatise, or newspaper column. The driving force is Churchill's vigorous poem, which evokes imitation, amendment, and counterblast. Altogether, apart from Churchill's alterations of his own work, I count nine new *Rosciads*, and a few ebullitions with other titles which claim kin with the idea or at least with the Roscian Tradition.

Immediate London reactions to Churchill included the *Churchiliad*, 1761. This is in prose and amounts to a 48-page hostile review, beginning with generalities and moving on to points of detail. At first the author reminds one of Laurence Sterne, but he presently declines to a pedestrian level and trails off into vapid querulousness. His style has colour, but it cannot disguise his plodding naivety. Three things in particular stick in his gullet. One is the idea that Churchill should be making money out of detraction. Another is that he should be combining the job of parson — though in reality a very loth and nominal parson — with the activities of theatre-critic, satirist, and (allegedly) indiscriminate calumniator. The third is his rating of Garrick as a nonpareil. Why, to praise Garrick, need Churchill attack Quin, who was a generation older and already retired? Quin had "long since resigned all pretensions to the chair of Roscius, in the very meridian of praise . . and here are you disturbing the manes of his theatrical reputation." The last generation thought him *then* what Churchill's Roscius, i.e. Garrick, is now: has there never been true appraisal before Churchill? The writer is especially pained at Churchill's disgusting poetic leap, in his opening couplet, from the original Roscius to the present day. "You have grossly forgot yourself."

> Roscius was a contemporary with Cicero, and died about seventeen hundred years ago [actually 1823 years]; then what could provoke thee to take no notice of the numberless great performers that have been since that period? This is a tacit confession, that this is either the most *meritorious*, or the most *impudent* age that has been since that time: but you seem to speak as if the chair was but just vacant, and bring the members of our stage as the only claimants.

Another anonymous riposte of the same year was the *Anti-Rosciad*, of 222 lines in heroic couplets. It is in character a defensive poem, aiming at impartiality but tamer and less witty than Churchill's. The tribunal device is employed for a rehearing of the case. The court is the Town and the judge Common Sense. We find Barry rated as second only to Garrick, and later Quin somewhat inconsistently given the same place. But the author makes the point, logical as far as it goes, that if malice and "Spight" are to usurp the place of judgment, no amount of merit, but only influence, can give security: "All must find foes in such a court, and there / Garrick, without a patent, miss the chair." Garrick's patent was the management of Drury Lane. Before Churchill's early death in 1764 there also appeared the *Rosciad of Covent Garden* (1762) and the *Smithfield Rosciad* (1763), the latter treating minor actors. Afterwards, in 1767, came the *Rational Rosciad*. The author of this poem writes in heroic couplets but, as befits a rationalist, dispenses with the fictive tribunal and all poetic machinery except a prayer to the muses for "Churchill's strength without his spite." What had been preliminary matter in earlier *Rosciads* is here expanded into a formal Part I, on stage-history and the merits of playwrights, whilst Part II deals with individual actors at both the main London theatres. An actor called Lee is said to be handicapped by managerial prejudice, "But if his hands by favour were unbound,/ By Truth he'd be our modern Roscius crown'd." Posterity can neither endorse nor belie this opinion, but may observe that Roscius has now got a crown. It will only be a matter of time before his chair becomes a throne.

Garrick, who reached fifty in 1767, kept the title by which his primacy was acknowledged, but for a variety of reasons such as stiffness, declining vigour, business disagreements, and the grudges of disappointed men, came under attack from several quarters. In consequence "Roscius" now appears as much in sniping as in laudatory contexts. Of two journalistic *Rosciads* by anonymous columnists which appeared in 1766, one was anti-Garrick. Two or three years later he was thought to have acted the dying King Richard too tamely, and an epigram called *Roscius Redivivus* was put into his mouth, in which he defended himself for not leaping about like a harlequin. However, he later made an effort to be physically more elastic, and comment ran thus:

> Who says that Roscius feels the hand of Time
> To blast his blooming laurels in their prime?
> With ever supple hands and pliant tongue,
> Roscius, like Hebe, will be ever young.

In this he much resembled his Roman original who, despite a lessening vocal power, remained always young in spirit: both actors were still performing towards seventy. The nastiest attack on Garrick came in 1772, when a disgruntled writer called Kenrick tried to smear him by suggesting a criminal liaison between him and Isaac Bickerstaffe ("Nyky"), a former collaborator and now a suspected homosexual who had just fled the country. Kenrick's poem was called *Love in the Suds*, "suds" at that time meaning something between "lurch" and "dumps," and the title was further explained as "being the Lamentation of Roscius for the loss of his Nyky." It was heavily undergirded by classical quotations and by the author's scholia, in which Garrick's brother is "the brother of Roscius," his house "the celebrated villa of Roscius," and so forth. Kenrick later apologized.

All these were London affairs, but the idea was spreading. Norwich, the county town of Norfolk, in 1768 acquired a royal patent for its ten-year-old theatre. The previous year some very young person published a *Roscius* on the local actors, claiming to "have made my Roscius on his sons comment." It is, as the author admits, the work of an "infant Muse." In Ireland a *Hibernian Rosciad* came out in 1765, and in Scotland a satirical *New Rosciad* in 1770. The latter, which is in Hudibrastic verse, takes advantage of the fact that the manager of Edinburgh's Theatre Royal was called David Ross. Identification was irresistible. The manager's pre-performance handouts are "Roscius' promises"; he gives foolish tips to an actress, "And Roscius tells her, by these rules,/ She'll pass upon Edina's fools." Another Edinburgh *Rosciad* appeared in 1775.

Then Garrick died, and the idea enters a third phase, lasting from 1779 to 1803, that is, until the rise of William Betty. We find the same variety of forms, and in many cases the same relationship to Churchill, but the dominating question now is – who is to succeed Garrick? And the most striking innovation is the announcement, perhaps the first of its kind in history, that the primacy of acting, the Chair of Roscius, must pass to a woman.

To speak first of the lesser wits of this period, they may be fitly represented by "Grubstreticus," who in 1780 wrote in Hudibrastic verse *A Parody on the Rosciad of Churchill*. He says he visited the theatre, apparently to see Shakespeare's *Henry VIII*, and sat in the gallery.

> I sought on high the bless'd abodes
> Of Nonsense, Noise, Love, Lice and Gods;
> And 'twixt two cook-maids stew'd in grease,
> By great good luck obtain'd a place.
> Some Tailors of unrivall'd stench,
> Sat sweating on another bench;
> And, as I listen'd to their chat,

Found this was Will, and Edward that.

These are lines, we may observe in passing, to the recitation of which the original Roscius, from his experience of Plautine prologues, would have done the richest justice. The tailors absurdly take the Earl of Surrey, in the play, to be a tailor like themselves, suing for payment of his bill, until a butcher's lad enlightens them: "That's Earl of Surry – play'd by Aiken." Grubstreticus presently passes to other actors, such as Wewitzer and Bannister, but reaches no very coherent conclusion except the then topical one of damning the French. He appends some other pieces of verse, however, one of which, dealing with a nonentity called Phillimore, momentarily reminds us of the greatest *Rosciad*:

> Roscius deceased, and Garrick likewise gone,
> Great Phillimore, the day is now thine own;
> Haste, and in triumph seize the vacant chair;
> Thine equal never yet was seated there . . . .

The feminine triumph occurs in *The New Rosciad in the Manner of Churchill*, 1785. This is in many ways the most ambitious poem of its kind, but is also the clearest, smoothest, and sanest, since 1761, though it is deficient in Churchill's rapier-work. It begins:

> Garrick deceas'd, ambition once again
> Produc'd fresh tumults in each players brain . . .
> Each pushes on to join the vacant throne,
> And each desirous is to reign alone.

Roscius' chair has now become a throne unequivocally. The tribunal idea is elaborately developed, and after some palaver with Shakespeare and Ben Jonson, in the course of which Shakespeare recalls his former verdict on Garrick, Sheridan is chosen as judge. There is a parade of actors from Covent Garden, Drury Lane, and the Haymarket, and then "Again in one, the three divisions mix'd,/ The Chair brought forward, and the standard fix'd." "Standard," of course, implies the standard of acting of the original Quintus Roscius. The semi-traditional historical survey is glossed over in a mere two lines, and then judgment begins. Some of the great names of English acting pass before us – the aged

Macklin, Kemble who "boldly claim'd the Throne, said 'twas his due," and the young Holman, here admonished by the example of an unnamed actor who "spouted forth with all the Roscian fire," but lost his head through over-eagerness. Hope, says the poet, "will weep till Holman's in the Chair." Then Bannister — "how oft he's toil'd/ To gain the vacant seat which Roscius fill'd!" The poem rises to its climax with the appearance of Sarah Siddons, probably the finest of all tragic actresses: "Here Shakespeare rose, acknowledging the Fair/ Would well supply th' important empty Chair." Predictably, murmurs of opposition arise: "the Chair to *Man* was ever giv'n." Spite and slander do their worst, but the judge delivers a decisive verdict in the now traditional form:

> 'Tis thou, great Siddons, shall possess the Chair,
> Nor quit it till thou place — an Equal there.

The final phase of the idea extends from 1804 to 1852. In this we find both some late stragglers following patterns already set, and also something again completely new. We might count as stragglers another regional work — an *Edinburgh Rosciad* written by one Logan and pertaining to the theatrical summer season in 1834 — and an anonymous *Mundus Dramaticus*, subtitled *The New Rosciad*, which appeared in 1852. Another echo of earlier practices was a magazine of theatre news and chatter published monthly in London from January to August of 1825 and called *The Roscius*.

What was entirely new was the notion of devoting a whole *Rosciad* to a single actor. The cause of this was the prodigy William Betty, who in 1803-4, as a boy in his earliest teens, took the country, and especially London, by storm. The craze, fanned by his sponsors with careful publicity, was intense but ephemeral. He seems to have been first drawn into the Tradition by a newspaper in Belfast, which said in a puff notice in 1803 that "he bids fair to rival the first tragedian of the age, and may not be unjustly styled, the Minor Roscius."[29] He soon became universally known as the Infant, or Young, Roscius, one or other of these expressions appearing on his playbills and in the titles of various short biographies written to satisfy, or inflame, public demand. From the first, however, and especially from the 1805 season, when the boy tried to repeat his former successes, he had against him two influential parties. On the one hand there were critics of real discernment, who could tell the difference between great acting based on mature understanding of a playwright's text, and Betty's charm and (admittedly remarkable) feats of memorizing, gesticulating, and declaiming. On the other hand there were the merely envious, especially those in some way connected with the theatre, who grudged him his celebrity and the fortune which accompanied it. In consequence the "rave" literature soon became tempered by a strain of admonition, pasquinade, and satire, and it is not surprising to find amongst this a new approach to the *Rosciad* idea.

In 1805, someone using the pseudonym of Peter Pangloss published the *Young Rosciad*. It is in Hudibrastic verse, and the author describes it as "an admonitory poem, well seasoned with Attic salt, *cum notis variorum*," — these last words taking us right back to the *Dunciad*. He divides his attack between Betty and his sponsors, on the one hand, led on by Fortune, Avarice, and Interest, and John Bull or the English public, on the other, who are the dupes of Fashion. "Blind leads the Blind ... Else how could Roscius gain such plauses?" The public are in fact throwing their money prodigally away, and this offends Justice and Common Sense, two powers whom Pangloss is not the first rosciadist to invoke. But there is hope:

> The Novelty is wearing off.
> Young Roscius is a new Religion,
> And Johnny Bull — 'tis *he's* the pigeon:
> He'll sicken soon of Schism, and then
> He'll soon come back to Church again.

To the theatrical and literary world the last two lines carried rich overtones of Quin and Garrick.[30] The author sums up his advice by telling Betty, before he acts, to learn to read, and in conclusion offers to become his tutor.

Betty fell from favour and quit the stage in 1808, but later made one or two attempts, which rumour multiplied, to execute a comeback. In this atmosphere there was published in 1812 one further *Rosciad*, describing itself as "a heroi-serio-comical poem," in two cantos. Its heroic couplets, in keeping with its date, are eight-tenths Pope and Churchill, one-tenth Gothic, and one-tenth Romantic.

> Roscius I sing, — not him of ancient fame,
> The mighty owner of th' applauded name;
> Nor he who still deserves Britannia's praise,
> The boasted Roscius of our fathers' days . . . .

Not Roscius nor Garrick, that is to say, but the *cher ami* of panting maids and, as we later learn, of more aged females too. The poem portrays him as very erogenous. Betty's evil genius, the matron Fashion, in the course of egging him on to attempt a return to the boards, turns aside to dwell bitterly on the lowness of public taste, which would as soon watch a circus as decent acting, and also on the execrable quality of the acting offered.

> But more than this my lab'ring soul forebodes, —
> I long to stock the stage with frogs and toads;
> With croaking concerts close a sylvan scene,
> And hold up grov'ling reptiles to be seen;
> Nor let a mimic train the crowd affront,
> *But show them nature if the actors won't.*

Amid elaborate mock-heroic machinery, with Impudence, Mimickry, and other such beings angrily demanding back what he has stolen from them, the unfortunate youth, in an addle of misgivings and pining ambition, is prodded forward. And Fashion leaves him at the green-room door.

"These motions of the mind, and these large strivings, a little handful of dust will soon lay to rest." Thus Virgil, treating of the animosities of bees.

Virgil was a child of eight when Roscius died. One spring day, some years ago, I took the country bus along the road which skirts the Alban hills, then walked by a side-road to Lanuvio. On a slope not far from some courses of prehistoric stones a dark-faced young man interrupted his seasonal work among vines and olive trees to pass the time of day, and produced from his vineyard hut a beaker of latin wine. In a narrow street near the market-place I bought something in a shop. They do not have many visitors, and the shop-girl offered to do the duty of cicerone. —*E il celebre attore Roscio?* — "I have never heard of him," she said, "but the Romans built a theatre in this town, and I will show you its ruins."

APPENDIX 1
A REGISTER OF REPUBLICAN ACTORS[1]

How extensive is the list of known republican actors? The theatrical history of the republic is a much-worked field, and one would naturally suppose that this question either was answered long since, or if not, could easily be answered now by analyzing the indexes of standard authorities on the Roman stage. But this appears not to be the case. Earlier in this century G. K. G. Henry made a deliberate count of named actors both for republican and imperial times, and published his results in a paper entitled "Roman Actors." This appeared in 1919.[2] It was more than a collection of names: it was a set of sketches and discussions, still eminently readable, and has been drawn on by several subsequent historians of the stage. But as a list it is far from satisfactory.

Henry dealt with about 75 actors all told, of whom a little under 50 belonged to the imperial epoch. He was aware that the latter figure could be increased, and probably in this part of his paper only aimed to include the more easily ascertainable or more interesting names. The literature and inscriptions of the empire contain in reality several hundred names of actors, and the figure is slowly increasing. Our present concern, however, is with the republic, and here Henry's list is more thorough. There was much for him to do, for the scholars of the previous century, for all their interest in the theatre, and zestful cataloguers though some of them were, had not given this aspect of stage history their fullest attention. Ribbeck's section on "Schauspieler" in *Die Römische Tragödie im Zeitalter der Republik* (1875), which admittedly covered only a limited field, treated no more than about eight actors, and could not have mustered even so many, but for the large-minded inclusion of Roscius, whose connection with tragedy is very slight compared to his dominant position in comedy. After conducting a new search, Henry wrote that "an examination of Latin literature brings to light some twenty actors mentioned at least by name belonging to the republican period." He did in fact find rather more than this, and if one takes the republic as extending down to 31 B.C.[3] and reckons into the count doubtful identities and anonymous performers referred to by Henry in passing, his list may be said to embrace as many as 37 actors all told. Recent standard textbooks on the Roman theatre, while perhaps not aiming to be exhaustive, are of interest as reflecting this general situation. Duckworth in his index includes about 24 republican actors, Margarete Bieber about 16, and Beare about 21.[4]

Three good tools already available in 1919 for the study of the ancient evidence were the inchoate *Realencyclopädie, CIL,* and O'Connor's *Prosopographia Histrionum Graecorum.* Today Degrassi's *ILLRP* helps with the inscriptions, O'Connor's catalogue has been supplemented by Iride Parenti, and an abundance of source-passages has been gathered together by Bonaria in his *MRF* and *RM.*[5] Furthermore, actors mentioned by Cicero have been treated in a number of separate studies, old and new.[6] There is, however, more to the question than the mere filling in of occasional gaps. We have to establish our terms of reference. Are we to include such a person, for example, as Decimus Laberius who, so far as we know, acted only once, and that by compulsion and under vehement protest? Henry does include him, as well as that Horatian pair Sarmentus and Messius Cicirrus, who are actors or ex-actors only by guess, not to speak of Dossennus (at Hor. *Epist.* 2.1.173), who is probably the stock figure from farce and should not be hypostatized into a flesh-and-blood *histrio.* There is too, as already indicated, the question of actors mentioned but not by name. In a strict prosopography it would be correct to omit them, but if the aim is to provide as useful an ancilla as possible to the study of Roman stage history, it would be better to bring them in. Such are, for example, the mime who attacked Accius and was sued for defamation, and the young female mime of Atina who about 70 B.C. found herself outside the protection of the law when (allegedly) assaulted by Cnaeus Plancius and some other youths.[7] There are also the anonymous actors whose existence is merely inferred – though pretty reliably inferred – from that of a guild (*koinon*) of Artists of Dionysus, such as the guild at Syracuse. In all doubtful or anonymous cases like these, it seems better to be inclusive than exclusive, but at the same time one needs to discriminate as clearly as possible between the known, professional actors and the others.

In trying to do this we are confronted with two problems of definition – the definition of "actor" and the definition of "republican." O'Connor, dealing with Greek actors, confined his treatment almost entirely to actors of comedy and tragedy, but it seems reasonable to include the mimes and their kind, and among these (because they cannot always be distinguished) the mimetic dancers, some of whom seem to be forerunners of pantomime, which did not reach Rome till the reign of Augustus. Despite the labours of Reich and Bonaria, it is by no means clear where to draw the line between a mime and a simple dancer, and even if we decided to draw it at, say, the point between speech and dumbshow, or the point between dramatic dancing and mere exhibition dancing, ancient allusions are in many cases too brief and vague to enable us to decide how to class a particular artist. On the other hand we should naturally want to exclude many, such as *kitharistai, kitharoidoi, auletai,* and so on, whom the Greek guilds were happy to recognize as Artists (*technitai*) of Dionysus completely on a level with fully fledged *komoidoi* and *tragoidoi*. The truth is that words like "actors" and "stagefolk" have in both ancient and modern times been vague and general rather than technical terms, and where one language does give a word some specialized use (such as *technites* in Greek), categorizations in other languages will not exactly correspond. The definition of "actor" for prosopographical purposes has therefore to be somewhat arbitrary. My own use of the term will be defined below.

"Republican," so far as time is concerned, gives one an easy lower limit of 31 B.C. The upper limit of 510 B.C. also seems obvious, but it lands us in another problem, of nationality and of geographical boundaries. If the enquiry is not to lose three-quarters of its point, all who performed in Rome must be included, whatever their place of origin. Those who may have performed in the Romanized towns of Italy, such as the mime-actress of Atina mentioned above, or the mime Protogenes whose grave was found near Amiternum in the heart of the Apennines, also form an integral part of the story. But where is the line to be drawn? What of an actor who is of Roman or Italian origin, or bears a Roman name, or acts in Latin, but performs overseas? What of Sicilians? What of actors abroad who perform in festivals held explicitly to the honour of Rome? What of actors from Magna Graecia who, although living within the republican time-span and vital to our understanding of the Roman theatre in all its forms, yet predate Roman rule in their own cities and have no personal connection with Rome? There are two interesting groups of this last kind in Athenaeus, who escape the mesh of *RE* by their obscurity and that of O'Connor through not being regular comedians or tragedians. They include Straton and Oinonas, with some others, and Kleon, Ischomachos, and Nymphodoros.[8] These still await classification in some work of reference. A more obvious test-case for my own purpose is that of Tarentum in the earlier part of the third century B.C., where it has been well observed that Drakon and Livius Andronicus belong to a single cultural history. They were in part contemporaries and shared the same background, though the former achieved his triumphs in Delphi and Delos and the latter in Rome.[9] In the twentieth century it has been increasingly realized that the history of the Greek and that of the Roman theatre are inextricably interwoven, and as far as actors are concerned, in the present state of the evidence it is once more impossible to draw other than a rather arbitrary line between them. Indeed if we were dealing with imperial times, it would be so arbitrary as to be almost meaningless. The long-term solution would be a single large prosopography of Graeco-Roman actors, or even of all Graeco-Roman stagefolk and other entertainers in general. The former might contain between one and two thousand names, the latter several thousands.

Nevertheless, since republican theatrical history, however we define it, will always have an interest of its own within the larger picture, it seems reasonable to assemble an actors' list, even if this does necessitate rule-of-thumb criteria. My own tentative procedure has been to put in capitals those who are republican actors according to a fairly strict definition, and in small letters those who, while not satisfying this definition, still have claims to consideration under it or are otherwise important to the stage-history of the period. Actor-producers and actor-managers are considered solely in their capacity as actors. *In capitals* are entered republican actors proper, that is: persons, named or anonymous, known or credibly believed to have appeared professionally in comedy, tragedy, satyr-drama, atellan, mime and mimetic dancing, together with a magode and the lysis-singers, and originating from or performing in republican Rome (510-31 B.C.) or other parts of Italy and Sicily ruled by the republic at the time in question. Also included are performers in any of the above dramatic genres in republican times who used Roman names (whatever their local associations may be), and the one or two so-called *rhomaistai*, who evidently presented some kind of Latin-language performance at certain Greek festivals. Total, 65 entries.

In small letters are entered other personages worthy of consideration alongside the strict list, i.e. persons who *may* belong to it but cannot be firmly so classified for lack of decisive evidence; anonymous members of theatrical guilds or groups, whom we cannot bring into focus as individuals; non-professionals known or believed to have appeared at least once in any of the genres stated; the two eponymous originals of Roman stagefolk, Salius and Ister; *choreutai* (as possibly dramatic) and a *chorodidaskalos*; actors in comedy or tragedy who performed specifically in honour of Rome at Greek festivals called Romaea (*Rhomaia*); a few *spurii*; and a miscellaneous group of three who, though outside the above categories, are too significant to be omitted, namely, Alexander of Laodicea (a Greek Artist of Dionysus who visited Rome under Sulla's auspices on behalf of his guild), Sempronius Tuditanus who was mad and seems to have had the delusion that he was an actor; and Jason of Tralles who acted the climax of the *Bacchae* before eastern potentates with the decapitated head of Crassus substituted for that of Pentheus. Total, 87 entries. Grand total, 152 entries.

Excluded are "actors" or "stagefolk" mentioned vaguely by ancient authors, without some sense of identity, office, or occasion; actors whose existence is wholly inferential from that of theatres or plays, or from the occurrence of *ludi scaenici*; anonymous prologue-speakers; anonymous actors in wall-paintings etc.; playwrights and other authors not known or credibly believed to have acted; stagefolk from or in parts of Italy and Sicily which were not under Roman rule at the time in question; musicians and recitalists who did not act (*tibicines, auletai, kitharistai, auloidoi, kitharoidoi,* and so forth); and such folk as conjurers, funambulists, and miscellaneous non-dramatic entertainers.

Method of Presentation

Each entry consists of a caption followed by six or seven numbered parts.

The caption gives the actor's name and function. Roman names are given in their Roman form, the Greek form usually being added if it occurs in the sources. Greek names which occur in both forms are given in both, the Roman form taking priority. Greek names occurring only in their Greek form in the sources are thus given, with the standard Latin transliteration added. By "function" is meant an actor's specialization within the profession, e.g. as an actor in tragedy or as a mime; and the evidence for this — the Latin or Greek technical term or other form of description in the sources — is given in brackets. Anonymous actors are arranged in the following order, and chronologically within each group:

(a) Anon. Actor(s) [without more precise specification].

(b) Anon. Actor(s) in tragedy.

(c) Anon. Actor(s) in comedy.

(d) Anon. Actor(s) in tragedy and/or comedy.

(e) Anon. Chorus-member(s).

(f) Anon. Mime(s) and/or mimetic dancer(s).

After the name and function, the information about each actor is arranged as follows:

(1) The century B.C., followed, where possible, by a more exact floruit or other indication of date. A hyphen between dates indicates duration. A solidus (oblique stroke) indicates the limits of uncertainty; it says nothing about duration.

(2) Place of origin and/or citizenship. Place-names are in general given in their Roman form.

(3) Place(s) where the actor is known to have performed, together with any necessary indication of circumstances.

(4) The ancient reference, and comments if necessary. If more than one reference is extant, I give the earliest one (or several in cases of doubt), followed by "etc."

(5) In the case of named actors, the reference in *RE*. "Not in *RE*" means that no separate entry for this person had appeared up to *RE* Suppl. XII (1970).

(6) References to any treatment of the actor in any of the following:

(a) Bonaria, *Fasti*

(b) Bonaria, *MRF*

(c) Bonaria, *RM*

(d) Henry

(e) O'Connor

(f) Parenti

(g) Spruit

(7) In a few cases I have added reference to further writings which help to solve problems or put the actor in his context. It did not seem necessary, however, to multiply allusions to the standard textbooks[10] or to general studies of Cicero's interest in the theatre which collect many of his remarks about individual stagefolk.[11] These are mentioned only in the most important cases.

Aesopus: see Clodius.

1 Agathodoros (**Agathodorus**).

Sub-dramatic entertainer in the Latin language(?) (*rhomaïstes*). (1) 2 cent. B.C. Fl. 172 B.C. (2) His birthplace is unknown but might well be a Latin-speaking area. (3) He is found performing on Delos.

(4) *IG* XI^2.133.81. (5) *RE* I.1 (1893) col. 747 s.v. Agathodoros 1, corrected by *RE* Suppl. I (1903) col. 23 s.v. Agathodoros 1. (6) —. (7) Hauvet-Besnault, *BCH* 7 (1883) 103 ff.; E. Capps, *TAPhA* 31 (1900) 115, 121-122; L. R. Taylor, *TAPhA* 68 (1937) 304 n. 53; Sifakis 20-21.

2 Agathokles (**Agathocles**).

Actor in comedy (*hypokrites*, context). (1) 2 cent. B.C. Fl. c. 150 B.C. (2) He was a citizen of Miletus. (3) He is found performing at Magnesia, some 27 miles away, being a winner at the Festival of Rome there.

(4) Kern 88a = Dittenberger, *Syll.*^{3} 1079. (5) *RE* Suppl. I (1903) col. 23 s.v. Agathokles 14a, cf. *RE* Suppl. X (1965) col. 6 s.v. Agathokles 14. (6) O'Connor 6.

Aisopos (**Aesopus**): see Clodius.

3 Alexandros (**Alexander**).

Lyrist and Artist of Dionysus (*kitharistes* and one of *tôn peri ton Dionuson technitôn*). (1) 1 cent. B.C. Fl. c. 81 B.C. (2) He was a citizen of Laodicea. (3) Where he performed is unknown. He was not himself an actor, but visited Rome about 81 B.C. on behalf of the Artists of Dionysus of Ionia and Hellespont and of the Pergamene Dionysus called D. Kathegemon.

(4) Inscr. originally published by M. Segre, *RFIC* 66 (1938) 253, inscr. A. (5) Not in *RE*. (6) —. (7) See p. 152 of this book; R. K. Sherk, *Historia* 15 (1966) 211-216, and *Roman Documents from the Greek East* (Baltimore 1969) 263-266 (which includes full Greek text).

4 **L. AMBIVIUS TURPIO.**

Actor in comedy (*actor, scaenicus*). (1) 2 cent. B.C. Fl. c. 185-160 B.C. and perhaps down to a little after 150. (2) He was doubtless of Roman or Italian origin but his birthplace is unknown. (3) He performed at Rome.

(4) Ter. prols. to *HT* and *Hec.*; didasc. to *HT*, etc. Cic. *De Sen.* 14.48, etc.   (5) *RE* I.2 (1894) col. 1804 s.v. Ambivius 4.   (6) Henry 337; Spruit 6, 26.   (7) Duckworth, see index; Bieber, *HGRT*² 153-154 and fig. 559; T. F. Carney, *P. Terenti Afri Hecyra* (= *PACA* Suppl. 2 [1963]) n. on didasc. (pp. 20-21) and on line 28 (p. 31); Beare 89, 164-166. Etc.

5   **AMPHIO (Amphion).**
Actor in tragedy (*tragoedus*).   (1) Probably 1 cent. B.C. Fl. probably c. 81/67 B.C.   (2) His birthplace is unknown.   (3) He apparently performed at Rome.
(4) Varro, *Sat. Men.* 367 = 369 Bolisani = Non. 55.33 Lindsay.   (5) Not in *RE*.   (6) —.   (7) C. Cichorius, *Römische Studien* (1922, repr. Darmstadt 1961) 215-216 (speculative).

Andronicus: see Livius.

6   **Anon.**
Actors? (among the Artists of Dionysus at Regium).   (1) Perhaps 3 cent. B.C.   (2) No birthplace is given for these *technitai*, but the birthplace would in many cases be Regium.   (3) The scene of their activities was Regium.
(4) *IG* XIV.615.   (5) —.   (6) —.   (7) Webster, *GB* 55.

7   **ANON.**
Actors (*histriones*).   (1) 3 cent. B.C. Fl. 207/204 B.C.   (2) Their birthplaces are unknown but they are likely to have been *peregrini*.   (3) They performed at Rome: the original actor-members of the guild founded under Livius Andronicus.
(4) Festus pp. 446-448 Lindsay.   (5) —.   (6) Spruit 54-57.   (7) E. G. Sihler, *AJPh* 26 (1905) 2-3; E. J. Jory, "Some Aspects of the Acting Profession at Rome" (unpubl. diss. London 1967) 144-158.

8   **Anon.**
Actor (*histrio*).   (1) 2 cent. B.C.? Fl. c. 200 B.C.?   (2) His birthplace is unknown.   (3) This *histrio* was probably a definite individual, performing at Rome, though the context in Plautus leaves open the possibility of a Greek, or even quite imaginary, ambience.
(4) Plaut. *Truc.* 931.   (5) —.   (6) —.   (7) W. B. Sedgwick, *CQ* 21 (1927) 88-89; P. J. Enk, *Plauti Truculentus* (Leiden 1953) 931 n.

9   **Anon.**
Actors (inferential among the Artists of Dionysus at Syracuse).   (1) 2/1 cent. B.C. The inscriptions have been dated c. 200/190 B.C. (see Webster) and also in 1 cent. B.C. (see Moretti, below).   (2) No birthplace is given for these *technitai*, but the birthplace would in many cases be Syracuse.   (3) The scene of their activities was Syracuse. Cf. Aristo (no. 51 below).

(4) *IG* XIV.12 and 13; etc. (5) —. (6) —. (7) L. Moretti, *Riv. di Fil.* 91 (1963) 38-45; Webster, *GB* 51; M. T. Manni Piraino, *Kochalos* 12 (1966) 204-206.

10   Anon.

Actors? (among *artifices* = Artists of Dionysus). (1) 2 cent. B.C. Fl. 186 B.C. (2) The *artifices* came from Greece. (3) They performed in Greece; and at Rome, in the games celebrated by M. Fulvius Nobilior.

(4) Livy 39.22.2. (5) —. (6) —. (7) H. D. Jocelyn, *Ennius* (Cambridge 1967) 16, n. 2; Webster, *HPA* 277, 279.

11   Anon.

Actors? (among *artifices* = Artists of Dionysus). (1) 2 cent. B.C. Fl. 186 B.C. (2) The *artifices* came from various parts of Asia (in the Roman sense). (3) They performed in Asia; and at Rome, in games celebrated by L. Scipio Asiagenus.

(4) Livy 39.22.10. (5) —. (6) —. (7) H. D. Jocelyn, *Ennius* (Cambridge 1967) 16, n. 2; Webster, *HPA* 277, 279.

12   Anon.

Actors (*akroamata*). (1) 2 cent. B.C. Fl. c. 170-160 B.C. (2) Their places of origin were various. (3) They performed at Rome and perhaps elsewhere, entertaining the young contemporaries of Scipio Aemilianus (but not Scipio himself).

(4) Diod. 31.26.7. (5) —. (6) —.

13   Anon.

Actors? (among *artifices* = Artists of Dionysus). (1) 2 cent. B.C. Fl. 167 B.C. (2) The *artifices* came from all parts (*ex toto orbe terrarum*). (3) They are found performing at Amphipolis in the victory show given by Aemilius Paullus.

(4) Livy 45.32.8. (5) —. (6) —. (7) Webster, *HPA* 277-278.

14   Anon.

Actors (*hypokritai*). (1) Fl. c. 2 cent. B.C., epigraphic dating. (2) Their birthplaces are not given. (3) They are found performing on the island of Paros, in the south-central Aegaean, being participants, perhaps winners, in a festival which may be the Festival of Rome.

(4) *IG*. XII.5.139. (5) —. (6) —.

15   Anon.

Actors (*scaenici artifices*). (1) 2-1 cent. B.C. Fl. c. 100 B.C. (2) Their birthplaces are unknown. (3) Each was honoured by conferment of the citizenship of one or more south Italian towns: Locri, Naples, Regium, Tarentum. Doubtless they gave performances there.

(4) Cic. *Pro Arch.* 10. (5) —. (6) —.

16 Anon.

Actors (*scaenici, explosi*). (1) 1 cent. B.C. Fl. c. 90/70 B.C. (2) Their birthplaces are not given. (3) They evidently performed at Rome, and they later rose to be *scribae*, in some cases eventually attaining equestrian status.

(4) Cic. 2 *Verr.* 3.184 (Greenwood in the Loeb edition takes *explosorum* wrongly of claqueurs). (5) —. (6) —.

17 Anon.

Actors (*in scaenam redierant ii, quos ego honoris causa de scaena decesse arbitrabar*). (1) 1 cent. B.C. Fl. c. 100-55 B.C. (2) Their birthplaces are not given. (3) They performed at Rome.

(4) Cic. *Ad Fam.* 7.1.2. (5) —. (6) —.

18 Anon.

Actors *qua* stage-vocalists? (*societas cantorum Graecorum et qui in hac sunhodo sunt*). (1) 1 cent. B.C. Fl. c. 85/55 B.C. (2) They came from Greek-speaking areas. (3) They performed at Rome, being possibly a group of expatriate *technitai*.

(4) *CIL* I^{2}2519 (cf. p. 844) = Degrassi *ILLRP* 771 = *AE* 1925 no. 127. (5) —. (6) —.

19 Anon.

Actors (*histriones*). (1) 1 cent. B.C. Fl. 76 B.C. (2) Their birthplaces are unknown. (3) They performed in Spain.

(4) Sall. *Hist.* fr. 2.70 Maurenbrecher = Macrob. *Sat.* 3.13.7. (5) —. (6) —.

20 Anon.

Actors? (among the Artists of Hilara Aphrodite at Syracuse). (1) 1 cent. B.C. Fl. 47/45 B.C. (2) The birthplace of these *technitai* is not given but may in many cases be Syracuse. (3) The scene of their activities was Syracuse.

(4) Two inscriptions in G. V. Gentil, *Arch. stor. siracus.* 7 (1961) 10 ff., reprinted with discussion by Moretti (see below). (5) —. (6) —. (7) L. Moretti, *RFIC* 91 (1963) 38-45.

21 Anon.

Actors (*scaenici artifices*; probably tragic actors — *cantata sunt quaedam . . . ex Pacuvi Armorum iudicio . . . et ex Electra Atili*). (1) 1 cent. B.C. Fl. 44 B.C. (2) Their birthplaces are unknown. (3) They performed at Rome.

(4) Suet. *Jul.* 84.2-4. (5) —. (6) —.

22 Anon.

Actors? (among the Artists of Dionysus at Naples). (1) 1 cent. B.C. Fl. 44/43 B.C. (2) Their birthplaces are not given. (3) They performed at Naples (and Rome?), and included Can(n)utius, q.v.

(4) Plut. *Brut.* 21. (5) —. (6) —. (7) Webster, *GB* 56.

23 ANON.

Actors, probably in comedy (*histriones*, context). (1) 3/2 cent. B.C. Fl. c. 205/185 B.C., in the year before the extant prologue of Plaut. *Amph.* (2) Their places of origin are unknown. (3) They performed at Rome. One of them acted Jupiter.

(4) Plaut. *Amph.* prol. 91-92. (5) —. (6) —.

24 ANON.

Actors in comedy (*grex*, context). (1) 3/2 cent. B.C. Fl. c. 205/184 B.C. (2) Their places of origin are unknown. (3) They performed at Rome, acting the *Asinaria* of Plautus.

(4) Plaut. *Asin.* prol. 3. (5) —. (6) —.

25 ANON.

Actors in comedy (*grex*, context). (1) 2 cent. B.C. Fl. 191 B.C. (2) Their places of origin are unknown. (3) They performed at Rome, in the original production of the *Pseudolus* of Plautus.

(4) Plaut. *Pseud.* 1334. (5) —. (6) —.

26 ANON.

Actor in comedy (*actor*, and context). (1) 2 cent. B.C. Fl. somewhat before 161 B.C. (2) His birthplace is unknown. (3) He performed at Rome: actor-manager of a play by Luscius Lanuvinus.

(4) Ter. *Phorm.* prol. 10. (5) —. (6) —.

27 ANON.

Actor in comedy (*komoidos*). (1) 2-1 cent. B.C. Lynched 91 B.C. (2) His place of origin was probably in Italy, but not Rome. (3) He is found performing in Picenum, perhaps at Asculum.

(4) Diod. 37.12. (5) —. (6) —.

28 ANON.

Actors in comedy (*histriones ... cum ageretur togata ... tota caterva ... cantorum ... actor*). (1) 1 cent. B.C. Fl. 57 B.C. (2) Their origin is unknown, but is likely to be Italian as they are found performing a *togata*. (3) They are found performing at Rome.

(4) Cic. *Pro Sest.* 118. (5) —. (6) —.

29 Anon.

Actor in comedy (context). (1) 1 cent. B.C. / 1 cent. A.D. Died between c. 48 B.C. and c. A.D. 15. (2) His place of origin is unknown. (3) He may have performed in Mytilene or at Rome.

(4) Crinagoras, *Anth. Pal.* 9.513. (5) —. (6) —. (7) A. S. F. Gow and D. L. Page, *The Greek Anthology: The Garland of Philip* (Cambridge 1968) 2.259.

30 Anon.

Actors in comedy (*komoidoi*). (1) Date unknown, republican period not excluded. (2) Their birthplaces are not given. (3) They were connected with Naples and Puteoli, and were either winners or in some other way recipients of honour.

(4) *IG* XIV 1114 (5) –. (6) Cf. O'Connor 563, where the plaque is (puzzlingly) taken to refer to a single actor. (7) Webster, *GB* 55.

31   ANON. son of . . . des.

Actor in tragedy (*tragoidos*). (1) 3/2 cent. B.C. Fl. towards 200 B.C. (2) He was a citizen of Syracuse. (3) He is found performing at Delphi.

(4) Inscr. at *BCH* 26 (1902) 266. (5) –. (6) O'Connor 510.

32   ANON.

Actors in tragedy and other *technitai* (*tragoidoi* etc.). (1) 2 cent. B.C. Fl. 167 B.C. (2) The birthplaces of these men are not given but may be assumed to be in the Greek world. (3) They performed in Greece; and also at Rome, taking part in the display in the Circus at the triumph of L. Anicius Gallus.

(4) Polyb. 30.22.12 = fr. 13 Dindorf = Athen. 14.615d. (5) –. (6) Bonaria, *Fasti* 218 and n.; Bonaria, *RM* pp. 174-175, no. 13.

33   Anon.

Actor in tragedy, perhaps also comedy, represented in the sculptured relief known as the "Dresdner Schauspieler." (1) The monument is probably to be dated c. 150 B.C./1 B.C. It may represent a contemporary actor but could conceivably be a copy of an original dating from 3 cent. B.C. (2) The actor's birthplace is unknown but would belong to the Greek world. (3) The same applies to the scene of his performances; he is fairly clearly a Greek *technites*, and the proposal (by Bulle) to identify him with Roscius does not seem well founded.

(4) –. (5) –, but cf. *RE* XIV.2 (1928) cols. 2082-2083 s.v. *Maske*. (6) –. (7) M. Bieber, *Das Dresdner Schauspielerrelief* (Bonn 1907); *HGRT*[2] fig. 307 and pp. 84 and 286, n. 32; T. B. L. Webster, *Monuments Illustrating Tragedy and Satyr-Play* (London 1962) 9-10, 109-110; Fleischhauer 110-111.

34   Anon.

Actor in tragedy (*tragicus*). (1) 2 cent. B.C. Fl. c. 125 B.C. (2) His birthplace is unknown. (3) He performed at Rome, if the reference in Lucilius (below) is drawn from a Roman context.

(4) Lucilius 567 Marx = 594 Warmington (*ROL* 3.184). (5) –. (6) –.

35   Anon.

Actor in tragedy (*histrio*, *agere*, context). (1) 1 cent. B.C. Fl. c. 100/91 B.C. (2) His birthplace is not given. (3) He performed at

Rome. In the passage in Cicero, Antonius is speaking, and claims to have seen this actor often. Some editors take the words as an allusion to Roscius, others to Aesopus: but it need not be to either of these.

(4) Cic. *De Orat.* 2.233, cf. Wilkins *ad loc.* (5) —. (6) —.

36 Anon.

Actor in tragedy (context). (1) 1 cent. B.C. Fl. c. 100/55 B.C. (2) His birthplace is not given. (3) He performed at Rome: the supporting actor said to have been accidentally killed by Aesopus.

(4) Plut. *Cic.* 5.3. (5) —. (6) See Henry 354.

37 Anon.

Chorus-members (*choroi, choreutai*). (1) 2 cent. B.C. Fl. 167 B.C. (2) They came from Greece. (3) They performed in Greece, but are also found performing at Rome, where they took part in the display in the Circus at the triumph of L. Anicius Gallus.

(4) Polyb. 30.22. 9-10 = fr. 13 Dindorf = Athen. 14. 615a. (5) —. (6) Bonaria, *Fasti* 218 and n.; Bonaria, *RM* 174-175, no. 13.

38 Anon.

(Mimetic?) dancers (*orchestai duo*). (1) 2 cent. B.C. Fl. 167 B.C. (2) They came from Greece. (3) They performed in Greece; but are also found performing at Rome, where they took part in the display in the Circus at the triumph of L. Anicius Gallus.

(4) Polyb. 30.22.11 = fr. 13 Dindorf = Athen. 14.615a. (5) —. (6) Bonaria, *Fasti* 218 and n.

39 Anon.

Mimes ?? (*sociorum, mimorum* — with or without the disjunctive comma). (1) 2 cent. B.C. (2) Fl. 160 B.C. (3) Their activity is at Rome, but they would be servitors rather than actors.

(4) Schol. *ad* Ter. *Hec.* 35 = prol. 2.27, *comitum*: p. 141 Schlee. (5) —. (6) Bonaria, *Fasti* 1158.

40 ANON.

Mime (*mimus*). (1) 2 cent. B.C. Fl. c. 136 B.C. (2) His birthplace is unknown. (3) He performed at Rome.

(4) *Rhet. ad Her.* 1.14.24; etc. (5) —. (6) Bonaria, *Fasti* 225 and n., 226 and n.; Bonaria, *RM* p. 176, no. 17.

41 Anon.

Mimes, at least for the nonce (slaves acting under direction of Eunus: *mimous ... epedeiknuto, di' hōn hoi douloi ... exetheatrizon*). (1) 2 cent. B.C. Fl. 135/133 B.C. (2) Their places of origin were probably various, including Sicily and Syria. (3) They performed outside the walls of a town in Sicily.

(4) Diod. 34/35.2.46. (5) —. (6) —.

42 ANON.

Mime? (*in scaena nominatim laeserat*). (1) 2 cent. B.C. Fl. c. 130/115 B.C. Warmington (*ROL* 3.15) would narrow this date to c. 117/115. (2) His birthplace is unknown. (3) He performed at Rome.

(4) *Rhet. ad Her.* 2.13.19. (5) —. (6) Bonaria, *Fasti* 226 and n., cf. Bonaria, *RM* p. 176, no. 17. (7) C. Cichorius, *Untersuchungen zu Lucilius* (Leipzig 1908, repr. Berlin 1964) 59 f.; W. Barr, *RhM* 108 (1965) 101-103.

43 Anon.

Mimes and other actors (*hoi apo skenes, mimoi, mimoidoi, mimoi gynaikes, orchestai, thymelikoi anthropoi*). (1) 2-1 cent. B.C. Fl. at various dates between c. 118 and 78 B.C. (2) Their birthplaces are not given. (3) They evidently performed at Rome: boon companions of Sulla both early and late in his life.

(4) Nicol. Damasc. *ap.* Athen. 6.261c = Jacoby *FGrH* 90.75; Plut. *Sull.* 2.2-3; 36.1-2. (5) —. (6) Bonaria, *Fasti* 237, 244, 245, 246, 248; Bonaria, *RM* p. 177, nos. 20, 25; p. 178, nos. 30, 32. (7) See pp. 141-167 of this book.

44 ANON.

Mime (*mimula*). (1) 1 cent. B.C. Fl. c. 70 B.C. (2) Her birth-place may have been Atina, near Arpinum. (3) She may have performed at Atina.

(4) Cic. *Pro. Planc.* 30-31. (5) —. (6) Bonaria, *Fasti* 298; Bonaria, *RM* p. 185, no. 64; Spruit 25.

45 Anon.

Mimes (*mimi, mimae*). (1) 1 cent. B.C. Fl. 44 B.C. (2) Their birthplaces are unknown. (3) The ordinary scene of their per-formances was presumably Rome; in the spring of 44 Mark Antony presented them with parcels of state land in Campania. Two or three such instances would be sufficient to account for Cicero's plurals.

(4) Cic. *Phil.* 2.101; see also 8.26; 10.22; 13.24; etc. (5) —. (6) Bonaria, *Fasti* 324, al.; Bonaria, *RM* p. 189, no. 88; p. 190, nos. 93 and 94.

46 ANTI(O)DEMIS.

Lysis-singer? (*Lysidos halkyonis*). (1) 2 cent. B.C. Fl. c. 150/135 B.C., rather than c. 195/185 as some have suggested. (2) She came from Paphos on the west coast of Cyprus. (3) She performed in Cyprus, and also, if hopes came true, at Rome. She is the earliest named female performer known in republican stage history, if the attribution to Antipater of Sidon is correct.

(4) Antipater of Sidon, *Anth. Pal.* 9.567; some, however, attribute this poem to Antipater of Thessalonica, Augustan period. (5) *RE*

Suppl. X (1965) col. 22 s.v. Antiodemis. (6) Bonaria, *Fasti* 222 and
n.; Bonaria, *RM* p. 175, no. 15. (7) Fleischhauer 153; Webster, *HPA*
205-206; A. S. F. Gow and D. L. Page, *Hellenistic Epigrams in the Greek
Anthology* (Cambridge 1965) 1, no. 61 and 2, pp. 82-83; see also p. 148
of this book.

47 **Antipatros (Antipater).**
Sub-dramatic entertainer in the Latin language (*rhomaïstes*)? (1) 2 cent. B.C. Fl. 173 B.C. (2) His birthplace is
unknown but might well be a Latin-speaking area. (3) He is found
performing on Delos.
(4) *IG* XI.²132.14. (5) *RE* Suppl. I (1903) col. 92 s.v. Antipatros
11a. This gives the date wrongly as 17 B.C. (6) —. (7) E. Capps,
TAPhA 31 (1900) 122.

48 **ANTIPHO (Antiphon).**
Actor in tragedy (... *in Andromacha* ...). (1) 1 cent. B.C. Fl. 54
B.C. (2) His birthplace is unknown. (3) He is found performing at Rome.
(4) Cic. *Ad Att.* 4.15.6. (5) *RE* I.2 (1894) col. 2526 s.v. Antipho
11. (6) Henry 356; O'Connor 36; Spruit 28, 32.

49 **Apollonios (Apollonius).**
Actor in tragedy (*hypokrites*, context). (1) 2 cent. B.C. Fl. c. 150
B.C. (2) His birthplace and citizenship are unknown. (3) He is
found performing at Magnesia, near Ephesus, being a winner at the
Festival of Rome there.
(4) Kern 88 a = Dittenberger, *Syll.*³1079. (5) *RE* II.1 (1895) and
RE II (1896) col. 123 s.v. Apollonios 48; emended at *RE* Suppl. X
(1965) col. 25 s.v. Apollonios 48, but "2 Jhdt. n. Chr." seems to be an
error for "2 Jhdt. v. Chr." (6) O'Connor 48.

50 **ARBUSCULA.**
Mime (*mima*). (1) 1 cent. B.C. Fl. 54 B.C. (2) Her birthplace is
unknown. (3) She is found performing at Rome.
(4) Cic. *Ad Att.* 4.15.6; etc. (5) *RE* II.1 (1895) and *RE* II (1896)
col. 421 s.v. Arbuscula; *RE* Suppl. X (1965) col. 40 s.v. Arbuscula. (6) Bonaria, *Fasti* 300 and n., 301-304, 311; Bonaria, *RM* p.
185, no. 66; Henry 379; Spruit 12, 24.

51 **ARISTO (Ariston).**
Actor in tragedy (*tragicus actor*). (1) 3 cent. B.C. Fl. 214
B.C. (2) His birthplace is not given but he seems to be a Syra-
cusan. (3) The indications are that he performed at Syracuse, and
perhaps also at Athens.
(4) Livy 24.2. (5) *RE* Suppl. I (1903) col. 135 s.v. Ariston 39b;
RE Suppl. X (1965) col. 43 s.v. Ariston 39b. (6) O'Connor 75, cf.
77. (7) Webster, *GB* 51.

52 Artemidoros (Artemidorus).
Actor in tragedy (*hypokrites*, context). (1) 1 cent. B.C. Fl. c. 100/90 B.C. (2) His birthplace is unknown. (3) He is found performing at Magnesia, near Ephesus, being winner at the Festival of Rome there.
(4) Kern 88c. (5) *RE* II.1 (1895) col. 1329 s.v. Artemidoros 18 (6) O'Connor 81.

53 C. Asinius Olympus.
(Mimetic?) dancer (*saltator*). (1) 1 cent. B.C. at earliest. Fl. after 42 B.C., perhaps in Augustan period. (2) His birthplace is unknown. (3) The indications are that he performed at Rome.
(4) *CIL* VI.10142. (5) *RE* Suppl. X (1965) col. 45 s.v. Asinius 21b. (6) Bonaria, *Fasti* 372 and n.; Bonaria, *RM* p. 191, no. 102.

54 ASKLAPIODOROS (Asclapiodorus).
Actor in tragedy (*tragaFudos*). (1) 1 cent. B.C. Fl. 100/75 B.C. (2) He was a citizen of Tarentum. (3) He is found performing at Orchomenus in Boeotia, being a winner at the Festival of the Graces there.
(4) *IG* VII.3195. (5) *RE* II.2 (1896) col. 1662 s.v. Asklapiodoros. (6) O'Connor 90. (7) P. Wuilleumier, *Tarente* (Paris 1939) 711.

55 L. ATILIUS PRAENESTINUS.
Actor in comedy (various parts of verb *agere*). (1) 2 cent. B.C. Fl. 166 B.C. and/or later. (2) He came from Praeneste. (3) He performed at Rome.
(4) Ter. didasc. to *Andr.*, *HT*, *Eun.*, *Phorm.*, *Adelph.* (5) Not in *RE*, but see *RE* II.2 (1896) col. 2076 s.v. Atilius 2. (6) Henry 341; Spruit 26.

56 Bacchis (Bakchis).
Mime? (conjectural). (1) 1 cent. B.C. Fl. 44 B.C. (2) Her birthplace is unknown. (3) She may have been booked to perform at Rome.
(4) Cic. *Ad Att.* 15.27.3, with Tyrrell and Purser *ad loc.* (5) *RE* II.2 (1896) col. 2792 s.v. Bakchis 4. (6) Bonaria, *Fasti* 319 and n.; Bonaria, *RM* p. 188, no. 86.

Bassiana: see Julia.

57 Bassilla.
Mime (*meimas*). (1) Formerly believed to be of 2 cent. B.C. (149/100 B.C.) but now accepted as of 3 cent. A.D. Fl. A.D. 200/250. (2) Her birthplace is unknown. (3) She may have performed at Aquileia in Venetia, as she was buried there.
(4) *IG* XIV.2324 and *add.* p. 704. Cf. under Julia Bassilla

infra. (5) Not in *RE*, but see *RE* Suppl. X (1965) col. 332 s.v. Iulia 559a. (6) Bonaria, *Fasti* 223 and n., cf. 224 and n., 1156 and n.; Bonaria *MRF*, 2. p. 211; Bonaria, *RM* pp. 175-176, no. 16; p. 269, no. 460; Henry 381; Spruit 87-88. (7) C. Corbato, *Dioniso* N.S. 10 (1947) 188-203; *SEG* (1957) p. 137, no. 630; Fleischhauer 120-121, 167.

Bassilla: see Julia.

58 **BURBULEIUS.**

Actor in tragedy or comedy (*histrio, scaenicus*). (1) 1 cent. B.C. Fl. c. 76 B.C. (2) His birthplace is unknown. (3) He performed at Rome. His teetering and gesticulation suggest tragedy rather than comedy.

(4) Val. Max. 9.14.5; etc. (5) *RE* III.1 (1897) col. 1060 s.v. Burbuleius 1. (6) Bonaria, *Fasti* 252 and n., 253; Bonaria, *RM* p. 179, no. 35; Spruit 28. (7) See p. 157 of this book.

59 **Caesennius Lento (Kaisennios Lenton).**

Actor (once) in tragedy? (*egit tragoediam*). (1) 1 cent. B.C. Fl. c. 50-43 B.C. (2) He probably came from Etruria. (3) His performance, if any, was at Rome.

(4) Cic. *Phil.* 11.13; etc. (5) *RE* III.1 (1897) col. 1307 s.v. Caesennius 6; cf. *RE* XVII.1 (1936) cols. 1238-1239 s.v. Nucula 1. (6) See Bonaria, *Fasti* 331; cf. Bonaria, *RM* p. 189, no. 92; Spruit 23. (7) Broughton, *MRR* 2. 540.

60 **L. Calpurnius Piso Caesoninus.**

(1) 1 cent. B.C. Consul 58 B.C. (2) His birthplace may have been Rome. (3) He probably performed, if at all, at Rome. Although Cicero's words at *De Prov. Cons.* 14 are most likely metaphorical, there *may* have been some stage-acting in Piso's past.

(4) Cic. *De Prov. Cons.* 14. (5) *RE* III.1 (1897) cols. 1387-1390 s.v. Calpurnius 90. (6) Bonaria, *Fasti* 289, 294, 295; Bonaria, *RM* p. 183, no. 58; p. 184, no. 61. (7) Broughton, *MRR* 2. 541-542.

61 **Can(n)utius (Kanoutios,-tias, Kannoutios,-tias).**

Actor? (one of the Artists of Dionysus). (1) 1 cent. B.C. Fl. 44/43 B.C. (2) He was of Greek origin, despite his Roman gentile name. (3) He performed at Naples (and Rome?). Plutarch's terminology suggests that he was an actor in comedy or tragedy, unless he is to be considered as a recitalist.

(4) Plut. *Brut.* 21. (5) *RE* III.2 (1899) col. 1485 s.v. Cannutius 1. (6) O'Connor 286.

62 **Cassius.**

Actor in comedy?? (*agentibus*). (1) 2 cent. B.C.? Fl. 161 B.C. or later. (2) His birthplace is unknown. (3) He performed, if at all, at Rome. His name appears in the mss. of Donatus, which read (apart from misspellings) *agentibus L. Cassio Atilio et L. Ambiuio.* Wessner followed

Wilmanns in deleting *Cassio*. As in other such instances, the inserted name could be that of a later actor-manager, though in this case it could also have come from a marginal adscript giving e.g. the name of some magistrate of the period.

(4) Donat. *ad* Ter. *Phorm.* praef. 6 = 2.346 Wessner. (5) Not in *RE*. (6) —.

63 CATIENUS.

Actor in tragedy (*actor, cantator*). (1) 1 cent. B.C. Fl. perhaps before 56 B.C. (2) His birthplace is unknown, but his name is of a type frequent among the Aequi, Vestini, and Sabines, and in Umbria and Picenum. (3) He doubtless performed at Rome.

(4) Hor. *Sat.* 2.3.61; cf. Cic. *Pro Sest.* 126; etc. (5) *RE* III.2 (1899) col. 1788 s.v. Catienus 1. (6) Henry 334, 360; Spruit 86, n. 53.

64 Charias (Charia).

Actor in tragedy (*hypokrites*, context). (1) 1 cent. B.C. Fl. soon after 86 B.C. (2) He was a citizen of Athens. (3) He is found performing at Oropus, on the Boeotian border with Attica, being a winner in the Festival of Amphiaraus and Rome there.

(4) *IG* VII 416. (5) *RE* III.2 (1899) col. 2132 s.v. Charias 6. (6) O'Connor 505.

Cicirrus: see Messius.

65 CIMBER.

Actor in tragedy (context). (1) 1 cent. B.C. Fl. c. 88 B.C. (2) His ultimate origin was probably Cimbric. (3) He performed at Rome.

(4) *Rhet. ad Her.* 3.21.34. (5) Not in *RE*, but see *RE* VI.A.1 (1936) col. 1038 s.v. Tillius 5.

66 CINCIUS FALISCUS.

Actor in comedy (*egisse comoediam*). (1) Middle of 2 cent. B.C.? (2) He came presumably from Falerii in Etruria. (3) He performed at Rome.

(4) *Excerpta de Com.* 6.3 in Donatus 1.26 Wessner. (5) *RE* III.2 (1899) col. 2557 s.v. Cincius 7. (6) Henry 342; Spruit 26. (7) See R. Syme, *Historia* 13 (1964) 114.

67 CLODIUS AESOPUS (Aisopos).

Actor in tragedy (*actor, agere, artifex, comicus, histrio, ludicra ars, tragicus, tragoedus, tragoidos*). (1) 2-1 cent. B.C. Fl. c. 100-55 B.C. (2) His birthplace is unknown. (3) He performed at Rome.

(4) *Rhet. ad Her.* 3.21.34; etc. (5) *RE* IV.1 (1900) col. 67 s.v. Clodius 16. (6) Bonaria, *Fasti* 528 and n., 1032; Bonaria, *RM* p. 202, no. 155 and p. 252, no. 387; Henry 352-355; O'Connor 18, cf. 17 and 383; Spruit 28, 32-33, 132. (7) F. W. Wright, *Cicero and the Theater*,

Smith Coll. Class. Stud. no. 11 (1931) 10-13. Duckworth 70, 74; Bieber, *HGRT*² 164; Beare 166, 371.

Copiola: see Galeria.

68   **L. Crassicius Pasicles or Pansa.**
Actor? (*circa scaenam versatus est*). (1) 1 cent. B.C. Fl. c. 50-30 B.C. (2) He was born at Tarentum. (3) He may have performed at Tarentum and Rome, but it is not certain that he went on the stage at all.
(4) Suet. *De Gramm.* 18; etc. (5) *RE* IV.2 (1901) col. 1681 s.v. Crassicius 2. (6) Bonaria, *Fasti* 357 and n.; Bonaria, *RM* p. 178, no. 29.

69   **Critonia (Kritonia? Kritonias?).**
Actress or actor in paratragic mime, or actor in tragedy; but perhaps a Varronian fiction (context). (1) 1 cent. B.C. Fl. probably c. 81/67 B.C. (2) Critonia's place of origin is unknown. The name is prima facie Roman, being the feminine form of the gentile name Critonius; if a Greek masculine, it seems otherwise unattested. (3) Critonia apparently performed at Rome.
(4) Varro, *Sat. Men.* 570 = Porph. ad Hor. *Sat.* 1.8.48. (5) Not in *RE*. (6) —. (7) C. Cichorius, *Römische Studien* (Leipzig 1922, repr. Darmstadt 1961) 216-218 (speculative).

70   **CYTHERIS (Kytheris).**
Also called Volumnia after her *patronus* Volumnius, and Lycoris (Lykoris, pseudonym). Mime (*mima*). (1) 1 cent. B.C.; she was born about 64 B.C. and was a figure of public note from 49 (at age 15) or earlier, until 37 B.C. or later. (2) She may have been born in Narbonese Gaul (see reference to Baca below). (3) She performed at Rome and perhaps elsewhere.
(4) Cic. *Phil.* 2.20; etc. (5) *RE* IX.A.1 (1961) cols. 883-884 s.v. Volumnius 17. (6) Bonaria, *Fasti* 304, 317, 393-418 and nn.; Bonaria, *RM* pp. 185-186, no. 70; p. 187, nos. 80-81; p. 188, no. 83; p. 190, nos. 94, 96; p. 191, no. 101; p. 192, nos. 107-108; Henry 397; Spruit 12, 22-24, 29, 89. (7) A. B. Baca, *CW* 60 (Oct. 1966) 49-51; S. Treggiari, *CW* 64 (Feb. 1971) 196-198.

71   **DEMETRIOS (Demetrius).**
Actor in tragedy or comedy (context). (1) 1 cent. B.C. Fl. c. 97/75 B.C. (2) His birthplace is unknown, but may have been Rome or some other Latin-speaking area. He is described as *Rhomaios*. (3) He is found performing at Argos.
(4) Inscr. at G. Vollgraf, *Mnemos.* 47 (1919) 252, A.5. (5) *RE* Suppl. X (1965) col. 136 s.v. Demetrios 32 f. (6) Parenti 128a, and see 562a. On the term *Rhomaios* see A. J. N. Wilson, *Emigration from Italy in the Republican Age of Rome* (New York and Manchester 1966) 99-121.

72 M. Demetrius (Demetrios).
Actor, and esp. mime? (*actor fabularum, dramatopoeos, histrio, modulator*, and worked *in schola mimarum*). (1) 1 cent. B.C. Fl. c. 35 B.C. (2) His birthplace is unknown: the idea of Comm. Cruq. that he was a Rhodian seems based on a confusion. (3) He performed at Rome.
(4) Hor. *Sat.* 1.10.18, 79, 90 with comments by Porph., Pseudo-Acr., and esp. Comm. Cruq. (5) *RE* IV.2 (1901) col. 2803 s.v. Demetrios 55. (6) See Bonaria, *Fasti* 383, 384 and n., 385.

73 DIONYSIA.
Mime or mimetic dancer (*gesticularia, saltatricula*). (1) 1 cent. B.C. Fl. c. 76-62 B.C. (2) Her birthplace is unknown. (3) She performed at Rome.
(4) Cic. *Pro Rosc. Com.* 23; etc. (5) *RE* V.1 (1903) col. 881 s.v. Dionysia 2. (6) Bonaria, *Fasti* 251, 275 and n.; Bonaria, *RM* p. 179, no. 34 and p. 181, no. 47; Henry 379, Spruit 17, 33.

74 DIPHILUS (Diphilos).
Actor in tragedy (*tragoedus*). (1) 1 cent. B.C. Fl. 59 B.C. (2) His birthplace is unknown. (3) He is found performing at Rome.
(4) Cic. *Ad Att.* 2.19.3; etc. (5) *RE* V.1 (1903) col. 1152 s.v. Diphilos 10. (6) Henry 356, where the date is wrongly given as 56 B.C.; Spruit 27.

75 DOROTHEOS (Dorotheus).
Actor in satyr-play (*hypokrites*, context). (1) 1 cent. B.C. Fl. 100/75 B.C. (2) He was a citizen of Tarentum. (3) He is found performing at Argos; also at Orchomenus in Boeotia, being a winner at the Festival of the Graces there.
(4) *IG* VII.3197.27. (5) *RE* V.2 (1905) col. 1570 s.v. Dorotheos 10; *RE* Suppl. X (1965) col. 180 s.v. Dorotheos 10. (6) O'Connor 163; Parenti 163. (7) P. Wuilleumier, *Tarente* (Paris 1939) 713.

76 Dossennus.
Sometimes wrongly described as an actor in comedy of the later 1 cent. B.C., on the strength of Horace as cited below. The allusion there is doubtless to the stock figure of farce (though Dossennus as a genuine personal name has recently been traced back to the 4 cent. B.C.).
(4) Hor. *Epist.* 2.1.173; etc. (5) See *RE* V.2 (1905) cols. 1609-1610 s.v. Dossennus. (6) Henry 361. (7) P. Zancani Montuoro, "Dossenno a Poseidonia," *ASMG* N.S. 2 (1958) 79-94.

77 DRAKON (Draco).
Actor in tragedy (*tragoidos*). (1) 3 cent. B.C. Fl. 280-271 B.C. (2) He was a citizen of Tarentum. (3) He is found performing at Delphi and Delos.

(4) Inscr. at H. Collitz and F. Bechtel, *Sammlung der griechischen Dialekt-Inschriften*, 3.2 (1905) 2564, line 50.   (5) *RE* V.2 (1905) col. 1662, s.v. Drakon 12; *RE* Suppl. X (1965) col. 180 s.v. Drakon 12.   (6) O'Connor 162.   (7) T. B. L. Webster, *Greek Theatre Production*[2] (London 1970) 97, 143, 146, 170.

78   Ecloga (Ekloge).

Mime (*mima*).   (1) 1 cent. B.C./1 cent. A.D. Her life falls somewhere between about 43 B.C. and A.D. 30, but she died at eighteen.   (2) Her birthplace is unknown.   (3) She may have performed in North Africa, Spain, or Rome, and seems to have been buried at Rome.

(4) *CIL* VI 10110, post-republican.   (5) *RE* Suppl. X (1965) col. 183 s.v. Ecloga 2.   (6) Bonaria, *Fasti* 364 and n.; Bonaria *RM* p. 190, no. 97; Spruit 12.

Eiranos: see Iranos.

79   Emphasis.

Mime? (the only evidence is that of her name).   (1) 1 cent. B.C.? Fl. c. 50 B.C.?   (2) Her birthplace is unknown.   (3) She may have performed at Rome.

(4) *CIL* I.[2]1359 = Degrassi, *ILLRP* 386, cf. fasc. 2, *add.* p. 385, no. 386, and p. 440.   (5) Not in *RE*, but see *RE* XXI.1 (1951) col. 18 s.v. Plautius 23 fin.   (7) C. Garton, *CR* N.S. 14 (1964) 238-239, but read now *filio*(?) instead of *patrono*.

80   Epinikos (Epinicus).

Actor in tragedy (*tragoidos*).   (1) 1 cent. B.C. Fl. soon after 86 B.C.   (2) He was a citizen of Athens.   (3) He is found performing at Oropus, on the Boeotian frontier with Attica, participating as *tragoidos* in the Festival of Amphiaraus and Rome there.

(4) *IG* VII 416.   (5) *RE* VI.1 (1907) col. 184 s.v. Epinikos 2.   (6) O'Connor 172.

81   EROS.

Actor in comedy (*comoedus*, *histrio*).   (1) 1 cent. B.C. Fl. c. 80/77 B.C.   (2) His birthplace is unknown.   (3) He performed at Rome.

(4) Cic. *Pro Rosc. Com.* 30-31.   (5) *RE* VI.1 (1907) col. 542 s.v. Eros 4.   (6) Henry 350; Spruit 26.

82   Euarchos (Evarchus).

Actor in comedy (*hypokrites . . . komoidias*; *komaFudos*).   (1) 1 cent. B.C. Fl. 100/75 B.C.   (2) He was a citizen of Coronea, most probably that in Boeotia.   (3) He is found performing at Orchomenus and Thespiae in Boeotia, and at Oropus on the Boeotian frontier with Attica. At Oropus he was a winner in the Festival of Amphiaraus and Rome.

(4) *IG* VII 417; 1760; 3195. (5) *RE* VI.1 (1907) col. 848 s.v. Euarchos 4. (6) O'Connor 186.

83 **EUCHARIS.**
Mime or (mimetic?) dancer (*ludos decoravi choro . . . Graeca in scaena*). (1) 1 cent. B.C. Fl. probably c. 80/40 B.C. Some would exclude the years before 60 B.C. and some (erroneously) give 1 or 2 cent. A.D. Eucharis died at fourteen. (2) Her birthplace is unknown but she was doubtless of Greek descent. (3) She performed at Rome.
(4) *CIL* VI 10096 = Degrassi, *ILLRP* 803. (5) *RE* XIII (1926) col. 499 s.v. Licinia 193; *RE* XV (1932) col. 1753 s.v. mimos; *RE* Suppl. X (1965) col. 188 s.v. Eucharis. (6) Bonaria, *Fasti* 282 and n.; Bonaria, *RM* p. 182, no. 52; Henry 380; Spruit 12. (7) See pp. 147 and 162 of this book.

Faliscus: see Cincius.

Focaeus: see Fufius.

84 **FUFIUS PHOCAEUS or FOCAEUS (Phokaios).**
Actor in tragedy (*tragoediarum actor*). (1) Probably 1 cent. B.C. Fl. before 56 B.C.? (2) He came from Phocaea, or perhaps from its colony Massilia. (3) He performed at Rome.
(4) Hor. *Sat.* 2.3.61, cf. Cic. *Pro Sest.* 126; etc. (5) *RE* VII.1 (1910) col. 203 s.v. Fufius 2. (6) Henry 360; Spruit 86, n. 53.

85 **GALERIA COPIOLA.**
Mime (*emboliaria*). (1) 1 cent. B.C.-1 cent. A.D. She was born about 93 B.C. and died in A.D. 9. (2) Her birthplace is unknown. (3) She performed at Rome.
(4) Plin. *NH* 7.158 (5) *RE* VII.1. (1910) col. 597 s.v. Galeria 1. (6) Bonaria, *Fasti* 247 and n., 293, 472; Bonaria, *RM* p. 178, no. 31; p. 184, no. 60; p. 203, no. 156, and cf. p. 218, no. 241; Spruit 12. (7) See p. 147 and p. 162 of this book.

Gallus: see Herennius.

Gallus: see Roscius.

86 **Glaukias (Glaucias).**
Actor in tragedy (*hypokrites*, context). (1) 1 cent. B.C. Fl. soon after 86 B.C. (2) He was a citizen of Thebes. (3) He is found performing at Oropus, on the Boeotian frontier with Attica, being a winner at the Festival of Amphiaraus and Rome there.
(4) *IG* VII.419; etc. (5) *RE* VII.1 (1910) col. 1398 s.v. Glaukias 5. (6) O'Connor 108; Parenti 108.

Hatilius: see Atilius.

87 **Herakleides (Heraclides).**
Mime (*biologos phos*). (1) Formerly believed to be of 2 cent. B.C.

(149/100 B.C.) but now accepted as of 3 cent. A.D. Fl. A.D. 200/250. (2) His birthplace is unknown. (3) He probably performed at Aquileia in Venetia, where he erected the memorial stone to Bassilla, q.v.

(4) *IG* XIV.2342 and *add.* p. 704. (5) Not in *RE.* (6) Bonaria, *Fasti* 223 and n.; Bonaria, *RM* pp. 175-176, no. 16, cf. p. 269, no. 460. (7) C. Corbato, *Dioniso* N.S. 10 (1947) 188-203; Fleischhauer 120-121, cf. p. 167; cf. *SEG* 14 (1957) p. 137, no. 630.

88   Herakleitos (Heraclitus).
Dramatic dancer? (*choreutes*). (1) 3 cent. B.C. Fl. 257 B.C. (2) He came from Tarentum. (3) He is found performing at Delphi.

(4) Inscr. at H. Collitz and F. Bechtel, *Sammlung der griechischen Dialekt-Inschriften* 3.2 (1905) 2566, line 46. (5) Not in *RE.* (6) —. (7) P. Wuilleumier, *Tarente* (Paris 1939) 715.

89   Herakleitos (Heraclitus).
Actor in tragedy (*hypokrites*, context). (1) 2 cent. B.C. Fl. c. 150 B.C. (2) He was a citizen of Malloea, in northern Thessaly. (3) He is found performing at Magnesia, near Ephesus, being a winner in the Festival of Rome there.

(4) Kern 88b = Dittenberger, *Syll.*³ 1079. (5) *RE* Suppl. X (1965) col. 321 s.v. Herakleitos 22. (6) O'Connor 219.

90   HERENNIUS GALLUS.
Actor in *praetexta?* — doubtless also in tragedy or comedy (*histrio*). (1) 1 cent. B.C. Fl. 43 B.C. (2) His birthplace is unknown. (3) He is found performing at Gades in Spain.

(4) Cic. *Ad Fam.* 10.32.2; etc. (5) *RE* VIII.1 (1912) col. 667 s.v. Herennius 27. (6) Henry 359; Spruit 47.

91   Hierokles (Hierocles).
Actor in comedy (*hypokrites*, context). (1) 1 cent. B.C. Fl. c. 100/90 B.C. (2) He was a citizen of Tralles, near Ephesus. (3) He is found performing at Magnesia, in the same area, being a winner at the Festival of Rome there.

(4) Kern 88d. (5) *RE* Suppl. X (1965), col. 322 s.v. Hierokles 23. (6) O'Connor 250.

Hilarus: see Ofilius.

92   HIPPIAS.
Mime (*mimos*). (1) 1 cent. B.C. Fl. 47 B.C. (2) His birthplace is unknown. (3) He performed at Rome.

(4) Cic. *Phil.* 2.62-63; etc. (5) *RE* VIII.2 (1913) cols. 1705-1706 s.v. Hippias 10. (6) Bonaria, *Fasti* 312 and n., 317; Bonaria, *RM* p. 186, no. 73; p. 188, no. 83; Spruit 23, 28.

Hister: see Ister.

Iallia: see Julia.

Ioulia: see Julia.

Iulia: see Julia.

Iason: see Jason.

93   Iranos (Eiranos, Iranus).
        Actor in comedy and tragedy (*komoidos, tragoidos*). (1) 1 cent.
B.C. Fl. c. 100/50 B.C.   (2) He was a citizen of Tanagra in Boeotia.
(3) He is found performing in his home town of Tanagra; and at
Oropus, some thirteen miles away on the Boeotian frontier with Attica,
participating as *komoidos* at the Festival of Amphiaraus and Rome
there. He performed, too, as a "herald" at the small place called
Acraephia, again in Boeotia, a little over twenty miles west and north of
his home.
        (4) *IG* VII 416; etc.   (5) *RE* Suppl. X (1965) col. 183 s.v.
Eiranos.   (6) O'Connor 261; Parenti 261.

94   ISIDORUS (Isidoros).
        Mime (*mimus*).   (1) 1 cent. B.C. Fl. 80/70 B.C.   (2) He was
probably a Sicilian by birth.   (3) He performed in Sicily.
        (4) Cic. 2 *Verr.* 3.78; etc.   (5) *RE* IX.2 (1916) col. 2060 s.v.
Isidoros 5.   (6) Bonaria, *Fasti* 254, 256, 257 and n.; Bonaria, *RM* p.
179, no. 36; Spruit 24, 28.

95   Ister (Hister, Istros).
        Actor (*epi skenen, technites*).   (1) 4 cent. B.C. Fl. 364
B.C.   (2) He came from Etruria.   (3) He performed in Etruria and at
Rome, and is the eponymous original of *histriones*.
        (4) Plut. *Quaest. Rom.* 107, cf. Val. Max. 2.4.4; etc.   (5) Not in
RE.   (6) Bonaria, *Fasti* 199 and n., cf. 196 and n.; Bonaria, *RM* p. 169,
no. 1; Spruit 7.   (7) B. Zucchelli, *Le denominazioni latine dell' attore*
= Stud. gram. e linguist. 4 (Brescia 1964) 29-48.

Istros: see Ister.

96   Jason (Iason).
        Actor in tragedy (*tragoidion hypokrites, tragoidos*).   (1) 1 cent.
B.C. Fl. 53 B.C.   (2) He was a citizen of Tralles, near Ephesus.
(3) He is found performing in Armenia.
        (4) Plut. *Crass.* 33; etc.   (5) *RE* Suppl. X (1965) col. 328 s.v.
Iason 12b; cf. *RE* XVIII.1 (1939) col. 1138 s.v. Orodes 1.   (6)
O'Connor 247.   (7) Sifakis 120; see also pp. 38-39 of this book.

97   Julia Bassilla.
        Names formerly read as Iallia and Bassiana. Possibly a mime.
(1) It is uncertain when she lived. 2 cent. B.C. (149/100 B.C.) has been

suggested, but 2 cent. A.D. is more probable. (2) Her birthplace is unknown. (3) She was held in honour at Tauromenium in north-east Sicily, and may have performed also at Rome. Bonaria in *MRF* implausibly sought to identify her with Bassilla, *supra*.

(4) *IG* XIV 1091 = Gruter, *Inscr.* III 1095, 5. (5) *RE* Suppl. X (1965) col. 332 s.v. Iulia 559a. (6) Bonaria, *Fasti* 224 and n.; Bonaria, *MRF* 2. p. 211; cf. Bonaria, *RM* p. 175, no. 16; cf. Spruit 87.

Kaisennios: see Caesennius.

98 Kallistratos (Callistratus).

Actor in comedy (*hypokrites*, context). (1) 1 cent. B.C. Fl. c. 100/75 B.C. (2) He was a citizen of Thebes. (3) He is found performing at Oropus, on the Boeotian frontier with Attica, being a winner in the Festival of Amphiaraus and Rome there; also in two festivals at Orchomenus.

(4) *IG* VII 419; etc. (5) *RE* X.2 (1919) col. 1737 s.v. Kallistratos 28; *RE* Suppl. X (1965) col. 346 s.v. Kallistratos 28. (6) O'Connor 283.

Kan(n)outias: see Can(n)utius.

Kan(n)outios: see Can(n)utius.

Kritonia, Kritonias: see Critonia.

Kytheris: see Cytheris.

99 D. Laberius.

Acted in mime on one occasion (*domum revertar mimus*). (1) 1 cent. B.C. He was born about 106 B.C. and died in the winter of 44/43 B.C. (2) He was probably born in or near Rome, perhaps at Lanuvium, where other members of his gens are found. (3) His constrained performance was at Rome.

(4) Cic. *Ad Fam.* 7.11.2; etc. (5) *RE* XII.1 (1924) cols. 246-248 s.v. Laberius 3; *RE* Suppl. X (1965) col. 357 s.v. Laberius 3. (6) Bonaria, *MRF* 1. pp. 9-103; *Fasti* 338-354 and nn., 469; Bonaria, *RM* pp. 5-9, 38-77, 103-130, 147-155; p. 183, no. 55; p. 185, no. 68; p. 186, no. 76; p. 187, nos. 78-79; p. 189, nos. 90-91; p. 193, no. 112; Henry 357; Spruit 39, 44-47, 143. (7) F. Giancotti, *Mimo e Gnome* (Florence 1967).

Lanuvinus: see Luscius.

Lento (Lenton): see Caesennius.

100 Leonteus.

Actor in tragedy (*tragoidos*). (1) 1 cent. B.C. or later. Fl. probably after 35 B.C. (2) He was a citizen of Argos. (3) It is not known where he performed. He may at some time have been in Rome as Iuba spent a period there.

(4) Amarantus and Iuba at Athen. 8.343e-f.   (5) *RE* XII.2 (1925)
col. 2040 s.v. Leonteus 4.   (6) O'Connor 313.

101 LEPOS.

Mime (*archimimus*).   (1) 1 cent. B.C. Fl. 45/30 B.C.   (2) His
birthplace is unknown.   (3) He performed at Rome.
   (4) Hor. *Sat.* 2.6.72; etc.   (5) *RE* XII.2 (1925) col. 2069 s.v.
Lepos.   (6) Bonaria, *Fasti* 390-392 and n.; Bonaria, *RM* p. 193, no.
117; Henry 361.

Leukios: see Lucius.

(Licinia) Eucharis: see Eucharis.

102 L. LIVIUS ANDRONICUS (Andronikos).

Actor, probably in both comedy and tragedy (*agere, suorum
carminum actor*).   (1) 3 cent. B.C. He was born perhaps about 284
B.C. (but the date is very uncertain) and died about 204.   (2) He came
from Tarentum.   (3) He performed at Rome, and perhaps before that
as a *technites* at Tarentum.
   (4) Cic. *Brut.* 71; etc. For the testimonia see A. Klotz, *Tragicorum
Fragmenta* (Munich 1953) 19-22.   (5) *RE* Suppl. V (1931) cols.
598-607 s.v. Livius 10a.   (6) Bonaria, *Fasti* 1161; Henry 334; Spruit 4,
5, 7, 8, 40, 54-57.   (7) F. Leo, *Geschichte der römischen Literatur* 1
(Berlin 1913) 71 f.; E. Fraenkel, *Plautinisches im Plautus* (Berlin 1922)
323 ff. = *Elementi Plautini in Plauto* (Florence 1960) 339 ff.; W. Beare,
Hermathena 54 (1939) 30-51, and *The Roman Stage*[3] (1964) 26-32 and
see index; Duckworth, see index; H. B. Mattingly, *CQ* N.S. 7 (1957)
159-163; T. B. L. Webster, *Greek Theatre Production* (London 1956)
97, and *GB* 57; Bieber, *HGRT,*[2] see index.

103 LUCCEIA.

Mime (*mima*).   (1) 1 cent. B.C., perhaps living on into following
century.   (2) Her birthplace is unknown.   (3) It may be assumed that
she performed at Rome.
   (4) Plin. *NH* 7.158.   (5) *RE* XIII.2 (1927) col. 1562 s.v. Lucceia
20.   (6) Bonaria, *Fasti* 1161; Bonaria, *RM* p. 218, no. 238; Spruit 12.

104 Lucius (Leukios).

Chorodidaskalos in tragedy.   (1) 1 cent. B.C. Fl. 97/75
B.C.   (2) His birthplace is unknown.   (3) He is found performing at
Argos.
   (4) G. Vollgraf, *Mnemos.* 47 (1919) 253, line 27.   (5) *RE* XII.2
(1925) col. 2263 s.v. Leukios 3.   (6) Parenti 318a.

105 Luscius Lanuvinus.

There is no ancient evidence for or against the modern suggestion
(see refs. to Beare and Carney below) that he may at some time have
been an actor, except that one of his own plays is known to have had an

actor-producer other than himself (Ter. *Phorm.* prol. 10). (1) Luscius lived in 3-2 cent. B.C. and was elderly by 166-160 B.C. (2) He was born in, or his family originated from, Lanuvium. (3) The scene of his activities was Rome.

(4) Ter. *Andr.* prol. 1-7, with Donatus *ad loc.* = 1.41 Wessner. (5) *RE* Suppl. VII (1940) cols. 419-420 s.v. Luscius 1a. (6) −. (7) Beare 114; T. F. Carney, *P. Terenti Afri Hecyra* (= *PACA* Suppl. 2 [1963]) p. 34. See pp. 41-139 of this book.

Lycoris (Lykoris): see Cytheris.

106 T. MACCIUS PLAUTUS.

Actor in comedy? mime? atellan? (*in operis artificum scaenicorum*; Plautus, *plotus, planipes*; *Maccus*, Maccius). (1) 3-2 cent. B.C. He was born about 254 B.C. and died in 184 B.C. (2) He was born at Sarsina in Umbria. (3) He performed in Rome, perhaps also in some Italiot-Greek city in association with *technitai*.

(4) Plaut. *Asin.* prol. 11; *Menaech.* prol. 3; etc. (5) *RE* XIV.1 (1928) cols. 95-126 s.v. Maccius. (6) Spruit 5, 56-57, 119. (7) F. Leo, *Plautinische Forschungen*² (Berlin 1912, repr. Darmstadt 1966) 63-86; Duckworth 49-51, 73, 380; Bieber, *HGRT*² 150-151; E. Paratore, *Plauto* (Florence 1961) 11 ff.; Beare, esp. 45-69. Etc.

107 Menodotos (Menodotus).

Actor in comedy (*hypokrites*, context). (1) 2 cent. B.C. Fl. c. 150 B.C. (2) He was a citizen of Pergamum. (3) He is found performing at Magnesia, a little over 90 miles to the south, being a winner in the Festival of Rome there.

(4) Kern 88b = Dittenberger, *Syll.*³1079. (5) *RE* XV.1 (1931) col. 916 s.v. Monodotos 4. (6) O'Connor 335.

108 MENOGENES.

Actor (*histrio, scaenicus*). (1) 1 cent. B.C. Fl. c. 61 B.C. (2) His birthplace is unknown. (3) It may be assumed that he performed at Rome.

(4) Val. Max. 9.14.5; etc. (5) *RE* XV.1 (1931) col. 917 s.v. Menogenes 2. (6) Bonaria, *Fasti* 220 and n., 221; Bonaria, *RM* p. 175, no. 114.

109 Messius Cicirrus.

Some have conjectured that he came from the stage; this is plausible, but there is no direct evidence for it. Cf. Sarmentus. (1) 1 cent. B.C. Fl. c. 38 B.C. (2) He apparently came from Oscan territory (Samnium or Campania). (3) He is encountered at Caudium.

(4) Hor. *Sat.* 1.5.52 ff.; etc. (5) *RE* XV.1 (1931) col. 1244 s.v. Messius 6. (6) Henry 377; cf. Bonaria, *Fasti* 381, and Bonaria, *RM* p. 192, no. 110. (7) A. La Penna, *Maia* N.S. 19 (1967) 154-158.

110 METROBIOS (Metrobius).

Lysis-singer (*lysioidos*). (1) 1 cent. B.C. Fl. c. 90-80 B.C. (2) His birthplace is unknown. (3) He apparently performed at Rome.

(4) Plut. *Sull.* 2.4; etc. (5) *RE* XV.2 (1932) col. 1474 s.v. Metrobios 1. (6) Bonaria, *Fasti*, 245, 248; Bonaria, *RM* p. 178, nos. 30, 32; Spruit 63. (7) See pp. 148, 160 f. and n. 67 in this book.

111 Metrodoros (Metrodorus).

(Mimetic?) dancer (*orchestes*). (1) 1 cent. B.C. Fl. c. 41 B.C. (2) His birthplace is unknown. (3) It is not known where he performed.

(4) Plut. *Ant.* 24. (5) *RE* XV.2 (1932) col. 1474 s.v. Metrodoros 5. (6) Bonaria, *Fasti* 374 and n.; Bonaria, *RM* p. 191, no. 103.

112 L. MINUCIUS PROT(H)YMUS (Prothymos).

Actor in comedy and tragedy (*agentibus*, sc. *Eunuchum*; *egisse tragoediam*). (1) 2 cent. B.C. Fl. 161-160 B.C. and/or later in the century. (2) His birthplace is unknown. (3) He performed at Rome.

(4) Ter. *Adelph.* didasc. (name absent in codex Bembinus); etc. (5) *RE* XV.2 (1932) col. 1956 s.v. Minucius 46. (6) Henry 342; Spruit 26.

113 Cn. Naevius.

Very likely acted in his own comedies and tragedies but the fact is not explicitly attested. (1) 3 cent. B.C. He was born about 270 B.C. and died about 201. (2) His birthplace was probably Capua, less probably elsewhere in Campania or at Rome. (3) His main activity was at Rome.

(4) Naevius *ap.* Gell. 1.24.2; Ter. *Andr.* 15; etc. For testimonia see A. Klotz, *Tragicorum Fragmenta* (Munich 1953) 30-31. (5) *RE* Suppl. VI (1935) cols. 622-640 s.v. Naevius 2. (6) Henry 336; Spruit 5. (7) H. T. Rowell, *MAAR* 19 (1949) 17-34; Duckworth 40-42, and see index; Bieber, *HGRT*^{2} 148-150, and see index. Beare 33-43, and see index.

114 C. Norbanus Sorix.

Mime (*secundarum*). (1) 1 cent. B.C./1 cent. A.D. He has been identified by some with Sorix, q.v., but is almost certainly to be dated later, in the early empire. (2) His birthplace is unknown. (3) He performed at Pompeii. The absence of any indication of mask with the bust suggests mime rather than comedy.

(4) *CIL* X.814; not regarded as republican by Degrassi, *ILLRP*. (5) *RE* XVII.1 (1936) col. 935 s.v. Norbanus 12. (6) Bonaria, *Fasti* 249 and n.; Bonaria, *RM* p. 206, no. 176, cf. p. 178, no. 32; Henry 355-356; Spruit 63. (7) B. Schweizer, *Die Bildniskunst der römischen Republik* (Leipzig 1948), see index; E. B. Harrison, *The Athenian Agora*,

VI, *Portrait Sculpture* (Princeton 1953) 13-16; Bieber, *HGRT*² 165, 323, and fig. 592; cf. p. 147 of this book.

Ofellius: see Ofilius.

115 M. OFILIUS HILARUS (Hilaros).

Actor in comedy (*comoediarum histrio*). (1) 2/1 cent. B.C.? Fl. c. 130/80 B.C.? (2) His birthplace is unknown. (3) He apparently performed at Rome.

(4) Plin. *NH* 7.184; *CIL* VI 23389 may be connected. (5) *RE* XVII.2 (1937) col. 2042 s.v. Ofellius 11. (6) Henry 360; Spruit 27.

Olympus (Olympos): see Asinius.

116 ORIGO.

Mime (*mima*). (1) 1 cent. B.C. Fl. c. 54/37 B.C. (2) Her birthplace is unknown. (3) She performed at Rome.

(4) Hor. *Sat.* 1.2.55; etc. (5) *RE* XVIII.1 (1939) col. 1059 s.v. Origo. (6) Bonaria, *Fasti* 304, 305, 411; Bonaria, *RM* p. 185, no. 67; Henry 379; Spruit 12, 24, 89.

117 PAMPHILUS (Pamphilos).

Actor (*histrio, tertiarum*). (1) 1 cent. B.C. Fl. 57 B.C. (2) His birthplace is unknown. (3) He performed at Rome.

(4) Val. Max 9.14.4; Plin. *NH* 7.54. (5) *RE* XVIII.3 (1949) col. 333 s.v. Pamphilos 13. (6) Bonaria, *Fasti* 284-286 and n.; Bonaria, *RM* p. 183, no. 54; Henry 355; Spruit 29. (7) See p. 157 of this book.

Pan(o)urgos: see Panurgus.

Pansa: see Crassicius.

118 PANURGUS (Panourgos).

Actor in comedy (*comoedus, histrio*; cf. *artificio comico*). (1) 2-1 cent. B.C. Fl. c. 93 B.C. (2) His birthplace is unknown. (3) He performed at Rome.

(4) Cic. *Pro Rosc. Com.*, esp. 27-31. (5) *RE* XVIII.3 (1949) cols. 870-871 s.v. Panurgos. (6) Henry 350; Spruit 32, 147, 162. (7) See p. 162 of this book.

Pasicles (Pasikles): see Crassicius.

Pellio: see Pollio.

Pellio: see Publilius.

119 Philokrates (Philocrates).

Actor in tragedy (context). (1) 1 cent. B.C. Fl. 100/75 B.C. (2) He was a citizen of Thebes. (3) He is found performing at Thespiae in Boeotia and at Oropus, on the Boeotian frontier with Attica, where he was a winner in the Festival of Amphiaraus and Rome.

(4) *IG* VII 417; etc. (5) *RE* Suppl. X (1965) cols. 533-534 s.v. Philokrates 7a. (6) O'Connor 485.

Phocaeus: see Fufius.

Piso: see Calpurnius.

Plancus: see Rubrius.

Plautus: see Maccius.

120 **P. Pollio or Pellio.**

Actor in comedy (*magnis comoediis . . . actores*). (1) 2 cent. B.C. 200/150 B.C. (2) His birthplace is unknown. (3) He presumably performed at Rome; his name is known only from Symmachus, and is probably a scribal error for T. Publilius Pellio, *infra*.

(4) Symmachus, *Epist.* 10.2. (5) Not in *RE*, but see *RE* XXIII.2 (1959) col. 1917 s.v. Publilius 14. (6) See Henry 337; Spruit 25.

121 **Polyxenos (Polyxenus).**

Actor in comedy (*hypokrites*, context). (1) 1 cent. B.C. Fl. soon after 86 B.C. (2) He was a citizen of Opus, on the coast of Locris, looking towards Euboea. (3) He is found performing at Oropus, some 43 miles to the southeast, on the Boeotian frontier with Attica, being a winner at the Festival of Amphiaraus and Rome there.

(4) *IG* VII 420. (5) *RE* Suppl. X (1965) col. 548 s.v. Polyxenos 10. (6) O'Connor 411.

122 **Po(m)pilius.**

Misnomer for C. Pomponius (see Festus 438 Lindsay) in some modern authorities, e.g. Bieber, *HGRT*² 159. The error probably arises from Festus' reference to the aedile M. Po(m)pilius in the near context.

123 **C. POMPONIUS.**

Mime (*mimus, saltat*). (1) 3 cent. B.C. He had reached old age by 211 B.C. (2) His birthplace is unknown. (3) He performed at Rome.

(4) M. Verrius Flaccus *ap.* Festus 436-438 Lindsay; etc. (5) Not in *RE*. (6) Bonaria, *MRF* 1. pp. 3-5; *RM* pp. 2, 35, 101, 173; Spruit 9-10. (7) R. W. Reynolds, *Hermathena* 61 (1943) 56-62.

Poplios: see Publius.

Prot(h)ymus (Prothymos): see Minucius.

124 **PROTOGENES.**

Mime (*mimus*). (1) 3/2 cent. B.C. Fl. c. 210/160 B.C. (2) His birthplace is unknown. (3) He may have performed at Amiternum, in the Apennines, some 56 miles north-east of Rome. He was buried near there.

(4) *CIL* I² 1861 = Degrassi *ILLRP* 804. (5) *RE* Suppl. X (1965) col. 670 s.v. Protogenes 11; cf. *RE* XV.2 (1932) col. 1744 s.v. *mimos*. (6) Bonaria, *Fasti* 208 and n.; Bonaria, *RM* p. 173, no. 5; Spruit 10, 28, 32.

125 **T. PUBLILIUS PELLIO.**

Actor in comedy (*egit*, *agit*). (1) 3-2 cent. B.C. Fl. 200 B.C. or later; conceivably (as Mattingly argues) as late as c. 144 B.C. (2) His birthplace is unknown. (3) He performed at Rome.

(4) Plaut. *Stich.* didasc.; *Menaech.* 404 (?); *Bacch.* 215; etc. (5) *RE* XXIII.2 (1959) col. 1917 s.v. Publilius 14. (6) Henry 336; Spruit 25. (7) T. Frank, *AJP* 63 (1932) 248-251; Duckworth 73-74; H. B. Mattingly, *Athenaeum* N.S. 35 (1957) 78-88; *Latomus* 19 (1960) 230-252; Beare 67, 164; etc.

126 **PUBLILIUS SYRUS (Syros).**

Mime (*mimicae scaenae conditor*, *mimos agere*, *scaenam tenet*). (1) 1 cent. B.C. Fl. c. 80 (or 83)-43 B.C. (2) He came from Syria, probably from Antioch. (3) He performed at Rome, perhaps also at Puteoli and other Italian towns.

(4) Cic. *Ad Fam.* 12.18.2; etc. (5) *RE* XXXIII.2 (1959) cols. 1920-1928 s.v. Publilius 28. (6) Bonaria, *MRF* 1.103-108; Bonaria, *Fasti* 355-363 and nn., 468 and n., 477? 480? 481; Bonaria, *RM* pp. 6-10, 71, 74, 78, 130-132, 155; p. 178, no. 28, cf. no. 29; p. 186, no. 76; p. 187, no. 79; p. 188, no. 84; p. 189, no. 90; p. 190, no. 95; pp. 201, 203; Henry 358; Spruit 33, 45. (7) F. Giancotti, *Mimo e Gnome* (Florence 1967); see also p. 148 of this book.

127 **Publius?** (Poplios? Only the first three letters of the name survive in the inscr.).

Magode (*magoidos*). (1) 1 cent. B.C. Fl. 84/60 B.C. (2) He probably came from Italy or Sicily; possibly from Rome, since the *-echaios* or *-emaios* with which his ethnic appears to end may conceal *Rhomaios*. (3) He is found performing at Delphi.

(4) Inscr. on pp. 7-8 of L. Robert, *Etudes épigraphiques et philologiques* (Paris 1938); see pp. 7-13. (5) Not in *RE*. (6) —. (7) Sifakis 104-105.

128 **Q. ROSCIUS GALLUS (Rhoskios).**

Actor in comedy, perhaps also in tragedy (*actor, agere, artifex, comici operis actor, comicus, comoedus, histrio, komoidos, ludicra ars, orchestes*). (1) 2-1 cent. B.C. He was born about 131 B.C. and died in 62 B.C. (2) We find him in his cradle at Solonium, which was probably the more level south-westward part of the *ager* of Lanuvium: doubtless he was born there. (3) The only place in which he is known to have performed is Rome.

(4) Q. Lutatius Catulus *ap.* Cic. *ND* 1.79 (this may date from some years before 100 B.C.); etc. (5) *RE* I.A.1 (1914) cols. 1123-1126 s.v. Roscius 16. (6) Bonaria, *Fasti* 248, 251; *RM* p. 178, no. 32; p. 179, no. 34; Henry 343 ff.; Spruit, see index. (7) H. Wiskemann, *Untersuchungen über den römischen Schauspieler Q. Roscius Gallus* (Hersfeld 1854); F. W. Wright, *Cicero and the Theater*, Smith Coll. Class. Stud. no.

11 (1931) 16-20; Duckworth 70, 74, 92, 93; Bieber, *HGRT*[2] 100, 164, 286, n.32; Beare 303-305, and see index; C. Garton, *New Theatre Magazine* 6 (1965) 6-12; and see pp. 158-188 of this book.

129 RUBRIUS "PLANCUS."

Actor (*histrio*). (1) 1 cent. B.C. Fl. c. 50/35 B.C. (2) His birthplace is unknown. (3) He evidently performed in Rome. The name "Plancus" was given to him as a cognomen because of his close resemblance to L. Munatius Plancus, the consul of 42 B.C.

(4) Plin. *NH* 7.55; etc. , (5) *RE* I.A.1 (1914) col. 1170 s.v. Rubrius 6; cf. *RE* XVI.1 (1933) col. 550 s.v. Munatius 30. (6) Spruit 29.

130 RUPILIUS.

Actor in tragedy (context). (1) 1 cent. B.C. Fl. c. 90/80 B.C. (2) His birthplace is unknown. (3) He evidently performed at Rome.

(4) Cic. *De Off.* 1.114. (5) *RE* I.A.1 (1914) col. 1229 s.v. Rupilius 1. (6) Henry 343; Spruit 28.

131 P. Rusticelius.

(Mimetic?) dancer, possibly pantomime (*saltator*). (1) His date is unknown. There is nothing to support Bonaria's suggestion (*RM* p. 271) that he may be pre-Varronian. If he was a pantomime his fl. doubtless falls after 22 B.C. (2) His birthplace is unknown. (3) The scene of his activities would be Rome and probably also Tibur, where the inscription concerning him was found. *Saltator* may be an indication of his calling (Muratori, Bonaria) or a cognomen (Orelli, Kajanto) or midway between the two.

(4) *CIL* XIV 3547. (5) *RE* Suppl. X (1965) col. 872 s.v. Rusticelius 4. (6) Bonaria, *Fasti* 1169 and n.; *RM* p. 271. (7) I. Kajanto, *The Latin Cognomina* (Helsinki 1965 = *Soc. Sci. Fen. Com. Hum. Lit.* 35.2) 418.

132 Sac(c)ulio (Sakoulion or Sakkoulion).

Actor?? (*gelotopoios*). (1) 1 cent. B.C. Fl. towards 42 B.C., when he was executed. (2) His birthplace is unknown. (3) He may have performed at Rome.

(4) Plut. *Brut.* 45. (5) *RE* I.A.2 (1920) col. 1689 s.v. Saculio; and Suppl. X (1965) col. 873 s.v. Sacculio. (6) Bonaria, *Fasti* 366; *RM* p. 191; Spruit 28, 87.

133 Salius.

Eponymous original of *salii* and *saltatores*. (1) He was regarded as having lived in the days of Aeneas. (2) He came from Arcadia. (3) He performed in Italy.

(4) Varro *ap.* Isidore, *Etym.* 18.50; etc. (5) Not in *RE*, but cf.

RE I.A.2 (1920) col. 1874 s.v. Salii 1. (6) Bonaria, *Fasti* 74; Bonaria, *RM* p. 162, no. 18; cf. p. 170.

Salutio: see Salvit(t)o.

134 SALVIT(T)O or SALUTIO.

Mime (*mimus*). (1) 1 cent. B.C. Fl. c. 48 B.C. (2) His birthplace is unknown. (3) He presumably performed at Rome.

(4) Plin. *NH* 7.54; etc. (5) Not in *RE*, but see *RE* IV.1 (1900) col. 1505 s.v. Cornelius 357; *RE* Suppl. X (1965) col. 874 s.v. Salvitto. (6) Bonaria, *Fasti* 308, 309 and n., 310, cf. 311; Bonaria, *RM* p. 186, no. 71; Spruit 28 (Salutio).

135 Sammula.

Mime? (1) Born in 1 cent. B.C. or earlier and said to have lived 110 years. (2) Her birthplace is unknown. (3) She performed at Rome. Pliny, without saying that she was a mime-actress, refers to her in a discussion of longevity where he seems to be concentrating on stagefolk (Lucceia, Galeria Copiola, Sammula, Stephanio).

(4) Plin. *NH* 7.159. (5) Not in *RE*. (6) —.

Sannio (Sannion): see Saunio.

Sarapio(n): see Serapio.

136 Sarmentus.

Scurra. Some have conjectured that he came from the stage; this is plausible, but there is no direct evidence for it. Cf. Messius. (1) 1 cent. B.C. Fl. c. 38 B.C. (2) He came from Etruria. (3) He was active at Rome and at Caudium.

(4) Hor. *Sat.* 1.5.52 ff.; etc. (5) *RE* II.A.1 (1921) col. 25 s.v. Sarmentus. (6) Bonaria, *Fasti* 381; Bonaria, *RM* p. 192, no. 110; Henry 376. (7) A. La Penna, *Maia* N.S. 19 (1967) 154-158.

137 Saunio or Sannio (Saunion or Sannion).

Clown, possibly something of a burlesque actor also (*satyrikon prosopon*, *gelotopoios*). (1) 2-1 cent. B.C. Fl. 91 B.C. (2) He came from Latium but was not a Roman. (3) He gave performances up and down Italy, including one at a town in Picenum, perhaps Asculum.

(4) Diod. 37.12. (5) Not in *RE*. (6) —.

138 Sempronius Tuditanus.

Not an actor, but seems sometimes to have suffered from the delusion that he was. (1) 2-1 cent. B.C. Fl. c. 80 B.C.? (2) His birthplace is not specified but the Sempronii Tuditani were an important Roman family. (3) The scene of his activities was Rome.

(4) Cic. *Acad. Pr.* 2.89; *Phil.* 3.16; etc. (5) *RE* II.A.2 (1923) col. 1439 s.v. Sempronius 89. (6) —.

139 Serapio (Sarapio).

Some (as Bonaria) have fancied him to be a mime, but he was in reality a victim-jobber, a slave in the employ of a hog-dealer. (1) 2 cent. B.C. Fl. c. 141/132 B.C. He is sometimes wrongly dated a century or so later. (2) His birthplace is unknown. (3) The scene of his activities was evidently Rome.

(4) Val. Max. 9.14.3; Quint. 6.3.57; etc. (5) *RE* I.A.2 (1920) col. 2394 s.v. Sarapio 1. (6) Bonaria, *Fasti* 311; Bonaria, *RM* p. 186, no. 72.

Sergios: see Sergius.

140 SERGIUS (Sergios).
Mime (*mimus*). (1) 1 cent. B.C. Fl. 47 B.C. (2) His birthplace is unknown. (3) He performed at Rome.

(4) Cic. *Phil.* 2.62. (5) *RE* II.A.2 (1923) col. 1688 s.v. Sergius 2. (6) Bonaria, *Fasti* 312 and n., 317; Bonaria, *RM* p. 186, no. 73; p. 188, no. 83; Spruit 23, 28.

141 L. Sergius (with or without the cognomen Turpio).
Actor in comedy (*egit*). (1) 2 cent. B.C.? Fl. in or after 160 B.C. (2) He was doubtless of Roman or Italian origin but his birthplace is unknown. (3) He performed at Rome. Some have taken the evidence as indicating that L. Ambivius and he together managed the third (and successful) production of the *Hecyra*. It seems more likely (especially in view of the singular verb) that he managed a subsequent production.

(4) Ter. *Hec.* didasc. as given by the Bembine codex. (5) Not in *RE*. (6) Spruit 26. (7) T. F. Carney, *P. Terenti Afri Hecyra* (= *PACA* Suppl. 2 [1963]) p. 23.

142 SORIX.
Mime (*archimimos*). (1) 1 cent. B.C. Fl. c. 80 B.C. (2) His birthplace is unknown, but his name or sobriquet is pure Latin. (3) He performed at Rome.

(4) Plut. *Sull.* 36. See also Norbanus *supra*. (5) See *RE* XVII.1 (1936) col. 935 s.v. Norbanus 12. (6) Bonaria, *Fasti* 248, 249 and n.; Bonaria, *RM* p. 178, no. 32; cf. p. 206, no. 176; Henry 355-356; Spruit 62-63. (7) See pp. 147-148 and 162 of this book.

Sorix: see Norbanus.

143 SPINTHER.
Actor (*histrio, secundarum*). (1) 1 cent. B.C. Fl. 57 B.C. (2) His birthplace is unknown. (3) He performed at Rome.

(4) Val. Max. 9.14.4; etc. (5) *RE* III.A.2 (1929) col. 1814 s.v. Spinther. (6) Bonaria, *Fasti* 284-286 and n.; Bonaria, *RM* p. 183, no. 54; Henry 355; Spruit 29. (7) See p. 157 of this book.

144 STATILIUS.
Actor in comedy (*histrio*, context). (1) 1 cent. B.C. Fl. c. 93

B.C.?   (2) His birthplace is unknown.   (3) He performed at Rome.
(4) Cic. *Pro Rosc. Com.* 30.   (5) *RE* III.A.2 (1929) col. 2184 s.v.
Statilius 1.   (6) Henry 343; Spruit 26, 32.

145 Straton (Strato).

Actor in comedy (*hypokrites*, context).   (1) 1 cent. B.C. Fl. c.
100/75 B.C.   (2) He was a citizen of Athens.   (3) He is found
performing at Thespiae in Boeotia and (soon after 86 B.C.) at Oropus,
on the Boeotian frontier with Attica, being a winner in the Festival of
Amphiaraus and Rome there.

(4) *IG* VII.416 and 1761.   (5) *RE* Suppl. X (1965) col. 925 s.v.
Straton 23.   (6) O'Connor 445.

146 Syrisca (Syriska).

Mimetic (??) dancer (*saltat*, context), if a real person.   (1) 1 cent.
B.C.? Fl. c. 50/43 B.C.?   (2) "Syrisca," whether it is her personal
name or merely an ethnic, indicates that she came from Syria.   (3) She
evidently performed in Italy.

(4) Appendix Vergiliana, *Copa*, line 1.   (5) Not in *RE*.   (6)
Bonaria, *Fasti* 307; *RM* p. 185, no. 69.

Syrus: see Publilius.

147 Tasurcus.

Actor in comedy or tragedy (*histrio*, and context).   (1) His date is
unknown.   (2) His origin is unknown.   (3) His activity would be at
Rome, as he is compared, to his disadvantage, with Roscius. He is known
from a single passage in Fronto, and corruption of his name is highly
probable. An allusion to Panurgus, q.v., was conjectured by Mai,
Frontonis Opera (1815) p. 219, n. 2; cf. Naber's edition (1867) p. 146
n. 9, and I. van Wageningen, *Scaenica Romana* (Groningen 1907) p. 29,
n. 5.

(4) Fronto, *ad M. Anton. Imp. de Eloquent. Lib.* 1. 16. A 392 Van
den Hout.   (5) Not in *RE*.   (6) Spruit 27.

148 TERTIA.

Mime (*mima*).   (1) 1 cent. B.C. Fl. 73-71 B.C.   (2) She was
probably born in Sicily.   (3) She performed in Sicily, and perhaps also
at Rome, since it appears from Cicero that Verres took her there.

(4) Cic. *2 Verr.* 3.78; etc.   (5) *RE* V.A.1 (1934) col. 822 s.v.
Tertia 1.   (6) Bonaria, *Fasti* 254-256, 257 and n.; Bonaria, *RM* p. 179,
no. 36 (Bonaria overlooks the allusion at *2 Verr.* 5.40); Spruit 12, 24,
29, 34, 89.

Tuditanus: see Sempronius.

Turpio: see Ambivius.

Turpio: see Sergius.

149 Valerius.

Stage-vocalist, probably actor (*cantabat ... scaenicus*). (1) 2/1 cent. B.C. Fl. c. 100 B.C.? (2) His birthplace is unknown. (3) He performed at Rome.

(4) Cic. *De Orat.* 3.86-87. (5) *RE* VII.A.2 (1948) col. 2296 s.v. Valerius 6. (6) Spruit 18, 32. (7) F. W. Wright, *Cicero and the Theater*, Smith Coll. Class. Stud. no. 11 (1931) 22.

Volumnia: see Cytheris.

150 VOLUMNIUS (Boloumnios), less correctly Volumnus.

Mime (*mimos*). (1) 1 cent. B.C. Fl. towards 42 B.C., when he was executed. (2) His birthplace is unknown. (3) It is likely that he performed at Rome.

(4) Plut. *Brut.* 45. (5) *RE* Suppl. X (1965) col. 1125 s.v. Volumnius 7a. (6) Bonaria, *Fasti* 366 and n.; Bonaria, *RM* p. 191, no. 100; Spruit 28, 87.

151 C. VOLUMNIUS.

Mime (*saltarit, secundarum partium*, context). (1) 3/1 cent. B.C.? (2) His birthplace is unknown. (3) He performed at Rome.

(4) M. Verrius Flaccus *ap.* Festus 438 Lindsay. (5) Not in *RE*. (6) Bonaria, *MRF* 1. p. 3. (7) H. Reich, *Der Mimus* I pt. 1 (Berlin 1903) 90.

Volumnus: see Volumnius.

152 ZOILOS (Zoilus).

Actor in comedy (*komoidias ... hypokrites*). (1) 1 cent. B.C. Fl. soon after 86 B.C. (2) He was a citizen of Syracuse. (3) He is found performing at Oropus, on the Boeotian border with Attica, participating in the Festival of Amphiaraus and Rome there.

(4) *IG* VII.420. (5) Not in *RE*. (6) O'Connor 207.

APPENDIX 2
A REGISTER OF AUGUSTAN ACTORS

In the eyes of archaeologists, who are the historians of edifice and artefact, the theatre in Augustan times experienced something of a boom. To the historian of literature and drama it fared contrariwise, that is, it underwent the beginning of a long process of decline from which the Roman stage was never quite to recover. This state of affairs could not be more forcibly underlined than it is by the fact that the opening of two new theatres at Rome in 13-11 B.C., increasing the number of permanently available theatre seats from an estimated 17,580 to over 38,000, that is to say, more than doubling the total,[1] postdates by some seventeen years the latest known presentation on the Roman stage of an identifiable new tragedy, the *Thyestes* of L. Varius Rufus, which had been produced in 29. What fortune did this paradox hold for the acting profession, both in its absolute numbers and in the nature of its specializations? It is not possible, in the discerpted and tattered state of the evidence, to answer this question fully or exactly, but we can perhaps make some progress towards collecting what evidence there is and seeing the scope and causes of uncertainty. From what is known we can form some conception of what may have been the case.

At the literary level, as with early and mid-Victorian drama in England, there was probably little contemporary awareness of a slump in drama, and actors, who in such a matter are like so many weathervanes to the Zeitgeist, need not on this account have been depressed either in numbers or in artistic integrity. Indeed "slump" is an oversimplifying and rather unjust term. The level of dramatic creativity in Rome and in the empire at large was probably near normal: it seems low only by contrast with those rare periods of exuberance such as Greek drama experienced in the fifth century B.C. and Rome in the second. Augustan playwrights were at work in both Latin and Greek,[2] and it seems a fair inference from the rate of theatre construction, a sketch of which will be given below, that a certain amount of new regular drama was expected to be performed, alongside revivals of old plays and the newly developed entertainment of pantomime. Old plays, with the passage of time, wavered between mustiness and classicality, but the accession of grandeur to the empire and the activity of scholars formed a pull in the latter direction, and wherever Greek was understood Menander at any rate seems to have remained fresh and green, as he was to do throughout imperial times. One sign of Augustan interest in him is the Lateran relief which shows him absorbed in the study of three comic masks.[3] This was based on a much older original at Athens, but the Augustan artist has rehandled the design; it is apparently he who has added the personified Scaena (Skênê) — unless the figure is that of the poet's beloved helper Glycera — on the right, to balance and in a manner bless his dramaturgical ponderings on the left. Some have thought it possible that the Roman public may even have had opportunities to see Old Comedy (Suet. *Aug.* 89.1), though hardly upon sufficient evidence. So far as contemporary dramatic performances in general are concerned, it is not improbable that old and new were mixed; this may not have been the case with the Oscan pieces[4] in which Augustus is believed to have taken an interest, but it probably was so at the Secular Games in 17 B.C., when Greek thymelic shows were done on the orchestra of Pompey's theatre, regular Greek plays in the Circus Flaminius or a part of it adapted for such purposes, and Latin plays, as the more elderly would recollect happening in Roscius' time, in front of a timber auditorium.[5]

Educated interest in the theatrical experience, in what it is that actors do, ran high. In Livy and Horace, in different ways, it emerges in the form of academic enquiry and speculation, or something analytical and didactic, as it had done in Aristotle more than three hundred years earlier. But the life of regular theatre is not sensed by them, any more than by him, as essentially a past phenomenon: rather to all three it is something which was found growing and is now fullgrown. This is, from Aristotle on, the common ancient attitude, held for instance by Lucretius with regard to the arts and sciences in general. Add to this that Virgil's recourse to the theatre for one of his most powerful images — *scaenis agitatus Orestes*[6] — is directly experiential: it is an appeal to the spectacle on stage, not to a written text.

It is beyond dispute, however, that notwithstanding such interest and an increasing number of days allotted to scenic performances, regular drama was being overhauled in popularity both by mime — the Greek mimes of Philistio, which were performed at Rome, coming eventually to rate comparison with Menander[7] himself — and by pantomime, which was introduced, or rather formally recognized, in 22 B.C., initially in both a tragico-mythical and comico-mythical variety. We need not here enter fully into the antecedents of pantomime, but its approach may be seen in the late republican era in both Greece and Italy. Its name is Greek, the two nuances of the word which seem best to justify it being "all-in-mime" and mime-of-the-whole-story," and two apparent Greek practitioners of it have been found as early as 84/60 B.C., though, curiously, the Greeks came to call it the "Italian" dance.[8] In Italy it might be regarded as an outgrowth of mime and the associated mimetic dancing, or better, perhaps, as an abstraction from this and from regular drama, especially tragedy and satyr-play, which contributed theme and mask.

When, in the Horatian travelogue of 38/37 B.C., Sarmentus asks Messius Cicirrus (Appendix 1, nos. 136 and 109) to "dance the Cyclops,"[9] which his bigness and ugliness would enable him to do without buskins or a mask, we seem to have *scurrae* using theatre language which borders very close upon, if it does not directly refer to, pantomime: it is just the kind of act which Bathyllus (Augustan register no. 22 below) might later have done in comico-mythical pantomime if he could be buskined up to the requisite height. And when Horace in 31/30 B.C. depreciates social chitchat such as whether "Lepos dances badly or not"[10] (no. 101 in Appendix 1, 36 in Appendix 2), he has convinced high authorities that he is talking about a pantomime,[11] though we have it expressly from Porphyrio that Lepos was an *archimimus* and, as such, a *speaking* actor.[12] From 22 B.C. pantomime was not only a huge success but could claim — and did claim through one of its executants — a measure of political significance as a pacifier or opiate of the common people,[13] functioning like the cruder circensian games to supplement and add zest to their daily bread.

An Augustan register, by contrast with that for the republic, should be empire-wide in its coverage. In the republican era the great majority of all known actors in the Graeco-Roman world have no Roman connections. They can therefore be kept separate, and have been separately treated, in effect, by O'Connor and Iride Parenti;[14] while the special interest which attaches to those Greek actors who are in some definite way connected with the young and thrusting Roman state justifies putting them in a Roman republican list of the kind which I have drawn up. From late republican and Augustan times on, however, known Greek actors without Roman connections are a distinct minority among actors as a whole. It is little trouble to include them, and it seems advantageous to aim at an empire-wide conspectus. This pragmatic advantage is endorsed by a serious historical consideration. From the time of Claudius we find the Greek guilds of Artists of Dionysus, who included virtually all self-respecting *tragoidoi* and *komoidoi*, united, perhaps federated would be a better word, into a world-guild, apparently with its headquarters at Rome. It can be inferred from a letter of Claudius and from other sources that the first steps towards this union had been taken during the principate of Augustus, and that he sustained, on an empire-wide basis, some or all of the privileges which these *technitai* had earlier won for themselves in their local guilds.[15] The tragic and comic actors whose existence in Augustan times is thus predicable happen not to be known to us by name, but it would have been misleading to omit them altogether from consideration, and they are therefore given a collective entry (no. 9 below).

There are other indications that the list of actors, if we could restore it in full, would be a long one. On the principle that where there were theatres there must also have been actors in employment, the profession in Augustan times is not likely to have been shrinking: it would seem, if anything, to have been perceptibly expanding. We do not find reports of theatres going out of use: instead we find evidence of many new theatres built and old ones renovated or developed, not only in Italy but in Greece, Gaul, Spain, and North Africa. With regard to the most famous of theatres, that of Dionysus in Athens, it is true that no structural changes have been traced for this period, but its use seems to have been continuous, while at Sparta the theatre was equipped for the first time to show regular plays, as opposed to non-scenic games and spectacles, by the building of a skene and proskenion which could when needed be rolled into position on rollers and wheels.[16] In Gaul the 12,000-seat theatre at Arelate (Arles) was probably begun in the late republic and finished under Augustus.[17] In Spain an elaborate theatre at Emerita (Merida) was built by Agrippa and completed in 18 B.C.[18] The sands of Tripoli saw the building of the theatre at Leptis Magna, dedicated in A.D. 1/2 and provided with a special box for the presiding magistrate in A.D. 10/14.[19] Theatres certainly or probably of Augustan date are found in northern Italy at Faesulae (Fiesole), Mediolanum (Milan), Augusta Taurinorum (Turin), and Augusta Praetoria (Aosta). Drawing nearer Rome, we find that in Campania a new theatre was built at Herculaneum and the larger and older of the theatres at Pompeii was extensively remodelled on the Roman plan.[20] Latium acquired two theatres in seaside towns. Agrippa built the one at Ostia, and Minturnae, which is known to have been staging scenic games already between 100 and 50 B.C.,[21] now erected its own permanent theatre a few years prior to or following the death of Augustus. There is another apparently Augustan theatre at Casinum.[22]

At Rome we encounter in Julius Caesar and Augustus a repetition of the Sulla-Pompey pattern of interest in theatrical affairs which had culminated in the building of the capital's first permanent stone theatre in 55 B.C. Caesar's friend the younger Balbus, who did for an actor in Spain (Appendix 1, no. 90) much what Sulla had done for Roscius (Appendix 1, no. 128) and Caesar in his ironic way for Laberius (Appendix 1, no. 99), built a new theatre not far from Pompey's, and the theatre which Caesar himself had begun was completed by his heir Augustus and dedicated to the memory of their deceased kinsman Marcellus.[23] Augustus also renovated Pompey's theatre.[24] Thus, after the Secular Games of 17 B.C. we hear little more of wooden theatres, the permanently available seating, as already indicated, being more than doubled in the ensuing six years. Vitruvius' book on architecture, written while the two new theatres were in building, puts it beyond doubt that theatre-construction on these lines was expected to continue.

Widespread interest in the theatre is also shown by Augustan portraiture and decorative art. Caius Norbanus Sorix, the mime *secundarum* at Pompeii, may have begun his career in republican times (Appendix 1, no. 114; Appendix 2, no. 41), but the vivid portrait bronzes of him are most convincingly dated as Augustan.[25] A dramatizing of the Perseus and Andromeda story, which had been handled in Roman tragedy by Andronicus, Ennius, and Accius, is intimated by the masks of the principals, with associated detail, in a marble relief from Naples and a wall-painting from Pompeii;[26] and tragic masks on medallions from the latter town are probably also Augustan.[27] Wall-paintings from Rome show an actor with a tragic mask, and a seated man holding a comic mask while an actor recites, though these have both been connected with semi-dramatic declamation rather than drama proper.[28] A thoughtful interest in comedy is also suggested by the Lateran relief of Menander mentioned earlier.[29] Moreover, in the fullest existing tabulation of masks and monuments illustrating New Comedy and Roman comedy, that by Webster, there are, on a rough count, nearly thirty entries — paintings, mosaics, reliefs, an antefix, a plaque, and ornaments on lamps, jugs, and Arretine ware — dated in the late first century B.C., early first century A.D., or as belonging to either century indeterminately.[30] Besides Pompeii and Boscoreale, they come from Naples, Rome, Milan, Corfu, Corinth, Athens, Tarsus, Egypt, and elsewhere — in fact they are scattered right across the Mediterranean. Not a few of these utensils and objets d'art are likely to be Augustan. Such things do not necessarily portray contemporary life, but they do bespeak contemporary *interest* and when added to the other evidence tell us much about the tastes and cultural atmosphere of the time when they were made and marketed. In such an atmosphere actors should have felt themselves to be in thriving business. There is little doubt that they were.

But turn now to current reference works on actors: the picture is in startling contrast. Of the 565 Greek actors, nearly all of them performers in tragedy or comedy, listed by O'Connor, how many belong to Augustan times? Two. They are Athenion and Leonteus (see register below, nos. 18 and 35). Of the additional 120 actors listed by Iride Parenti in her supplement to O'Connor, how many are Augustan? One (Babyllius, see register, no. 20). In addition these catalogues offer, between them, about seven other actors dated to the first century A.D. without more precise specification. This is no belittling as slipshod the work of those prosopo-graphers: they tell pretty much what is known. The Athenian theatre archives, and especially the so-called fasti, didascaliae, and victor-lists, impressive even in ruin, provide something like a motion picture of the theatre from the fifth to the second century B.C., but they stop short at about 141. Other Greek festival records of a fairly elaborate kind run into the following century, but for Augustan times we are dependent on short, chance inscriptions and on allusions in literature. For actors at Rome these latter sources are the only ones available; there was no government-sponsored inscriptional archive, and inscriptions attesting ludi scaenici were spasmodic, depending on the initiative of the sponsoring magistrate or others involved on any given occasion. Henry in his "Roman Actors," drawing on both literary and epigraphic sources, collects information on a total of twelve Augustan stagefolk, if we allow him the inclusion of Gabba (see register, 31) — we cannot allow him Princeps, who was only a piper. Additional material has been gathered by Bonaria; it is, however, not set out in prosopographic form but in the form of mimic and pantomimic fasti.

In compiling my own register I have reviewed the work of all these and supplemented it where I could. A minuter combing of ancient literature might yield more names, and future epigraphic (and papyrological) discoveries, as explained below, could yield many more. Future additions can also be expected from improved methods of dating. For there is a fair number of actors, both Greek and Roman, attested in inscriptions whose dates are as yet either wholly uncertain or known only to the century. These I have had for the most part to leave aside.

Clearer light on the gap between what is known and what was the case can be obtained by chronological analysis of the catalogues of O'Connor and Iride Parenti. It soon becomes evident that our prosopographical knowledge of Greek actors is strongest for the third and second centuries B.C. and next strongest for the fourth. And if we divide the period 121 B.C. – A.D. 60 into four terms of about 45 years each (with one slight overlap), the following picture emerges:

121-75 B.C.	about 117 actors known
76-31 B.C.	3 actors known
31 B.C. – A.D. 14	3 actors known*
A.D. 14 – 60	about 4 actors known*

*There are also about 7 actors assigned to the first century A.D. without more precise dating.

This effectively demonstrates that the paucity of names for the Augustan period is part of a wider picture. The wider picture might seem at first sight to betoken the virtual collapse of the acting profession or at any rate the profession of *tragoidoi* and *komoidoi*, in about 75 B.C. Needless to say, we hear nothing elsewhere of quite such a drastic event. Rather, it betokens the relative lack of detailed festival records from that point onward for some time.

Is there hope that such records could yet come to light? The strongest ground for hope lies in the progress actually made in the twentieth century between 1908 and 1961. For if we break down the figure of 117 actors attested for the years 121-75 B.C. we find that to O'Connor, writing in 1908, only 69 were known, whilst his supplementer in 1961, drawing largely upon material, mostly epigraphic, discovered in the interim, was able to add 48 more. Roman actors, because of the lack of methodical contemporary record, will probably always have to be gleaned in ones and twos from scattered sources, as in the register following, but for Greek actors in the late republic and the empire there is always the hope that more festival records will turn up and substantially fill out the picture.

The Register

In this register the information about each actor is presented in the same order as in my republican list, and the reference books cited are the same. The rest of the methodology is the same, except on two points. (1) Whereas in the case of republican actors the criteria of selection included some definite tie with Rome, more definite, that is, than the mere fact of performing within the bounds of the empire — and this entailed the exclusion of several hundred Greek actors lacking such a tie — in the present list that criterion is relaxed and the field is empire-wide. (2) Second, performers in pantomime are included.

Where there are positive grounds for thinking that the careers of republican stagefolk continued to, or beyond, 31 B.C., I have brought them into the list, but where such evidence is lacking they are omitted even though, as in the case of Origo (Appendix 1, no. 116), they may have survived long enough and indeed have been listed in certain modern authorities as Augustan.[31] In the same way I have omitted actors found performing in the reigns of Tiberius and later emperors, however likely it may be that they began to act earlier, unless there is reasonable evidence that they did.

In capitals are entered Augustan actors proper, that is: persons, named or anonymous, known or credibly believed to have appeared professionally in comedy, tragedy, mime (of various kinds), mimetic dancing, and pantomime — including a mistress of interludes (48) and a dancer of Roman pieces (49), in both cases apparently pantomimic — at any place in the empire between 31 B.C. and A.D. 14. There must also have existed in this period professionals performing in atellan and satyr drama, and there were doubtless also lysis-singers, magodes and their kind, and *rhomaistai*: these would have been included if directly attested, but I have not found any. No actors, by the way, are recorded as performing at Greek "festivals of Rome" (*Rhomaia*) in this period. Total, 21 entries.

In small letters are entered other personages worthy of consideration alongside the strict list, that is, persons who *may* belong to it but cannot be firmly so classified for lack of decisive evidence, anonymous members of guilds or groups who cannot be brought into focus as individuals, non-professionals known or credibly believed to have appeared at least once in any of the genres mentioned above, and a few *spurii*. Total (including 6a and 15a), 33 entries. Grand total, 54 entries.

Excluded are stagefolk not within these categories, e.g. musicians and recitalists who did not act and miscellaneous non-dramatic entertainers or exhibits such as Lycius the dwarf.

Classifying by genres, we find the following of interest under tragedy: 8, 9, 15, 18. The following under comedy: 1, 6a, 7, 8, 9, 19, 20, 38, 39, 52. The following under mime and mimetic dancing: 10, 17, 23, 26, 28, 29, 32, 34, 36, 37, 41, 42, 45, 46, 47, 50. And the following under pantomime: 11, 12, 13, 14, 21, 22, 33, 40, 43, 44, 46, 48, 49, 51.

1   **ALEXANDROS** (Alexander).
        Actor in comedy (mask of comic slave on his gravestone).   (1) 1
cent. B.C./1 cent. A.D. Fl. probably c. 25/1 B.C.   (2) He was a citizen
of Athens, of the deme Sphettos.   (3) He presumably performed at
Athens.
        (4) *IG* III.2028.   (5) Not in *RE*.   (6) Webster *HPA* 272-273, and
*MNC*² p. 14, p. 51 AS 4, and plate IIIb.

2   **Anon.**
        Actors (*omnium linguarum histriones*).   (1) 1 cent. B.C. − 1 cent.
A.D. They belonged to the Augustan period in general.   (2) They were
of varied ethnic origin, as attested by their various languages.   (3) They
performed at Rome, in games sometimes given with separate staging in
the individual wards of the city.
        (4) Suet. *Aug.* 43.1, apparently drawing on Augustus' own
record.   (5) −.   (6) Bonaria, *Fasti* 424; Bonaria, *RM* p. 194, no. 121.

3   **Anon.**
        Actors (*acroamata et histriones ... etiam triviales ex circo
ludios*).   (1) 1 cent. B.C. − 1 cent. A.D. They belonged to the
Augustan period in general.   (2) Their origin is not given.   (3) They
performed at Rome, and probably also elsewhere.
        (4) Suet. *Aug.* 74.   (5) −.   (6) Bonaria, *Fasti* 426.

4   **Anon.**
        Actors, of equestrian rank (*ad scaenicas ... operas et equitibus
Romanis aliquando usus est*, sc. *Augustus*).   (1) 1 cent. B.C. Fl.
between 31 and 22 B.C., when the practice was stopped by resolution of
the senate.   (2) They were Roman citizens.   (3) They performed at
Rome.
        (4) Suet. *Aug.* 43.3.   (5) −.   (6) −.

5   **ANON.**
        Actors (*histriones*).   (1) 1 cent. B.C. Fl. 17 B.C.   (2) Their origin
is not given.   (3) They performed at Rome, at Augustus' Secular
Games: the more mature of the actors concerned − such as did *not*
survive to take part in the next celebration of the Secular Games in A.D.
47. Compare following entry.
        (4) See Suet. *Claud.* 21.2.   (5) −.   (6) Bonaria, *Fasti* 585.

6   **ANON.**
        Actors (*histriones*).   (1) 1 cent. B.C. − 1 cent. A.D. Fl. 17 B.C. −
A.D. 47.   (2) Their origin is not given.   (3) They performed at Rome,
at Augustus' Secular Games, presumably as adolescents, and survived to
take part in Claudius' celebration of the Secular Games in A.D. 47. They
included Stephanio, q.v.
        (4) Suet. *Claud.* 21.2.   (5) −.   (6) Bonaria, *Fasti* 585.

6a Anon.
Actor in comedy (context). (1) 1 cent. B.C./1 cent. A.D. Died
between c. 48 B.C. and c. A.D. 15. (2) His place of origin is
unknown. (3) He may have performed in Mytilene or at Rome.
(4) Crinagoras, *Anth. Pal.* 9.513. (5) —. (6) —. (7) A. S. F.
Gow and D. L. Page, *The Greek Anthology: The Garland of Philip*
(Cambridge 1968) 2.259.

7 Anon.
Actors in comedy (*komoidoi*). See Appendix 1, no. 30. Augustan
period not excluded.

8 Anon.
Actor in tragedy, perhaps also in comedy, the "Dresdner Schauspieler." See Appendix 1, no. 33. Augustan dating is a possibility.

9 Anon.
Actors in tragedy and actors in comedy (predicable in the world
guild of Artists of Dionysus, with their synagonists; or among the
forerunners of these). (1) 1 cent. B.C./1 cent. A.D. Fl. 31 B.C./A.D.
14. Claudius writing in A.D. 47 to the world guild confirms privileges
earlier "granted by the deified Augustus." (2) They came from all
over the Greek-speaking world, not excluding Italy and
Sicily. (3) Their places of performance were equally widespread.
(4) Texts at Viereck, *Klio* 8 (1908) 413 ff., *POxy* 2476, 2610; and
A. Rehm, *Milet* 1.3. (Berlin 1914) no. 156. (5) —.
(6) —. (7) Pickard-Cambridge, *Festivals*[2] 297.

10 Anon.
Mime-actors, on one or two occasions; of equestrian rank (*equites
R. matronasque ad agendum mimum produxit in scaenam*). (1) 1
cent. B.C. Fl. c. 19-16 B.C. (2) They were Roman citizens and
citizens' wives. (3) They performed at Rome, in shows arranged by L.
Domitius Ahenobarbus as praetor and consul.
(4) Suet. *Ner.* 4. (5) —. (6) Bonaria, *Fasti* 440, 458; *RM* p.
195, no. 131.

11 ANON.
Pantomimes (*pantomimi duo*) (1) 1 cent. B.C./1 cent. A.D. Fl.
between 22 B.C. and A.D. 14. (2) Their origin is not
given. (3) They performed at Rome. Bonaria would identify them
with Pylades I and Bathyllus I, but there seems insufficient warrant for
this.
(4) Quint. 6.3.65. (5) —. (6) Bonaria, *Fasti* 488; Bonaria, *RM*
p. 195, no. 128.

12 Anon.
Pantomimes (*context*). (1) 1 cent. A.D. Active from the days of
Bathyllus I and Pylades I to at least c. A.D. 63. (2) Their places of

origin would be various. (3) They performed at Rome: *successores*, continuing the "house" of Bathyllus and Pylades. They included Sophe, q.v., and may have included other "Theorobathylliani" (cf. *CIL* VI.10128) and "Theoriani" (cf. *CIL* IV.1891). See also Hylas, Nomius, and Pierus *infra*.

(4) Sen. Younger, *NQ* 7.32.3. (5) —. (6) Bonaria, *Fasti* 509, 511, 513; Bonaria, *RM* p. 195, no. 127.

13 Anon.

Pantomimes and other artists (*akruamata, pantomimi*). (1) 1 cent. B.C. Fl. 3/2 B.C. and a little earlier. (2) Their places of origin are not given. (3) They are found performing at Pompeii, in shows given by A. Clodius Flaccus in his first and third duumvirates. Pylades I was among those taking part on the former occasion.

(4) *CIL* X.1074. (5) —. (6) Bonaria, *Fasti* 496; Bonaria, *RM* p. 200, no. 147.

14 Anon.

Pantomimes, including amateurs of equestrian rank and ladies of note (*es ten orchestran . . . esechthesan*, and context). (1) 1 cent. B.C. Fl. 2 B.C. (2) Their places of origin are not given. (3) They participated in a pantomimic concourse or festival sponsored by T. Quinctius Crispinus Valerianus, praetor in 2 B.C., possibly also in one led the same year by Pylades I. These concourses evidently took place at Rome: the current belief (Bonaria as cited below) that they took place at Naples is unjustified.

(4) Dio Cass. 55.10.11. (5) —. (6) Bonaria, *Fasti* 497 and n.; Bonaria, *RM* p. 200, no. 148.

15 Antigonos (Antigonus).

Actor in tragedy (*tragoidos*). (1) 1 cent. B.C.? Fl. perhaps c. 20 B.C. (2) His place of origin is unknown. (3) He is associated with Didyma, the former Branchidae, 11 miles south of Miletus, and may have performed in the theatre of the latter town.

(4) Inscr. at A. Rehm, *Die Inschriften von Didyma* (Berlin 1958) 50.1A. 25. (5) Not in *RE*. (6) —.

15a Anti(o)demis.

See Appendix 1, no. 46.

16 Antipatros.

Sub-dramatic entertainer in the Latin language (*rhomaïstes*)? See Appendix 1, no. 47. The date 17 B.C. given by *RE* Suppl. I (1903) col. 92 s.v. Antipatros 11a is an error for 173 B.C.

17 C. Asinius Olympus.

(Mimetic?) dancer (*saltator*). See Appendix 1, no. 53. He died as a child, but it is very possible that his short life overlapped with the Augustan period.

18 **ATHENION (Athenio).**
Actor in tragedy (context). (1) 1 cent. B.C. Fl. c. 50/1 B.C. (2) His place of origin is unknown., (3) The scene of his activities is uncertain, but he was the instructor of Leonteus, who came from Argos. Leonteus being a *tragoidos*, Athenion presumably was one likewise, *pace* Dieterich in *RE*, who records him solely as a tragic poet.
(4) Athen. 8.343e (citing Amarantus?). (5) *RE* II.2 (1896) col. 2041 s.v. Athenion 7. (6) O'Connor 12, cf. 313.

19 **ATIMETUS (Atimetos).**
Actor in comedy (*comoedus*). (1) 1 cent. B.C./1 cent. A.D. Fl. 31 B.C./A.D. 14. (2) His place of origin is unknown, but his name (ambivalent like our "priceless") is Greek. (3) He evidently performed at Rome. He was probably a member of Augustus' household, his name appearing in an erasure on the monument of Livia.
(4) *CIL* VI.2217 = 3926, cf. 3933. (5) Not in *RE*. (6) Spruit 86, n. 55.

20 **(T?) BABYLLIOS (Babyllius).**
Actor in comedy (*komoidos*). (1) 1 cent. B.C./1 cent. A.D. Fl. c. 20 B.C./c. A.D. 20. (2) His provenience is uncertain, but it was a Greek city yielding an ethnic in *-deus*. (3) He appears to have performed at Gortyn, in south central Crete.
(4) Inscr. at *BCH* 60 (1936) 23, and *REG* 49 (1936) 241 (L. Robert). (5) *RE* Suppl. X (1965) col. 94 s.v. Babyllios. (6) Parenti 102a.

21 **Bacchylides.**
Pantomime (*pantomimus*). (1) He is given as 1 cent. B.C. with an implied fl. of 22 B.C. (2) His place of origin is not given. (3) He is named by the Suda lexicon as an initiator, along with Pylades, of pantomime at Rome. But fairly obviously the name is a slip for Bathyllus, q.v., the error arising partly by homoeoteleuton (*Pyladou. . . Bacchylidou*), or by a confused reading of some passage such as Athen. 1.20c-d, where the poet Bacchylides and Bathyllus are mentioned near together. No variant is recorded.
(4) Suda, s.v. *orchesis*. (5) Not in *RE*. (6) Bonaria, *Fasti* 486 and *RM* p. 195, no. 127, records the reference without quotation or comment.

22 **BATHYLLUS (Bathyllos) I,**
so designated to distinguish him from a namesake of the later 1 cent. A.D. Pantomime (*histrio, orcheseos tragikes eisegetes, pantomimos, -us, saltare*, etc.) (1) 1 cent. B.C. (– 1 cent. A.D.?) His career at Rome began in 22 B.C. and may have lasted into the Christian era. (2) He came from Alexandria. (3) He performed at Rome. It is probable that he is identical with C. Theorus, q.v., though the full name

C. Theorus Bathyllus is not found, and its existence is not proved by adducing "Theorobathylliana" on a bone docket, *CIL* 6.10128.

(4) The earliest literary references are Crinagoras, *Anth. Pal.* 9.542; Sen. Elder, *Controv.* 3, praef. 10 and 16; 10, praef. 8; Phaedr. 5.7. Note also the bone docket cited above and the Pompeian graffiti mentioning C. Theorus. (5) *RE* III.1 (1897) cols. 137-138 s.v. Bathyllus 7; *RE* Suppl. X (1965) cols. 95-96 s.v. Bathyllos 7; *RE* Suppl. X (1965) col. 950 s.v. Theoros 3. (6) Bonaria, *Fasti* 486, 487, 493, 500-505, 507, 511, 513; Bonaria, *RM* pp. 11, 12; p. 195, no. 127; p. 196, no. 133; pp. 198-199, nos. 141, 143 ff.; Henry 362; Spruit 80. (7) O. Weinreich, *SHAW* Jahrg. 1944-1948, 46 ff. (known to me only from following). Bonaria, "Dinastie" 224 ff., esp. 231-232.

23 **C. CAESONIUS PHILARGYRUS** (Kaisonios Philargyros).
Mime (*moschologos*). (1) 1 cent. B.C./1 cent. A.D. Fl. c. 25 B.C./A.D. 25. (2) His place of origin is unknown. He was probably a Roman citizen and became also a citizen of Gortyn, in south central Crete. (3) He evidently performed at Gortyn, this being where he was honoured.

(4) Inscr. at *Ann. Epigr.* 1926, 39 = L. Robert, *REG.* 49 (1936) 242. (5) *RE* Suppl. X (1965) col. 120 s.v. Caesonius 7a. (6) Bonaria, *Fasti* 433 and n,; Bonaria, *RM* p. 195, no. 126.

Caracuttis: see Julius.

Caracuttius: see Julius.

24 **Castor** (Kastor).
Actor? (*histriones...gladiatores*). (1) 1 cent. B.C. Fl. c. 20 B.C. (2) His place of origin is unknown. (3) The scene of his activities was Rome, but the precise nature of his *scientia* is uncertain: ancient guesses say acting or gladiatorial fighting; modern guesses include grammar and general erudition.

(4) Hor. *Epist.* 1.18.19 with scholia. (5) *RE* X.2 (1919) col. 2346 s.v. Kastor 2. (6) Bonaria, *Fasti* 438, 439; Bonaria, *RM* 195, no. 130.

Celsus: see Furius.

Copiola: see Galeria.

Corocotta: see Julius.

25 **L. Crassicius Pasicles or Pansa.**
Actor? (*circa scaenam versatus est*). See Appendix 1, no. 68. His fl. extends to about 30 B.C.

26 **Dionysius** (Dionysios).
Mime (*hethologus = ethologos*, if his epitaph has been rightly supplemented). (1) Of imperial but uncertain date. Some have re-

garded him as potentially Augustan, but the formula *Aug. n(ostri) verna* in his epitaph is chiefly associated with a later period, c. A.D. 193/235. He died at the age of 28.   (2) The term *verna* indicates that he was born in some branch of the emperor's household; and he was buried at Rome.   (3) Presumably he performed at Rome.

(4) *CIL* 6.10129.   (5) Not in *RE*.   (6) Bonaria, *Fasti* 430; Bonaria, *RM* p. 194, no. 123.

27   **Docilis or Dolichus(-os).**

Actor? (*histriones...gladiatores*).   (1) 1 cent. B.C. Fl. c. 20 B.C.   (2) His place of origin is unknown.   (3) The scene of his activities was Rome, but the precise nature of his *scientia* is uncertain: ancient guesses say acting or gladiatorial fighting; modern guesses include grammar and general erudition.

(4) Hor. *Epist.* 1.18.19 with scholia.   (5) *RE* V.1 (1903) col. 1251 s.v. Docilis.   (6) Bonaria, *Fasti* 438, 439; Bonaria, *RM* p. 195, no. 130.

Dolichus (Dolichos): see Docilis.

28   **Ecloga (Ekloge).**

Mime (*mima*). See Appendix 1, no. 78. Her life falls somewhere between about 43 B.C. and A.D. 30, but she died at eighteen.

29   **Eucharis.**

Mime or (mimetic?) dancer (*ludos decoravi choro ... Graeca in scaena*). See Appendix 1, no. 83. Some authorities implausibly date her in 1 or 2 cent. A.D.

30   **L. FURIUS CELSUS (Phourios Kelsos).**

Pantomime (*mython orchestes*).   (1) 1 cent. B.C./1 cent. A.D. Fl. c. 25 B.C./A.D. 25.   (2) His place of origin is uncertain, but he was a Roman citizen, of the Falerna voting-district (which included Capua and Puteoli), and became also a citizen of Gortyn in south central Crete.   (3) He performed at Gortyn.

(4) Inscr. at *Ann. Epigr.* 1926, 39 = L. Robert, *REG* 49 (1936) 241.   (5) *RE* Suppl. X (1965) col. 241 s.v. Furius 51b.   (6) Bonaria, *Fasti* 432 and n.; Bonaria, *RM* p. 194 no. 125.

31   **(A?) Gabba.**

Gelotopoios. As in the case of Sarmentus the *scurra* and Messius Cicirrus in late republican times, some have wished to connect this jester with the stage, but there is no good warrant for doing so.   (1) 1 cent. B.C. Fl. before the death of Maecenas in 8 B.C. He may have outlived Augustus but this is not certain.   (2) In regard to origin, Plutarch calls him a Roman: Martial, though speaking with obvious paradox, calls him *rusticus.*   (3) The scene of his activities was Rome.

(4) Mart. 1.41.4; 10.101. Etc.   (5) *RE* VII.1 (1910) cols. 418-419 s.v. Gabba.   (6) Henry 375.

32   GALERIA COPIOLA Mime (*emboliaria*).
        See Appendix 1, no. 85. Her last appearance onstage, a token
appearance presumably after long retirement and allegedly at the age of
103 or 104, was at votive games given in A.D. 9 to celebrate Augustus'
recovery from sickness.

Hedymus (Hedymos): see Nedymus.

33   HYLAS.
        Pantomime (*histrio, pantomimus, saltare*).   (1) 1 cent B.C./1 cent.
A.D. Fl. c. 22-18 B.C. and perhaps till c. A.D. 14.   (2) He came from
Salmacis in the territory of Halicarnassus in Caria.   (3) He performed
at Rome.
        (4) *CIL* VI.10115; Suet. *Aug.* 45.4. Etc.   (5) *RE* IX.1 (1914)
cols. 115-116 s.v. Hylas 3; *RE* Suppl. X (1965) cols. 327-328 s.v. Hylas
3.   (6) Bonaria, *Fasti* 489, 490, 494, 495, 508, 512; Bonaria, *RM* p.
12; pp. 196-199, nos. 132-134, 143, 144; Henry 365; Spruit 119, 121.

Ila: the Italian form of the name Hylas, q.v.

34   C. Julius Caracutti(u)s (Ioulios Karakoutti(o)s); the cognomen may be a
        variant of Corocotta.
        Mime (context).   (1) 1 cent. A.D.? Fl. in days of Augustus/
Tiberius? He has also been assigned to about 3 cent. A.D.   (2) His
place of origin is unknown.   (3) He performed at Rome, his
entertainment of "senate, matrons, and royalty" being mentioned by his
widow in his epitaph. His burial also was at Rome.
        (4) *IG* XIV.1683.   (5) *RE* Suppl. X (1965) col. 331 s.v. Iulius
196a.   (6) Bonaria, *RM* p. 204, no. 164.

Kaisonios: see Caesonius.

Karakouttios: see Julius.

Karakouttis: see Julius.

Kelsos: see Furius.

35   LEONTEUS.
        Actor in tragedy (*tragoidos*). See Appendix 1, no. 100. His career
almost certainly overlapped with the Augustan period.

36   Lepos.
        Mime (*archimimus*). See Appendix 1, no. 101. His fl. may be as late
as 30 B.C.

37   Lucceia.
        Mime (*mima*). See Appendix 1, no. 103. She may have lived into
Augustan times and into 1 cent. A.D.

38   Milanio.
        Actor in comedy (*comoedus*).   (1) 1 cent. B.C./1 cent. A.D., thus

possibly Augustan. (2) His place of origin is unknown; the name is ultimately derived from Greek *melas*. (3) He presumably performed at Rome, this being where he was buried.

(4) *CIL* VI.6252. (5) Not in *RE*. (6) Spruit 86, n. 55.

39 NEDYMUS (Nedymos), alias Hedymus (Hedymos).

Actor in comedy (*comoedus*). (1) 1 cent. B.C./1 cent. A.D. Fl. probably about the change of era. (2) His place of origin is unknown. (3) He presumably performed at Rome, where he was buried.

(4) *CIL* VI.4436. (5) Not in *RE*. (6) Spruit 86, n. 55. (7) Webster, *GB* 58.

40 NOMIUS (Nomios).

Pantomime (context). (1) 1 cent. B.C./1 cent. A.D. Fl. 10 B.C./A.D. 14? (2) He came from Syria. (3) He performed at Rome.

(4) *CIL* VI.10115; Sen. *Controv.* 3, praef. 10 *Nomio* Buecheler *nomimi meo* codd. (5) *RE* Suppl. X (1965) cols. 415-416 s.v. Nomius 2. (6) Bonaria, *Fasti* 508, 515; Bonaria, *RM* p. 198, no. 143; p. 199, no. 146; Henry 365.

41 C. NORBANUS SORIX.

Mime (*secundarum*). See Appendix 1, no. 114. He is more probably of early imperial than republican date, and may well be Augustan.

Olympus (Olympos): see Asinius.

Pansa: see Crassicius.

Pasicles (Pasikles): see Crassicius.

Philargyros, -us: see Caesonius.

42 Philistio (Philistion).

Mime-actor as well as mime-writer? (descriptions include *komoidos, skenikos*, and perhaps *mimos*). (1) 1 cent. A.D. Fl. A.D. 8. (2) He came from a city in western Asia Minor, variously given by the sources as Sardis or Magnesia in the province of Asia, or Prusa or Nicaea in Bithynia. (3) The scene of his activities was Rome.

(4) Mart. 2.41.15. Etc. (5) *RE* XIX.2 (1938) cols. 2402-2405 s.v. Philistion 4. (6) Bonaria, *Fasti* 516-540, 1137; Bonaria, *RM* p. 12; 202-203, no. 155.

Phourios: see Furius.

Pierus: see Pileius.

43 M. PILE(I)US PIERUS.

Pantomime (context). (1) 1 cent. B.C./1 cent A.D. Fl. 10 B.C./A.D. 14? (2) He came from Tibur. (3) He performed at Rome, also at Pompeii.

(4) *CIL* VI.10115. Etc. (5) *RE* Suppl. X (1965) col. 542 s.v. M.

Pileus Pierus. (6) Bonaria, *Fasti* 508, 514; Bonaria, *RM* p. 198, no. 143; p. 199, no. 145; Henry 365.

44 PYLADES I,

so designated to distinguish him from later namesakes. Pantomime (*choreuon, orchestes, pantomimos, -us, saltare*). (1) 1 cent. B.C. − 1 cent. A.D. Fl. 22 B.C. − 2 B.C., by which time he was very old. (2) He came from Cilicia. (3) He performed at Rome and also at Pompeii.

(4) Boeth. *Anth. Pal.* 9.248; Antipat. Thessal. *Anth. Plan.* 290; Sen. *Controv.* 3, praef. 10; *CIL* X.10115; *CIL* X. 1074? Etc. (5) *RE* XXIII.2 (1959) cols. 2082-2083 s.v. Pylades 2; see also *RE* III.1 (1897) cols. 137-138 s.v. Bathyllus 7. (6) Bonaria, *Fasti* 484-499, 508, 511; Bonaria, *RM* pp. 11, 12; pp. 195-198, nos. 127, 132-134, 143; p. 200, nos. 147-149; p. 203, no. 158; cf. p. 204, no. 162; Henry 362, 382; Spruit 80. (7) Bonaria, "Dinastie" 224 ff., esp. 237-239.

45 Quintia.

(Mimetic?) dancer (context). (1) 1 cent. B.C./1 cent. A.D. Fl. probably in the Augustan period. (2) Her place of origin is not given. (3) She performed at Rome, apparently in the Circus Maximus (*magno notissima circo*).

(4) *Priap.* 27. (5) *RE* Suppl. X (1965) col. 864 s.v. Quinctius/-a 76. (6) Bonaria, *Fasti* 429; cf. Bonaria, *RM* p. 192, no. 122.

46 P. Rusticelius

(Mimetic?) dancer, possibly pantomime (*saltator*). See Appendix 1, no. 131. His date could be Augustan but there is nothing to confirm this.

47 Sammula.

Mime? See Appendix 1, no. 135. Her long life may have overlapped the Augustan period.

48 SOPHE.

Mistress of pantomimic interludes (*theorobathylliana arbitrix imboliarum*; the first word may be a quasi-cognomen). (1) 1 cent. B.C./1 cent. A.D. Fl. after 22 B.C., but very probably within the Augustan period. (2) Her place of origin is not given; her name is Greek. (3) She performed at Rome.

(4) *CIL* VI.10128. (5) Not in *RE*. (6) Bonaria, *Fasti* 513; cf. Bonaria, *RM* p. 199, no. 143; p. 218, no. 241; Henry 380.

Sorix: see Norbanus.

49 STEPHANIO.

Dancer of Roman pieces (*togatarius; primus togatus*, coni. *togatas, saltare instituit*). (1) 1 cent. B.C. − 1 cent. A.D. Fl. 17 B.C. − A.D. 47 and after. (2) His place of origin is unknown. (3) He performed at Rome.

(4) Plin. *NH* 7.159. Etc. (5) *RE* III.A.2 (1929) col. 2350 s.v. Stephanio 1. (6) Bonaria, *Fasti* 450, 451, 557; Bonaria, *RM* pp. 12, 13; pp. 197-198, no. 138; p. 206, no. 177; cf. p. 211, no. 202; Henry 382; Spruit 118.

50 Telethusa.
(Mimetic?) dancer (*circulatrix*, and context). (1) 1 cent. B.C./1 cent. A.D. Fl. probably in the Augustan period. (2) Her place of origin is not given. Her name is Greek, formed from the present participle of *telethao*, but possibly familiarized by Ovid (*Met.* 9.682, etc.). (3) She evidently performed at Rome.
(4) *Priap.* 19. (5) *RE* Suppl. X (1965) col. 927 s.v. Telethusa 2. (6) Bonaria, *Fasti* 428, cf. 701; Bonaria, *RM* p. 194, no. 122.

Theorobathylliana: see Sophe.

51 C. THEORUS (Theoros).
Pantomime (*victor pantomimorum*). (1) 1 cent. B.C. − 1 cent. A.D. Fl. perhaps c. 10 B.C. − A.D. 14. (2) His place of origin is not given. His name is Greek. (3) He performed at Rome, perhaps also at Pompeii. On the question of his identity with Bathyllus I, see under the latter.
(4) *CIL* VI.10115. Etc. (5) See *RE* III.1 (1897) cols. 137-138 s.v. Bathyllus 7; *RE* Suppl. X (1965) cols. 95-96 s.v. Bathyllos 7; *RE* Suppl. X (1965) col. 950 s.v. Theoros 3. (6) Bonaria, *Fasti* 508-510, 513; Bonaria, *RM* pp 198-199, no. 143; Henry 365. (7) Bonaria, "Dinastie" 224 ff., esp. 231-232.

52 Tyrannus (Tyrannos).
Actor in comedy (*komoidos*). (1) 1 cent. B.C./1 cent. A.D.? Augustan? (2) His place of origin is unknown. His name is Greek. (3) He evidently performed at Rome, and he was buried there on his death at the age of eighteen.
(4) *CIL* VI.6253 = *IG* XIV.2050. (5) *RE* Suppl. X (1965) col. 954 s.v. Tyrannos 1 a. (6) Spruit p. 86, no. 55.

APPENDIX 3: TABLE OF ROSCIADS

Listed here are the twenty-one Rosciads known to the writer, together with certain other ebullitions closely related to the Rosciad idea.

No.	Date	Author	Title
1.	1750	Anon.	*The Rosciad, a Poem*
2.	1753	Anon.	*The Ancient Rosciad*
3.	1761	Anon. (Charles Churchill)	*The Rosciad. By the Author*
4.	1761	Anon. (Thomas Morell?)	*The Anti-Rosciad*
	1761	Anon.	*The Churchiliad: or, a Few Modest Questions* . . .
5.	1762	Anon. (H. J. Pye?)	*The Rosciad of C-v-nt G-rd-n*
6.	1763	Anon.	*The Smithfield Rosciad*
7.	1765	S(arah) K(ing)	*The Hibernian Rosciad*
8.	1766	Anon. (John Potter?)	*The Rosciad, or a Theatrical Register,* article in the *Public Ledger*
9.	1766	Anon.	*The Theatrical Register; or, Weekly Rosciad,* column in the *London Chronicle*
10.	1767	F-B-L-.	*The Rational Rosciad. On a More Extensive Plan* . . .
	1767	Anon.	*Roscius . . . Examination . . . of all the Principal Performers belonging to the Norwich Theatre*
	c. 1769	Anon.	*Roscius Redivivus,* an epigram
11.	1770	Anon.	*A New Rosciad, for the Year MDCCLXX* (Edinburgh)
	1771-72		*"Be dumb, ye Criticks . . . Who says that Roscius feels the hand of Time? . . .,"* complimentary verses
	1772	Anon. (William Kenrick)	*Love in the Suds . . . the Lamentation of Roscius for the loss of his Nyky*

12.	1775	Anon.	*The Edinburgh Rosciad for 1775*
	1780	Pseud. "Grubstreticus"	*A Parody on the Rosciad of Churchill*
	1780	Pseud. "Grubstreticus"	Verses on Phillimore
13.	1785	Anon. (J. H. Leigh)	*The New Rosciad, in the Manner of Churchill*
	1787	Anon.	*The Garriciad, a Poem: being a Companion to the Rosciad of Churchill*
	1788	Anon.	*The Modern Stage Exemplified, in an Epistle* . . . The *European Magazine* called this a "pseudo-Rosciad."
14.	1799	More Kotzebue	*The Minor Rosciad*
15.	1801-02	Anon.	*The Theatrical Repository; or Weekly Rosciad*
16.	1802	George Butler	*The Rosciad*
17.	1805	Anon.	*Roscius in London. Biographical Memoir of . . . Betty* . . . (There were many such memoirs.)
17.	1805	Pseud. "Peter Pangloss"	*The Young Rosciad, an Admonitory Poem* . . .
18.	1805	Anon.	*The Prose Rosciad*
19.	1812	Pseud. "K.L.M.N.O.P.Q."	*The Rosciad: a Heroi-Serio-Comical Poem*
	1825	Anon.	*The Roscius*, nos. 1-7, a monthly theatrical magazine
20.	1834	W. H. Logan	*The Edinburgh Rosciad; for the Summer Season 1834*
21.	1852	Anon.	*Mundus Dramaticus (The New Rosciad)*

NOTES

1: PERSON, PERSONA, PERSONALITY

1. Juv. *Sat.* 7.232-236.
2. "Fascination ... scraps of knowledge," P. Green, *Juvenal: The Sixteen Satires* (London 1967) 175. The other quoted words are from J. D. Duff, *Fourteen Satires of Juvenal* (Cambridge [1898] reset reprint 1970) 287-288.
3. Keeping the attention fixed inside the dramatic illusion has indeed been a feature of criticism common to many periods: take for example A. C. Bradley's *Shakespearean Tragedy* (first publ. 1904), G. Wilson Knight's *The Wheel of Fire* (first publ. 1930), H. B. Charlton's *Shakespearian Comedy* (first publ. 1938), H. D. F. Kitto's *Greek Tragedy: A Literary Study* (first publ. 1939), and Northrop Frye's *Anatomy of Criticism* (first publ. 1957). For recent emphasis on the centrality of praxis as taught by Aristotle and for a protest against alleged foisting of the "tragic hero" concept on to ancient drama, see especially J. Jones, *On Aristotle and Greek Tragedy* (New York [1962] 1968) 43-47.
4. *Prosopographia Imperii Romani, saec. I II III*, edd. E. Klebs, H. Dessau, P. de Rohden (Berlin 1896-1898); second edition, edd. E. Groag and A. Stein (Berlin and Leipzig 1933-). The *Prosopography of the Later Roman Empire*, edd. A. H. M. Jones, J. R. Martindale, J. Morris, 1, A.D. 260-395 (Cambridge 1971). 2, A.D. 395-518, is in process of compilation and publication.
5. Bonaria, *MRF*, of which fasc. 2 is devoted to the fasti; and the same author's *RM*, which contains a condensed version of the fasti on pp. 167-274. For O'Connor and Parenti see below and Abbreviations.
6. See Abbreviations.
7. G. K. G. Henry, "Roman Actors," *SPh* 16 (1919) 334-384.
8. Notably the Ph.D. thesis by E. J. Jory, "Some Aspects of the Acting Profession at Rome" (Univ. of London 1967; copy in the library of University College): pp. 233-244 list "all the actors known or suspected to have taken part in Latin performances of comedy and tragedy." A published

item of great value is the index to J. E. Spruit's *De Juridische en Sociale positie van de Romeinse Acteurs* (Assen 1966).

9. Schol. on Eur. *Med.* 922. See further D. W. Lucas' commentary in his edition of the *Poetics* (Oxford 1968) 158-159.

10. Pollux 4.143-154.

11. *Corp. Fab. Aesop.* 1.1, ed. A. Hausrath, corr. H. Haas (Leipzig 1957) 27 (version 3)= Halm 47, Chambry 43.

12. See esp. Arist. *EN* 3.2.1 (1111b). The key word is *proairesis*, traditionally rendered "moral choice" or (as in J. E. C. Welldon's translation) "moral purpose." The more recent translation by J. A. K. Thomson (London 1955, repr. 1963) limits the matter to "deliberate choice" here, but finds itself obliged to say "right choice" at 6.2.2 (1139a).

13. Character revealed by pattern of choices, *Poet.* 6.1450b8-9; natural to place *personae* on a moral scale, 2.1448a1-5; tragic *personae* should be better than ordinary men, 2.1448a16-18, 15.1454a16-17 and 1454b8-9.

14. *Poet.* 15.1454a33-36.

15. C. Garton "Characterization in Greek Tragedy," *JHS* 77 (1957) 247-254.

16. Cf. *Concise Oxford Dictionary*[5] (Oxford [1964] 1967) s.v. function.

17. Cf. Garton (above, n. 15) 250.

18. Arist. *Poet.* 6.1450a21.

19. See esp. Cic. *De Off.* 1.114.

20. H. D. F. Kitto, *Greek Tragedy: A Literary Study*[3] (London 1961, repr. 1966). This book originally appeared in 1939.

21. S. T. Coleridge, *Biographia Literaria*, ed. G. Watson (London 1965, repr. 1967) 168-169.

22. Or possibly "Glory to the Only God"; Coleridge (above, n. 21) 289. The words are wrongly translated in the Watson edition as "The glory of God alone."

23. Shelley made his mind up early: see his Notes on *Queen Mab*, esp. that on 7.135-136, " . . . belief is utterly distinct from and unconnected with volition. . . . Belief is a passion, or involuntary operation of the mind. . . ." etc.

24. Plut. *Solon* 29.5; a garbled version of the same incident at Diog. L. 1.59.

25. Cf. A. W. Pickard-Cambridge, *Dithyramb, Tragedy, and Comedy*[2] (Oxford 1962) 77 – the inserted paragraph by T. B. L. Webster, the reviser.

26. Ter. *Hec.* prol. 1.4-5 and prol. 2.40-41.

27. Quint. 6.3.65.

28. Macrob. *Sat.* 2.7.15.

29. Suet. *Aug.* 45.4.

30. Hor. *Sat.* 2.3.60-62, Pseud.-Acr. and Porph. ad loc.; see Appendix 1, nos. 63 and 84.

31. See section 9 of the ancient *Life* of Aeschylus. The sentence is suspect, but we need not doubt the tradition that over-impressionable

beholders of Aeschylean drama felt sensations of horror, cf. *Life*, section 7.

32. Juv. *Sat.* 3.175-176.

33. The primary source on this eccentric is Cic. *Phil.* 3.16; cf. Val. Max. 7.8.1 and Lactant. *Div. Inst.* 3.23 (Migne, *PL* 6.422 - 423).

34. Plut. *Cic.* 5.4.

35. Cf. Pickard-Cambridge, *Festivals*² 305: "In addition to the title ἱερονείκης which could be used of any victor in sacred games or belonging to a ἱερὰ σύνοδος, we find περιοδονείκης used to indicate a victor in all the four great festivals of Greece, and πλειστονείκης of one who broke the record in the number of his victories; παράδοξος is constantly used of the victor and παραδοξονείκης is found." Some of these terms came to be latinized and used in Italian contexts; see, for example, *CIL* IX.344 = Bonaria, *Fasti* 885 = Bonaria, *RM* p. 232, and see the word *hieronica* in lexicons.

36. Polyb. 30.22.12= fr. 13 Dindorf= Athen. 14.615a.

37. For the ruin of the Orestes role see Lucilius 567 Marx = 594 Warmington (*ROL* 3.184). On Aesopus and Roscius see Cic. *De Orat.* 1.258 and 124.

38. Cic. *Tusc. Disp.* 2.16.38, cf. p. 195-196 below; and *Ad Fam.* 7.1.

39. *Rhet. ad Her.* 1.14.24; 2.13.19; the mime actor is no. 40 in Appendix 1.

40. The facts are known from Aristoph. *Acharn.* 377-382 (with schol.) and other passages.

41. For *hoious dei* see Arist. *Poet.* 25.1460b34. Sophocles' gentility and poise of temperament are attested by the ancient *Life* and by Aristophanes and Ion of Chios.

42. Aristoph. *Frogs* 1471.

43. Cic. *De Off.* 1.114.

44. Quint. 11.3.178-181.

45. Plin. *NH* 7.54; Val. Max. 9.14. 4; Quint. 6.3.57.

46. Val. Max. 9.14.5, cf. Plin. *NH* 7.55. C. Scribonius Curio (consul 76 B.C.) was very like Burbuleius in his delivery and was nicknamed after him. For a lively sketch of Curio see Cic. *Brut.* 216-217. Cf. p. 157 below.

47. Sen. *Epist.* 80.7-8.

48. John Jones (above, n. 3) 60.

49. Jones (above, n. 3) 61.

50. *Hamlet* 2.2.562.

51. For the ritual preliminaries to the Great Dionysia see Pickard-Cambridge, *Festivals*² 59-63, with references there given. The phallus is mentioned by Plutarch, *De Cupid. Divit.* 527d; he does not say explicitly that he is speaking of Athens but there is every reason to suppose that his words applied there.

52. Liv. 7.2.3.

53. Festus 436f. Lindsay (the right order of the clauses is uncertain); Servius on *Aen.* 8.110; cf. Duckworth 13.

54. Livy mentions many cases of *instauratio* between 216 and 179 B.C.

The clearest statement of principle is at Cic. *De Har. Resp.* 2.23. Cf. L. R. Taylor, *TAPhA* 68 (1937) 292; Duckworth 77-78.

55. For an exemplary discussion of this feature of the Roman theatre see J. A. Hanson, *Roman Theater-Temples* (Princeton 1959).

56. Aug. *De Civ. Dei* 6.5.

57. Gell. 6.5.7-8.

58. *Oxford Dictionary of the Christian Church* (Oxford 1957) s.v. intention.

59. Plut. *Crass.* 33.2-4. Plutarch's word for "finale" is *exodion*, which is well-attested in this sense. B. Perrin, in the Loeb edition, is doubly in error in translating *exodion* as "farce" here and trying to explain with reference to the satyr-play which followed three tragedies at the Great Dionysia. Plutarch did not throw away his great moments like this.

60. See below, p. 150.

61. See below, p. 152.

2: TERENCE'S ANTAGONIST: THE BACKGROUND

1. See for example H. B. Mattingly, "The Terentian Didascaliae," *Athenaeum*, N.S. 36 (1959) 148-173, and "The Chronology of Terence," *RCCM* Ann. 5 (1963) 12-61; slightly earlier were M. R. Posani, "La figura di Luscio Lanuvino e la sua polemica con Terenzio," *RAL* 7.4 (1943) 151-162, conveniently summarized by H. Marti in *Lustrum*, Jahrg. 1963, Bd. 8 (1964) 18; and L. Gestri, "Due frammenti di Luscio Lanuvino e la cronologia terenziana," *SIFC*, N.S. 23 (1949) 153-178, of which the substance is given in the above-mentioned volume of *Lustrum*, p. 20. Among older work on Terence the following may be noted as highly relevant to Luscius: P. Fabia, *Les Prologues de Térence* (Paris 1888), and the same scholar's *P. Terenti Afri Eunuchus* (Paris 1895); and E. Fraenkel, "Zum Prolog des terenzischen Eunuchus," *Sokrates* 6 (1918) 302-317.

2. Duckworth 61-65 and see index s.v. "Luscius Lanuvinus"; Beare 114-115 (but see also 96-106); W. Kroll in *RE* Suppl. VII (1940), cols. 419-420 s.v. Luscius Ia; and Schanz-Hosius, *Geschichte der römischen Literatur.* I⁴ (Munich 1927, repr. 1959) 125.

3. Ribbeck CRF^2 (Leipzig 1873, repr. Hildesheim 1962) pp. 83-84.

4. Ribbeck uses an inferior text of Donatus to that of Wessner, and even then skimps on his quotation of it. Further fragments have been proposed by Posani (above, n.1), who bases himself on Ter. *Phorm.* 14-16 and 9-11a. *POxy* XXXVIII (1971) 2825 sheds much new light on the original of Luscius' *Phasma*; see below, pp. 103 ff.

5. Both edited by P. Wessner as *Donatus: Commentum Terenti* 1 (1902,

repr. Stuttgart 1966); 2 (1905, repr. Stuttgart 1966), .and 3.1 (1908, repr. Stuttgart 1966), this last volume containing Eugraphius.

6. J. F. Mountford, *The Scholia Bembina* (Liverpool and London 1934); a selection of the other scholia in F. Schlee, *Scholia Terentiana* (Leipzig 1893), where the fullest but also the most unreliable information on Luscius occurs in what Schlee calls the *commentarius recentior*. Schlee's work has been heavily criticized (see references, especially to the articles by E. K. Rand, in *Lustrum* Jahrg. 1961, Bd. 6 [1962] 153-154), but no one has troubled to supersede it. I have found no evidence that the removal of its deficiencies would increase our knowledge of Luscius. The principal life of Terence (that by Suetonius, used by Donatus) does not mention Luscius.

7. A synopsis of views advanced over the half-century 1909-1959 is given by H. Marti in *Lustrum*, Jahrg. 1963, Bd. 8 (1964) 20-23. Marti's conclusion is that it has not been shown that the didascalic dates need be abandoned.

8. Mattingly, as cited in n. 1 above. Marti (above, n. 7) cites five different proposed orders for the plays. Mattingly himself proposed two different orders at different times.

9. Don. ad Ter. *Andr.* prol. 6 = 1 p. 43 Wessner.

10. One of the mss. (T) of Donatus refers to him in the dative as Lucio Lauino (Don. ad Ter. *Andr.* prol. 4 = 1 p. 41 Wessner). This can hardly be taken as evidence for the praenomen Lucius, though he may well have been called that.

11. See Dziatzko-Kauer edition of Ter. *Phorm.* (Leipzig 1913, repr. Amsterdam 1967) pp. 220-221.

12. F. G. Allinson, Loeb edition of Menander (1921) 359, 448; OCD^1 (1946) s.v. Luscius (OCD^2 [1970] offers "Luscius Lanuvinus [?Lavinius]"). Edmonds, II p. 633 and p. 53; C.A.P. Ruck, *IG II^2 2323: The List of the Victors in Comedies at the Dionysia* (Leiden 1967) 48.

13. The only indication apart from circumstantial evidence is his cognomen Lanuvinus, which does not seem very likely to have been retained from a former servile status. However, in later times, Praenestinus occurs as the cognomen of a freedman.

14. *CIL* $I.^2 1332$ = VI.21696 = Degrassi, *ILLRP²* 928.

15. *CIL* $I.^2 182$ = XIV.3154; $I.^2 183$ = XIV.3155; $I.^2 184$ = XIV.3156 = Degrassi *ILLRP²* 859.

16. Naevius' *Ariolus*: Ribbeck CRF^2 pp. 9-10, Warmington *ROL* 2 pp. 80-81. It is not easy to translate *inanem volvulam madidam* convincingly.

17. M. Aurelius ap. Fronto, *ad M. Caes. et invicem*, 2.8.3 = p. 31 Van den Hout. Lanuvium shared this characteristic with Naples.

18. This is a guess based on a visit to the place which I made a few years ago. Lanuvio has a present population of around 4,000.

19. Livy 41.16.1-2. On the religious background in general, see A. E. Gordon, *The Cults of Lanuvium, Univ. of Calif. Publ. in Cl. Arch.* 2.2. (Berkeley 1938) 21-58.

20. Suet. *Vit. Ter.* 6: *colore fusco*. Lanuvines themselves were prover-

bially sun-tanned.

21. It would require skilled co-ordination of site-study, artefacts, and literary (including mythological) records. A systematic beginning on the artefacts (period c. 775-550 B.C.) has now been made by P. G. Gierow in *The Iron Age Culture of Latium* 1 (Lund 1966).

22. Diomede. Their real beginnings as a township are better gleaned from Gierow (see previous note).

23. Agnes K. Lake, "The Archaeological Evidence for the 'Tuscan Temple,' " *MAAR* 12 (1935) 89-149; see 129-130.

24. See Webster, *MNC*[2] IT58 (p. 138).

25. Juv. *Sat.* 3.173.

26. G. B. Colburn, *AJA* Ser. 2, vol. 18 (1914) 377.

27. For Lucius Aelius Stilo Praeconinus see *RE* I.1 (1893) cols. 582-583 s.v. Aelius 144. For his father the *praeco* see Suet. *Gramm.* 3.

28. Cic. *Pro. Rosc. Com.* 43-46; *RE* XIII. 2 (1927) cols. 1865-1866, s.v. Luscius 2; R. Syme, "Senators, Tribes and Towns," *Historia* 13 (1964) 108.

29. Asconius 81; *RE* XIII.2 (1927) cols. 1865-1866, s.v. Luscius 1; Syme (above, n. 28) 119.

30. *RE* XIII.2 (1927) cols. 1865-1866 s.v. Luscius 3; Syme (above n. 28) 108.

31. *CIL* XIV.2119.

32. *CIL* XIV.2118.

33. I have compiled the list from scattered sources. There is as yet no published prosopography of Lanuvium.

34. As by Beare 114, and T. F. Carney, *P. Terenti Afri Hecyra*, *PACA* Suppl. 2 (Rhodesia 1963) p. 34.

35. See discussions by C. M. Kurrelmeyer in *The Economy of Actors in Plautus* (Graz 1932), by L. R. Taylor in "The Opportunities for Dramatic Performances in the Time of Plautus and Terence," *TAPhA* 68 (1937) 284-304, and by Duckworth 76-79.

36. Ter. *Hec.* prol. 2.43.

37. Ter. *Hec.* prol. 1.4.

38. Ter. *Hec.* prol. 2.40-42.

39. Livy 34.44 and 54; Val. Max. 2.4.3; Vitruvius 5.6.2; cf. H. D. Jocelyn, *Ennius* (Cambridge 1967) 18, n. 3.

40. See plan (after Canina) in J. A. Hanson, *Roman Theater-Temples* (Princeton 1959) 120, illustr. 16. My estimate is of seating-capacity, not of number of rows. For some calculations see T. P. Wiseman, *Historia* 19(1970) 72.

41. Hor. *Sat.* 1.10. 76-77.

42. See Webster, *HPA* 279.

43. See notes on the censors of these years in Broughton *MRR*.

44. Liv. 40.51.3; Webster (above, n. 42) 279.

45. Liv. 41.27.5.

46. Polyb. 30.22.12= fr. 13 Dindorf= Athen. 14. 615a-d.

47. A meaning of *topographos* not recognized in LSJ or its Suppl.; cf. Webster, *HPA* 164, 177, 278.

48. Cf. Vitr. 5.6.9 and 7.5.2; Webster, *HPA* 162-166, 278-279, and *GB* 57; Bieber, *HGRT*² 124-125 and figs. 471-474.

49. Cf. Webster, *HPA* 301.

50. For bibliographic information on this episode see n. 30 to p. 148.

51. Festus pp. 446-448 Lindsay.

52. Most recent discussion, with references, in E. J. Jory, "Some Aspects of the Acting Profession at Rome" (unpubl. diss., London 1967) 145 ff.

53. Jory (above, n. 52) 149-150.

54. By E. G. Sihler in "The Collegium Poetarum at Rome," *AJPh* 26 (1905) 1-21. On p. 13 Sihler involves himself in a contradiction when saying that the low rating of Terence in the canon of Volcacius reflects *collegium* opinion: for Luscius is there rated even lower. The same contradiction appears in Duckworth 46.

55. Hor. *Sat.* 2.6.36-37.

56. Cic. *2 Verr.* 3.184; see no. 16 in Appendix 1.

57. Text, photograph, and discussion in E. J. Jory "P. Cornelius P. L. Surus: an Epigraphical Note," *BICS* 15 (1968) 125-126 and plate 13.

58. Ter. *Andr.* prol. 17.

59. As recorded in Suet. *Vit. Ter.* 5. Suetonius thinks of the land as a rich man's pleasure garden, and as so used by Terence, which it probably was not.

60. As recorded by Porcius Licinus ap. Suet. *Vit. Ter.* 5.

61. Ter. *Phorm.* prol. 19.

62. The story that Caecilius "vetted" the manuscript of the *Andria* is not incompatible with this.

63. For *actor* so used, see Ter. *HT* prol. 12, *Phorm.* prol. 10.

64. See E. J. Jory *"Dominus Gregis?" CPh* 61 (1966) 102-104.

65. By H. D. Jocelyn, *Ennius* (Cambridge 1967) 12-23.

66. Quoted at Gell. 1.24.2; translation by Janet Lembke, *Arion* 6 (1967) 378 — a version which I admire, despite its failure to render *Romai* in the last line.

67. Donat. *De Com.* 63 = 1. 26 Wessner.

68. Ter. *Hec.* prol. 2.7.

69. Ter. *Hec.* prol. 2.20-21.

70. The tradition transmitted by St. Jerome's *Chronicle.*

71. Ter. *Phorm.* prol. 9-10.

72. Above, nn. 44 and 45.

73. Webster, *HPA* 279.

74. Polybius (above, n. 46).

75. Agathodoros: see Appendix 1, no. 1. Antipatros: see Appendix 1, no. 47.

76. Novius: *IG* II².2325, col. 8; Pickard-Cambridge, *Festivals*² 112.

77. Duckworth 385.

78. E. W. Handley, *Menander and Plautus: a Study in Comparison*, Inaug.

Lect. at Univ. Coll. London (London 1968) 8.

79. Gell. 1.24.3, "et numeri innumeri simul omnes conlacrimarunt." I give William Beare's fine translation of this line (Beare 66-67).

80. Duckworth 394.

81. Duckworth 46-49, with references; cf. Beare 86-90.

82. Skill *in argumentis*, Varro ap. Charisius, *G.L.* 1.241.28 Keil; *gravitas*, Hor. *Epist.* 2.1.59.

83. Ribbeck, *CRF²* 58-62; Warmington, *ROL* 2 pp. 518-521; cf. K-T II 333 (pp. 121-122).

84. Volcacius Sedigitus, Morel, *FPL* p. 46; Gell. 2.23.11.

85. K-T II 334 (pp. 122-123).

86. Ribbeck, *CRF²* pp. 62-63; Warmington, *ROL* 2. pp. 522-533.

87. Webster, *HPA* 274.

88. Duckworth 47.

89. Warmington, *ROL.* 2 p. 522, n. *a*, following Nonius 233.12 (152-154).

90. *Thesaurus* and *Phasma*. For possible discarding of these two titles earlier in Roman theatre history see the two following studies.

91. Ter. *Andr.* prol. 20.

92. Ter. *Andr.* prol. 21.

93. Ter. *Andr.* prol. 21.

94. See below, pp. 94-96.

3: LUSCIUS: THE THESAURUS

1. Every increase in our knowledge of Greek New Comedy helps our understanding of Roman comedy, and this applies even to those Roman plays of which the Greek source is unknown or (as in the case of the *Thesaurus*) uncertain.

2. I am not concerned here with the traces of possible *fabulae incertae*.

3. Ter. *Eun.* prol. 9-13 as printed in the Oxford text by Kauer and Lindsay (1926 and repr.).

4. Don. ad Ter. *Eun.* prol. 10 = 1. p. 273 Wessner.

5. Schol. Bemb. ad *Eun.* prol. 11 = p. 13 Mountford. Eugraphius (see Don. 3. 1. p. 91 Wessner, cf. p. 89) summarizes the plot more briefly than Donatus, without mentioning the slave, but likewise points out how Luscius has violated ordinary judicial usage. Also, like the Bembine scholiast, he appears to regard the old man as the finder.

6. Apparently first noticed by Leo, *RhM* 38 (1883) 322.

7. Suda s.v. *Kratês*; cf. Meineke 1.58 ff.

8. Plaut. *Trin.* 17-18.

9. Kock II p. 142; Edmonds II pp. 42-43, 52-53.

10. Kock III pp. 276-277; Edmonds II pp. 632-635; discussion by H. Dohm, *Mageiros= Zetemata* 32 (Munich 1964) 120-122.

11. Kock III pp. 358-359; Edmonds III A pp. 294-295.

12. The inscription is *IG* II².2323 = IX.2.975, the list of victors in comedies at the Athenian Dionysia. As read by Kirchner in *IG* II² (date 1931), line 169 in col. 3 shows that in a celebration which took place in 181 B.C. a poet whose name is lost won second place among the new plays with a comedy whose title (in the dative case) ended in -αξομένοις. Now there is only one such comedy known to us, namely the *Diadikazomenoi* of Dioxippos, and Koehler in *IG* IX.2.975 (date 1883) seemed on very strong ground in proposing a supplement to this effect. Hence the poet is assigned by Edmonds III A pp. 292-293 to New Comedy, as indeed he had already been by Meineke on general grounds. C. A. P. Ruck, however, in his recent study *IG II² 2323: The List of the Victors in Comedies at the Dionysia* (Leiden 1967) claims to be able to read -ραξομένοις at the critical point (col. III, line 276), which would rule out Dioxippos' play (see pp. 14 and 45 of Ruck's monograph). Ruck is probably correct on this point, though his work has been searchingly criticized by Paul Roesch (*AC* 37 [1968] 732-733). Kaibel in *RE* V.1 (1903) col. 1151 s.v. Dioxippos 3 favoured a New Comedy date, though W. Kraus in *Der Kleine Pauly* 2 (1967) col. 95 s.v. Dioxippos, adducing other conjectural epigraphic evidence, argues for a date in the mid-fourth century. The question seems not yet closed.

13. Kock II p. 557; Edmonds III A p. 118. Edmonds' translation seems dubious.

14. K-T II pp. 78-79; Kock III pp. 67-69; Edmonds III B pp. 630-633.

15. The hyperbole has been taken by K-T II p. 79 to suggest a mendacious *miles* as the speaker; but the ordeal could be of various other kinds, e.g. the result of a shipwreck or marooning or a term in the quarries, or a parasite exaggerating his plight while his patron was away (cf. Plaut. *Stich.* 155 ff.)

16. The former is quite imaginable for Luscius' *Thesaurus* as we know it from Donatus; the latter could have occurred e.g. in the original of the *Aulularia*, with "Megadorus" as the *senex amator* and "Euclio" as the *parcus senex*.

17. Assumed as certain or probable by, for example, Ribbeck, *CRF*² p. 84 "Menandrum Luscii auctorem fuisse probabilis est virorum doctorum coniectura"; Kock III p. 67, following Meineke; E. Fraenkel, *Sokrates* 6 (1918) 308; F. G. Allinson, Loeb Menander (1931) p. 359; T. B. L. Webster, *SM*² 148; Edmonds, III B pp. 629-631. P. Fabia, *P. Terenti Afri Eunuchus* (Paris 1895), n. on prol. 10 (p. 79) writes: "L'original était aussi, selon toute vraisemblance, une comédie de Ménandre: puisque Térence ne nomme pas l'auteur du *Thesaurus*, c'est l'auteur du *Phasma*." Cf. the same author's *Les Prologues de Térence* (Paris 1888) 268-269. K-T II p. 77 reserves judgment.

18. Fronto in Strato's *Musa Puerilis= Anth. Pal.* 12.233 (third cent. A.D.).

19. Pap. Brit. Mus. 2562, ed. H. I. Milne in *Greek Shorthand Manuals* (London 1934) 38. *Thesauros* occurs in tetrad 330, *Phasma* in tetrad 334. Cf.

K-T I p. 150.

20. For the view that the *Aulularia* is Menandrean see the authorities cited by W. E. J. Kuiper, *The Greek Aulularia* (Leiden 1940) p. 8, n. 1; more recently, Webster *SM²* 120-127, W. Ludwig, "Aulularia-Probleme," *Philologus* 105 (1961) 247-262, and F. Klingner, *Studien zur Griechischen und Römischen Literatur* (Zurich 1964 [1956]) 114-125 (this last known to me only from *Lustrum* Bd. 10 [1966] 195).

21. Choricius 32.73 (p. 360 Foerster-Richsteig); cf. Kuiper (above, n. 20) 8-9, K-T II p. 51, and Ludwig (above, n. 20) 253.

22. An argument warmly espoused by G. Jachmann, cf. Kuiper and Ludwig (previous n.).

23. This view was defended by A. Krieger, *De Aululariae Plautinae exemplari Graeco*, Diss. (Giessen 1914); so more recently H. J. Mette in *Lustrum*, Jahrg. 1965 Bd. 10 (1966) 16, 91-95, 195-196.

24. Cf. Kuiper (above, n. 20) 11-16. The case for Menander's *Apistos* as source for the *Aulularia* is put by Webster at *SM²* 120-127, and the equivalence of the two plays is elsewhere regarded by him as a fact (see his *Studies in Later Greek Comedy* [Manchester 1953] 67); additional arguments by K. Gaiser, *WS* 79 (1966) 191-194.

25. For example J. Sargeaunt in the Loeb Terence I (1912 and repr.) p. 239 assumes ten years, whilst Edmonds III B p. 631 assumes nine years. Neither comments.

26. Webster *SM²* 148.

27. Dziatzko sensibly reserved judgment on this point, see the Dziatzko-Hauler ed. of Ter. *Phormio* (fourth ed. Leipzig 1913, repr. Amsterdam 1967) p. 89, n. on line 3 ff.

28. Schol. Bemb. ad *Eun.* prol. 11 = p. 13 Mountford.

29. The single fragment of the *Thesauros* of Dioxippos could fit in at this point, if that were the source-play.

30. Beare 114.

31. Webster *SM²* 148. So P. Fabia, *Les Prologues de Térence* (Paris 1888) 269 visualizes the scene as "devant les juges."

32. Ribbeck *CRF²* p. 84. Correct text at Don. ad Ter. *Eun.* prol. 10 = 1 p. 273 Wessner (published 1902, repr. 1966).

33. Kock III p. 67; Edmonds III B p. 630.

34. K-T I, *Epitr.* frag 6, κριτής (47 and 50), δίκας λέγοντες (52).

35. Compare Menander's phrase τὸν παρατυγχάνοντα at K-T I, *Epitr.* frag. 6, line 58. The use of the verb *capere* confirms that the proceedings are thought of as private; cf. P. J. Enk, *Plauti Mercator* (Leiden 1966) 736n. I cannot agree with Enk that the word *iudex* necessarily tells in the opposite direction.

36. F. Leo, *Plautinische Forschungen²* (Berlin 1912, repr. Darmstadt 1966) 100.

37. E. Fraenkel, "Zum Prolog des terenzischen Eunuchus," *Sokrates* 6 (1918) 302-317, esp. p. 308. I am indebted to Prof. W. G. Arnott for drawing

my attention to this article. P. Fabia, *Les Prologues de Térence* (Paris 1888) 270 pointed out that if (as he assumes) the *epistula* clinches the young man's case, there would be nothing for the *senex* to say at all unless he spoke first.

38. K-T II pp. 77-78.

39. Fraenkel (above, n. 37).

40. So P. Fabia, *P. Terenti Afri Eunuchus* (Paris 1895), n. on prol. 10 (p. 79). P. Fabia, *Les Prologues de Térence* (Paris 1888) 270 assumes that the *iudicium* forms the finale of the comedy. We have no reason to suppose this.

41. See F. Schlee, *Scholia Terentiana* (Leipzig 1893) 165, *ursos ... introducebant*.

4: LUSCIUS IN THE STEPS OF MENANDER: THE PHASMA

1. The *Phasma*, whose source is known, is much more directly benefited by recent papyrological advances than the *Thesaurus*. Cf. previous chapter, n. 1.

2. For a comparative consideration of the apparition-theme in ancient drama generally, see Ruby Mildred Hickman, *Ghostly Etiquette on the Classical Stage* (Cedar Rapids 1938) = Iowa Studies in Class. Philol. 7. Pages 150-159 are devoted to New Comedy and the Roman adaptations of it. However, there is need of a fresh treatment, taking in new material and studying the whole within the setting of the psychology of the irrational. The question of how far Greek and Latin distinguish terminologically between ghosts and other apparitions also needs further study.

3. Polyb. 30.22.12 (= fr. 13 Dindorf) = Athen. 14.615a. See above p. 55.

4. Monimos is not known from literary sources. The facts and inferences in this paragraph are primarily based on the two allusions to him in *IG* II².2323, recently re-edited by Carl A. P. Ruck as *IG II² 2323: The List of the Victors in Comedies at the Dionysia* (Leiden 1967): see p. 15 (col. 4, lines 383-392) and p. 48. An earlier revival of the *Phasma* is known to have taken place some eighty-eight years before, in about 255 B.C., but there may have been many other performances unknown to us.

5. *Sikyonioi*: photographs of the papyrus fragments are given by A. Blanchard and A. Bataille, "Fragments sur papyrus du ΣΙΚΤΩΝΙΟΣ de Ménandre," *RecPap* 3 (1964), plates 6 to 13. The papyrus Didotiana was originally published, with photographs, by H. Weil, *Monuments Grecs* 1 (1879), no. 8; description and text at K-T I pp. 1x-1xi, 143-145.

6. Don. ad Ter. *Eun.* prol. 9.3 = 1 p. 272 Wessner. Among the best aids to study of the *Eunuchus* prologue are P. Fabia, *Les Prologues de Térence* (Paris 1888) and *P. Terenti Afri Eunuchus* (Paris 1895); and E. Fraenkel, "Zum Prolog des terenzischen Eunuchus," *Sokrates* 6 (1918) 302-317. Since Ribbeck other fragments of Luscius (from unspecified plays) have been

proposed: *Phorm*. 9-11a and 13-15 (neither passage very convincingly) by L. Gestri, "Due frammenti di Luscio Lanuvino e la cronologia terenziana," *SIFC* N.S. 23 (1949) 153-178; another study of Luscius is M. R. Posani, "La figura di Luscio Lanuvino e la sua polemica con Terenzio," *RAL* 7.4 (1943) 151-162. I regret that these latter two rather inaccessible papers are known to me only from summaries by H. Marti in *Lustrum*, Jahrg. 1963, Bd. 8 (1964) 15, 18, 20.

   7. Wessner prints *ex vicino quodam*. I owe knowledge of Kassel's convincing emendation to Professor E. G. Turner. Corruption was caused by *apud vicinum proximum* following. It makes much better sense for the plot summary to say nothing about the girl's paternity. (However, it could have been Donatus himself, or even his source, and not a later scribe, who fudged the story at this point.) See also n. 44 below.

   8. So, surprisingly, E. Fraenkel in *Sokrates* 6 (1918) 311. The point is discussed by E. G. Turner, "The *Phasma* of Menander," *GRBS* 10 (1969) 307-324: see p. 321.

   9. Cf. Turner (above, n. 8) 309 and 323-324. Turner shows that we cannot exclude the possibility that the two fathers are one and the same person (children who were homopatric but not homometric being allowed to marry each other by Attic law; cf. Nepos, praef. 4).

   10. Edmonds III B pp. 750-751.

   11. For discussion, photographs, and bibliography see S. Charitonidis, Lilly Kahil, and R. Ginouvès, *Les Mosaïques de la maison de Ménandre à Mytilène* = *AK* Beiheft 6 (Berne 1970), esp. 12, 60-62, 65-68, 72-77, 81-82, 91-92, and plates 8.2 and 24.2. Mme Kahil records great indebtedness to the work of T. B. L. Webster, E. G. Turner, and others. For further discussion by Mme Kahil and Prof. Turner see *Entretiens Hardt* 16, *Ménandre* 1 (Vandoeuvres Genève 1970) 36-39. See also Webster, *MNC*² ix and 301, and his review of *Les Mosaïques* ... in *JHS* (forthcoming). Where these authorities have disagreed with each other I have not found it possible to be absolute.

   12. Mme Kahil, *Mosaïques* (above, n. 11) 72.

   13. Mme Kahil, *Mosaïques* (above, n. 11) 65.

   14. Mme Kahil, *Mosaïques* (above, n. 11) 67.

   15. For the parchment fragments the best edition up to 1971 was Del Corno (1966) 567-581; review by W. G. Arnott, *CR*, N.S. 18 (1968) 33-35. See also K-T I pp. liv-lv, 134-137, cf. Edmonds III B pp. 748-755, though Turner (above, n. 8) and others have shown that many of the proposed supplements and inferences are invalid or questionable. For the papyrus fragments see *POxy* XXXVIII (1971) 2825. For a tentative (and to some extent controversial) reconstruction of the plot of the play, see Turner (above, n. 8). Professor Turner with great kindness supplied me with an advance text of both these last two items, and my own account of the fragments is everywhere beholden to his.

   16. As seen by Turner (above, n. 8) 321, this seems to render untenable

Webster's belief (*SM*² 101-102) that the exposition-speech of Petr. 1b is spoken by Pheidias himself in the *third* act. Webster also refers to it as written on papyrus, which is an error.

17. For a defence of either view see *Entretiens* (above, n. 11) 36-39. Among other scholars Webster has maintained that the mosaic scene was staged, and W. G. Arnott that if it was staged it cannot be a shrine scene.

18. Cf. Turner (above, n. 8) 323-324.

19. My English is based on Del Corno's Greek text. The supplements to Petr. 1a given in K-T I pp. 136-137 may be provisionally accepted, and are included in the translation.

20. The last part of this speech is not on the parchment. It is known from a quotation by Clement of Alexandria. The vulgarism in the middle of the fragment, though its punch-word is not on the parchment, is rendered certain by Marcus Aurelius 5.12.

21. By Turner (above, n. 8) 318.

22. Text as in Del Corno. In some places adequate supplements have not been established. In what follows, where necessary I set in square brackets what I take to be the approximate sense, sometimes availing myself of the supplements in K-T I pp. 134-135.

23. The difficulty of supposing him still in conversation with the servant is the sudden stage-clearing at line 8.

24. It can hardly be (as has been proposed) the goddess to whom the pseudo-shrine is supposedly (or even really) dedicated, since line 25 refers to this goddess as if she is someone else.

25. Text as in Del Corno. As before I give conjectures or sense-links in square brackets in translation, partly following supplements printed in K-T I p. 135.

26. If (as Turner thinks) the couple next door took the girl in because of their own childlessness, the case for a τίτθη as foster-mother becomes weaker than ever. However, I doubt if the reason was childlessness, because this would make their son younger than the fosterling, whereas the sequel (which seems to portray him as for a time in love with her) suggests that he is older.

27. This is conjectured by Turner, who compares Hamlet. However, the number of scenes available to show this development would be much more restricted in Menander.

28. In *POxy* XXXVIII (1971) 2825.

29. Just conceivably it may be taking place simultaneously. I have assumed throughout that the slave is telling (more or less) the truth. If he is not, we should have to modify the reconstruction, but the ultimate outcome is the same.

30. In B the interpretation and bracketed words given are mostly based on suggestions by Turner and others in *POxy* (above, n. 28). The last line of B col. i is known from a quotation in Athenaeus.

31. By E. W. Handley.

32. Unless he suspects his neighbour of paternity of the *Phasma*, in which

case he might want to wash his hands of that family altogether.

33. I neglect, as unlikely, the possibility that besides, or instead of, these Menander would introduce a confession scene in yet a third household.

34. Turner (above, n. 8) 309 argues that this is very possible.

35. Supplements in the translation are based on suggestions in *POxy* XXXVIII, p. 13, or by Turner, except that phrases of my own are used at the beginning and end.

36. Suggested by Turner as the most plausible festival which will fit the space on the papyrus.

37. There is great uncertainty here.

38. The sense-supplements in the translation are mainly my own. Parts of two further lines are preserved but the sense is obscure.

39. For some suggestions on the act-structure see Turner (above, n. 8).

40. Gell. 2.23.11: "illud Menandri de vita hominum media sumptum simplex et verum et delectabile." I quote from Warmington's translation of this passage.

41. Turner (above, n. 8) 308 rightly sees that "Ghost" is a bad translation for the title of this play, though his remarks on pneumatological terms need qualification, and on p. 323 he speaks of this play as a play about a ghost.

42. Webster *SM*[2] 101, cf. K-T I p. 135. Del Corno 567, 575, drops the *nutrix* from his text, but retains her tentatively in his notes.

43. F. Leo. *RhM* 38 (1883) 322.

44. Kassel's emendation for the manuscript reading *ex vicino quodam* (with variants *vicio* and *vitio*) fits perfectly here. As to my split anapaest in the first line, and one or two other non-classical features in the verse, it hardly seems worth eliminating them as we do not know to what period this *argumentum* belongs. Note in Plaut. *Rud.* Arg. 1 "reti piscator de mari extraxit vidulum," where "mari extrax" is an anapaest.

45. Plut. *Quaest. Rom.* 6.

46. It was argued at length by Kuiper, *The Greek Aulularia* (Leiden 1940) 77, 128, that Plautus, in order to comply with Roman custom, made radical structural alterations in the case of the *Aulularia* and turned the original (Greek) plot into something of a muddle. Kuiper made similar proposals about the *Epidicus, Rudens, Cistellaria,* and *Bacchides.* In general he carried speculation much too far; for rejection of his case on the *Aulularia* see W. Ludwig, *Philologus* 105 (1961) 44 ff. On the general question of prohibited degrees in marriage in Greek and Roman comedy see C. W. Keyes, "Half-sister Marriage in New Comedy and the *Epidicus*," *TAPhA* 71, 217 ff. and E. Fraenkel, *Elementi plautini in Plauto* (Florence 1960) 434-435. These writers both stress that legal non-prohibition and actual sentiment were not necessarily coextensive.

47. Ter. *Andr.* prol. 15, *Hec.* prol. 47.

48. Dziatzko-Hauler were rightly open-minded about this in their edition of the *Phormio* (Leipzig 1913, repr. Amsterdam 1967), n. on prol. line 3.

49. Don. ad Ter. *Adelphoe*, praef. 4 = 2 p. 4 Wessner.

50. Atilius Fortunatianus ap. Caesius Bassus, *G.L.* 6.255 Keil.

51. Adopted by Dziatzko and others.

52. See P. Fabia, *Les Prologues de Térence* (Paris 1888) 268, and *P. Terenti Afri Eunuchus* (Paris 1895), n. on prol. 9 (p. 79); E. Fraenkel, "Zum Prolog des terenzischen Eunuchus," *Sokrates* (1918) 305.

53. "Ex alia in aliam linguam ad verba expressa translatio sensus operit, et velut laeto gramine sata strangulat:" from the preface to Evagrius' Latin translation of St. Athanasius' life of St. Antony; quoted by St. Jerome, *Epist.* 57.6. St. Jerome agrees with Evagrius and for that matter with Terence, to whose practice he refers a little earlier (57.5): "Terentius Menandrum, Plautus et Caecilius veteres comicos interpretati sunt; numquid haerent in verbis, ac non decorem magis et elegantiam in translatione conservant? Quam vos veritatem interpretationis, hanc eruditi *kakozêlian* nuncupant." *Kakozêlia* is a nice Greek equivalent for the *obscura diligentia* of Luscius.

54. Kuiper's phrase.

5: LUSCIUS: THE UNNAMED PLAYS

1. Among the opponents of this dating the most extreme is probably H. B. Mattingly, "The Chronology of Terence," *RCCM* Ann. 5 (1963) 1.12-61, who would bring the *HT* down as far as probably the autumn (ludi Romani) of 151 B.C. His thesis on Terentian chronology has not found general support.

2. E. Fraenkel, "Zum Prolog des terenzischen Eunuchus," *Sokrates* 6 (1918) 310.

3. See for example, George B. Duckworth, "The Dramatic Function of the *servus currens* in Roman Comedy," in *Classical Studies Presented to Edward Capps* (Princeton 1936) 93-102, and his *NRC* 106-107, 225, and index s.v. "running slave"; also H. Marti in *Lustrum*, Jahrg. 1963, Bd. 8 (1964) 18, 24, 31, 36. The question of the origins of the *servus currens* has recently been complicated by discovery of his presence in Menander's *Aspis* 399 ff.

4. Duckworth 106.

5. See Eugraphius on Ter. *HT* prol. 31 = Don. Comm. Ter. 3.1 (Leipzig 1908, repr. Stuttgart 1966) p. 157 Wessner.

6. The wording suggested could be an iambic senarius or the end of a trochaic septenarius. The Greek original, if any, may have contained ἐξίστασθε or παραχωρεῖτε.

7. W. W. Buckland, *A Text-Book of Roman Law*, third ed., rev. by P. Stein (Cambridge 1963) 198, summarizing a view of Ihering's but referring directly to *Dig.* 41.2.1.3.

8. W. W. Buckland (above n. 7) 168 (with references), showing that both *furiosi* and *insani* passed into the *cura* of a *curator*. The relevant passage in Gaius came in the lacuna before 1.197.

9. Contrast Ter. *HT* prol. 1.

10. H. B. Mattingly (see n. 4 above) would put it as late as 149/148.

11. E. Fraenkel (n. 2 above) 310. The source-play would presumably contain the word ἔλαφος.

12. F. Leo, *Plautinische Forschungen*[2] (Berlin 1912, repr. Darmstadt 1966) 162 n. 3, cf. the Dziatzko-Hauler edition of the *Phormio* (Leipzig 1913, repr. Amsterdam 1967), n. on prol. 6 ff. (p. 90). E. Fraenkel (above n. 2) 310, more cautiously says "a dream or vision."

13. See T. B. L. Webster, *Studies in Later Greek Comedy* (Manchester 1953) 130.

14. For some different uses of dream and hallucination in Greek New Comedy see Menander's *Dyskolos* 407 ff. and *Theophoroumene*, with discussions by E. W. Handley, *The Dyskolos of Menander* (London 1965) pp. 203-204 and *BICS* 16 (1969) 88-101.

6: THE THEATRICAL INTERESTS OF SULLA

1. Suet. *Aug.* 89.1.

2. See for example T. F. Carney, *A Biography of C. Marius* (*PACA*, Suppl. 1, n.d., about 1962) 71-72.

3. From Sulla himself, e.g., his attitude to the aedileship, his feeling for Metrobius, and some of his dealings with the Artists of Dionysus. From his friends, his jesting temperament and conviviality (and contrast *optime cantasse dicatur*, Macrob. *Sat.* 3.14.10, with Nero's *vox caelestis*, etc.). From his enemies, e.g., the hostile presentation in Plut. *Sull.* 2, with *legousin* and *dokounta*, and the denigrating plurals at 33.2.

4. Cic. *Brut.* 111 and the commentary by A. E. Douglas (Oxford 1966) ad loc.

5. Cassiod. *Chron.* ad 115 B.C. (Migne, *PL* 69 [Paris 1865] col. 1224): "L. Metellus et Cn. Domitius artem ludicram ex urbe removerunt, praeter Latinum tibicinem cum cantore, et ludum talarium" (s.v.1.). The interpretation of this has been much controverted. T. Frank, *CPh* 26 (1931) 11-20 denied that *artem ludicram* referred to the legitimate stage at all; against him W. M. Green, *CPh* 28 (1933) 301-302. Further discussion at B. Zucchelli, *Le denominazioni latine dell' attore = Studi grammaticali e linguistici* 4 (Brescia 1964) 19-20, 45, and J. E. Spruit, *De Juridische en Sociale positie van de Romeinse Acteurs* (Assen 1966) 58-63, who points out that there was no lack of stagefolk at Rome in Sulla's youth.

6. See T. F. Carney, "The Death of Sulla," *A Class.* 4 (1961) 64 ff., with full medical discussion. The incidence of venereal syphilis before the fifteenth century is, however, very uncertain. For two rival views see the papers by C. W. Goff and C. J. Hackett in D. R. Brothwell and A. T. Sandison (edd.), *Diseases in Antiquity* (Springfield, Illinois 1967); a map on p. 161 shows the disease as probable round the shores of the Mediterranean in the Bronze Age and Graeco-Roman times.

7. As claimed by R. Büttner, *Porcius Licinus und der litterarische Kreis des Q. Lutatius Catulus* (Leipzig 1893). For a spirited denunciation of the idea see E. Badian in *Historia* 6 (1957) 324, n. 50, and 11 (1962) 221, with references there given.

8. For Catulus' stepbrother, C. Julius Caesar Strabo, see Ribbeck, TRF² (Leipzig 1871, repr. Hildesheim 1962) 227-228. As for Amphio(n), his *patronus*, after he was freed, is usually taken to have been the younger Catulus only, but the fact that Cicero (*De Orat.* 2.155) puts a pointed allusion to Pacuvius' *Amphio* into the mouth of the elder Catulus gives some slight ground for thinking that it was he who originally bought and named Amphio(n) (cf. *RE* XIII.2 [1927] col. 2068, s.v. Lutatius 3). Catulus' son-in-law was Hortensius, nephew of the mad Tuditanus. For *Roscius exoritur* see Catulus *ap.* Cic. *N.D.* 1.79.

9. *Auct. de vir. illustr.* 72.4.

10. Cic.*De Off.* 2.58.

11. His praetorship was probably in 97 B.C., not 93 as commonly believed: see E. Badian, "Sulla's Cilician Command," *Athenaeum* 37 (1959) 279 ff.; cf. T. R. Broughton, *MRR* Suppl. (New York 1960) 20-21.

12. On the censors' ruling of 115 B.C., see above, n. 5. On Accius' politics see B. Biliński, *Accio ed i Gracchi*, Accad. Pol. di Scienze e Lettere, Bibl. di Roma, Conferenze, fasc. 3 (1958); Biliński perhaps over-accentuates the class struggle.

13. Appian, *BC* 1.99.464. For Sulla's monetary arrangements see Gell. 2.24.11.

14. This is probable, not certain. For a neat presentation of the evidence, see D. Magnino, *Plutarchi Vita Ciceronis* (Florence 1963) 44, n. on 13.2. For a discussion of varying views see H. Hill, *The Roman Middle Class in the Republican Period* (Oxford 1952) 160-161. L. Roscius Otho's law restoring the front seats to the knights has recently been dated in 68 rather than 67: see U. Scamuzzi, "Studio sulla *Lex Roscia Theatralis*," *RSC* 27 (1969) 144 ff.

15. Cf. M. Bonaria, *RM* 5. The post-Sullan actor mentioned above is Diphilus (Cic. *Ad Att.* 2.19.3).

16. The point was well made by W. Warde Fowler, *Social Life at Rome in the Age of Cicero* (1908, repr. London 1964) 316-317: "It is possible that both Sulla and Caesar, who also patronized the mimes, may have wished to avoid the personal allusions which were so often made or imagined in the exhibition of tragedies, and have aimed at confining the plays to such as would give less opportunity for unwelcome criticism."

17. See below, pp. 153-156.

18. Plut. *Pomp*. 9.3.

19. Plut. *Sull*. 2.2 and 30.5. Many anecdotes bear this out. Cf. Val. Max (6.9.6), who, however, mistakenly thought that Sulla outgrew these habits.

20. In his burlesques or farces: see next paragraph.

21. Plut. *Sull*. 13.4; 14.5. A. E. Raubitschek, "Sylleia," in *Studies in Roman Economic and Social History in Honor of Allan Chester Johnson* (Princeton 1951) 49-57.

22. The only ancient notice of these sketches is Athen. 6.261c. For a fair statement of the evidence (a) that the sketches were atellans or attellan-like, and (b) that they may have burlesqued mythology, see C. A. Van Rooy, *Studies in Classical Satire and Related Literary Theory* (Leiden 1965) 153. The foundations of this view were laid by B. L. Ullman in *SPh* 17 (1920) 379 ff. See also H. Bardon, *La Littérature latine inconnue* (Paris 1952) 1.152. F. Leo, *Ausgewählte Kleine Schriften* (Rome 1960) 1.252, the article originally published as "Die römische Poesie in der sullanischen Zeit," *Hermes* 49 (1914) 161-195, noted that Sulla's pieces were apparently still available fifty years after his death.

23. App. *BC* 1.101.472.

24. Eucharis: *CIL* VI.10096 = Degrassi, *ILLRP* 803; see Appendix 1, no. 83. Copiola: Plin. *NH* 7.158 (she may have been slightly older); see Appendix 1, no. 85, and Appendix 2, no. 32.

25. *CIL* X.814; Bieber, *HGRT*² 165 and figs. 592 a-b. Cf. Appendix 1, nos. 114, 142, and Appendix 2, no. 41.

26. On the limitations of the early mime libretto see Bonaria, *RM* 1-5.

27. This detail about Publilius Syrus is given by Plin. *NH* 35. 199. On the white chalk in relation to imported slaves see Juv. 1.111 and commentators. For discussion of Publilius' dates see *RE* XXIII.2 (1959) col. 1921 s.v. Publilius 28, cf. Bonaria, *RM* 131; and F. Giancotti, *Mimo e Gnome* (Florence 1967) 137-143.

28. Antiodemis, as described by Antipater of Sidon, *Anth. Pal.* 9.567; but some prefer to attribute to Antipater of Thessalonica, in Augustan times. It has been objected to me that lysis-singers were always male, but the description of Antiodemis as "a halcyon of Lysis" seems to throw doubt on this. See Appendix 1, no. 46.

29. Cf. Lily Ross Taylor, *Roman Voting Assemblies* (Michigan 1966) 29-31, 124-125.

30. Appian, in a difficult and controverted passage (BC 1.28.125), appears to assign such an event to 106 or 111 B.C. Most scholars believe, however, that Appian's remark is a confused echo of the theatre-demolition carried out in the mid-second century B.C. The theatre was begun in 154. The date of its demolition was fixed with probability as 151 by E. T. Salmon, *Athenaeum* 41 (1963) 5-9.

31. Alba Fucens put up a statue to Sulla, *CIL* I².724 = IX.3918. For its contemporary theatre, and the relationship of this to Pompey's, see B.

Andreae, "Archäol. Funde u. Grabungen im Bereich der Soprintendenzen von Nord- u. Mittelital., 1949 bis 1959," in *JDAI* 74 (1959) cols. 210-211.

32. If Bieber's exposition in her *HGRT*[2] is correct. See esp. p. 146, "With the Atellana not only the types and jokes but also their [the Oscans'] temporary stage buildings came to Rome. This simple stage had a world-wide historical significance. It migrated together with the farce — now become Oscan Atellana — to Rome. Here it became the stage of Plautus and it combined in the first century B.C. with the Greek theatron to produce the Roman theater structure. . . ."

33. Clodius Aesopus: see Appendix 1, no. 67. The others included Galeria Copiola, now aged about forty.

34. For a summary account of the Artists of Dionysus and their guilds, together with the Greek text of seventeen of the relevant inscriptions, see Pickard-Cambridge, *Festivals*.[2] 279-321.

35. Cf. Poland in *RE* V.A.2 (1934) cols. 2474 ff., s.v. *technitai*, esp. col. 2500, and see n. 38 below.

36. Pausanias 1.20.4 has the report that Sulla was to blame: according to Appian *Mithr.* 38 it was Aristion (Athenion).

37. This is at present a guess, but one that may, when more is known, be verified by archaeology.

38. *IG* II[2].1338; Pickard-Cambridge, *Festivals*[2] 295-296, Greek text at 317-318.

39. E.g. by Fiechter and Dörpfeld. Against them see A. W. Pickard-Cambridge, *The Theatre of Dionysus at Athens* (Oxford 1946) 142, n. 1; 177, n. 4; 180, 247, 270.

40. On this guild and the theatre at Pergamum see Pickard-Cambridge, *Festivals*[2] 279-321; Webster, *HPA* and *Greek Theatre Production*[2] (London 1970), index; R. K. Sherk, below, n. 43.

41. Plut. *Sull.* 11.1. For a Roman attempt to carry out a somewhat similar mechanical exercise see Val. Max. 9.1.5, Plut. *Sert.* 22.

42. These are mentioned at App. *Mithr.* 63.

43. Inscr. originally published by M. Segre, "Due lettere di Silla," *RFIC* 66 (1938) 253-263; for text, bibiography, and discussion see R. K. Sherk, *Roman Documents from the Greek East* (Baltimore 1969) 263-266.

44. Plut. *Sull.* 19.6.

45. J. Day, "The Value of Dio Chrysostom's Euboean Discourse for the Economic Historian," *Studies in Roman Economic and Social History in Honor of A. C. Johnson* (Princeton 1951) 233. For Sulla's stay at Aedepsus see Plut. *Sull.* 26. 3-4 and Strabo 10.1.9 = c.447. Segre (above, n. 43) 256, n. 3 agrees that the Artists at Aedepsus were a branch of the Isthmian-Nemean guild.

46. *IG* VII.413; text, discussion, and bibliography at R. K. Sherk (above, n. 43) 133-138.

47. *IG* VII.419.

48. *IG* VII.416.

49. *IG* VII.420.

50. Above, n. 5; cf. App. *BC* 1.28.125. The relation between *technitai* and *scaenici artifices* is briefly discussed by Webster *GB* 38, and more fully by E. J. Jory, "Some Aspects of the Acting Profession in Rome" (unpubl. diss., London 1967) 20-27, cf. 144-158.

51. Commodus: Hdn. 1.13.8.

52. Plut. *Sull.* 2 and 36 (broadly confirmed by Val. Max. 6.9.6); Macrob. *Sat.* 3.14.10: Nicol. Damasc. ap. Athen. 6.261c; cf. Bardon (above, n. 22) 152. Sallust, however, denies that Sulla was remiss in his duties (*Bell. Jug.* 15.3).

53. The association of Verres and Mark Antony with mimes is well known; for Catiline see Q. Cicero, *Comm. Pet.* 10.

54. Cic. *Brut.* 216; Val. Max. 9.14.5; Plin. *NH* 7.55.

55. If the relationships proposed in *RE* VIII.A.1 (1955) col. 162, s.v. Valerius 266, and col. 243, s.v. Valeria 389, are accepted. In this event both Hortensius, who was teased with the name of Dionysia, and the Messalla who was nicknamed Menogenes became kinsmen of Sulla by his marriage to Valeria. The key passage is Plut. *Sull.* 35.4 (whatever the right text may be). See R. Syme, *JRS* 45 (1955) 158.

56. Plin. *NH* 7.54; Suet. *Jul.* 59; Marius Mercator, *Liber subnotationum in verba Juliani* cap. 4. On this last see n. in Migne, *PL* 48, col. 130, corrected by M. Ihm in *RhM* 44 (1889) 529-531. Cf. *TLL* and *Onomast.* s.v. *Durio.* The senior Lentulus (Spinther) mentioned above may have contributed in 70 B.C. to the annual celebration of the *victoria Sullana*: see H. B. Mattingly, *Num. Chron.* 16 (1956) 199-200; cf. Broughton *MRR* Suppl. (1960) 19.

57. Plutarch (*Sull.* 2.1) describes it as *deinôs pikran*.

58. For Sulla's hair see Plut. *Sull.* 6.7 and iconography. For Roscius a reliable inference may be drawn from Cic. *Pro Rosc. Com.* 20.

59. This at any rate is how I would interpret his *decorum* and *venustas*. For the former see Cic. *De Orat.* 1.129 and 132 ("Roscio, quem saepe audio dicere, caput esse artis decere; quod tamen unum id esse, quod tradi arte non possit"); also 2.242. *Perfectus, perfecte* is used of him by Cic. *De Orat.* 1.129 and by Festus and Paul the Deacon. For his *venustas* see Cic. *Pro. Arch.* 17, *De Orat.* 1.129 and 251; Gell. 5.8.4. Cf. Cic. *De Orat.* 1.129 *delectet*.

60. Several actors are credited with pleasing the *populus*, the *nobiles*, etc., but these expressions do not have quite the same proud ring as *populus Romanus*. For the true force of the latter, see Tac. *A*.1.33, "For the memory of Drusus was held in great honour by the Roman People" ("quippe Drusi magna apud populum Romanum memoria"). Almost the only actor or entertainer I can find spoken of in comparable terms is an undated Cn. Pompeius Astipa, *daeliciae* [sic] *populi Ro.* (*CIL* VI.10151, an epitaph).

61. Macrob. *Sat.* 3.14.13.

62. Macrob. (above, n. 61), Plut. *Sull.* 36, cf. 2-3 and perhaps 33.2; cf. Val. Max. 8.7.7: "principum familiaritates amplexus est."

63. Plut. *Sull.* 26.3-4 (with acknowledgments to Perrin's translation);

Macrob. *Sat.* 3.17.11 (on Sulla's sumptuary law).

64. Plaut. *Pseud.*: *pulmentum* (220), *olivum* (210), *pisces* (169), *perna* (166), *tergora* (198), *sumen* (166), *agninae lactes* (319, cf. 329-330), *callum* (166), *glandium* (166), *aqua* (157, 166), *nux* (371), *vinum* (183), *montes frumenti* (189), *penus annuos* (178). The Cook (803-836) carries the same food-motif to a farcical extreme. For the sweet drinks see 741.

65. Cic. speaks of his *purissima et castissima vita* and his *abstinentia, Pro Rosc. Com.* 17; cf. 18: *purior, pudentior*. We have to remember, of course, that it is an advocate for the defence who is speaking.

66. Cic. *Ad Fam.* 9.22. See Ribbeck, *CRF²* (Leipzig 1873, repr. Hildesheim 1962) p. 90, and L. Rychlewska, *Turpilii Comici Fragmenta* (Wratislava 1962) 67. In my opinion these scholars are both wrong in making it a young man's role.

67. J. D. Salinger, in a story in *For Esmé with Love and Squalor, and other stories* (London 1953) 182-183. For Metrobius see Plut. *Sull.* 2 and 36, and for Catulus, Cic. *ND* 1.79. Plutarch's description of Metrobius (in Sulla's last years) as *exôros*, "past his first bloom," has been widely mistranslated as "past his prime." This has led to the astonishing portrayal, in Peter Green's novel *The Sword of Pleasure* (Cleveland 1957), of Metrobius at that time as an effeminate person in his *seventies*. Joanne Daly's *An Actor in Rome* (London 1971) is handicapped by the same misunderstanding.

68. For *cullei Lanuvini* see Cic. *Ad Fam.* 9.22.4, though the expression has troubled copyists. The sex associations help to explain why for some scholars the name of Lanuvium itself came to have ribald overtones; see the recondite monograph *Ciceros Brief an Paetus ix. 22* (Giessen 1929) by W. Wendt, esp. 35-37. Cf. also, however, Lewis and Short, s.v. *nefrens*.

69. Plaut. *Pseud.* 214; Cic. *Pro. Rosc. Com.* 20. Roscius in all likelihood was acting Ballio in Sulla's lifetime, as Cic. says *tractare consuevit*, and the speech probably dates from soon after Sulla's death.

70. Plaut. *Pseud.* 229.

71. Plut. *Cic.* init.

72. Sulla/sibylla: Peter, *HRR²* 1.195; Macrob. *Sat.* 1.17.27, Charis. 1 p. 110 Keil, both quoted in full by Peter; further ancient speculation in Diomedes. In modern times too there has been much discussion of the origin of Sulla's name. W. Schulze, *Zur Geschichte der lateinischen Eigennamen²* (Göttingen 1964, repr. Berlin etc. 1966), rejects the derivation from *sura* on account of the manifestly short first vowel of the name when it is written in Greek, and classes it as an Etruscan name. So I. Kajanto, *The Latin Cognomina* (Helsinki 1965) 106. Cf. J. Reichmuth, *Die lateinischen Gentilicia und ihre Beziehungen zu den römischen Individualnamen* (Zürich 1956) 66: "In the case of Sulla the modern derivation from *surula* (dim. of *sura* = calf of leg) is no better than the ancient one — shortening from Sibylla or meaning 'yellow.'" I had thought of connecting the name with the IE root which appears in Avestan *sūra* and Vedic *sū́ra*, = brave, heroic, hero, with cognates in Irish and Gaulish (on this word see G. Dumézil, *Eranos* 52 [1954] 109, n. 1);

Sulla himself would have liked this, but there is the same difficulty over the quantity of the first vowel. See further n. 73 below.

73. Plut. *Sull.* 2.1. Plutarch's hint about the direct signification of "sulla" or "syllas" is very obscure; and the name was a puzzle to Quintilian (1.4.25). It seems just conceivable that the Athenians were playing on something suggested to them by the name itself when they said Sulla was mulberry and barley. This is what must have been at the back of Daniel Wyttenbach's mind when he said (*Lexicon Plutarcheum* [Oxford 1830, repr. Hildesheim 1962] 2.1454) that there is a Greek word *syllas* meaning *genus placentae*.

74. Plut. *Sull.* 22.4; 29.6.

75. Peter, *HRR*² 1.198-199; Cic. *De Div.* 1.33.72.

76. Cf. n. 79 below.

77. App. *BC* 1.105.492. On the ring given to Roscius see Macrob. *Sat.* 3.14.13. This was an *anulus aureus* (which would be good Latin for Sulla's kind of ring too, cf. Plaut. *Pseud.* 56, so that a thought-connection is by no means ruled out; cf. Sen. *De Ira* 8.6). For Sulla's relationship with Roscius in his closing years see Plut. *Sull.* 36.1, and on his illness and death see T. F. Carney, "The Death of Sulla," *AClass.* 4 (1961) 64 ff.

78. Cic. *De Orat.* 2.233.

79. Probably in 68 B.C.; see above, n. 14.

80. For the honour bestowed on the actor Herennius Gallus in Spain in 43 B.C. see Asinius Pollio ap. Cic. *Ad Fam.* 10.32, which brings out the irregular and autocratic nature of the act on that occasion. But Sulla was a regular autocrat. For the remark made to Augustus see Macrob. *Sat.* 2.7.19. For Paris see Juv. 7.89 and J. D. Duff ad loc. For the third-century appointment see Hdn. 5.7.7.

81. We may neglect the remote possibility that he was brought home along the rougher Latin Way.

82. App. *BC* 1.73.340.

83. So, at least, her name was understood, and in my opinion correctly. For discussions of its meaning see A. E. Gordon, "The Cults of Lanuvium," *Univ. of California Publications in Class. Archaeology* 2, 2 (1938) 35-37, and (better) G. Dumézil "IUNO. S.M.R.," *Eranos* 52 (1952) 105-119, esp. 112, n. 2. For the denarius see Sydenham, *CRR* 771, p. 126; but the date should be 80 B.C. rather than 78 or 77 (see M. H. Crawford, "The Coinage of the Age of Sulla," *NC* 7th Ser. 4 [1964] 144).

7: HOW ROSCIUS ACTED BALLIO

1. Cic. *Pro Rosc. Com.* 20.

2. Macrob. *Sat.* 3.14.13.

3. Cic. *Pro Rosc. Com.* 19.

4. Cic. *Pro Rosc. Com.* 23.

5. Macrob. *Sat.* 3.14.13.

6. Cic. *Pro Rosc. Com.* 30.

7. On Satyros see Aeschines 2.156-157 and O'Connor 429. On Alexandros the Sphettian see *IG* III.2028 and Webster *MNC*² AS 4 (p. 51). For Stratocles and Demetrius see Quint. 11.3.178-181. On Pellio see Plaut. *Bacch.* 214-215 and E. Fraenkel, *Elementi plautini in Plauto* (Florence 1960) 240-241. For the coins of Q. Pomponius Musa see Sydenham *CRR* (rev. ed. 1952) nos. 821, 821a, 822.

8. E.g. Plaut. *Pseud.* 447 (*paedagogus*), cf. 933 (*magister*), 1193 (*praeceptor*); Ter. *Andr.* 192 (*magister*); Ter. *HT* 889 (*veterator*).

9. James Boswell, *Life of Johnson*, Oxford Standard Authors (London 1904 and often repr.) 2, p. 24 (*anno* 1776).

10. On the etymology and congeners of *phallos* see, for example, *RE* XIX.2 (1938), col. 1681, s.v. *phallos*; O. Stotz (work cited in n. 18 below) p. 19; Edmonds, II.719; Aristoph. *Birds* 1529; and Herodas 6.69.

11. Cic. *Ad Fam.* 9.22.1 Cicero's comment is: "totus est sermo verbis tectus, re impudentior."

12. For *ballio* as a military term connected with *balneum* see A. von Premerstein in *Klio* 3 (1913) 38; cf. R. Cavenaile, *Corpus Papyrorum Latinarum* (Wiesbaden 1958) 106, V (pp. 212 ff.); Robert O. Fink, *Roman Military Records on Papyrus* (Cleveland 1971) 106-114, 534. For Viriballum see Ptol. 3.2.3.

13. On doubling in general see F. Schmidt, *Über die Zahl der Schauspieler bei Plautus unt Terenz* (Erlangen 1870); H. W. Prescott, articles and reviews in *HSPh* 21 (1910) 31-50; *CPh* 18 (1923) 29 ff.; *TAPhA* 63 (1932) 121-125; *CPh* 29 (1934) 350 f.; *CPh* 36 (1941) 281-285; C. M. Kurrelmeyer, *The Economy of Actors in Plautus* (Graz 1932); Duckworth 94-98; Webster, *HPA* 266f., 281.

14. Now in the Metropolitan Museum, New York; illustr. at Bieber, *HGRT*² fig. 473.

15. Now in the Naples Museum; illustr. at Bieber, *HGRT*² fig. 324.

16. E. Fraenkel, *Elementi plautini in Plauto* (Florence 1960) 136-142, shows that the scene between Ballio and his male slaves (*Pseud.* 133-170) is to be taken as a free Plautine and romanizing development of something much more circumscribed in his Greek source, and that most of the sequel, including the courtesan-parade and *flagitatio*, until Ballio leaves the stage, is probably pure Plautine invention, romanizing and (by Greek standards) coarsening the whole ethos of procurer and courtesanship. The chances are that Roscius accepted the implications of this for his acting, though I do not think for a moment that he would lend countenance to any differentiation, of the kind so beloved of modern scholars, between "Plautinisches" and "Unplautinisches."

17. Cic. *Brutus* 290.

18. Otto Stotz, *De Lenonis in Comoedia Figura*, Diss. (Darmstadt 1920), see esp. pp. 20-48.

19. By Burt Shevelove and Larry Gelbart; performed at the Strand Theatre, London, in 1963-1964.

20. Pollux, *Onomasticon* 4.143-145.

21. My count is based on material collected in Webster, *MNC²*.

22. Webster, *MNC²* AV 3 (p. 56).

23. Webster, *MNC²* EG 3 (p. 175).

24. Webster, *MNC²* ZV 1 (p. 96).

25. Webster, *MNC²* UJ 30 (p. 234).

26. Webster, *MNC²* IT 85 (p. 327). It is uncertain whether this is a leno (mask 8 in Pollux) or one of the old men (mask 3 in Pollux).

27. Webster, *MNC²* DM 1 (p. 70).

28. Plaut. *Pseud.* 967.

29. Cic. *Pro Rosc. Com.* 20.

30. Cic. *De Orat.* 3.221.

31. Cf. Northrop Frye, *Anatomy of Criticism* (New York 1969) 164-165.

32. Webster, *MNC²* MT 9 (p. 80).

33. Cic. *Ad Fam.* 9.22.4.

34. Plaut. *Pseud.* 767-789.

35. Val. Max. 7.7.7. Macrob. *Sat.* 3.14.12.

36. Bieber, *HGRT²* fig. 561a (from ms. C= Vat. lat. 3868).

37. L. W. Jones and C. R. Morey, *The Miniatures of the Manuscripts of Terence* (Princeton 1930-1931) fig. 730 (from ms. F).

38. Jones and Morey (above, n. 37), figs. 727 (from ms. P), 728 (from ms. C), 729 (from ms. O) and 730 (from ms. F).

39. Jones and Morey (above, n. 37), fig. 729 (from ms. O).

40. Karl E. Weston "The Illustrated Terence Manuscripts," *HSPh* 14 (1903) 37-54; Bieber, *HGRT²* 164. Tac. *Dial.* 20 at first sight militates against belief in continuity of the art of gestus, but it implies at least that the public in the first century A.D. believed that it knew what the gestus of Roscius was like. No doubt gestus had subsequently become more sophisticated, but it need not have changed fundamentally. It should also be noted that many scholars have disputed Jones and Morey's contention that the originals of the miniatures in the Terence mss. cannot date from before late antiquity: see authorities cited by Mme L. Kahil in *AK* Beiheft 6 (1970) 102-103.

41. On the *flagitatio* see the discussion by Hermann Usener, "Italische Volksjustiz," *Kleine Schriften* 4 (1913, repr. Osnabrück 1965) 356-382 = *RhM* 56 (1900) 1-28. For *Pseud.* 360 ff. Usener proposed reassigning the parts to give a "strophe," 360-362, with reviling by Pseudolus alone; an "antistrophe," 363-365, with reviling by Calidorus alone; and an "epode," 366 ff., with reviling by both. His arguments, however, are not fully cogent.

42. Loeb edition of Plautus by P. Nixon, vol. 4 (1932) 188-189.

43. Webster, *MNC²* XT 8 (p. 67).

44. Webster, *MNC*² MT 32 (p. 84).
45. Varro, *De L.L.* 7.81, "cum leno ... secundum parietem transversus iret."
46. Above, n. 26.
47. Webster, *MNC*² ZT 20 (p. 92).
48. Cic. *Pro Rosc. Com.* 20.
49. Plaut. *Pseud.* 767-789.
50. Cic. *De Sen.* 70.
51. Cf. Cic. Pro Rosc. Com. 17.
52. C. Fundilius Doctus, *CIL* XIV.4275; illustr. at G. Fleischhauer, *Musikgeschichte in Bildern*, Bd. 2, Lieferung 5 (Leipzig 1964), Abb. 62.

8: THE BACKGROUND TO THE *PERSONAE* OF SENECA

1. L. Herrmann, *Le Théâtre de Sénèque* (Paris 1924) 391, 470.
2. C. W. Mendell, *Our Seneca* (New Haven-London 1941) 10.
3. P. Ure, "On Some Differences between Seneca and Elizabethan Tragedy," *Durham Univ. Journal* 41 (1948) 18.
4. H. Drexler, *Gnomon* 3 (1927) 452.
5. See pp. 15-16 above, and C. Garton, "Characterization in Greek Tragedy," *JHS* 77 (1957) 248-249.
6. R. Bridges, "The Influence of the Audience on Shakespeare's Drama," *Stratford Shakespeare* 10 (Stratford-on-Avon 1907), 321 ff.
7. W. Zürcher, *Die Darstellung des Menschen im Drama des Euripides* (Basle 1947) 131.
8. W. Schadewaldt, "Sophokles, Aias und Antigone," *Neue Wege zur Antike* 1. Reihe, 8 (1929) 72.
9. J. F. Gronovius, n. on *Medea* 25: "At ars est poetae...." N. T. Pratt draws attention to this in *Dramatic Suspense in Seneca and in His Greek Precursors* (Princeton 1939) 67.
10. W. Steidle, "Bemerkungen zu Senecas Tragödien," *Philologus* 96 (1944) 250; G. Müller, "Senecas *Oedipus* als Drama," *Hermes* 81 (1953) 447.
11. Cic. *Tusc. Disp.* 2. 16. 38.
12. Sen. *Epist. Mor.* 8. 8.
13. Demetrius, *On Style* 169.
14. Virg. *Aen.* 4.660: "sic, sic iuvat ire sub umbras."
15. Cf. Pratt (above, n. 9) 103 ff.
16. Cf. Pratt (above, n. 9) 34.

9: THE ROSCIAD IDEA

1. The works of modern scholarship to which I am most indebted in this discussion are: Joseph M. Beatty, "The Battle of the Players and Poets," *MLN* 35 (1919) 449-462, and "Churchill's Influence on Minor Eighteenth Century Satirists," *PMLA* 42 (1927) 162-176; Richmond P. Bond, "*-IAD*: a Progeny of the *Dunciad*" *PMLA* 44 (1929) 1099-1105 (his n. 12 collects the titles of nineteen *Rosciads*, the fullest list up to that time), and *English Burlesque Poetry* 1700-1750 (Cambridge, Mass. 1932); Wallace C. Brown, *Charles Churchill* (Lawrence, Kansas 1953); Douglas Grant ed., *The Poetical Works of Charles Churchill* (Oxford 1956); James Laver ed., *The Poems of Charles Churchill* (London 1933); Carola Oman, *David Garrick* (London 1958); Giles Playfair, *The Prodigy* (London 1967); Robert C. Whitford, "Gleanings of Churchillian Bibliography," *MLN* 43 (1928) 30-34.

2. Lucil. 567 Marx = 594 Warmington.

3. Hor. *Sat.* 1.5.63-64.

4. Pers. 5.8-9.

5. See Juv. 3.96-97.

6. It was first published in 1928 by the Rev. Montague Summers in his edition of John Downes' *Roscius Anglicanus*. The latter work (1708) is a prose record of Restoration plays and actors, with comments and criticisms. If the *Satyr* is at all closely connected with Downes, as it may be, we have here a very near approach to the *Rosciad* idea. *Roscius Anglicanus* (without the *Satyr*) has more recently (1969) been reprinted by the Augustan Reprint Society, publ. no. 134, University of California, Los Angeles.

7. Brown (above, n. 1) 34.

8. Arist. *Poet.* 1448a. The best and oldest surviving Greek manuscript (A = cod. Parisinus 1741, of the tenth or eleventh century) represents the name of this poem as *Deiliad*, i.e. lay or epic on cowards. Above the word, the hand of a later "corrector" recommends the spelling *Dêliad*, i.e. lay or epic of the island of Delos. Editors have varied in their choice. The most recent, D. W. Lucas (ed. Oxford 1968) prefers *Deiliad*, but it is problematic which reading was more familiar to Pope, and whether he was aware of the double tradition.

9. Bond, "*-IAD*" (above, n. 1) 1099.

10. Hor. *Epist.* 2.1.82.

11. Cic. *Pro Rosc. Com.* 23.

12. Cic. *Pro Arch.* 17.

13. Cic. *De Orat.* 1. 129.

14. Cic. *Brut.* 290.

15. I quote from Robert Ainsworth, *Thes. Ling. Lat. Compend.* (2nd ed. 1746 and 3rd ed. 1751), s.v. Roscius; and Adam Littleton, *Ling. Lat. Lib. Dict. Quadripertitus* (4th ed. 1715) s.v. Roscius.

16. Roscia, daughter of Sidonius Apollinaris: see his *Epist.* 5.16.5.

17. See the entry of Paulus under *Rosci* (p. 367) in Festus' *De Verborum*

Significatu, ed. W. M. Lindsay (Leipzig 1913, repr. Hildesheim 1965).

18. *Scholia in Horatium . . . in Codic. Paris. Lat. 17897 et 8223 obvia . . .*, ed. H. J. Botschuyver (Amsterdam 1942) p. 424 (n. on *Epist.* 2.1.79).

19. Puttenham, *Engl. Poesie* 1.14 (Arb.) 48, quoted in the *OED* s.v. "histrion."

20. Sir Richard Steele in *Tatler* 167 (May 4, 1710).

21. *3 Henry VI* 5.6.10. Pope's edition appeared in 1725. The Quarto and Folio editions of this play both had versions of "Rossius."

22. George Anne Bellamy, quoted by Carola Oman (above, n. 1) 88.

23. Carola Oman (above, n. 1) 84.

24. Cl. Fr. Fraguier, "Recherches sur la Vie de Q. Roscius le Comédien" (1717), publ. in *Mém. de Litt. tirez des reg. de l'Acad. Royale des Inscr. et Belles Lettres*, tome 4 (Paris 1746) 437-456. This Académie was incorporated in the Institut de France in 1795.

25. For a synopsis see the Table of Rosciads in Appendix 3.

26. The editions by James Laver (1933) and Douglas Grant (1956) and the biography by Wallace C. Brown (1953). See above, n. 1.

27. The title is listed by Bond, "*-IAD*" (above, n. 1), n. 12. Professor Bond informs me that he has no further knowledge of it.

28. Brown (above, n. 1) 40-41.

29. *Belfast News Letter*, quoted by Playfair (above, n. 1) 29.

30. Quin's nose had been put out of joint by the young Garrick's new style of acting, which had swept the public off its feet. Quin consoled himself with the hope that the public would soon tire of such novelty and return to orthodoxy. He compared Garrick's success to that of the evangelical preacher George Whitfield, saying, "Garrick is a new religion; Whitfield was followed for a time; but they will all come to church again." Garrick replied in some verses beginning *"Pope Quin, who damns all churches but his own,/* Complains that Heresy infects the town," and ending, "When Doctrines meet with gen'ral approbation,/ It is not *Heresy*, but *Reformation*." For further detail see Carola Oman (above, n.1) 44. Considering how thoroughly Garrick was destined to eclipse Quin, the reminiscence of this story by Peter Pangloss in the *Young Rosciad* is not altogether happy.

APPENDIX 1: A REGISTER OF REPUBLICAN ACTORS

1. This Register supersedes my "Roman Republican Actors: A Conspectus," published in *SPh* 63 (1966) 473-498. The numbering has been completely revised.

2. See Abbreviations: Henry.

3. As in Broughton, *MRR*.

4. See Abbreviations: Duckworth, Bieber, *HGRT*², and Beare.

5. For full titles of all these works see Abbreviations.

6. E. Bertrand, "Cicéron au Théâtre," *Annales de l'univ. de Grenoble 9* (1897) 83-208; F. W. Wright, *Cicero and the Theater*, Smith Coll. Class. Stud. no. 11 (1931); W. A. Laidlaw, "Cicero and the Stage," *Hermathena* 94 (1960) 56-66; Lidia Winniczuk, "Cicero on Actors and the Stage," *Atti del. I Congresso Internaz. di Studi Ciceroniani* 1 (1961) 213-222.

7. *Rhet. ad Her.* 1.14.24 and 2.13.19; Cic. *Pro Planc.* 30-31.

8. Athen. 1.19 f. and 10.452 f.

9. Cf. T. B. L. Webster, *Greek Theatre Production*² (London 1970) 97, 143, 146, 170.

10. By Duckworth, Margarete Bieber, and Beare.

11. See n. 6 above.

APPENDIX 2: A REGISTER OF AUGUSTAN ACTORS

1. The evidence is controverted, but I have given conservative figures. See J. Weiss in *RE* V.A.2 (1934) col. 1286 s.v. Theatrum Balbi, and U. E. Paoli, *Das Leben im Alten Rom* (Bern 1948) 304, n. 4.

2. Evidence for Roman tragedy at Schanz-Hosius, *Geschichte der römischen Literatur*. II 4 (Munich 1935, repr. 1959) 292-293. For Greek tragedy note Cn. Pompeius Macer (see *RE* XXI.2 [1952] col. 2277 s.v. Pompeius 92) and C. Asinius Pollio (Serv. *Ecl.* 8.10, which may however be a misunderstanding). Cf. A. Lesky, *A History of Greek Literature*, transl. by J. Willis and C. de Heer (New York 1966) 809.

3. Bieber *HGRT*² 89-90 and nn.; fig. 317a.

4. Strabo 5.233. See also register, no. 2. P. Frassinetti, *Le Attellane* (Rome 1967) 14. If Suet. *Aug.* 89.1, mentioned above, does not refer to Greek Old Comedy it must refer to republican Latin comedy, such as that of Terence.

5. *CIL* VI.32323; Bonaria *MRF* 2. p. 45; Bieber *HGRT*² 184. The phrasing of the inscription suggests, to my mind at any rate, that the wooden theatre by the Tiber and the arrangement in the Circus Flaminius were structures of some durability, and not purely *ad hoc*, as is often assumed.

6. Virg. *Aen.* 4.471.

7. In joint gnomologies and in a *synkrisis* of the two poets, all probably composed in 4/6 cent. A.D. (see *RE* XIX.2 [1938] cols. 2403-2404). However spurious or misconceived these may be they are genuine testimony to the mimographer's reputation. The omission of Philistio from both the first and second editions of the *OCD* was unpardonable.

8. Pantomime artists in 84/60 B.C.: (1) Dyrrachinos, see L. Robert, *Études épigraphiques et philologiques* (Paris 1938) 11; Daux, *BCH* 63 (1939)

169. (2) Ploutogenes, see F. Hiller von Gaertringen, *Inschriften von Priene* (Berlin 1906) 113; L. Robert, *Hermes* 65 (1930) 114-117. Cf. Sifakis 104-105.

9. Hor. *Sat.* 1.5.63.

10. Hor. *Sat.* 2.6.72.

11. Schanz-Hosius, *Gesch. der röm. Lit.* II 4 (Munich 1935, repr. 1959) 295 and n. 8.

12. Porphyrio on Hor. *Sat.* 2.6.72. He could of course be mistaken.

13. Macrob. *Sat.* 2.7.19.

14. O'Connor and Parenti: see Abbreviations.

15. For Augustus' relations with the Artists of Dionysus and the probable Augustan origin of the world-guild, see the supplemented text of papyrus *BGU* 4.1074 as given by P. Viereck, *Klio* 8 (1908) 415, with comments at 418; *POxy* XXVII (1962) 2476, and XXXI (1966) 2610; Pickard-Cambridge, *Festivals*[2] 297.

16. Athens: A. W. Pickard-Cambridge, *The Theatre of Dionysus in Athens* (Oxford 1946) 247. Sparta: Bieber *HGRT*[2] 122, with references.

17. Arelate: Bieber *HGRT*[2] 199-200, with references.

18. Emerita: Bieber *HGRT*[2] 202, with references.

19. Leptis Magna: Bieber *HGRT*[2] 206-207, with references; A Neppi Modona, *Gli Edifici Teatrali Greci e Romani* (Florence 1961) 147.

20. Faesulae: Neppi Modona (above, n. 19) 114; Mediolanum, 122; Augusta Taurinorum, 122; Augusta Praetoria, 123. Herculaneum: Bieber *HGRT*[2] 186, with references; Neppi Modona (above, n. 19) 105. Pompeii: Bieber *HGRT*[2] 170-172, with references; Neppi Modona (above, n. 19) 91, 94.

21. *CIL* I.[2] 2687 = Degrassi *ILLRP* 727.

22. Ostia: Bieber *HGRT*[2] 191, with references; Neppi Modona (above, n. 19) 107. Minturnae: Bieber *HGRT*[2] 193, with references; Casinum: Neppi Modona (above, n. 19) 107.

23. Rome, theatres of Balbus and Marcellus: Bieber, *HGRT*[2] 184, with references.

24. Augustan restorations of Pompey's theatre: *Res Gestae* 20, cf. Bieber *HGRT*[2] 181.

25. Cf. Bieber *HGRT*[2] 165, with refs. and figs. 592 a-b.

26. Bieber *HGRT*[2] 157 with figs. 570, 571.

27. Bieber *HGRT*[2] 159 with figs. 575, 576.

28. Bieber *HGRT*[2] 165 with fig. 593.

29. Above, n. 3.

30. Webster *MNC*[2]: AT 25 (p. 56); ZL 5 (p. 88); EL 24 (p. 100); FB 1 (p. 112); AL 2, AL 3 (p. 160); XL 1 (p. 167); NB 4, NB 5, NB 6, NB 7, NB 8 (p. 182); NP 4 (p. 185); NP 49, NP 50, NP 51 (p. 191); IL 5, IL 7 (p. 202); IM 5 (p. 209); IT 65, IT 66 (p. 220); IV 8, IV 9, IV 10 (p. 222); IP 3 (p. 325); IV 19 (p. 328); JM 5 (p. 329).

31. Schanz-Hosius, *Gesch. der röm. Lit.* II 4 (Munich 1935, repr. 1959) 293.

INDEX

1: Scene from Act 2 of Menander's *Phasma*, the original of Luscius Lanuvinus' play (see pp. 99 ff.). Mosaic at Mytilene, third century A.D.

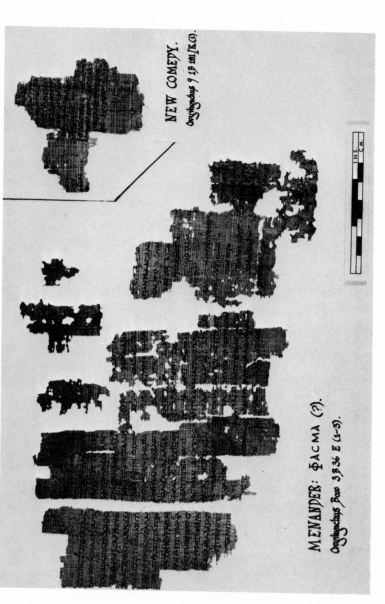

NEW COMEDY.

Oxyrhynchus 9 *JB* 131 [R(?).

MENANDER: ΦΑΣΜΑ (?).

Oxyrhynchus Boox 3 B 36 E (1-3).

2: Papyrus fragments of Menander's *Phasma*, the original of Luscius Lanuvinus' play (see pp. 103 ff., 112 ff.). Early 1 cent. A.D.

3: (a) Goat, showing *hirquina barba*, Plaut. *Pseud.* 967
(see pp. 186-187).

3: (b) Roman stilus from Lanuvium (see p. 47).

4: (a) Medallion struck in 1805 in honour of William Betty,
the Young Roscius (see pp. 226-228).

4: (b) Figures of Andronicus (?), Demosthenes, Roscius, and
Cicero, on frontispiece of John Bulwer's *Chironomia*, 1644.